GEOGRAPHIES FOR ADVAN

EDITED BY EMERITUS PROFESSOR S.H. BEAVER M.A. F.R.G.S.

GEOGRAPHY OF POPULATION
Second edition

GEOGRAPHIES FOR ADVANCED STUDY
Edited by Emeritus Professor Stanley H. Beaver, M.A., F.R.G.S.

GEOGRAPHY OF POPULATION
Second Edition

BY

J. BEAUJEU-GARNIER

*Professor of Geography at the
University of Paris 1 (Sorbonne)*

TRANSLATED BY

S. H. BEAVER

*Emeritus Professor of Geography,
University of Keele*

LONGMAN
London and New York

Longman Group Limited London

Associated companies, branches and representatives
throughout the world

Published in the United States of America
by Longman Inc., New York

English translation © Longman Group Limited 1966, 1978

First published 1966
Second edition 1978

ISBN 0 582 48569 X cased
ISBN 0 582 48570 3 paper

Library of Congress Cataloging in Publication Data

Beaujeu-Garnier, Jacqueline
Geography of population.—2nd ed.—(Geographies
for advanced study).
1. Population geography
I. Title   II. Series
301.32   HB1951   77-30726
ISBN 0 582 48569 X
ISBN 0 582 48570 3 Pbk

Printed in Great Britain by
Whitstable Litho Ltd., Whitstable, Kent

Preface to the First Edition

This volume is the result of fifteen years devoted to research in the subject of world population. It is derived from the reading of a wide range of literature, from innumerable calculations made from diverse statistical sources, from many discussions not only with the most eminent specialists in many disciplines but also with peasants, workers, breadwinners, wives, children and others during the course of worldwide travel. Though it has recourse to figures—for how else can one 'prove' one's theories?—there is no rate, no percentage, which does not reflect an impression gained from personal study of the problem.

A large two-volume work has already been published on the world's population.[1] It represented the culmination of the first stage of this research, and I hesitated for a long time before drafting this present synthesis, which, bearing in mind the variability, even the absence, of documentation for a large part of the globe, might appear to be presumptuous. Thus the reader will find in these pages many question marks, many expressions of doubt, many pointers to further research, which will enable him, whilst familiarising himself with the experiences and outlook of human societies, to become aware of the limits and uncertainties of our knowledge and of the immense task which confronts us in the understanding of the present state of humanity and in the foreshadowing of its future.

I hope also that the reading of these pages will help all those who are concerned with the world's future to understand the gravest of our problems, which is the population explosion and its effect on the urgent necessity to give all men the right to be adequately fed, to work and to live a decent life.

This book is published simultaneously in France and in England. The English edition has been prepared by my colleague, Professor S. H. Beaver, who has been much more than a mere translator, and at the same time a wise interpreter and a geographical guide whose many helpful suggestions I gratefully acknowledge. Finally, both

[1] J. Beaujeu-Garnier, *Géographie de la Population*. 2 vols. Paris, 1956–58.

Professor Beaver and I are grateful to Professor Germain d'Hangest, who has reviewed the whole translation, adding certain touches of style which have not altered the geographical truth but have made it easier to comprehend!

J. BEAUJEU-GARNIER

Preface to the Second Edition

When the first edition was published, Geography of Population was a pioneer work. A work of this type had never before appeared in Geography. Since then, many other volumes have been published dealing with the geography of population in a more or less exhaustive way. Furthermore, demographers, historians, physicians, sociologists, ethnographers as well as geographers have continued to publish research monographs at a greater or lesser level of generalisation while statistical materials have become more and more useful, notably by the increased frequency and regularity of population censuses which have become the general rule in almost every country. It was thus necessary to completely revise the second edition. This is what has been done.

All the source material has been gone over again. My conclusions have been studied in the light of this and revised. Recent trends in demographic evolution, greatly variable between continents and countries, have been recorded. It is therefore a new picture of world population and its problems which is given to the reader. The previous edition was published when the World possessed three thousand million inhabitants. This one could have been entitled, like the French edition, 'four thousand million people'!

I would like to thank Odile Andan and Jean-Jacques Boislaroussie who helped to put together some of my new material and Jeanne Tiem who redrew several of the maps.

J. BEAUJEU-GARNIER

Contents

Maps and Diagrams

List of Plates

We are indebted to the following for permission to reproduce copyright photographs: Radio Times Hulton Picture Library (Plate 20); U.S. Information Service (Plate 23); Aerofilms Ltd. (Plate 28); and Novosti Press Agency A.P.N. (Plate 34).

PART I

INTRODUCTION

CHAPTER ONE

What is Population Geography?

It is commonplace to say that the modern world is evolving at a pace hitherto unknown; and among the many aspects of this accelerated evolution, demographic facts are not the least important or engrossing. In 1800 there were about 900 million people, in 1976 more than 4,000 million—a prodigious and dramatic multiplication indeed! One may well ask how far this human tide will go, and how long our small planet will be able to contain and above all to feed these millions. There are other distressing questions too, for in this demographic development all parts of the world do not follow the same rhythm, and the economic and, doubtless, the political face too of tomorrow's world will result in a large measure if not entirely from the bulk and, still more, from the efficiency of these different masses of people.

The subject impinges ever more sharply upon our awareness, and, as geographers, we can add our contribution to the study of these burning and difficult questions. If the demographer measures and analyses the demographic facts, if the historian traces their evolution, if the sociologist seeks their causes and repercussions by the observation of human society, it is the business of the geographer to describe the facts in their present environmental context, studying also their causes, their original characteristics and possible consequences. In so doing, the geographer borrows from several disciplines within the social sciences, but regroups the material in the light of his avowed object of relating all phenomena to a given situation, as revealed by the earth's surface—a fascinating perspective but a delicate and complex operation.

Even for simple description, and certainly for more advanced studies, the geographer must have recourse to the statistician. Numbers are the irreplaceable key to precision and to the comparisons which are the gateway to classification: one can say that population is dense or sparse, that a city is large or small but we can get no further without statistics—statistics for today, for yesterday, statistics to show evolution in time and in space. Anything which helps to explain the geography of our times is within the province of the geographer.

A geographical study of population thus takes on a threefold aspect: the distribution of people over the globe, the evolution of human societies and the degree of success which they have achieved.

The most elementary fact is the *distribution* of population. It would seem obvious that the natural environment, with its massive and sometimes fearful power and its often violent contrasts, should be a determining factor. But the social geographer catalogues the climate, notes the relief, evaluates the biological possibilities of the environment, records, like a doctor, the reactions of the human organism and then finds that neither in terms of numbers nor of distribution is population slavishly controlled by the physical environment. He must have recourse to other explanations. History appears indispensable, and many are the events that matter; wars that ravage and migrations that sweep across continents, mixing races and civilisations; periods of peace, conducive to many fertile developments but also to the weakening of societies; the action of powerful individuals who pacify, upset, regulate, or discover and invent; the psychology of the masses, their desires, their spirit of adventure, their 'malthusianism' or their fertility, their slow conquest of the soil and their sudden spurts of invention, their movement from the populated parts to the wide open spaces.

The presence of man anywhere is thus essentially transitory and changing. It is the result of a double *evolution*, a development *in situ* and innumerable displacements. The growth of populations is in the first place a function of the demographic factors which are part of the field of population geography: marriage, births, illness, deaths, age and sex composition—these are not just accidental; when one has evaluated them, one cannot explain them without again considering the physical, biological, economic, technical and psychological factors. The combination of these demographic factors demonstrates some of the fundamental characteristics of a population, for example the natural increase which furnishes probable indications of its future evolution, the age-composition, of vital importance in evaluating the internal dynamism of the group. Sometimes, however, the result of the evolution does not conform to the simple budget of internal demographic phenomena, as in Ireland, for example, where despite a natural increase of births over deaths, the population has diminished by one half in little more than a century, or in the United States, where until 1913 the total increase was greatly superior to the natural increase. These two countries provide typical examples of these anomalies, which force us to consider migration—migration of all kinds and of different rhythms—daily, seasonal, temporary or permanent, national or even inter-continental. Such movements of people have many consequences, demographic and economic certainly, but also racial, moral, technical and medical.

Human societies exist and change, but they are also active in impressing their mark, with greater or less force, on their own environment—houses, forest clearings, cultivated fields, factories, routeways. What are these *activities*? How can man guide them towards a successful end? How are they distributed within a society? Are they adapted to the natural conditions or how are they supported? To answer these questions it is necessary to know not only the age and sex composition of the group being studied, but also something of their health, their physical aptitudes and their technical and intellectual equipment, and in addition the nature and amplitude of their action and the state of their realisation. The result is the outline of a complete human geography.

Such is the object of this book. Based upon a detailed regional study of the world's population already published,[1] it tries to analyse the more general aspects of the subject whilst giving local examples in as much detail as possible.

[1] J. Beaujeu-Garnier, *Géographie de la population.* 2 vols. Paris 1956–58.

CHAPTER TWO

Demographic Sources and Uncertainties

All population study rests on a considerable volume of documentation. No man is identical with any of his fellows; each has a will of his own, is capable of initiative and lives in conditions which are always changing; and it is dangerous to rely on any single example in order to generalise or to deduce the future from the past, and it is even risky to compare two statistical series which are apparently similar. Figures are indeed essential, but interpretation and pertinent comment are vital. What comparison is there between the African labourer who removes earth in a basket and his United States counterpart driving an enormous bulldozer? And yet both are building a road. Or what comparison between an undernourished Indian, racked with tropical diseases, and with an expectation of only forty-two years' life, and a well-fed Swede, leading a much more healthy existence and with an expectation of seventy years? Yet each figures as a person in the demographic statistics of his country.

Prudence and suspicion are necessary when one embarks on human geography, for the official statistics of even the most advanced countries are not free, for various reasons, from serious errors, whilst in other countries the statistics are embryonic, the methods of collection experimental and the people primitive. Even the criteria utilised are often different and one is confronted by tables with similar nomenclature but different meaning. The difficulties should certainly not be underestimated.

Statistical documentation

To handle so complex a subject one must have economic as well as demographic statistics. The monthly or annual publications of different countries are of considerable value but more general publications, such as those of the former League of Nations and now the United Nations[1] have the merit of assembling and often of critically

[1] *Annuaire statistique de la Société des Nations*, Geneva; *Demographic Yearbook* prepared by the Statistical Office of the United Nations, New York; also *Statistical Yearbook*, United Nations, New York.

comparing and presenting in a uniform manner the dispersed and fragmentary material. One very interesting summary has been made for the period 1906–36 of the natural population trends of the world.[1] On certain aspects—social, medical, economic, psychological—the up-to-date studies made by U.N.O., the Food and Agriculture Organisation (F.A.O.), the UNESCO, and the World Health Organisation, are indispensable. And in recent years systematic bibliographies have begun to appear.[2] But the main bases of demographic documentation are the census and the national register ('*état civil*' in France); unfortunately these two sources cannot escape severe criticism.

Censuses are compiled by many diverse methods which greatly influence the value of the results obtained. Certain countries employ methods which are theoretically very efficient: in France, every member of the adult population must fill up a form on the same night and the papers are collected from the houses shortly afterwards; in the U.S.A. the enumerators visit all dwellings, a process which by reason of the area to be covered may take several weeks. But other more uncertain procedures are employed, such as the 'declaration'; in India for example, before the war, and in African territories under European administration, heads of families were summoned to declare their composition to the authorities; in several Latin American countries the people must attend at an office to register themselves. It is obvious that negligence or the desire, for one reason or another, to give false information can give rise to errors.

The methods of conducting the census are not the only source of errors; the results are published only after long delays due to the difficulty of classifying and elaborating; besides the lack of homogeneity in different fields of enquiry is a great hindrance.

Until recently the frequency of censuses was extremely variable; certain countries held them at regular intervals, sometimes every five years (France, Japan, Denmark, Honduras) others every ten years (U.S.A., U.K., Canada, Mexico, Egypt, India, Belgium, Spain, Burma, Chile), in yet other cases the periodicity was inconstant—ten or twenty years in Brazil, five or ten in Venezuela. It must be added that domestic or international political events have often interrupted

[1] H. Bunle, *Le mouvement naturel de la population dans le monde de 1906 à 1936*. Institut national d'études démographiques. Paris, 1954.

[2] As a result of initiative taken by the International Union for the Scientific Study of Population: H. T. Eldridge, *The materials of demography*, 1959 (in English), and J. C. Chasteland, *Démographie*, 1961 (in French).

the regularity of the sequence; thus in France the census of 1916 did not take place, neither did that of 1941, whilst after the war the rhythm was completely upset—censuses in 1946, 1954, 1962, 1968, 1975.

Other states have no regular census interval; in the huge territory of Russia, the last five censuses were in 1879, 1926, 1939, 1959, 1970; in Bolivia, censuses took place in 1882, 1900, 1950, 1976; some countries, oddly enough have had regular censuses in the past but have abandoned the practice, e.g. Uruguay between 1908 and 1963; finally there are countries which have but recently entered the statistical field, as with the famous Chinese census of 1953.

It also happens that censuses do not affect all individuals in the same way; in South Africa, the European population is enumerated every five years, the Africans (and only from a more recent date) every ten years. During the colonial period, in many African countries, only the European population was regularly counted, whilst the natives were roughly estimated. In Latin America, in some cases, the forest-dwelling Indians do not figure at all. A monumental enquiry into the British colonial empire showed how fragmentary were the data and how misleading the figures, even when they did exist.[1]

It is not enough merely to assemble the data; certain criteria must be adopted in publication. But in this field too homogeneity is absent. Thus classification by age-groups is not systematic. The interval of five years is that most commonly adopted, but whilst some countries like Germany, Canada, U.S.A., Japan, Australia, systematically divide their population into five-year age groups, others do this only for the younger groups—Egypt up to twenty-nine years, the U.K. up to thirty-four years and over fifty-five; and sometimes the grouping is in ten-year stages. It is the same with the lower age-limit assigned to the active population—this varies from ten years of age in Greece and Panama to fourteen in Canada and fifteen in New Zealand, whilst France, Czechoslovakia, Switzerland and many others do not give a lower limit at all. One could multiply these examples many times.

Side by side with the census, the 'national register' is the main means of ascertaining a country's population; but it has not everywhere the same character nor the same value.

A few European countries (Denmark, Finland, Netherlands, Nor-

[1] R. R. Kuczynski, *A demographic survey of the British Colonial Empire, 1948–1953*. 4 vols.

way, Sweden) have established what is called a 'permanent register of population'; each individual has his particular dossier, which is opened at his birth, follows him around and is closed with his death. Such a register gives a perfect understanding of the population of a country. In France, one merely records the important events in the life of individuals in registers.

The institution of the national register is often recent: in Bolivia it was begun in 1940; often it does not exist. It is not obligatory in the Indian sub-continent; it applied only to the European population over a great part of Africa before the attainment of independence; although it is theoretically obligatory in Brazil, tests have shown that certain liberties have been taken with the law, since in many areas the births enumerated are fewer than the number of baptisms recorded in the church registers.

A large part of the world's population is thus very badly known; though the Chinese census has brought one-fifth of the world's population at a single stroke into official statistics, the amount of uncertainty is still considerable. Satisfactory mortality statistics exist for only 23 per cent of the African population, 44 per cent of that of Asia, 50 per cent of South America, 85 per cent of Europe, 87 per cent of Oceania and 98 per cent of North America. Statistics of births are not very much better—only 75 per cent in Nicaragua, 80 per cent in Peru, 86·5 per cent in Puerto Rico, 98 per cent in Canada and the U.S.A.

In the present state of things, one can distinguish several groups of countries in accordance with the value of their statistical documentation; Western Europe and the countries of 'white' civilisation throughout the world (U.S.A., Canada, Australia and New Zealand, Argentina) have satisfactory statistical services, as also has Japan and probably, in recent years, the U.S.S.R. Some countries have elaborate statistics but the liability to error is frequent and important: such is the greater part of Latin America. Others have had until recently but fragmentary statistics or none at all, such as the majority of African countries and those of the Middle East and China.

It is only fair to say that international organisations have made great efforts to remedy these defects, by encouraging the taking of censuses at regular ten-year intervals (1960, 1970), and many countries have adopted this rhythm (24 countries out of 40 in the Americas, for example, with the remaining 16 having used the year 1975), and in establishing the international rubrics and classification to which countries are invited to conform in the matter of the data collected and its abstraction. Meanwhile there has developed a growing interest in what is undoubtedly the major problem of our time, namely population growth and its variations, trends and consequences. It is interesting to note that of the twenty or so specialist demographic periodicals published in various parts of the world, three-quarters have commenced since 1945. Indeed, in addition to the Demographic Yearbook and the periodical Bulletins of the United Nations, some fifteen countries now have their national or international demographic publications, amongst which the following are the best known: the French review *Population*, from 1945, the *Population Bulletin* in the United States, also from 1945, and the principal English-language journal, *Population Studies*, which began in 1947. Bibliographical volumes have collected together masses of information; we may note those by J. C. Chasteland (1961), W. Zelinsky (1962), C. Legeard (1966), and especially the well-known *Population Index*. This last has been appearing since 1937; it includes upwards of 2,000 references in each annual issue. At the same time there has been a considerable outpouring of other demographic literature, including studies of the censuses of certain countries, and descriptions of population phenomena in different parts of the globe or in individual territories.

Demographic knowledge has thus made great progress in the last two decades, if only because of the resumption of censuses in the Soviet Union and the entry of China into the family of countries making systematic efforts in this direction, and one may expect the situation to improve notably in the next few years, so that studies in this highly important field may become more and more firmly based.

Noteworthy errors and omissions

Each type of information necessary for the geographical study of population is more or less difficult to obtain, and each has its own particular troubles. There are many causes of errors and inaccuracies, both in censuses and in national registers. First there are the omissions, and conversely the double entries, which rise from very varied motives which may be simple negligence or a deliberate intention to deceive. Fiscal and electoral motives are often important. In France, Corsica would appear to have had 246,000 inhabitants in 1968 and 220,000 in 1975, according to the official censuses, for many of its citizens reside in other départements of France but continue to be recorded in their native island. Further research, however, directed towards the planning of economic development, shows that in fact the island's population is only 140,000. In Brazil, a perusal of the successive censuses shows that the 1900 enumeration was seriously lacking, whilst that of 1920 was as much as 50 per cent in excess in the northern part of the country.

Inadequate census returns are very common—a person's age is omitted, or the state of marriage or celibacy, or the date of birth; in France, it has been ascertained that errors are most numerous in the southern departments, and amongst young persons and women. Some families do not state the number of their children, others do not give their ages. Many old people exaggerate by declaring themselves 'centenarians'. In countries where a national register does not exist, as in Africa, one gets an abundance of ages expressed merely in round figures, 20, 25, 30, but often lack of precision goes even further, and a child will be recorded as born 'after the fire', or 'before the famine'.

Births are not always registered when they occur in far-off or inaccessible areas; and certain countries have for long almost systematically ignored female births. Even in areas where the national register functions normally, delays in registering vary a great deal, from one day in the most populated areas of the U.S.A. to sixty-two days in New Zealand and ninety days in the wilderness of Brazil. It follows that some infants who die before being registered are not enumerated. In certain cases, live births are registered only if the child lives for at least twenty-four hours (Spain, Cuba, Honduras, Bolivia). Elsewhere, registration depends (as in the U.S.A.) on race, for the blacks are more negligent than the whites; or on the difference between the more conscientious population of the towns and the more negligent inhabitants of the countryside; or on the age of the mother (for both young and old women are less interested in registering births than those aged between twenty and forty); or on the degree of literacy (the least exact registrations are made by mothers who had but little schooling). Besides, registration of births in the United States only began in 1915 in the north-eastern States and the whole territory was not brought into line until 1933; detailed studies have shown that even now one or two per cent of the total births do not enter the statistics; this deficiency is of course most important in the larger states, with sparse and mainly rural population.

The registration of *deaths*, too, can give rise to many errors. One of the most frequent and important is that relating to the mortality of young infants and still-births. Sometimes still-births are only registered as deaths. Certain countries, in order to distinguish between abortions and still-births, have adopted certain criteria, but these are not uniform.

Causes of death are not the object of systematic study in most countries. The World Health Organisation, in response to a worldwide enquiry, has received replies from only thirty-one countries, representing 540 million people, or no more than one-fifth of the world's population. Even if all the countries having the necessary information had replied, the result would still only have comprehended one-half of the world's population. The data must be accepted with great caution; certain causes of death are not declared and often even the medical registration is lacking. In France, in 1936 no less than 21 per cent of the reports were unusable, and in 1947, 8 per cent. In England, a report is made by a doctor on each case of death, and this much improves the quality of the statistics. However, despite the obvious deficiencies, a brief glance at the demographic annual of U.N.O. enables one to ascertain some interesting facts: the proportion of deaths from infectious and parasitic diseases per 100,000 inhabitants is 6·5 in Denmark, 7·8 in New Zealand, 6·3 in Australia, 7·8 in the U.S.A.; in contrast to these most favoured countries, the figure is over 59 in Portugal, 239 in Colombia and 318 in Salvador.

Statistics of *marriages* are also full of snares, for some countries include free unions ('informal' marriages) with legal marriages, and as the demographic result of both is the same, the annual statistical summaries prefer to group them together. In some countries the proportion of free unions is considerable; it is equal to that of legal marriages in Paraguay, Peru and Sri Lanka, and three times as great in Haiti. In general, 'marriages' of this type are very frequent in the whole of Latin America; many countries do not bother to distinguish between legal and 'free' unions and these differences obviously have an effect on the divorce statistics, for the dissolution of a 'free' marriage gives rise to no legal process and so escapes the census. Furthermore, some countries such as Brazil, Chile, Colombia, Spain, which are dominantly Catholic, do not permit divorce.

The evaluation of *migrations*, whether within a country or from one country to another, is also a tricky business. For international migrations, a questionnaire is addressed to all governments by the International Labour Organisation. One can base one's estimates on port statistics, frontier controls, immigration cards, passports, change of address registers, files of labour permits, social security cards, and transport tickets, but the data are not uniform for all countries. Outside Europe, port and frontier statistics give about 70 per cent of the information, but in European countries it is mainly change of residence data which is used. Nevertheless, the disparity between the sources of information is such that appreciable differences are recognisable: thus in 1952 the figure for Germans going to Argentina or Australia may vary by 100 per cent, depending on whether one takes the emigration statistics of the country of origin or the immigration statistics for the country of destination; and almost as great an error occurs with respect to Canada or the United States.

The *occupations of the active population* are difficult to compare. Some countries do not ask for this information within censuses, others do not always include it in their published abstracts, and the classification is in any case far from being homogeneous. Most countries retain a traditional division into agriculture, mining industry, commerce, etc., but many others are adopting a grouping into primary, secondary and tertiary (only the content of each of these groups is not absolutely fixed). In certain cases, statistics are published of socio-professional groups or social classes, especially in countries behind the 'Iron Curtain', but one can hardly make valid comparisons, for information of this sort is rare.

It must be emphasised too that even in the terms employed it is difficult to get agreement. The word 'worker' means something very different in the case of an old industrial country like England, a highly mechanised country such as the U.S.A., or a country in course of economic transformation. The workers in England are classified as 20 per cent skilled, 60 per cent semi-skilled and 20 per cent labourers, but in the engineering industry these proportions are 38, 47 and 15 respectively.

Finally, the notion of *rural* and *urban* population, which appears at first sight so simple, is in fact quite unsatisfactory. The distinction is founded upon most diverse criteria. Sometimes 'urban' means those who live in places having a certain form of administration—as in South Africa, Tunisia, Brazil, the U.K. and the U.S.S.R. Another criterion is agglomeration in places of a certain minimum size—but the critical figure is 250 in Denmark, 2,000 in France, 20,000 in the Netherlands, 30,000 in Japan and 40,000 in Korea. The two criteria combined, total numbers and administrative organisation, are used in Canada, the U.S.A., Norway and Turkey. Finally, in the former Belgian Congo, the only grouping which counted was of non-natives —if there were 100 Belgians in one place, they were 'urban'. Economic criteria are also used: Peru takes the importance of the settlement and the major activity of its inhabitants; Israel brings in the 'urban aspect'; Italy takes a non-agricultural working population of over 50 per cent. To add to the confusion, some countries have modified their classification from time to time; Norway and Sweden have changed it since 1930, Spain since 1950, the U.S.A. between 1940 and 1950.

Lest this list of difficulties is in danger of becoming too discouraging, it is here ended so that the study of the geography of population may be begun.

PART II

MAN AND SPACE

CHAPTER THREE

The Great Human Masses

In 1976 the world's population, according to the available statistics, was about 4,000 million. It is not necessary, however, to have recourse to statistics to realise what diversity underlies this figure, what contrasts it implies in the density of the human groups, what minute differences in their localisation and structure, what racial complexity even—although this last notion is far more easily grasped theoretically than in the facts themselves.

RACIAL COMPLEXITY

Though it is necessary to make reference to the different races of mankind, the difficulty of this subject is very evident.

The notion of 'race'

The notion of 'race' is ill-defined. Most specialists nowadays agree in distinguishing three great human stocks; white, yellow (in which is included the American Indian branch, the so-called 'redskins') and black. But there is no unanimity even on this elementary classification based on the apparently incontestable criterion of skin colour. Some see evidence of a fourth stock, the brown, in the most ancient African inhabitants, the pygmies of the virgin forests of west-central Africa, who are less than 1·5 m tall, are mesocephalic, with brown skin and crinkled hair, and are related to the Negritoes of Asia and Oceania. However, this group is of small numerical significance.

Within each of these great stocks there are striking variations. A Scandinavian bears little resemblance to a Mediterranean: both are indeed 'white' but the one is small, with brown eyes and hair and a dull complexion, and generally brachycephalic, the other is tall and fair with blue eyes and a rosy complexion, and dolichocephalic. Similarly a Congolese, small and short-limbed, very hairy, and prognathous, is very different from a Nilotic, very tall and slender and with finely sculptured features. The great human stocks are themselves composite and divide into many branches; attempts have been made to parcel these up into more restricted groups known as 'races'. Thus, the black Africans comprise two great branches, the palaeo-negritoes, the first wave of peoples to invade the continent, and the Blacks who came later and who are themselves divided into four great races—Sudanese, Guineans and Congolese, South Africans, and Nilotic.

In order to categorise these races, a number of criteria are used in combination: external, readily recognisable features such as height, complexion, eye and hair colour, degree of hairiness, sleekness of hair, shape of the nose; bodily measurements such as cephalic index (i.e. the ratio of the length of the skull to its breadth; thus are defined three great groups, brachycephalic (broad-headed), dolichocephalic (long-headed) and mesocephalic; and internal characteristics ascertained by the measurement of certain parts of the skeleton, or by blood-analysis. The results, however, are often uncertain or contradictory, and it is easy for racial theorists to draw misleading conclusions.

We need only follow the prehistorians in their researches into the peopling of Europe, and in particular of Western Europe which, for thousands of years, was the remotest corner of the known world, to be convinced of the inextricable mixture that has taken place, to which the thousand-and-one faces of the inhabitants bear witness. The same thing is observable in the market squares of the peripheral parts of Asia—Middle East, India, Indochina, etc. Further, we need only read the works of the ethnologists to understand how difficult is racial classification; the Bushmen, who were the second occupants of the African continent after the Pygmies, are yellow-skinned people of mongoloid race; now lost amongst the blacks, they are reduced to a few thousands and confined to the Kalahari district; in the Ethiopians, even more than in the Nilotics, negroid bodies and a black skin are associated with European-type faces, which bear witness to a very ancient cross-breeding; and what we shall say of the Peuls, one of the most troublesome enigmas of black Africa?

Finally, even the term 'race' itself is employed in very disputable manner in some cases: thus the famous 'Bantu' are a group speaking related languages but without physical unity, and the name is often used in Africa to denote a common civilisation rather than an anthropological area. Similarly the term 'Arab' has lost all racial significance, and the original characterisations are found only in certain Bedouin tribes.

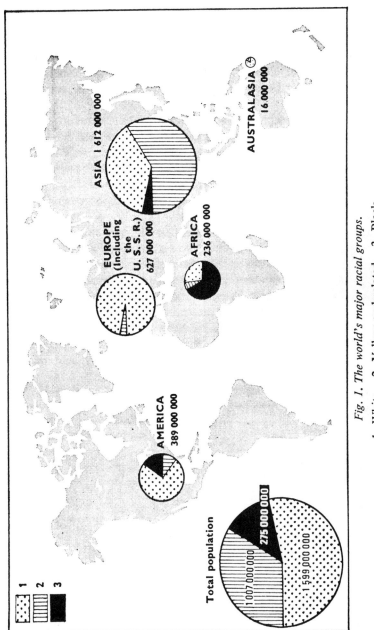

Fig. 1. The world's major racial groups.

1. White.   2. Yellow and related.   3. Black.

The subdivided circle in the left-hand corner shows the proportions in the world as a whole, and similarly for each continent.

The Middle East is a good example of the confusion between communities of different types, racial, religious, linguistic; there are Arabic-speaking Christians and Muslims who are Arab neither by race nor by speech; even the Jewish 'race', one of the most closed communities of all, does not escape contamination—in southern Morocco there are certain 'mellahs' (Jewish quarters) peopled by judaised Berbers.

Though the geographer who studies the population of a region may be led, in order to explain certain forms of habitat, the aptitudes of a given community, or other civilisation characteristics of the present day, to follow the paths of the specialists in their researches into population, and the varied contributions which they have produced, he is outside his proper field in systematically penetrating this often deceiving labyrinth.

Even with regard to the most elementary human differentiation represented by skin colour, systematic classification is almost impossible, partly because of the innumerable cross-breedings which have given every imaginable tint of brown, and partly because of the impossibility of scientific discrimination between the mixtures. There is the famous dictum: 'In the United States, a drop of black blood makes one black; in South America, a drop of white blood and one is considered white.' According to the whim of the legislators, the

Major Human Stocks in 1960 (millions)[1]

	White	Yellow and related groups[2]	Black[3]
Europe (excluding U.S.S.R.)	418	—	—
U.S.S.R.	186	23	—
Asia (excluding U.S.S.R.)	624	930	58
North America	182	1	17
Central and South America	112	42	36
Africa	64	10	162
Oceania	13	1	2
Total	1599	1007	275

[1] Since this date, many countries have ceased to classify their nationals according to race, and it is thus impossible to give more recent overall figures.
[2] People of E. and S.E. Asia and American Indians.
[3] Including half-castes.

half-breed is either a separate class, as with Eurasians in the areas of old European colonisation in south-east Asia, and the 'coloured' people of South Africa, or is included in the favoured group as in the countries of Latin America, or is judged of inferior caste. But in order to obliterate the disparities amongst their people, certain states have simply dropped the grouping from their statistics; thus Mexico has not for several decades published figures of the racial composition of the population.

With all these reservations, it is still worthwhile to cite the latest statistical estimates of racial grouping.

Whites appear to be the dominant element, and though Europe is the greatest essentially white continent, Asia contains the greatest numbers, for the majority of the peoples of the Indian peninsula and of the Middle East are classed as white.

The great crossroads of humanity

Certain parts of the world are veritable melting-pots where the great human stocks are juxtaposed and inextricably mixed. In general historical vicissitudes have produced this cohabitation, which has been fertile, more or less, in its production of mixed breeds. The north-east of South America and South Africa offer two contrasting examples of such regions.

The extreme complexity of the population of *Indian Latin America* stems from a colonisation which was at the same time exploration and peopling, from the widespread absence of racial prejudice, from the varied combinations of latitude and altitude which provided a wide variety of natural environments.

The 'Indian' substratum was here much denser than in North America. Its origin appears complex: the discovery of the remains of more ancient occupants shows that the first migrations go back no further than between the twentieth and tenth centuries B.C. and were effected from North East Asia across the Behring Strait; but local ethnographic, linguistic, ethnic and pathological analogies, sometimes backed up by legend and tradition, support the idea of subsidiary, more or less localised waves of Melanesians, Polynesians and Chinese moving towards lower California and the coasts and western mountains of central South America; and perhaps even Australian aboriginals amongst the Onas tribe of Tierra del Fuego. By the time of the European conquest there were some 12 million inhabitants. The first white occupants settled in regions where the Indians—who

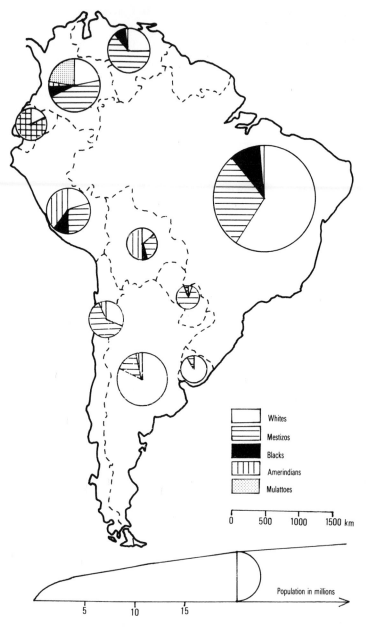

Whites

Mestizos

Blacks

Amerindians

Mulattoes

0   500   1000   1500 km

Population in millions

5   10   15

Fig. 2. The major racial groups of Latin America.

provided an immediate labour supply—were particularly numerous. But hard labour rapidly reduced these fragile people in the most accessible areas; in 150 years they had disappeared from the Antilles, from the plains of the Orinoco, and from the lower Amazon. And so, on the recommendation of Father Bartolomé de Las Cases, the Iberians, frightened by the demise of the Indians and already accustomed to using black labour, began the importation of African slaves from 1510 to Hispaniola (Cuba), and from 1538 to Brazil. This cruel traffic, which decimated the finest races of Africa, was accompanied by grievous losses of human life which necessitated constant further supplies in order to maintain the labour supply of the plantations and mines. From the beginning of the sixteenth century to the progressive abolition of slavery in the nineteenth (Argentina suppressed the importation of 'ebony wood' in 1813, Brazil officially in 1831 and effectively by 1852; slavery disappeared from Haiti as early as 1804, in 1853 from Bolivia, Colombia and Venezuela, and in 1888 from Brazil) this system must have been responsible for the introduction of some 20 million blacks into the Americas. In Latin America there remained 3 million at the time of the abolition of the slave trade, and there are more than 20 million now, to which number a further 50 per cent must be added for mulattoes (half-castes).

The whites themselves arrived in several waves; the colonial period had brought poor peasants as well as managers, administrators and clerks. The total can scarcely have exceeded a few hundreds of thousands but these first arrivals mingled with the natives. At the end of the eighteenth century, there were in certain parts of Latin America ten times more coloured people, pure or half-caste, than white. The second stage begins with independence and the end of slavery. From 1810 to 1950, perhaps 12 million Europeans have settled in Latin America, many fewer than in North America, for the greater distance, the less favourable climate, and the presence of certain fearful diseases such as yellow fever, discouraged the newcomer or hindered his final settlement. It was especially the southern territories, with a more temperate climate, which profited from this white immigration. Finally the Asiatics have come in again, but this time in small numbers. In the course of recent decades some 200,000 Japanese have settled in Brazil, 25,000 Chinese coolies in Cuba, and also real Indians from India, and also Javanese, in some of the Antilles and in the former Guianas.

From these multiple migrations, distributed essentially by geographical circumstances, can be recognised what have been called the 'Four Americas'. In the north-east of South America, that is on the extensive fringe which extends from north-east Brazil to the roots of the isthmus of Panama, is 'mixed America'; in the hot and humid coastal plains blacks predominate whilst the interior and the uplands are the domain of the Indian; half-castes, mulattoes and 'Zambos' (Negro-Indian mixtures) are frequent; whites are present but not numerous, Asiatic Indians appear in Guyana and Japanese in Surinam. This is the most varied human melting-pot in the whole world. In the parts of Brazil which fall within this zone, one may suggest, on the basis of statistics, descriptions and personal experience the following classification: white, or mainly white, 45 per cent, black 16 per cent, Indian 3 per cent, half-castes of all varieties 36 per cent. In Colombia, blacks and mulattoes form 35 per cent of the population.

Races of the West Indies (percentage)

	White	Black	Mulattoes	Asiatics
Cuba	75	24	—	1[1]
Haiti	—	98	—	—
Dominican Republic	13	19	68	—
Puerto Rico	73	4	23	—
Virgin Isles	9	69	22	—
Jamaica	1·6	74	24·3	—
Tobago		100		
Trinidad	—	—	—	33[2]
Barbados	7	70	—	—
Bahamas	15	85	—	—

Source: A. Viatte in *Encyclopédie de l'Amérique Latine*, 283–322
[1] Chinese.   [2] Hindus.

In the north, in the islands, is 'Brown America', where the rapid and almost complete extinction of the Indians and the existence of several great slave markets contributed to the formation of a population in which black is abundant. The record is held by Haiti with 98 per cent blacks running their own state and having for a time thought of excluding whites. Elsewhere the proportion of mulattoes is high and the palest of them pass as white; in Cuba, the 'whites', less numerous than the blacks in 1840, now comprise 75 per cent of the population, and in Puerto Rico 73 per cent.

In the west, the distance from Europe, and the presence of mountain refuges, for long the seat of indigenous communities of whom some were famous, like the Incas, have allowed the preservation of 'Red America'; its area coincides with the isthmian chains and with the Cordillera and high plateaux of western South America. This zone commences even north of the Rio Grande, in the most inhospitable and remote regions of southwestern U.S.A., and continues to the end of Tierra del Fuego. The most reliable sources permit the following tabulation:

States	*Population with Indian blood per cent*	*Of which Pure Indian per cent*
Mexico	88	33
Costa Rica	49	2
Nicaragua	81	4
Panama	60	10
Honduras	85	40
San Salvador	92	40
Guatemala	97	67
West Indies	—	—
Bolivia	85	51
Peru	93	46
Equador	70	50
Guianas	—	2·4
Venezuela	—	3·7
Colombia	—	8
Brazil	15	4
Paraguay	93	6
Chile	75	10
Argentina	—	1
Uruguay	—	—

Lastly, Argentina forms the pivot of the fourth section—'White

America'. Here, the Indians, who even at first, were never numerous, have been decimated, almost exterminated (in Argentina there are 98 per cent whites), or completely assimilated, e.g. in Uruguay and in the south or south-eastern states of Brazil, where the whites are 86·9 per cent, the blacks 6·7 per cent, and the half-castes 4·5 per cent.

South Africa offers a picture similar and yet different. Within a total of 25·5 million inhabitants, there are 71 per cent Bantu, 17 per cent European, 2.8 per cent Asiatic and 9.2 per cent 'Coloured' (half-caste). It is the progressive occupation of the territories that has produced this variety. First the incoming of the whites, the Boers, descendants of the original Dutch settlers, and later the British, penetrating into the interior in waves—the 'treks' which began in 1834; then the occupation of the rich mineral-bearing regions, and the importation of Asiatic labour for the plantations of Natal; and lastly the multiplication of the blacks, their infiltration into towns and their

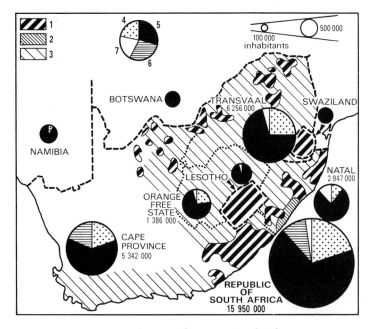

Fig. 3. Population and races in South Africa.

1. Native reserves.   2. Areas with Asiatic population dominant.   3. Major white areas (with working population of Coloured near Cape Town, Black elsewhere). Subdivision of circles: 4. White.   5. Black.   6. Coloured.
7. Asiatic.

employment as manual labourers in all branches of economic activity, and the confinement of some of them in the meagre native reserves. At the end of the eighteenth century there were 15,000 whites in South Africa; in mid-nineteenth century, 150,000; in 1904, 1,120,000 (between these last two dates, in 1867, diamonds had been discovered); at present, a little over 3 million. The half-castes are not numerous, and are made up of the descendants of the slaves of the old Cape colonists, the remnants of the Hottentots and the 'coloured' half-caste Europeans.

Here, in contrast to what happens in South America, racial classification is solidly established and enumerated, and legislation prohibits all marriage and even sexual intercourse between whites and other groups. A policy of 'apartheid' (complete separation of black and white communities) has been adopted, but is difficult of full realisation in present economic and territorial circumstances.

Of the Asiatics, 82 per cent are grouped in a belt ninety miles by thirty miles stretching north and south of Durban; they actually make up 31 per cent of the population of this city. The 'Coloured' people are strongly localised (90 per cent) in the locality of their origin, i.e. Cape Province, and indeed 25 per cent of them are to be found in Cape Town and environs. According to the census of 1951, they were actually more numerous than the Europeans in Cape Province. The whites are mainly in the west and south of Cape Province and in southern Transvaal. As for the Bantus, their major domain is the south-east where are found the native reserves which stretch, surrounded by European lands in the Low Veld, from Port Elizabeth to the Mozambique frontier, and in the north west, along the frontier which separates the Republic from Botswana. In pursuance of the apartheid policy adopted by the white Afrikaners, reserves totalling 160,000 sq. km. have been conceded since 1973, making eight Bantu states containing 14 million inhabitants. These states enjoy a certain degree of autonomy and will in time become independent: Transkei has had a government since 1956 and a legislative assembly since 1963, and in 1976 it hoisted its own flag.

The towns are the points of contact if not of mixing; they attract the non-white because of the economic enterprises created by the whites. Since 1946, there have been as many black as white urban dwellers, and if all the non-whites are included, the proportion of whites has recently decreased to about 30 per cent.

In other parts of the world one finds a greater or less degree of 'cohabitation' or living together. In the southern U.S.A. black and white, though equal in law, in fact practise racial segregation; in Soviet Asia the russification of the territories has provoked large migrations of whites who mingle freely with the 'yellow' natives; in the Indian sub-continent black and white mix. But certain major physical features mark the boundaries of major racial stocks—the Sahara, for example, despite many infiltrations, is substantially the barrier between black and white in Africa, whilst the great mountain chains of central Asia and southern China almost sever white from yellow.

If one discounts the great colonial movements of the last few centuries, the domain of the white race is confined to Europe, the Mediterranean lands and southern Asia, that is one-eighth of the world's land surface. Recent migrations and conquests have permitted the whites to triple this domain, even leaving aside those areas where they do not practically form the total population (for example Latin America, with the exception of Argentina). The white races, and especially the European sections thereof, have until now revealed themselves largely as conquerors, and their territory has grown from 17 per cent to 50 per cent of the world's land surface. This fact, pregnant with meaning, has been the main happening of the last two centuries; it may well be that the 'coloured awakening' will be the key to the world of tomorrow.

Disparity between continents

Of the 3,967 million people in the world in 1975, more than half were in Asia (56·7 per cent):

Population of Continents in 1964 *and* 1975 (millions)
(*Estimated*)

	1964	1975
Africa	276	403
America	459	550
Asia	1,823	2,255
Europe	440	473
Oceania	17	22
U.S.S.R.	230	254

GENERAL DISTRIBUTION

Two maps side by side show first the areas of the different countries reduced to easily comparable geometrical forms, and secondly the population of these countries also represented by geometrical shapes corresponding in size to the numbers of inhabitants. These two maps show strikingly the differences between the various parts of the world.

In all, Eurasia has three-quarters of the world's population; the Old World contains 86 per cent and the New World only 14 per cent. Other disparities appear also: two-thirds of the world's people live on one-seventh of its area. Some 3,000 million (about eleven-twelfths of the world's total) occupy the northern hemisphere, which is more favourable for living than the southern, both in the Old World (93·5 per cent in the northern hemisphere) and in the young Americas (72 per cent in the northern hemisphere). Of course this is partly due to the inequality of the extent of land in the Old World as against the New, and in the northern hemisphere as against the southern; however, if one considers not only total numbers but density, one is forced to look for other causes as well.

Latitude and population

If we divide the globe into belts limited by equidistant parallels of latitude, enormous differences in population appear. Though there is much land north of 60°, as in North America and Asia, the population here is very small. The strongest concentrations are found in the northern hemisphere between latitudes 60 and 20, that is in the temperate zone and at the northern limits of the tropical zone.

The most important region is the 'underbelly' of Asia, bordering the Pacific and Indian Oceans from northern China to the western limits of the Indian subcontinent; if we add the peninsular and island fringes, which are mostly swarming with humanity, 2,170 million people, 54 per cent of the world's population, live in this region. The second great belt comprises peninsular Europe, with Russia as far as the Urals; here dwell 600 million people, 15 per cent of the world's total. The third region is eastern North America, on the Europe-facing Atlantic fringe, which has 130 million. If we add the 3 per cent represented here, we see that the three great concentrations, of which the last two are entirely in the temperate zone, and the first is largely tropical, extending actually to the equator in the Indonesian islands, contain three-quarters of the world's population.

It is also in the temperate zone that are to be found the other note-worthy but smaller concentrations—the northern and southern extremities of Africa, south-eastern Australia, the states and provinces grouped around the Plate estuary, the western fringe of the U.S.A.—totalling about a hundred million people. Indeed the importance of the temperate latitudes in the localisation of the spreads of population, both dense and sparse as well, is remarkable, as is the relative void of the intertropical latitudes (except for parts of the East Indies).

Finally, the remaining 6 or 7 million people are dispersed over the lands of the globe in knots or strings controlled by exceptional circumstances—groups in the high basins of Mexico, central America and the Andes, on the littoral fringe of eastern and north-eastern Brazil, in the cleared and conquered lands of São Paulo, in oases at the foot of the Andes; in Africa, along the ribbon of the Nile, and local concentrations in the coastal regions of the Gulf of Guinea, in Zanzibar and in the vicinity of Lake Victoria; in the Middle East and Asiatic Russia, on coastal fringes, in valleys, or in concentrations around mineral fields and newly-developing centres of industry, interrupting but locally the vast expanse of sparsely peopled terrain.

Opposed to these relatively densely peopled lands are the vast spaces in which there may be less than one person to the square kilometre, such as the glaciated solitudes in the high latitudes of North America and Asia, north of the sixtieth parallel, the Scandinavian areas north of the Arctic circle, the great open spaces in the heart of the different continents, such as central Asia or the country east of the Caspian sea, the Sahara, the Kalahari, the centre of Australia, and of Amazonia, and long sinuous ribbons coinciding largely with the great mountain zones of the world.

The thousand and one variations on this theme can find no simple and uniform explanation.

Truth and fiction about population density

Density, the number of people per square mile (or kilometre or any other unit) is a means at once convenient and misleading for the evaluation of the differences in population distribution. On average there are 29·3 persons per sq. km. in the whole world, but Oceania has only 2·4, Africa 12·8 and the Americas 13·7, amongst the least peopled continents, whilst Asia has 80·7 and Europe (excluding the

U.S.S.R.) has 95. Densities are thus variable enough on a continental scale, but they become much more so with a reduction in the areas to the size of individual states. Here the first place is held by the Netherlands with 368 people per sq. km., followed by Belgium with 322, Japan (292) and the United Kingdom (219). It seems that small states and particularly island states have dense population, for example Taiwan (435) and Puerto Rico (347); although the island of

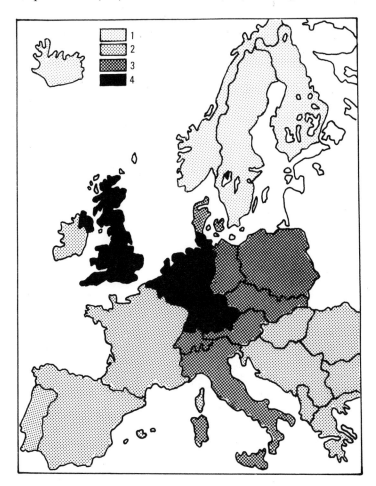

Fig. 4. Density of population in western Europe.
Density per sq. km.: 1. Under 20 persons;   2. 20 to 100;   3. 100 to 200;
4. Over 200.

Java, with 606, is easily in the lead, it is but a part of Indonesia whose average density is only 86, including as it does the large and sparsely peopled island of Kalimantan (Borneo). In contrast, amongst the world's giant states, China has 88, the U.S.S.R. has only 11·4, Canada 2·3, U.S.A. 22·6, Brazil 12·6 and Australia 1·8.

These are only overall values; they are of least significance when the area involved is vast and has marked environmental differentiation. Though the huge Soviet Union, extending into two continents, has but 11·3 people to the square kilometre the density is even lower, at 2·8 in the Asiatic portion whilst reaching 28·6 in European Russia; the Chinese average is 88, but the deltaic plains of the Yang-tse-Kiang and the Hoang Ho have over 500 and the interior high plateaux of Tibet only 1·2, with 2·6 in Tsing Hai and 3 in Sinkiang. Even if the state is small the contrasts can be just as striking: Egypt averages 37 persons per square kilometre but the narrow ribbon of settlement nourished by the waters of the Nile has over 600. In the extremely varied regions of western Europe density values are even more contrasted, alpine valleys or even those of lower mountains like the mining valleys of South Wales containing bead-strings of villages which contrast with the solitude of the intervening mountains. Conversely, homogeneity within the natural environment is often linked with an even distribution of population. In Europe the great plain of northern Germany and Poland averages 36 persons per square kilometre except along the rivers and coasts and in the vicinity of towns; in the great central plains of North America, densities of 3 per square kilometre in Canada west of the Great Lakes and 11 in the U.S.A. west of the middle Mississippi, are found with remarkable regularity over wide areas. Thus, it is rare that regions of even density coincide with a political unit, and the larger the unit, the less likely is the coincidence.

This is not the only difficulty. Just as all the human beings enumerated are not uniformly distributed, so they have not all the same capacity for action, the same wealth, the same needs. How can one compare the 326 people per square kilometre of England and Wales, of whom but 3 per cent derive their income from agriculture, and of whom only 22 per cent are under fifteen years of age, with the 606 of Java, of whom four-fifths are rural and 40 per cent children? In both cases the territory is well populated but the mode and standards of life are profoundly different and a cartographic representation of the two types of population would only show a part of the fundamental differences between them.

The calculation of 'economic density' has been proposed, using as a basis the net cultivable area in relation either to the total population or to the number of rural inhabitants. Another basis suggested is the 'standard land-unit', the coefficients for which enable account to be taken of different modes of land use. Others have attempted to calculate 'indices' based on the calories produced by countries having a strong agricultural dominance, or on productivity, or on the values of the national incomes. All these methods have their interest in showing up this or that aspect of population density, but none is of undisputed absolute value and above all none escapes from the criticism that, being applied to large and complex areas, it distorts a phenomenon which is essentially localised and variable.

Extreme density values

The above remarks have shown the great inequality of population distribution. The apparent significance of latitude has already been noted; one might add to it the repulsive effect of the great continental masses—the heart of Eurasia, of Africa, the great plains and plateaux in the middle of North and South America, and of Australia, as opposed to the fringes of greater or less depth, much more densely peopled. In Europe, excluding Scandinavia, the average densities are 120 per square kilometre to the west of a line from Denmark to Italy, only 90 to the east thereof, with about 30 in European Russia. In North America, at the latitude of New York, densities reach over 100 in the north east, 50 to the south of the Great Lakes and less than 10 west of the Mississippi. The heart of Africa, whether desert as in the Sahara or impenetrable equatorial forest, is also largely empty (3 persons per square kilometre in central Africa in general, with less than one in some forested areas and in the Sahara).

However, the amplitude of the scale of local densities is attributable especially to the mode of grouping of the individual people, and to the difference, fundamental though becoming less and less precise in fact, between rural and urban population. What a contrast, for example, between the vast central plains of the United States, with their prosperous mechanised agriculture, and the rice fields of the Far East, tilled with meticulous care! These two types of rural exploitation represent just about the two extremes of human density in areas of continuous cultivation; in a village in Yunnan 500 or 600 persons live on the same space as a family farm of five or six people in the United States.

The greatest rural concentrations would appear to be attained in

Java, where there are 1,038 persons per square kilometre on the rich soils of the Klaten district, more than 700 on those of Cheribon and Sukohardjo, and in China, where the fertile red earths of Szechwan support innumerable hamlets giving densities of over 700. It is the Far East which seems to hold the records both for absolute density and for its extent; almost all the deltaic and coastal plains of monsoon Asia bear more than 300 peasants to the square kilometre and this has been called a 'vegetable civilisation' for life there depends on the harvest which supplies food, clothing and constructional materials. Only in the Nile valley does a comparable situation exist: the valley and the upper delta have between 400 and 600 persons per square kilometre. There is no limit to rural congestion other than the possibility of survival, and the capacity of these teeming masses to withstand privations, and to adapt themselves to concentrated misery, seems almost infinite; nevertheless a density of 1,000 would seem to be the absolute maximum.

It is quite otherwise with urban agglomerations, where conditions are very different both in the form and grouping of the dwellings and in the origin of the resources which support them. For the town, the only problem is the space necessary for the disposition of houses and ancillary buildings, in accordance with agreed standards. It would be vain to fix limits or even to suggest figures for overcrowding: Paris, one of the most congested cities of the western world, had over 34,000 persons per square kilometre; the population is only half as dense in London, one-fifth as dense in New York. English town-planners in their conception of New Towns, have envisaged an ideal density of 5,000 persons per square kilometre (or 20 to the acre); in contrast, some of the densities encountered in the old quarters of certain towns in other continents appear quite fantastic—200,000 per square kilometre, for example, in the casbah of Algiers, and even 290,000 per square kilometre (1,174 to the acre) in the town of Victoria in Hong Kong.

We may note in passing a small cartographic problem. The representation of the distribution of population will vary greatly according to whether one considers an overall density or a mean rural density with appropriate symbols for the towns.

Regional gradations in distribution

Europe, the most populous of all the continents in relation to its size is also the one in which the distribution is most even; there are no central deserts, but only an increasing sparsity of population in the northern regions. For the trio Sweden, Norway and Finland, the mean density is only 15·2 per square kilometre and though there may be permanent dwellings beyond the Arctic circle they are but small and con-

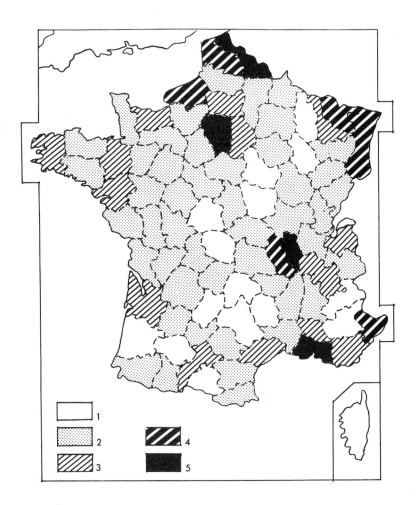

Fig. 5. Population density by départements in France, 1975.
Density per sq. km: 1. Under 40 persons; 2. From 41 to 92 (national average); 3. From 93 to 149; 4. From 150 to 299; 5. From 300 to 500. The département of Seine has 21,820 per sq. km.

sist solely of a special group, the Lapps. But it is worth while under-lining the dissymmetry which prevails on both sides of the Atlantic in respect of the northern limits of population; Oslo and Stockholm flourish in the same latitude as the Canadian Arctic desert, and in no other part of the world, except in the U.S.S.R., does normal human occupation extend so far towards the pole.

In the remainder of the continent, three facts are noteworthy: (1) the continuity of the spread of population which extends more or less everywhere; (2) its fragmentation by physical features which are numerous but of small size, nowhere presenting massive barriers to human penetration (in the Austrian Alps 50 per cent of the pre-Alps are inhabited and it is necessary to get into the high mountains to find as much as 80 per cent of the land inhospitable); (3) the existence of a diagonal belt of denser population extending from England to Italy via northern France, Belgium and the Netherlands, and western Germany; here densities are almost constantly above 200 persons per square kilometre and the towns are more numerous and more popu-lous than almost anywhere else; on the contrary, towards the south west, both in France and in the Iberian Peninsula, and to the east, in Eastern Europe, the population is spread less thickly. The French anomaly is striking: the country has only 97 persons per square kilo-metre but is bordered by states more intensively peopled; even moun-tainous Switzerland has 155 to the square kilometere and only the Iberian Peninsula is less peopled.

The U.S.S.R. extends across Europe and Asia, and presents two very different types of population distribution. West of the Urals the population is more numerous and in the vast central plains the den-sity is higher—over 50—along a wide belt which runs from the Ukraine, eastwards towards Sverdlovsk and south-eastwards along the shores of the Black Sea to countries beyond the Caucasus. In the northern plains the population decreases rapidly, as in neighbouring Scandinavia. In Asia, it is the valleys and basins, especially within a 1000-km wide belt along the southern frontier, which have become most peopled; the northern territories are harsher than in Europe and still more sporadically populated (only 6 per 10 square kilometres in central and north-eastern Siberia). The remote Pacific coast has a narrow fringe rather more populous. In all, 48 per cent of the popul-ation of the U.S.S.R. is gathered in 6 per cent of the territory, and 6 per cent of the people are scattered through two-thirds of the country.

In the southern portion of Asia, that is beyond the mountain backbone which marks the division between U.S.S.R. in the north, China and India in the south, two types of distribution are also encountered. To the west of the Indian peninsula, in the semi-desert crossroads of the Middle East, the people are grouped along the banks of rivers: Lebanon and Israel (163 persons per square kilometre) belong to the densely peopled Mediterranean coastlands whilst Iraq stretches along Mesopotamia. One can speak of an oasis population in the broadest sense, with vast empty spaces in between. Overall densities are low—19 to the square kilometre—but if they are calculated on the basis of utilisable land (which forms but 5 per cent of the whole) they rise to more than 300.

With India opens a new world—that of teeming human masses. As in Europe but on a much larger scale, nature has prepared a fragmented base; as in Europe, but in much greater profusion, people are spread throughout—in the greater and lesser plains, along the mountains, in the basins, on the deltas; numerous on the islands, more numerous still on the coastal margins, they only thin out with the onset of the massive brutality of central Asia. There are 300 persons per square kilometre in the Japanese archipelago, 435 in Taiwan, 183 in the Indian Republic, but only 7·4 in Laos; 339·4 in Shantung, 378·5 in Kiangsu, in Eastern China, but only 1 in Tibet. In detail, some curious variations appear, for all the south-eastern deltas are not equally peopled (over 450 rural people per square kilometre in the Tonkin delta but only 65 in the Irawaddy delta), and fertile Java (606) lies cheek-by-jowl with almost empty Borneo (65).

In Africa the most striking feature is the general symmetry of the distribution, especially in the whole western half. The relatively densely peopled northern and southern fringes, Maghreb and South Africa between Cape Town and Durban, are separated by two desert areas, the Sahara and south-west Africa, from tropical Africa, where, on each side of the relatively empty Congo basin astride the equator, are to be found somewhat greater densities. The distribution of these latter is remarkable, especially in the great subcontinental bulge which borders the Gulf of Guinea; alternating bands extend E.–W. parallel to the coast. The coast is irregularly but fairly populated with over 20 per square kilometre on an average; similar densities are found in a belt some 700–800 km to the north, along a zone extending from Cape Verde to northern Nigeria; in between, there is a relatively sparsely populated belt commencing 150–250 km from the coast. It would appear that this anomaly is not conditioned by any natural geographical factors.

The eastern half of Africa has no such symmetrical E.–W. distribution. In the north the peopling resembles that of the Middle East—the ribbon along the Nile oasis, amidst the sand and rocks of the desert, runs through the Sudan and Egypt to a delta which has nothing of the richness of the great Asiatic deltas and in fact has a low and wide fringe still scarcely tamed by man. In the centre, the mountains and especially the surroundings of the great lakes, appear as favoured areas where the population flourishes, high above the plains, which are relatively empty except along the coast. In the southern part of Africa the dissymetry is sharp, between the west, with its near-desert north of the coastal fringe, and the east which is much more densely peopled, both in a 200-km wide belt along the coast and in clusters in the interior. In all, Africa is, of all the three Old World continents, the least populated, and is not much more so than the Americas.

The American New World, elongated almost from one polar circle to the other, contains the emptiness not only of the vast glaciated Canadian northlands and Alaska (in Canada 90 per cent of the population lives less than 300 km from the U.S. frontier) but also of the impenetrable virgin forests of the equatorial Amazon basin (mostly in Brazil). It so happens that the greatest breadth of both continents is found in these particularly inhospitable latitudes. In the U.S.A. as in Canada more than three-quarters of the population is concentrated in the eastern half. The great estuaries and embayments of the U.S. coast from Boston to Washington are bordered by an almost continuous belt of cities which is unrivalled elsewhere in the world—a veritable 'Megalopolis' with 40 million people. The shores of the Great Lakes and the valley areas in general have also dense agglomeration, and in this country where the newly-formed States were often delimited by rivers, it is common to find States with their frontiers more densely peopled than their interior—as with Arkansas, Missouri and Kentucky for example. The mountains on the other hand are sufficiently large and high to have hindered human penetration; but their edges and their interior basins are relatively well populated, and the detailed distribution offers some curious shapes, such as the N.E.–S.W. alignment in the Appalachian valleys parallel to the axes of the mountain folds, and the geometrical pattern of the great plains which comes to an abrupt stop at the foot of the Cordillera.

Beyond the Mexican frontier there is a remarkable change. In the

West Indies there is a density rare in the Americas; though Cuba (79 persons per square kilometre) and the Dominican Republic (96) are but moderately peopled, Haiti with 166 and Puerto Rico with 347 are more like areas of the older continents. In the Central American isthmian zone, mountains play a dominant role; their slopes, high basins and valleys are much more sought after by the rural and by the urban population than the coastal plains, which are often almost empty as in Lower California (where the contrast with the State of California is truly remarkable) and in eastern Yucatan. In Mexico, 50 per cent of the population lives on the high central plateaux at elevations of over 1800 m; in Costa Rica, 70 per cent dwell in the high valleys in and around the capital city.

This pre-eminence of the mountain settlement, as opposed to the low population of the coasts, is found again south of Panama. In South America, on the east coast, there is population only between the mouths of the Amazon and latitude 40°S; on the west coast the population is sparse or non-existent around the Tropic and only becomes dense in the temperate latitudes of Chile. A second remarkable fact is the discontinuity of the settlement, and the isolation of one group from another. This is the continent of empty frontier zones (hence the difficulty of boundary-demarcation problems). Finally, the interior of South America is almost completely empty; a vast and long triangle of solitude stretches from the plains of the Orinoco to the interior of north-eastern Brazil and right down to the Tierra del Fuego, scarcely interrupted by a diagonal which joins the high plateaus of Bolivia to the town-clusters around the Plate estuary via the oases of the Tucuman district. The physical opposition presented by the abrupt and lofty mountains of the western Cordillera, and the broader plateau massifs of the east is reflected in the two main types of population distribution—nodes or ribbons, very precisely delimited, in the basins and valleys of the western mountains, and vast clusters and bands of almost continuous population, thinning out towards the interior, in the east, around the Plate Estuary, Rio de Janeiro and São Paulo, Bahia and Recife.

Australia, the last continent, which is also the world's largest island, has less than 2 persons (actually 1·8) to the square kilometre. Within a territory only slightly smaller than the U.S.A. it has but one-eighteenth of the latter's population. Moreover, this small population is very unequally distributed; 74 per cent of the inhabitants are concentrated in the south-eastern states on some 26 per cent of the territory, the six State capitals contain more than half the population, and the urban population amounts to 85 per cent of the whole. Conversely the centre of the continent is utterly empty except for a few mining centres and some stock-raising stations. In Western Australia the density is only 0·42 persons per square kilometre whereas it reaches 16 in the State of Victoria with the most favoured environment of the whole continent.

CHAPTER FOUR

Factors in Population Distribution

The rapid description in Chapter 3 of the distribution of mankind over the globe suggests immediately the fundamental importance of certain factors; the role of the physical environment is incontestable, but though it forms the inescapable basis it is capable of modification and adaptation. On the one hand, historic and economic events play their part; on the other, man himself is by no means passive and powerless: endowed with a body and a mind, he enjoys a double privilege, for his organism has a certain natural suppleness which permits a considerable degree of adaptation, and his ingenuity gives him the possibility of combating, scientifically and technically, his external surroundings.

MAN AND THE NATURAL ENVIRONMENT

Among the physical elements whose role is most clearly marked are high latitudes, mountain masses, great deserts, the hot-wet regions, and of course water. Moreover, the influence of each of these factors is not simple, and the human body is subjected to multiple forces which exercise their influence at the same time on the vegetable and animal kingdoms and on the possibilities of exploitation and transport, and in consequence react with double effect upon man's activities.

The 'elasticity' of the human body

The human body can adapt itself to its natural environment. Perhaps an adaptation wrought over thousands of years is to be seen in the distribution of black and white races, for the white man is particularly the habitant of the temperate zone and the black man of the hot regions. The latter is undoubtedly better adapted than the former to life in the hot countries; the strong pigmentation of his skin forms a sort of screen which puts him 'in the shade', so to speak, and allows him to work naked, and thus reduces the amount of salt loss through evaporation; the great number of sweat-glands, which give him greater capacity for perspiration, the multiplicity of sub-cutaneous blood capillaries which are dilatable and increase the peripheral blood circulation—these things permit him to maintain more easily his thermal equilibrium.

Other adaptations can be seen on the individual scale: for example, the human body has the power of thermal regulation which enables it to maintain a constant interior temperature despite great external variations; the alpinist can, by methodical training, overcome mountain sickness and proceed quite normally at elevations of over 3,000 metres—an ability which the Indian of the Andes enjoys through inheritance.

All the same, the capacity for adaptation seems to obey certain laws: biological suppleness is greater when health is good; it is easier for young people than for babies and the aged. Individuals with healthy stomachs, not over-addicted to alcohol, and accustomed to a rough and healthy life can accommodate far more changes than others. Representatives of a society characterised by cushioned comfort and perfect hygiene are the first victims when transplanted into primitive conditions. Just as man can lose the habit of walking, so he can lose his resistance to climatic change and to the assault of microbes. Finally, there is also the question of affinities; a Mediterranean adapts himself more readily to a tropical climate than a northern European; the white man, in general, withstands cold climate better than hot, especially when heat is combined with high humidity.

Adaptation, however, does not necessarily mean integration. Often the transplanted man survives but his descendants reveal their weaknesses. The most remarkable examples of integration are the whites in the tropical environment of the West Indies, of intertropical Latin America, and of northern Australia—but in all these cases 'Mediterranean' man was involved. Another is provided by the Negroes now installed in the industrial cities of northern United States, who show the adaptation, albeit relatively recent, of tropical man to a temperate environment.

Man and high latitude

The most redoubtable enemy of mankind would appear to be cold, especially when it attains, even seasonally, extreme values. A very low mean annual temperature is actually less unfavourable; on the contrary, vegetation prefers a warm season opposed by an extremely cold season.

In the southern hemisphere, outside the completely ice-covered Antarctica, the continents end more than 40 degrees from the Pole, and the extremity of South America is the only area with a 'high latitude' environment; narrow and tapered, it enjoys a maritime climate and the Fuegians have managed to survive with monthly minima of —4°C (25°F), maxima of 9°C (48 °F)—a range of only 15°C (23°F). In the northern hemisphere, on the other hand, large continental territories extend beyond the sixtieth parallel; they are most populated in western Europe, under the influence of an oceanic climate which itself is largely controlled by the warm Atlantic ocean currents. The traditional people of these lands are few in number and consist of specially adapted races—Eskimos and Lapps for example. In Canada, the limit of the populated area coincides roughly with the January isotherm of —20°C (—4°F); in the east, it scarcely goes beyond the edge of the temperate forest, in the centre, it coincides with the prairies, though in the west it reaches more northerly latitudes in the warmer climate of the Pacific fringe, and Alaska now has over 300,000 people, grouped mainly in the sheltered parts of the southern coast, and with 'natives' forming only 10 per cent. In the north of Soviet Russia, similarly, a new colonisation has added to the sporadic and precarious encampments a series of new towns, especially on the shores of the deep Arctic embayments—Kirovsk, founded in 1930, with 332,000 inhabitants, Vorkuta, founded in 1943, with 60,000, Igarka and the polar stations of Nordvik and Ikson.

In these regions the enemy is not only the cold which affects the circulation and provokes congestion, leading to frostbite followed by gangrene, which in turn leads to loss of energy, a progressive torpor and ultimately death; in addition the long polar night and the feebleness of the oblique rays of the sun are responsible for the extreme poverty of the native inhabitants and the precariousness of their resources, and for the vitamin deficiencies which react unfavourably in growth and reproduction. These factors are responsible, far more than the rigours of the temperature, for the very low fertility of certain of the polar people. The native peoples are physiologically adapted: sub-cutaneous fat protects them from variations in temperature, and their hairy system is well developed. They use all the resources of their environment with an ingenuity that only poor people possess; they consume much fat and oil, and the raw flesh and entrails of their kill; the seal provides food and clothing and light; they build their igloos of snow; seasonal migrations allow them to take advantage of the long daylight and of animal resources. However, natural adaptation was not always so remarkable—the Fuegians used to live naked, warming their rare infants in contact with their breast.

The unadapted man who penetrates such an environment feels the effects very much. The hallucinated narratives of the polar explorers of the heroic age bear eloquent witness—amputations, scurvy and wholesale deaths were the lot of these pioneers. Technical mastery has not suppressed the difficulties, it has merely enabled them to be overcome on occasions. It is impossible to conceive a general peopling of these lands, but the permanent establishment of certain important communities has certainly become possible. Without reckoning the advanced military bases or polar scientific stations, some 250,000 people have settled in Alaska since 1933; the Soviets have established more than a million individuals on the northern solitudes of Asiatic Russia in the last thirty years. A veritable artificial environment has been created in which ultra-violet rays, insulated houses and special vitaminised food help to neutralise the effect of the climate. Even an embryonic agriculture has been developed thanks to the transformation of the soil by the removal of stones, treating with lime, introducing bacteria, and fertilising and planting with species specially adapted to the vegetal rhythm of these high latitudes. It is the triumph of powerful and efficient but costly technology, of which the use can be but limited and determined by particular incentives.

Man and mountains

The role of altitude is much more complex. In the different climatic zones, relief introduces variety and gradation. If the relief is composed of bold mountain chains, steep slopes, narrow gorges, sterile and unstable rock, then whatever the altitude, it will oppose human occupation; but if there is a wide valley, an open basin, then new conditions arise for man to exploit. Located in a cold region, the mountains accentuate the cold and the humidity and repulse man, but if they rise in the torrid zone or among the deserts they become a haven of coolness, providing an environment which is reflected in the distribution of population. The analysis of the influence of relief is thus a delicate matter. The influence is a function of altitude, latitude, and, in detail, of aspect, steepness and the nature of the terrain.

Altitude exercises an absolute control over atmospheric pressure, which affects the human organism. Mountain sickness is well known; it affects some people at 1,800 m and might lead to death beyond

7,500 m. The mountaineer accustomed to height lives easily at more than 3,500 m in the Himalayan valleys or on the high plateau of the 'roof of the world' and even at more than 5,000 m in the Peruvian Andes. But altitude is not the only limiting factor; it combines with several others.

Mountains that repel. In temperate lands, altitude by itself does not operate to limit human occupation of mountains; cold and the poverty of resources paralyse life before altitude comes into play. In the European mountains, which are favoured by their small size and their situation in a densely peopled environment, permanent habitation does not rise above 300 m in the north of the British Isles, 600 m on the western sides of the mountains of southern Norway and little more than 900 m on the eastern side, less oceanic but drier and sunnier. At the other extreme, Trevelez (1,740 m) in Alpujana, is the highest village in Spain (if one excepts Soldeu in Andorra). In the northern pre-Alps, very wet and cool, the highest settlements reach 1,400 m (the general average limit is about 900 m); they reach 1,600 m in the central Alpine range of France, and 1,800 m in drier Austria. The three highest permanent villages in the Alps are about 2,000 m, but they are exceptionally situated on shoulders of wide valleys eroded in slate. Progress towards Mediterranean latitudes is not accompanied by a more intensive and higher settlement of the mountains, for the period of vegetative growth is then restricted not only by the length of the cold season but also by the summer drought; in the Portuguese Sierra d'Estrela, there are only three frost-free months, and two of these are completely rainless.

The slightest variations may be of significance in this marginal type of habitat; aspect and exposure are of great importance particularly for settlements at high elevations. In the upper Valais, 86 per cent of the population lives on the 'adret', i.e. the south-facing slope exposed to the sunshine.

In similar latitudes of north eastern U.S.A. the high and forested massifs are uninhabited and settlements, strung out along the larger valleys, more rarely in smaller valleys, hardly rise above 400 m in central Vermont, or 600 m in the interior of New York State. In the Appalachians the geometrical alignment of the valleys is faithfully followed by that of the settlement pattern. Forest covers the crests and the narrower incised valleys, whilst man utilises the alluvial floors of the larger valleys, and the flat-floored 'coves', for his habitations.

Mountains that attract. In the intertropical regions, by contrast, relief is an important climatic corrective, for mountains right on the Equator can be temperate and even cold. The great mountain backbones of central and western America, both North and South, though interposing an abrupt barrier to oceanic influences, rise up in great terraces, and contain high basins favourable for settlement, amply watered and with flat floors which are often covered with the fertile products of vulcanicity. These basins have been, since before Columbian days, the scene of human concentration, and they remain centres of population, more accessible from the Pacific coast, so that the political frontiers have been pushed westwards over the Andes, well into the empty zones of the Atlantic slope.

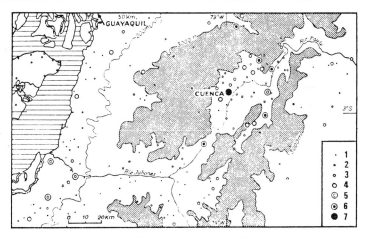

Fig. 6. Settlements in part of Peru.
Size of settlements: 1. Hamlets.   2. Under 500 inhabitants.   3. From 500 to 2000.   4. From 2000 to 5000.   5. From 5000 to 10,000.
6. From 10,000 to 50,000.   7. Over 50,000 inhabitants.

In Mexico, the population becomes very sparse below 1,000 m; climate and mineral resources, now as in the past, are responsible for this. On the high 'Mesas' tropical diseases are powerless and rainfalls more abundant, the fertile soils are derived from volcanic lavas, and mineral exploitation is intense and profitable. In Colombia, the Andean chains contain 98 per cent of the population, in Equador, 85 per cent, and in Peru 62 per cent; in Bolivia, 75 per cent of the population live at over 3,000 m, and La Paz, at 3,641 m, is the world's highest capital city, whilst the mining town of Potosi is at

4,100 m. The Indians are adapted to this altitude and climate, which perhaps explains their anxious passivity and unwillingness to descend to the coastal plantations, where they know that malaria, intestinal parasites and other miseries would await them. It is much the same in East Africa, where the highlands, with 65 people per square kilometre, overlook the almost empty Congo basin; *anopheles* and the tsetse fly disappear at these altitudes and cattle-raising can flourish. Similarly it is in the mountains that the southern Asiatics place their summer 'resorts' such as Darjeeling and Dalat.

In the dry regions also, mountains may figure as fortunate zones because they attract rainfall and so offer pasturage for animals, the possibility of irrigation in basins or on terraces, and above all because they create water reserves for the bordering arid plains. In monsoon Asia this rain-making function is vital; the monsoon wind blows over a plain such as the Indus and it remains insufferably dry, but when that same wind encounters the mountains it produces deluges, the highest rainfalls in the world, as much as 7,500–10,000 mm (300–400 in) a year. 'Arabia felix' displays its garden, cultivated lands and its coolness above a coastal fringe which is arid and deserted.

The negative role of relief. Mountains give rise to a special environment on their flanks which can either attract or repel settlements. If one may speak of a 'mountain environment' it is also true that there is a 'peri-montane' environment. Often around mountains there is quite a zone of human settlement. In Japan for example, on the population map, the mountains stand out as bare spaces in the midst of the overpopulated fringing and coastal plains. One could almost make a hydrographic map of the world's mountains simply by mapping the dense population of the valleys and the empty spaces between. To fly by night, for example, over the mining valleys of South Wales is to get an unforgettable impression of the lights of the valleys gleaming on the black background of the empty interfluves.

In many countries the coalfields, always densely populated, are situated at the foot of mountains or uplands, as in Europe, the U.S.S.R. and the U.S.A. Elsewhere, the geological structure permits the occurrence of powerful springs at the base of the mountains, as in the Bekaa, between the Lebanon and Anti-Lebanon ranges. On the fringe of mountains, the accumulated rock debris may play a varied part, according to the nature of the rocks, and the circumstances of climate and so of erosion: sterile stony plains as in the sub-Himalayan foothills or in the Lannemezan cone at the foot of the Pyrenees, are poorly peopled; alluvia formed from volcanic debris, as in Indonesia, are amongst the most densely peopled areas of the world.

The abundance of water in the mountains permits the irrigation of neighbouring or even distant plains; what would Egypt be without the mountains at the double head of the Nile, or California without its water resources in the Sierra Nevada, or Andalusia without its mountain rim? It also offers unlimited possibilities for the production of hydroelectric power, which in turn, through irrigation enables more life to be supported. At the very foot of the mountains, chaplets of villages and towns make use of sites which are favoured either by water resources or by facilities for travel (passes and cross-roads). In the United States, Denver and Pueblo lie at the eastern gateways into the mountains, whilst on the western side the ribbon-like plains of the Sacramento and San Joaquin, of Portland and Seattle and the narrow Pacific coastal plain, form a double fringe of densely-peopled territories.

Man and the desert

The lack of water is another great natural obstacle to human existence, and the desert can best be compared with the ocean. Oases have precise outlines like islands, and they often support an exceptionally dense population (1,200 per square kilometre in the palm-oases of Djerid, in the Sahara) in the midst of immense spaces that can only be crossed with some danger. Lack of water dehydrates the human body especially when it is accompanied by high temperature; if it is prolonged, it causes hallucinations—as with explorers deceived by mirages—torpor, and death. It is necessary to drink up to 12 litres a day to combat this, and often the white inhabitants wrap their infants in wet cloths to protect these frail creatures.

Traditionally, the people of the desert are renowned for their sobriety, their patience in times of scarcity, their capacity for rapid recuperation at the time of 'rebic',[1] all of which qualities bear witness to an adaptation to the environment. They are in constant struggle against the scarcity of water; nomadism has enabled them to utilise to the full the rare rains, either by rhythmic migrations following the seasons, as on the edge of the Sahara, or by exceptionally close observation of occasional storms, which are immediately followed, as in the Arabian desert. But the development of cultivation on the periphery of the deserts, and the existence of political frontiers—both

---

[1] 'rebic' : abundance of food after an occasional rainstorm.

evidence of the 'civilisation' of the desert's edge—reduce the possibility of movement and accelerate the process of permanent settlement. Another aspect of the struggle is the procuring of water in the midst of the desert. There are numerous and varied examples of this, such as the utilisation of the natural floods of rivers, as in Egypt and Mesopotamia, the use of *foggaras*, wells, barrages, canals and aqueducts. Modern techniques are enabling water to be provided by more and more complex works such as the gigantic dams of Soviet central Asia and south-western U.S.A., barrages of all sizes built by hand in China, very deep bore-holes, made for oil but often yielding water, as in northern Sahara, improved forms of covered culverts and underground canals as in the Israel Negev. Finally, other methods have been evolved such as dry-farming, and the adaptation of plant species (e.g. *Kochia* from the Australian desert planted in the Egyptian Libyan desert), just as in the polar regions, by a *tour de force* man has brought lawns and crops into the middle of the burning desert—witness the neighbourhood of the oilfields of the Sahara and Arabian deserts.

The expansion of human settlement in the desert is thus a possibility but it is strictly limited by the quantity of water available and is thus controlled by natural conditions and technical progress. Grandiose plans have been made in the Sahara, in Palestine, in Egypt and in Asiatic Russia but they are all either delayed or shelved; perhaps they will be realised one day. Attempts have also been made to provoke artificial rain but the method is not yet perfected. At all events, it would appear that of all the environments naturally hostile to man, the desert is the one in which most progress has been made and is still likely to be made.

Man and the hot, wet lands

The great regions of hot, wet climate in the world are those which, like the Congo Basin, have a mean annual temperature of over 26°C (79°F), more than 1500 mm (60 in) of rain a year, and a relative humidity of between 77 and 92 per cent; such regions coincide exactly with the zone of equatorial forests, impenetrable, indestructible, hostile in every way to human life. Here, vegetation is uncontrollable and every conceivable parasite flourishes. The soil, if deprived of its protective mantle, rapidly loses its apparent fertility; leached and encrusted, it can only support meagre and infrequent harvests, and fallow must last four or five times longer than cropping. Man is but a marginal being, menaced and infested. In Equatorial Africa, nine-tenths of the population are attacked by intestinal parasites; in India 100 million were a prey to malaria which, until the remarkable progress of the last thirty years, used annually to account for 2 million deaths. In America, in Africa, in Australia, the hot, wet regions cover 28 per cent of the surface of the continents but carry only 8 per cent of the world's population, with average densities of only 6 persons per square kilometre. In such an environment innumerable enemies lie in wait for the human, but it is the exuberance, the super-abundance, of the vegetable and microbe kingdoms which is most difficult to conquer.

Nevertheless, in similar latitudes in tropical Asia there are teeming millions; one-quarter of humanity living on 8 per cent of the utilisable land surface of the world, with densities averaging 70 to the square kilometre. Java, with the densest rural population in the world over a large area, is the outstanding example of this anomaly. But Java is an island, narrow and slender, easily penetrable and withal mountainous; streams flow freely down the slopes of the volcanic cones which furnish fertile debris; and a suggestion of seasonal differentiation appears as a result of the monsoon. Java thus has special physical conditions, and the contrast with the neighbouring but massive island of Borneo seems very striking. Minute gradations of climate and soil may alter the possibility of human settlement; and perhaps certain cultures and ways of life might permit man to adapt himself to such regions. The hypothesis has been put forward that a well-maintained system of irrigation in former times permitted a numerous population to live in regions which subsequently became malarial owing to the derangement of the water system; the ruined civilisations of Sri Lanka, and the relics buried under the vegetation of Yucatan, certainly give food for thought.

Though the difficulties of adaptation to such an environment are complex, they are far from being insurmountable. It is no longer a question of remedying deficiencies but, on the contrary, of restraining or suppressing certain elements which make life impossible. A choice is often difficult to make, but if the method selected is appropriate, progress can be rapid and considerable, as the following example shows.

The struggle against malaria. Malaria was one of the most widespread endemic diseases in the world. Though the presence of water is indispensable for the egg-laying female, the great variety of species of *anopheles* makes their development possible in a wide variety of physical conditions. Some lay their eggs in the still, muddy water of paddy-fields; others prefer clear and sunlit water; yet others are equally at home in brackish or in fresh water, and some are even content with the water collected in holes in trees or in the hollows of leaves. Thus the struggle has been a long and difficult one; deforestation or an alteration in the water regime might provoke the appearance of another species of mosquito with different habits. The systematic use of DDT has furnished a radical solution, perhaps even too radical, for the destruction of the undesirable *anopheles* has entailed that of useful insects also and there is a risk of indirectly altering the whole regional biological complex. Be that as it may, the method has certainly been crowned with success: regular spraying with insecticide, together with the introduction of fish which eat the mosquito larvae, and the medical treatment of infected individuals, have almost caused malaria to disappear from many regions. Moreover, the reduction in the necessity for taking quinine has allowed the birth rate to rise, as in Sri Lanka. The scale of this operation has extended far beyond the hot, wet regions—into the desert oases, and the low marshy plains of the Mediterranean, for example—but it shows that powerful modern technical aids can succeed where primitive defence methods and the empirical solutions of the past have only given partial results. The development of agricultural colonisation and the growth of large towns in regions formerly noted for their deadly unhealthiness are witnesses of the victories over the natural environment; and the list is not yet closed.

The varied role of water

The role of water is infinitely complex and diffuse; it does not characterise any specific parts of the globe but creeps in everywhere and reappears at every step. Though the absence of water may be an insurmountable obstacle, and its excess may offer grave inconvenience, the techniques of irrigation and drainage—that is, the control of water—are widespread, as we have seen, from the most primitive processes to the most grandiose modern schemes. But water enters in other ways into human life. To compare the climate of Great Britain, which has 210 persons per square kilometre, with the interior of Canada or Siberia, in the same latitude, is to realise the influence of the great maritime environments; even large lakes may have their own influence, as in the case of the Great Lakes of North America.

Water is also important as a means of transport and of penetration, and as the source of supplementary foodstuffs—but this brings us into the economic field. It is easy to see on a population map the greater density in coastal areas than in hinterlands (in Brittany 120 as against 60 per square kilometre), the settlement spreading from the rivers of eastern Canada, laid out on the 'range' system (rows of townships lying between successive meridians six miles apart), or the coincidence, in the United States, of certain State boundaries with populated valleys which served as means of penetration and became the favoured centres of colonisation. Moreover, many of the world's great cities are ports. Even in natural environments which are unfavourable and almost deserted by man, the presence of water introduces slight differences: amongst the sparse population of the Congo basin, there are more numerous settlements on the borders of Lake Mweru, for example, where, in the marshy and tse-tse infested plains, fishing provides an additional resource.

Geology and soils

Locally, within a region homogeneous in its climate and relief, the nature of the rocks and the soil cover is reflected in possible variations. The slopes of even dangerous volcanoes are sometimes swarming with people, as in Java, Japan, Sicily and Central America, where the decomposition of the lavas and ashes gives rise to fertile soils; the bareness of many areas of limestone, which lets the water through like a sieve into its depths, contrasts with the lush verdure of crests and summits made of crystalline rocks or sandstones, which are impermeable; whilst friable and crumbling rocks especially in stormy climates, yield rough, unstable and inhospitable ridges—often known as 'badlands'. The same contrasts exist in lowlands, where limestones are generally cultivated whilst the damp clay vales bear grassland and woods.

The effect of the solid rocks may be masked by a superficial cover: the fertile loams of central Europe and the loess terrains of the basins of northern and central China, with their high fertility and dense population, contrast with the vast northern regions covered with morainic debris or with glacial drift—as in large areas of northern Europe (including the greater part of the British Isles) and of North America—and with the thick but leached and easily lateritised soils of the intertropical lands. Here again, natural conditions and economic development are closely associated and are strongly reflected in population densities.

Physical environment and natural regions

To detach the physical elements in order to examine separately their respective roles is to falsify the geographical reality. In effect, all the elements function in a complex manner, reacting on each other and creating, within the great natural realm, a whole series of minor regions. The most important element determines the general character—for example, climate in the polar regions and the deserts, relief in the great mountain and plateau areas of the globe. When no physical element is dominant, the subtle balance of the different factors which are present provides a more fragmented framework. The variations are notably fewer and less conspicuous in the great plains of central U.S.A. or the even vaster plains of the U.S.S.R. than in the fragmented landscapes of western Europe. The conditions offered to man are thus extremely varied, and frequently political frontiers as well as population densities are affected.

England, dominated by a temperate oceanic climate, offers to the inhabitants low mountains covered with heathland suitable only for sheep, thin strips of limestone scarpland, sometimes covered with poor pasture and sometimes with wheat-fields, vales and plains where, according to the permeability of the soil, are found verdant pastures or prosperous arable farms. The slightest minor variation in the soil is sufficient to produce a 'micro' natural region which generations of ingenious farmers have exploited in an original way: the mosaic of Norfolk is a good example.

One could cut out an area the size of England from the great wheat-fields of the Dakotas or of the Ukraine, or from the Mato Grosso of Brazil, and the uniformity would be far greater. But when a railway traverses such uniformity, or when a town appears, the distribution of population is immediately modified. So natural conditions form but a background and the natural region is only a framework of greater or less extent, more or less precisely defined, within which complex economic factors play their part.

ECONOMIC FACTORS IN POPULATION DISTRIBUTION

Man is not just passive within his natural environment. He is active in proportion to his ingenuity, his numbers and his technical efficiency. Since we cannot separately examine every human enterprise in order to see its repercussion on the map of population density, we may attempt to establish a parallelism between the growth in the complexity of activities and the intensity of the peopling.

There is on the earth's surface a whole gamut of material civilisations ranging from the most elementary to the most complex; and this enables us to form a vivid picture of the general evolution which, extending over thousands of years, has affected some human groups more than others. Thus the general statements outlined for the present day may be applied to the successive phases of the past, and history linked to geography.

The natural economy

In primitive societies the effectiveness of man, deprived as he is of powerful aids and consumed by privation, is slight; the elasticity of the margin is slight and the number of the population is strictly limited by the potentialities of the local environment. The individual leads a marginal existence as to food and lodging, clothing and other needs. His consumption, meagre and often uncertain, cannot be reduced without danger to his survival. A precarious equilibrium between resources and consumption characterises such communities, and over the years, periodic famines have acted as demographic controls. In any case a large area is needed to furnish even the barest needs, and long migrations in the pursuit of fresh resources are often necessary, often almost continuous; local reserves, once consumed, are replaced but slowly if at all.

The simplest case is furnished by tribes living solely on natural products—the gatherers, hunters and fishermen. In these cases not only are the resources limited, but the people possess no proper technical means of utilizing them. One calls to mind the hunting methods of the pygmies in the African forests, or the Indians of the Amazon basin, before fire-arms came to their aid; and even with the possession of these arms, survival is still more or less hazardous. The Australian aboriginals would eat everything edible, animal or vegetable—at least 300 species of plants, whilst caterpillars, ants and locusts, which are the pests of settled agriculture, constitute a not inconsiderable part of their diet; even certain poisonous plants, after suitable treatment, are eaten.

Basically rural societies

Because man does not in general like to be the slave of chance, most societies, even very primitive ones, are preoccupied with basing their subsistence on the stronger foundations of animal-raising or agriculture. In their most primitive forms both these activities are large consumers of space, and the stock-raisers merely transpose the problem, for they use part of the natural resources through the intermediary of their herds, usually consuming milk and its products rather than meat. It is especially the vast steppes, on the fringes of the deserts, which have been traditionally used in this way, and some of them, as in central Africa and in the Near and Middle East, are still so used. Nomadism or semi-nomadism are the ways of life adapted to this primitive and extensive herding; they are not accompanied by high densities.

Primitive agriculture represents a more direct contact of man and the soil, even though it is based on the shifting cultivation of burnt-over patches ('ladang'). The lack of fertiliser, the primitiveness of the methods, the debility of the labour force, often female, and the rapid exhaustion of the soil impose an exceptionally long rhythm of rotation: in tropical Africa some five to twelve years of fallow ensue after only three years of cultivation, whilst in the dry interior of north-eastern Brazil, cultivation for one to four years is followed by twenty years of fallow. Manioc (cassava) in Brazil and in equatorial Africa, millet and sorghum in the Sudan and in the Deccan of India, are the basic food plants. This system also is hardly conducive to high population densities—3 to 5 persons per square kilometre appears to be the limit in Rhodesia, 5 to 10 in equatorial Africa. The necessity for long fallows is not the only cause; the lack of labour (much of which is occupied with other affairs) is also a hindrance to cultivation; the women, on whom often devolves the task of cultivating the crops, lack energy, whilst the migration of the young men to the towns also helps to paralyse the agricultural effort. Amongst the Turumba of Middle Congo 27 per cent of the total human task is concerned with agriculture, 4 per cent with clearing land, 13 per cent with transport and 56 per cent with the preparation of the products (drying, threshing, retting, hulling or peeling, and milling).

Some purely rural populations, however, have acquired such skill in the exploitation of the soil that densities reach much higher values. It only needs animal-raising and the use of manure to be associated with soil tillage for the agriculture to be completely transformed. Thus, in West Africa, the enclosed 'tapades', regularly manured, bear a harvest every year; the terraced mountain slopes of the Kabre, also regularly manured, bear population densities of 100 to 200 persons per square kilometre.

Nothing else comes near the remarkable success of the rice-cultivators. In black Africa, from the meagre densities of the interior one passes suddenly into the rice-fields of the marshy regions, fertilised by river floods, where, as with the Dyola, there are 120 persons per square kilometre. In far-eastern Asia, thanks to the same cereal, occurs the miracle of a veritable ant-heap of humanity, with the greatest rural densities in the whole world, from 300 to 1,000 persons per square kilometre. Rice is one of the most accommodating plants in the world; many different types of soil are suitable, and it is not even hindered by a slight salinity of the water; it likes heat but is grown quite far into the temperate zone where the summer is hot enough; it likes moisture during the period of growth, but dryness at harvest time—and this corresponds exactly to the alternating seasons of the monsoon climate. In certain parts of China as many as three harvests a year are obtained and it is not rare to find rice being harvested throughout the year. The water which floods the paddy-fields often brings with it fertilising elements, and it is particularly valuable when it is muddy with loess or organic debris, for this solves the problem of the maintenance of soil fertility. Another advantage possessed by rice is the size of the yield—it produces two to two-and-a-half times more grain to the acre than wheat, two-thirds more than barley and one-third more than maize. Moreover, it is a food of high value, especially when consumed in the husk; for this external covering of the grain contains four-fifths of the fat, mineral substance and vitamins. Rice is thus the cereal which allows the greatest number of people *not* to starve on the smallest possible space; and the type of cultivation is one of the main factors in rural population density.

All communities based on a subsistence economy—including those which in former times on the European plains were supported by temperate cereals such as wheat and rye—are closely subject to the risks of the harvest; the slightest climatic aberration, or the attack of a disease or an insect pest, is immediately reflected in the food intake and then in the demographic curve. In central India there is a saying 'one year in three has a poor harvest, one year in seven there is a famine'.

In all the forms of rural exploitation so far dealt with, one can say that the population lives essentially on what the local soil produces. The role of transport, commerce and allied activities created by the urban world appear to have been originally negligible, even though nowadays there is some penetration of these influences almost every-where. Thus the fundamental consequences of rice-cultivation are of very ancient origin, though now some of the rice is traded and replaced by less costly grains in the poor areas, or supplemented by other products in the better areas.

Man and the land in advanced societies

In complex societies, agriculture forms but a part of the resources at the disposal of the population and the average density in a country or region has only a remote relationship to the productivity of the soil or the intensity of the agricultural effort. In France, the value of agricultural output is only 6 per cent of the gross national product, and only 12 per cent of the population work in agriculture. In the United States the comparable figures are 3·6 and 3 per cent, in the U.K. 3·1 and 3 per cent; that is, the density of the agricultural working population per sq. km. is low when compared with that of the total working population. In France these figures are respectively 5·5 and 36·5 per sq. km., in the United States 0·3 and 8·5, and in the U.K. 3·1 and 101·8. The difference is more accentuated as the econo-mic evolution becomes more adavnced. The case of the United King-dom is a little exceptional, for agricultural production is nowhere near sufficient to meet the national demand. A comparison with a less-advanced economy like that of Brazil shows the difference at once: here 44·3 per cent of the working population is in agriculture, and the value of the agricultural output represents 18 per cent of the GNP; the density of the agricultural working population is 1·5 per sq. km. and that of the total working population 3·5 (these figures are so low by reason of the vast extent of Brazil and the low overall density of population).

In effect, the development of a modern economy based on industry and commerce is reflected, profoundly and in many ways, in the structure of rural life. Sometimes that structure already existed, and its transformation was effected in the last century as in Europe; in other cases the transformation is happening now, or is about to happen, as in communist states, or in the developing countries; and when the economic evolution takes place over a whole new country—as in Australia, most of the U.S.A., Canada and Soviet Asia—the rural world takes on a highly original aspect.

In such countries agricultural output is either, as in the U.S.A., greatly superior to the national requirements and so gives rise to exports, or else, as in the U.K. much below, so that imports are necessary. It is no longer a question of food crops and a subsistence economy; in the U.S.A. one farmer fed fifteen people in 1950 and forty-eight now. The fact that the agricultural communities are only a small part of the whole creates new opportunities for them.

Technical competence. The more complex the civilisation and the greater its material power, the more technology permeates all forms of activity, including the cultivation of the soil. In the first stage, new methods of cultivation and new and better hand-implements favour the growth of rural population. The improvement of crop rotation and of implements and the increased use of manure were responsible for the growth of rural population in the European plains in the seventeenth and eighteenth centuries, by reducing and then removing the risk of famine. In the second stage, on the one hand the rural density becomes too great and there must be some displacement or absorption by other than agricultural activities, on the other the improvement of production thanks to better techniques releases some of the manpower, which can disperse by emigration. At the same time the growth of manufacturing supplies the rural population with ever better and better tools; the local craftsmen, outmoded, quit the villages. This is what happened in western Europe during the nine-teenth century. Finally, the progress of mechanisation replaces human labour and there is a generally rising standard of life, which the farmers must share. They must therefore increase their resources, and for this they have three choices, either separately or simultane-ously: to increase the land at their disposal, to increase their yields, or to improve the nature or the quality of their harvests. It is this stage that has been reached in agriculture in the countries of north-west Europe.

According to the stage of technical development reached, the same sort of agriculture can carry very varied population densities; in the wheatlands of Leon, in Spain, where the methods are traditional, the density is 75 per square kilometre; in the medium-sized holdings of Beauce, mechanised on a typical European scale, the density is 20; but over the vast wheatlands of north-central U.S.A. it falls to 10. It is estimated that to cultivate a hectare (2·47 acres) of wheat requires between eight and fifteen days of labour a year by traditional methods; with complete mechanisation only one is required. In the U.S.A. densities are eight times higher in the cotton lands of the Old South, teeming with coloured labour, than in California, where the new cotton lands are highly mechanised. One kilogramme of rice requires three hours of peasant labour in the Far East, and 1·6 minutes of the time of the Louisiana farmer.

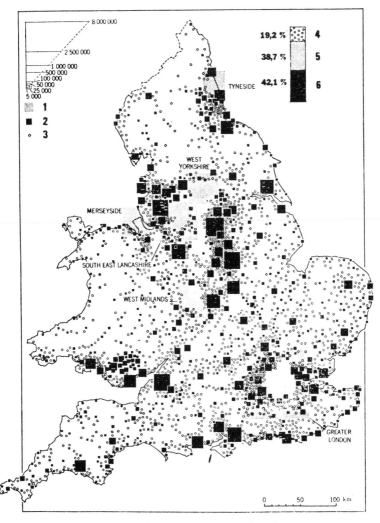

Fig. 7. Population of England and Wales.

1. Conurbations. **2.** Other towns. **3.** Rural population (one symbol equals 5000 persons). *Classification of population.* **4.** Rural. **5.** The six conurbations. **6.** Other urban centres.

Predominant influences in the diversification of the rural population pattern are thus the nature of the agriculture and the technical skill of the exploitation—the latter of which may depend partly on the adaptability and financial capacity of the people under consideration, and partly on the length of time over which the development has taken place.

Specialisation. The nature of agriculture may be determined by the natural environment but other influences may also be at work. In primitive rural societies, the subsistence economy offers little choice. Thus only fifty years ago every French département produced wheat, even the most mountainous ones and those on the Mediterranean, for the Frenchman was above all a bread-eater. With the development of transport, regions were no longer obliged to produce all their needs; they could choose, could specialise and exchange products. Thus there came about an adaptation of cropping to the natural conditions: the great fertile plains grew wheat and sugar beet exclusively while the mountains gave preference to stock-raising, and these transformations were accompanied by movements of people.

Material progress, however, sets in motion an evolution rather more complex than this. The development of certain lines of transport creates special movements of foodstuffs towards the great urban centres of consumption. The rising standard of life has a double role; it makes consumers more 'choosy' and favours certain labour-consuming productions like fruit and vegetables (it takes 400 days of labour to produce one hectare of tomatoes), and it also encourages the farmers to increase their profits by practising a more intensive cropping; finally, by the perfection of new methods, the control of the natural environment is partially eliminated: irrigation, land reclamation and the large-scale use of chemical fertilisers have transformed the appearance of large areas. So one sees the development, around the great cities, along the main lines of communication, and in valleys, of specially favoured belts of market gardening, accompanied by very diverse population densities. In New Jersey the cultivation of fruit and vegetables carries densities four times greater than in the corn belt of Iowa; and the dairying zone is seven times more densely peopled than the wheatlands of north Dakota. Between 1851 and 1911 the population of the cereal-growing county of Suffolk, in East Anglia, diminished by 16 per cent, whilst that of the Vale of Evesham, with its fruit and vegetable farming, increased by 90 per cent.

Agriculture and population distribution

In short, it may be said that whether we are concerned with essentially agricultural communities or with those in which agriculture is but a secondary activity integrated into a complex overall economy, several factors play a part in determining the density of the population.

In mainly agricultural societies the factor which is generally fundamental is the possibility of survival, that is, the capacity of the region, at the existing stage of technical development, to provide the food necessary for a certain number of people. If this number is appreciably exceeded a new equilibrium must be sought. Formerly it was famine which was the great regulator, but happily there are now other solutions: the growth of the territory occupied, by clearance or by conquest (this explains the great outburst of deforestation and reclamation in western Europe in the Middle Ages, the accelerated growth of rice-fields in the Far East during the past century, which has paralleled the population growth, and the incessant warfare between African tribes before the colonial period), the increase in production, either by better methods of cultivation (manures, fertilisers, better implements, new rotations) or by the improvement of the cultivated areas (e.g. by irrigation) and finally the emigration of excess population. Presentday China, which provides an excellent example of the use of all these means of increasing the national food supply, has recorded a 20 per cent increase in overall yields.

In those communities where agriculture is only a secondary activity, the conditions of equilibrium are founded on a much more complex basis and are much more supple. The farmer no longer produces only for his own sustenance but for profit, which he uses as he pleases. The density of population thus tends to evolve in response to diverse factors of which the most important would seem to be the standard of life in the country as a whole. In effect, in a poor country where the revenue is low and does not rise, rural progress is slight and the appearance of the landscape changes but little. Such a situation may become paroxysmic during a period of economic difficulty; thus in Austria, much reduced in area after the 1920 treaties, the population of the poor Alpine mountain zone increased immediately, thus reversing a long term reduction due to migration to the plains and the great cities; in the United States, during the great depression of 1929–35, some two million urban refugees returned to the land, and the number of farmers who abandoned their farms and went to the towns was six times less than in the few previous years.

In a country with a high standard of living, the farmers are sustained by the general prosperity and their own desire not to be left behind. The high income so much sought after may be derived either from the scrupulously careful exploitation practised by some densely-peopled countries like Denmark or the Netherlands and in certain types of agriculture such as market gardening, or from the exploitation of very large farms, as in central North America. In the first case the agricultural population is quite dense (11 to the square kilometre in the Netherlands); in the second it is much sparser (0·3 only).

The influence of the standard of living stands out in glaring fashion if one considers rice cultivation in the Far East and in the United States, for example. The cultivation of one hectare of rice in the Tonkin delta requires more than 400 days of hard manual labour; the same area on a mechanised American farm, seven days. In south-east Asia 500 to 600 people live on the produce of an area equal to a farm which is exploited by five or six people in the United States. The arable lands of Iowa are about one-half those of France, but the number of farms is twelve times smaller and the agricultural labour force only one-twentieth.

All this underlines the importance in the distribution of population of what one might call the 'quality' of rural life—which includes economic, technical, social and psychological aspects. But to an increasing extent the countryside is no longer evolving as an autonomous unit, and many other powerful factors are penetrating to all parts of the globe.

The role of transport in the evolution of societies

The growth of means of transport is fundamental in the present distribution of people over the globe. Transportation has exerted a direct or indirect influence on almost all human groupings, and has transformed the map of the world during the last two centuries. Sea transport has permitted the discovery of new lands, and the establishment of cheap, long-distance trade routes; great ports have flourished, others have sprung up, and a world map showing the major cities emphasises the importance of the seaboard. The development of continental transport, in its turn, has rendered possible the birth of modern civilisation through *concentration*, i.e. the gathering of raw materials, means of production, foodstuffs, the growth and multiplication of resources, and so of people, in one place. Cities of ever-increasing size and extent, industrial regions ever more monstrous have been nurtured by the railway, the road, and navigable water-ways; this is often obvious on the map from the tentacles which spread out from population nuclei, carrying with them long ribbons of suburban growth along the major lines of communication. This phenomenon is particularly noticeable in the plan of towns which, as in the United Kingdom and in new countries, have not suffered from the choking collar of fortifications which for so long hampered the cities of Europe.

The influence of transport has not only been on the economic side. By the movements and the mixing which it has aided, it has affected the whole outlook of mankind. Instead of being isolated, knowing only our own environment, and living simply on the produce of our own fields and our own craftsmen, we have become capable of comparing our lot with that of others, and so choosing. Transport has created new needs but has also provided the means of satisfying them; it has permitted the specialisation of production, and since its influence has not been evenly felt either in space or in time, two important consequences have ensued.

An increasing contrast became manifest in the nineteenth and early twentieth centuries between the regions already reached by modern transportation methods, and those not so affected. The former became the scene of great activity, in which industry played an ever-increasing part, and the great cities expanded at an accelerating pace; they drew raw materials and foodstuffs by the shipload from other parts of the world, to which they exported coal, machinery, and textiles. Western Europe took the lead in this progress, accompanied by certain other regions, amongst which the United States soon held pride of place. This movement touched the rest of the world but sporadically, and more or less slowly. Certain countries, like the communist states, have endeavoured to make up for their late start by new methods; but it remains true that at the moment the contrast between the advanced and the retarded countries has never been greater.

Within the countries which are emerging from the colonial period, the role of transport stands out vividly; the superimposition of one form of civilisation over another produces the striking contrast between modern cities linked to the rest of the world by sea and by air, and the remote countryside where the traditional way of life survives, whilst along the few lines of communication is a fringe of mixed development with plantations, exportable crops, and the exploitation of mineral resources.

This contrast between different parts of the world, and in particular between different parts of the same country, has been responsible for considerable movements of people, which we shall deal with under the heading of migration. Every day thousands of people, caught up in this stream, quit their homes to migrate from the country to the town, from the less favoured regions to those which have a reputation for greater prosperity, and from the countries with a stagnant economy to those more dynamic.

In these movements, the role of lines of communication has been studied in great detail. The existence of a railway line largely determines the peopling of a new country, for colonisation closely follows the route, later spreading further away from the axis. This was the case with the great transcontinental lines of North America, where rail construction and land grants moved together, with the Trans-Siberian railway across Asiatic Russia, and with the recent rail developments in the new China. Though nowadays the regions traversed may be entirely occupied, a ribbon of greater density still clings to the routeway.

In old countries where railways were built across a countryside already peopled and organised in the traditional economy, the influence was different: a concentration of people in the most important towns on the line whilst smaller intermediate places lost inhabitants, a fillip to the development of a narrow discontinuous fringe but also to the depopulation of a belt some five to ten miles wide on each side, whilst areas further afield remained unaffected.

Canals and roads also have their related centres of activity. Along waterways the distribution is very characteristic: the Thames estuary is a good example. Here, on both waterfronts, are the warehouses and the industries which need heavy bulk transport, such as power stations, gas works, cement and paper factories, oil refineries, whilst in the streets immediately behind are smaller and more specialised industries such as engineering and chemicals, with the dwellings of the workpeople still further inland, along the roadways which run parallel to the river banks. In new countries the construction of an air-strip is often the first link in a chain which ends in the creation of an isolated island of colonisation in the interior, from which the occupation of a greater area may proceed.

It is especially in areas which are difficult for human occupation—the vast and thinly peopled expanses—that the role of transport is clearly marked. Thus in Northern Australia where the density is three people to 100 square kilometres, the only two centres are Darwin, a port, and Alice Springs, the rail-head serving the southern grazing region; these two small urban centres contain one-fifth of the entire population, and the rest of the people are mainly in areas near to these centres or within easy reach of the railway line. In the interior of Brazil, the construction of railways has been accompanied by the building of small new towns and by the development of the already existing mining and agricultural centres; the prosperity of the more ancient centres of colonisation not served by the railway line has quickly become jeopardised by the growth of these more favoured rivals.

There remain huge areas of the globe in which the development of resources has scarcely begun because of the absence of means of transport, and all the plans so far prepared or envisaged for the 'underdeveloped' countries have in their forefront a solid basis of means of communication.

Industry and population

One major result of the development of transport, as we have seen, is the possibility of concentration in all its various forms. Dispersed local crafts have been replaced by clusters of factory industries. The example of the textile industry of western Europe is typical: village craftsmen preparing locally produced wool, linen or hemp were progressively called to the towns in the nineteenth century by the construction of mills, and more and more of the raw material—cotton, wool, jute—had to come from overseas. So it happened on the flanks of the Pennines, in Flanders, in Champagne, in Saxony and in Lombardy, where the countryside lost much of its population whilst the towns multiplied and swelled. Roubaix, centre of the French woollen industry, had 8,000 inhabitants in 1802 and 124,000 in 1901, of whom two-thirds had been born outside the town.

It was coal which provided the motive power for the first modern developments, and it is not surprising that in the countries where the industrial revolution took place it was the coalfields, worked at first by primitive means, later much improved, that attracted the various industries. All the coalfields of north-west Europe took part in this development. Here grew the human ant-heaps with their innumerable mining villages and their towns with metallurgical, textile, and chemical industries. These 'black countries' which, from Lancashire to the Ruhr and from Silesia to St Etienne, mark the edges of, and depressions within, the old hercynian mountain massifs, have more than 1,000 persons per square kilometre over considerable areas. Their age is now such that they must be rebuilt and rejuvenated if they are to retain their people. Somewhat similar are the basins of the Donetz and the Urals in the U.S.S.R., and the Appalachian fringes in the United States, great centres of industrialisation. But in other countries there are coal-fields much more recently exploited, or still merely scraped by primitive methods, as in India and China; they have hardly succeeded as yet in attracting manufacturing industries. Brazilian coal from the south feeds industries 1,600 km to the north, near the great cities and the iron mines.

Outside the coal-fields, certain other minerals of fundamental importance, and widespread abundance, like iron ore, have attracted and retained a labour supply, whilst others, much more precious, like gold and diamonds, have been responsible for veritable 'rushes' and for the peopling of many large areas which are otherwise relatively inhospitable. In the French part of Lorraine, it was only after 1879 that it became possible to use the phosphoric ore for steel-making; but from that date the mining and industrial towns multiplied rapidly. In the United Kingdom similar centres established on the same mineral resource, as Scunthorpe and Corby, are flourishing. It was the mirage of gold which attracted the Iberians to Latin America, and encouraged them to penetrate into the interior and to build towns of which Ouro Preto is one of the most famous; it was gold too which prompted the often audacious penetrations of the mountains of western North America, and which was responsible for the demographic upsurge in Australia, where 554,000 people arrived between 1851 and 1860 in a country which in 1850 held only 405,356 all told. Gold again peopled the Rand in South Africa, where, beside Johannesburg, in a dozen towns are gathered a million and half people, of whom 350,000 work in the gold mines, and two hundred miles or so to the south-west the diamond fields of Bloemfontein, Kimberley and the lower Vaal are also more densely populated than the extensive farmlands which surround them.

One must, as in the case of agriculture, consider the *nature* of industry. With extractive industry or constructional work the attached population is numerous but fluctuating, linked as it is with the life of the mines or the duration of the works and with the possibility of selling the extracted ore. In South American countries, the non-ferrous metal mines, copper and others, suffer wide fluctuations in employment which, because of dependence on exports, reflect the state of the international market. Oil-well drilling and the construction of dams need but a transitory labour supply; the actual pumps and generating stations require very few men.

On the contrary, there is great diversity amongst the transformation industries. The regions of textile manufacture, engineering and light industries are abundantly populated and often take the form of town-clusters with associated industrial villages and small factories; whereas heavy metallurgy and the chemical industries employ relatively few men in much larger installations. The former use male and female labour indifferently, and have much more flexibility in their location, for their raw materials are generally of light weight; the latter demand almost entirely male labour and they are much more directly related to sources of raw materials and cheap transport, especially by water. Thus the physical aspect of the older textile areas such as Lancashire, southern New England, central Hondo in Japan, is characterised by high population density over extensive areas whilst the chemical complexes, very active but recently located in new areas, have but few people—as for example the two great centres of oil refining and petrochemicals in France, the lower Seine and the Etang de Berre.

The role of technology is equally important. Normal technical progress ensures that as an industry develops its production will be achieved with a diminishing manpower. Thus in France the Renault company produced 63,000 cars with 30,000 workers in 1938 and 543,000 with 61,435 workers in 1960. The same sort of difference is to be found between countries in which technology is well advanced and those which are at a more elementary stage of development: in the United States a road will be built by half a dozen technicians and a battery of powerful machines, in India, with a multitude of men and women armed with shovels and carrying baskets of earth and stones on their heads.

There does not exist, however, in this realm the same simple relationship as in rural life. The growth of individual technical skill does not entail a diminution in the number of inhabitants in relation to the area considered—a striking contrast to what so often happens in essentially rural districts. On the contrary, as the development of material civilisation increases, so industries become more complex, more ramified and interlinked, and so the urban concentrations can become ever larger and larger. There are no other limits to the expansion of these conurbations than those imposed by the possibilities of food transport and the planning of the occupied space in such a way as to allow the inhabitants to lead more or less normal lives.

Here also, the historical stages are well marked. In old countries which developed early, the first stage was that of dispersed craftsmen; then came the development of isolated nuclei of industrialisation based on coal, on basic raw materials, and later along the main lines of communication. Progressively, as one factory industry attracted another, the small centres grew and multiplied. Finally, thanks to new discoveries and progress in many directions, but particularly those of transport, methods of production, materials and universal education, there has come about a dispersion of industry. The use of hydroelectricity has brought industry into the mountains; in Germany they build factories in the country, and in the United Kingdom new industries are directed into the 'Trading Estates'; whilst in France, there is a policy of decentralisation, which forbids the establishment of new industries in the already congested urban areas such as Paris and the cities of the north and encourages their dispersion to the major urban centres of the country districts.

In the newer countries, industrial developments are implanted in the rural areas and sometimes even in the middle of virgin territory, using the mineral resources newly discovered or but recently reached by means of transport; the development of the great industrial complexes of Asiatic Russia—the Kuzbas, Karaganda, Irkutsk and Tashkent—is typical of this revolution which plants towns and housing estates in the midst of vast spaces which but yesterday were empty steppes and now are covered with cereals or cotton. In the Sahara and Arabian deserts, the towns arising from the exploitation of petroleum duplicate the traditional oases; in the Andes and in the Atacama desert, the centres of extractive industry form more or less detached nuclei, as do the mining and smelting centres in the solitudes of Western Australia. But in the Republic of India, the great Tata metallurgical complex, using coal and iron almost side by side, has developed amidst a village-studded countryside and the works at Jamshedpur and Asansol are surrounded not only by specially-built workers' housing estates but by a mass of seemingly endless and utterly miserable collections of tin shacks.

Urban development

The town appears at first sight to be one of the major elements in the distribution of population. It is customary to oppose town and country, urban and rural population, and though we have already noted (p. 13) that statistics of the two are often of unequal value and difficult to compare, it is nevertheless true that a division exists, both

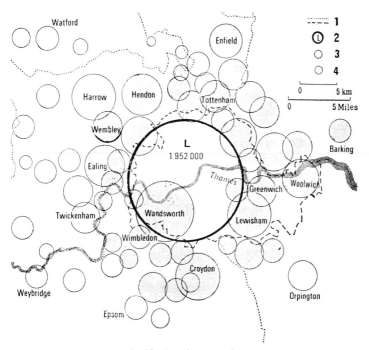

Fig. 8. The London conurbation.

1. County boundaries (pre-1964).   2. London (population of city and inner ring).   3. Towns of the middle ring.   4. Towns of the suburban ring.

on the ground and on the map, between the scattering of isolated farms, the multiplicity of villages, more or less compact and of greater or less importance, and the rarer and larger concentrations which are the towns. This purely formal distinction takes no account of the occupation of the people who reside in these different types of habitat.

Geographers have devised many methods, both quantitative and

qualitative, of defining towns, and it is difficult to give a single definition for a reality which has a thousand different forms. However,
concerning ourselves only with the distribution of population, we
must insist on several facts.

An urban group is distinguished from the rural environment by its
density and compactness. Even in countries where the towns extend
into infinite residential suburbs, as in the United States, there is

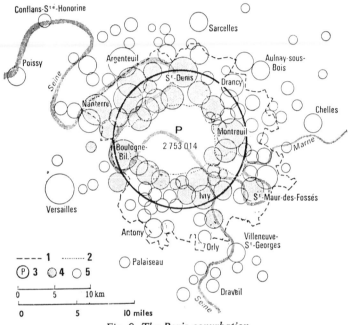

Fig. 9. The Paris conurbation.

1. Boundary of Seine département. 2. City limits. 3. Paris—
population of the 20 arrondissements. 4. Towns of the urban fringe.
5. Towns of the suburban ring.

always a point at which they give way to fields and to rural terrain in
which the built-up surface is proportionally very small. Thus Los
Angeles spreads its villas and gardens for 75 kilometres, until
finally, they disperse over the hills and eventually disappear. At the
opposite extreme are the ancient cities, for long encircled by protective
walls, which end with brutal suddenness against the neighbouring
fields; for a long time such great capitals as Madrid and Rome rose

straight from an almost deserted countryside, and it is only recently that they have begun to spread.

In some areas the conglomeration of towns is such that many of them cover an immense area almost without interruption. The seven conurbations of Great Britain contain 35·4 per cent of the population on 4 per cent of its area. The vast nebulae which encircle most of the world's great capitals such as Moscow, Paris and Tokio are similar.

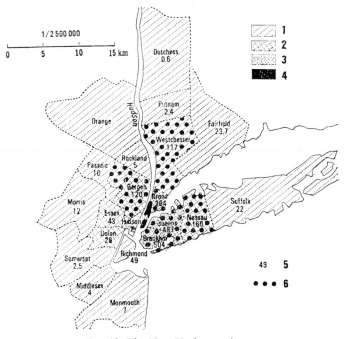

Fig. 10. The New York conurbation.

Density: 1. Under 6,000 persons per sq. km. 2. From 6,000 to 40,000. 3. From 40,000 to 100,000. 4. Over 200,000.

Journey to work. 5. Number of people (thousands) working in Manhattan. 6. More than 100,000 people working in Manhattan.

But first prize must surely go to the constellation of cities—now known as 'megalopolis'—which fringes the north-east coast of the United States in an almost unbroken belt from north of Boston to south of Washington.

In general it is possible to distinguish a central and more densely peopled nucleus and a peripheral residential area of greater or less width and extended star-like along the lines of communication. In the greatest agglomerations appears the phenomenon of the 'city', a relatively unpeopled core surrounded by a ring of much greater density. In London, the real heart of the metropolis—the famous 'City'—had 128,129 inhabitants in 1801 and only 4,771 in 1961. In Liverpool, the mean density in 1931 was 8,625 persons per square kilometre but whilst the central area had 14,550 to the square kilometre the inner ring had double this figure, a middle ring a density similar to that of the core, and a wide outer ring only 4,000.

The influence of towns on the distribution of population is thus exercised directly through the concentration of people but also indirectly through the swarms of suburbanites scattered over their peripheral countryside, often far from the centre, in dormitory suburbs or satellite towns, and through the demand for food which entails a large rural labour supply for the market gardens and dairy farms. In Brazil, they have actually created market-garden 'colonies', often in the hands of Japanese, to improve the vegetable supplies of the large cities; in China the traditional peasant would often use town refuse or night soil to improve the output of his garden, and the towns were encircled with girdles of exceptionally flourishing crops. In Western Europe there is hardly a city which has not its belt of market gardens and glasshouses.

The less need a country has for labour to work in its fields, the greater the urban dominance. This is the case not only in old, industrialised countries, but also in areas of recent colonisation. In the former, as in the United Kingdom, after a long period of urbanisation the town-dwelling population is one of the highest in the world (81 per cent), but the urban system, the heritage of a long tradition, remains very complex, with a whole hierarchy of towns in which small and medium ones actually have, between them, more people than the great cities. On the contrary, in the recently colonised territories the urban population is equally overwhelming but it is the large cities which contain most and the role of the very few secondary centres is of much less importance. Thus, in Australia the urban population amounts to 85.5 per cent, with 61.5 per cent in the six State capitals. In California 80·7 per cent of the population is town-dwelling, and two-thirds of these are in the three great agglomerations of San Francisco, Los Angeles and San Diego. In the Soviet Far East the urban population again reaches 80 per cent of the total, and similarly in the central Asiatic regions of recent industrialisation and mineral exploitation.

By way of contrast, the role of towns is much less important in the old countries with a rural tradition; but there are many shades of variation between the two extremes of Europe and European Russia on the one hand, with a multiplicity of small or medium-sized townships, and central Africa on the other, where towns are only exceptionally present. In the former, the towns are survivals; they were founded progressively in accordance with the needs and capacity of a solidly-constituted rural society, and are in course of being adapted to new circumstances. In the latter, they were created by the colonists and imposed from without on a rural environment which had existed until then without having felt the need for towns. The urban population represents only one-third of the total in the countries of eastern Europe and the Mediterranean and only 10 to 15 per cent in central Africa, and its spatial distribution is noticeably different.

The current trend towards urbanisation is affecting much more strongly those parts of the world that are under-urbanised than those in which towns and cities are already well developed. At the beginning of the present century, only 13·6 per cent of the world's population lived in towns of over 5,000 inhabitants; by 1950 the percentage had risen to 28·2 and in 1975 it was 41; it may well reach 55 per cent by the year 2000. It is the Third World that is now becoming the main sphere of urbanisation; the great rush from the countryside to the towns is explained by the liveliness of the urban economy and the improvement in transport facilities. At the same time we have witnessed an increase in the relative importance of large towns; the proportion of the total urban population living in towns of over 100,000 rose from 40 per cent in 1900 to 63 in 1975 and may well reach 75 per cent by the end of the century. The growth rate of the large towns is thus four times that of the total population and nearly twice that of the overall urban population.

In short it is transport and a variety of functions and resources which have favoured the growth of towns. Industry constitutes one of the bases of their activity but it is not the only one; commerce, administration and the multiplicity of so-called 'tertiary' activities occupy in general a greater number of the inhabitants and offer them resources which have nothing to do with the original natural environment.

The fundamental basis of trade

It is tempting to draw a certain parallelism between the degree of urban concentration and that of trading or marketing: in effect, market towns are at once centres of production, transformation and organisation; they offer the maximum of highly concentrated resources, directly and indirectly, both in the inventive and in the speculative field. This is so, in varying degree, in almost all the towns of the world. On the national scale, the United Kingdom, which formerly dominated international commerce, was for long the typical case; no other country could boast of such a density of population accompanied by so high a standard of living. Japan provides at the present time a comparable example.

In a closed community, the number of people is more or less limited, but the wider the possibility of complex trade, the greater is the possibility of peopling a region up to a limit that knows almost no bounds. The masses can be fed with food brought from the ends of the earth, paid wages by factories which use American cotton to make cloth for sale to West Africa, or by petroleum companies which, having their headquarters in London, pump oil in Iran for sale to Italy. It is even possible to live by simply levying a duty on intense traffic, as Hong Kong does, acting as an entrepôt for the greater part of the trade between the western world and communist China. At this stage, the distribution of population is relieved of all link with the natural environment, and the supremacy of the economic environment is complete.

THE IMPORTANCE OF HISTORY

In an examination of the importance of the natural environment or the role of economic conditions, one never finds a uniform situation or general laws without numerous exceptional cases; perhaps this is the main lesson of the previous pages. Another conclusion is the importance of the idea of evolution; the same physical or economic element can play a completely different role according to the period, or to the state of development of the community concerned. The age and vicissitudes of human occupation are traceable also in the present distribution pattern; these underlying influences are always there, and in certain cases they may even undoubtedly take pride of place.

Age of peopling

The duration of human occupation is of fundamental importance; populations living in the same place for a long time, even though they may develop but slowly, will end by becoming more and more numerous. In India, where one could hardly say that until recent decades the conditions for demographic development were excellent, tens of millions of people accumulated slowly in the course of centuries. Western Europe, before the great stride forward of the eighteenth century, offers another example of this very slow rise of the demographic curve. It seems that one need not seek elsewhere for the cause of the difference between the high densities of Europe and the much lower densities of North America or Australia, although both of these continents are now peopled by white races with a similar type of civilisation and standard of life. But in the early nineteenth century, at the moment when the great demographic upsurge began, France already had 50 persons to the square kilometre whilst the United States had 0·5 and Australia only one person to 10,000 square kilometres. The rapidity of subsequent progress, in which many factors have combined to the detriment of Europe and in favour of other continents, has still not succeeded in obliterating the consequences of this profound initial inequality.

Another example may be found in a comparison of population densities in the several Indochinese deltas; in the north, the Tonkin delta, very early occupied, has more than 500 people per square kilometre, whilst on the contrary the eastern distributaries of the Mekong have scarcely 200, the low plains formed by the Thai rivers a little over 150 and those of the Irawaddy barely 70. Yet these deltas enjoy similar natural conditions, and the same rice grows in the same paddy-fields. Minor historical circumstances explain, at least in part, these differences. The Cochinchina delta was conquered by the Annamese, at the expense of the Cambodians, in 1757, but it was scarcely before 1850 that the occupation was complete, and the cultivated surface still only represents two-fifths of the total, for man, less pressed here by sheer necessity, has made fewer elaborate arrangements to overcome the deficiencies of the natural environment. Thus whilst five peasants work on one hectare of land in the Tonkin delta, only one-and-a-half on average are employed in the Cochinchina delta, and before political conditions made migration—whether seasonal or permanent—impossible, the call of the southern areas was a con-

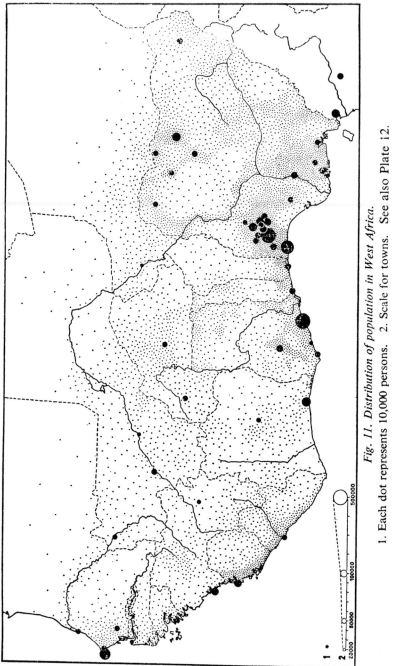

Fig. 11. Distribution of population in West Africa.

1. Each dot represents 10,000 persons.   2. Scale for towns.   See also Plate 12.

stant one. It is the same in lower Burma where colonisation on an intensive scale only began after the middle of the nineteenth century; the area under paddy multiplied more than sevenfold between 1866 and 1940 whilst the population quadrupled. In Siam too it was only after the end of the eighteenth century that the Burmese advance obliged the Siamese to descend towards the delta, and it is mainly during the twentieth century that a considerable extension of the rice-fields has taken place, also demanding seasonal migratory labour.

The age of the peopling thus seems linked with the density of population; it is not only that the older the settlement the greater the population, but even the distribution is different. The age-long application of careful techniques has enabled the old peasant societies of eastern Europe and the Far East to make use of every patch of land and to penetrate the remotest valleys; a population with its roots in the remote past has a tendency to adapt itself very closely to the natural environment, and to occupy every conceivable locality. In Europe, in face of the demographic crises of the Middle Ages, and to cater for their growing needs without any technical progress, the peasants were forced to cut down the forests and to settle even up the steep slopes of the mountains. On the contrary, in a new country, the newcomers, few in numbers, tend to squander or at least to be prodigal with the resources of the virgin country which opens out in front of them. So huge farms were delimited, like those of the Boers penetrating into the South African interior, carved out of an almost uninhabited savana and drawing their boundaries at a distance of half-an-hour's horse ride from a centrally placed landmark. It is to this sort of squandering of space and of the natural resources that must be attributed the damage caused by soil erosion in the great plains of the United States, where extensive grain-growing left vast expanses of bare soil; the exhaustion of the coffee lands of São Paulo in Brazil offers a similar case.

This notion of vast spaces at the mercy of a handful of men has protracted consequences; it crystallises in the form of great estates, and frequently results in extensive exploitation which is self-perpetuating and necessitates the employment of much machinery to replace the absent men. Thus the very low densities in the new and recently occupied countries are maintained, often intentionally: Australia, which prides itself on the possession of some of the largest agricultural machines in the world, has voluntarily reduced its population expansion until recent years, providing the best example of a new country poorly populated.

It may be asked—and this is one of the most pressing of the world's present problems—whether countries like Australia will be able to remain almost empty, or to retain an agricultural economy based on extensive farming, whilst a few thousand miles away there are countries swarming with half-starved millions; the 'white Australia' policy seems rather a gamble in the light of the over-population of the countries which border the western Pacific.

Cycles in the distribution of population
It would nevertheless be false to conclude that the oldest-established populations are always the most dense. In many countries of the world there are examples which contradict this rather simple 'law'. Some of them are by no means easy to explain and one may ask why a

Fig. 12. Hill-villages and modern colonisation in Italy.
(From 1/100,000, sheet 159.)

region which was formerly prosperous and densely peopled is now almost abandoned by mankind.

The cycles of occupation of the plains of central and southern Italy are quite remarkable: these areas are well cultivated and famous in the classical Roman period, but gradually they were lost—in the words of the Latin historians—through the abuses brought about by the 'latifundia' system; their agricultural regime was upset, they became infested with malaria, and were abandoned for centuries, whilst the medieval villages perched themselves on hilltops overlooking the coastal plains. However, the drainage and improvement works undertaken during the last century-and-a-half, but particularly during the last thirty years, have now permitted a reoccupation, and the rectangular plots and the white cuboidal blocks of the colonists' houses bear witness to the renewed presence of peasant cultivators right up to the sea coast.

A somewhat similar evolutionary cycle is being worked out in Mesopotamia, famous in ancient times for its fertility and its cities. The derangement of the hydrological system allowed the desert to advance, and it is now being pushed back again thanks to the irrigation and reclamation works recently undertaken. Other regions have not been so fortunate, and in Yucatan the great ruins which bear witness to the flourishing civilisation of its Mayas are now swallowed up beneath an impenetrable jungle on the low and malarial plains. There has been much speculation as to the reasons for this decay, just as scholars have sought for possible climatic variations to explain the changes which have undoubtedly come about in certain parts of North Africa and the Sahara between prehistoric and even classical times and the present day. In Asia also there are traces of similar variations; in Sri Lanka the 'centre of gravity' of the population has changed, for formerly the population was most dense in the dry belt, where intensive irrigated rice cultivation was practised through a system of small reservoirs. These were destroyed during the Tamil invasion in the middle of the thirteenth century, and as a result the area became malarial and the towns were abandoned to become buried in the forest; in this province there are now only 14 persons to the square kilometre. On the other hand modern colonisation has gradually developed the wet western coastal plain and slopes, on the basis of tea and rubber plantations, and this area now has over 200 to the square kilometre.

The changes may sometimes be much more rapid. In the territories surrendered by East Germany to Poland in 1945, the evacuation of the existing population and its replacement by Polish colonists resulted not only in a reduction in density but also a change in the pattern of distribution; a peasantry of small proprietors took the place of the former large estates.

Finally, in the new countries where a colonisation of varying duration has permitted the opening up of new lands, we have the beginning of the first cycle of occupation.

Changes in local circumstances have their natural repercussion on the distribution of population, and though one can sometimes blame changes in the natural environment, such as climatic variations, as often as not it is the vicissitudes of political events which have been the controlling factor, either directly by provoking mass migrations, or indirectly by creating such changes in the conditions of life as have fundamentally disorganised the traditional social structure. The destruction of systems based on water-control, irrigation or drainage, is particularly fraught with dire consequences, for it can render sterile or unhealthy the most fertile areas of the world. Happily the converse is also true, for systematic reclamation schemes and efforts designed to improve land management can render an area habitable or can increase its present density of population.

The relation between wars or forms of government, and the distribution of population, is also evident in certain cases.

Relationships between civilisations

Every civilisation is linked with a certain form of land occupation, but no civilisation is everlasting, and in the world there are many forms of civilisation which have had, and still have, many contacts. This also has its effect on the distribution of population and enables us to explain apparent anomalies on the population map.

The harsh mountains of Kabylia, lacerated by winter cold and summer drought, have over 100 persons to the square kilometre on an average, and as much as 246 in the central ranges, though the Algerian average is hardly more than 40. The area has served as a refuge, first for the sedentary Berbers fleeing before the invasion of Arab nomads, then for Algerians during the conquest and occupation of the plains by Europeans. Other similar mountain refuges contain the Kabré, small cultivators of central Togo (120 to the square kilometre); the Alaouites, the Druses, the Maronites, protecting their religious faiths in the Lebanon mountains where the density is twice that of the country as a whole. In other cases it is the desert which has served as a protective barrier between races or religions: the Mozabites have established their pentapolis in the isolated valleys of the bastion of M'zab, in the heart of the Sahara.

In all these cases, and in many others, the need to escape from persecution or massacre, or the unwillingness to submit to contact or assimilation, has caused the former inhabitants to flee for the sake of peace, seeking refuge in the most inaccessible, often inhospitable places, yielding place to the incoming conquerors. Such are the reasons for the inverse relationship between population density and the quality of the natural environment which one sometimes encounters.

It is also the conflict between two civilisations which is responsible for the depopulation of certain parts of black Africa where the expeditions of the slave traders and their procurers ravaged the population for a long time. North of the Gulf of Guinea, in the coastal belt, in contact with the sea, rice-fields and plantations flourish, succeeded towards the interior by a depopulated zone in which slave-trading was practised; this belt separates the high coastal densities from the dense areas of the north where the climatic conditions are less favourable but where there existed, from the thirteenth to the nineteenth century, ancient black kingdoms, like the Mossi kingdom in the west and that of the Hausa in the east, well organised and strong enough to resist the raiders and to gather local forces around them.

Different civilisations, however, when confronting each other do not always clash, and often exist quite happily side by side. Thus the Europeans who colonised parts of Africa at the end of the nineteenth century, developed a network of towns, creating new and artificial centres of population and commercial activity. Most of such towns are either ports or mining centres.

Finally, in a region where a single type of civilisation has evolved on the spot, far-reaching modifications are nevertheless produced which march in step with certain events: increased security, and measures for the improvement of health on the low plains (as in Italy) lead to the dispersion of people and the abandonment of the old fortified towns or villages on the hill tops; the development of transport and of modern industry has also, as we have seen, given rise to new patterns of population distribution.

THE DYNAMISM OF POPULATION DISTRIBUTION

Whether it be natural conditions, the economic environment or the facts of history, their part is more varied and complex than any given example might reveal. Though one may admit that in primitive societies there is apparent a certain immobility, because the possibility of change is limited, it is quite otherwise as soon as technical progress manifests itself, or a new need arises, or certain political or military events occur. Many recent factors have determined that during the last century the distribution of mankind has changed as never before, owing first to the vast increase in numbers, and secondly to extraordinary technical progress.

The general human cover is thickening all over the globe—but it is thickening particularly in certain areas and becoming thinner in others. Never before has there been such a great contrast between the countryside and the great urban agglomerations, or between the rural areas worked by machines and those which must still employ hand labour. Technical progress is enormous but it remains the privilege of certain countries only, or of limited regions.

At the same time the limits of the habitable areas are changing; but if one puts the accent on recent conquests by modern equipment, on cities rising in the desert or on the edge of the polar regions, one must not forget that these conquests are often substitutions rather than creations. Relict groups, naturally, adapted to such areas, disappear, like the Fuegians at the southern extremity of South America; the Eskimo of the Canadian North are transformed as they approach the artificial centres created by the white man; the villages in the high mountains of old-established areas lose their populations and die. But at the same time virgin lands are cleared and put under the plough; such was the case in the great plains of North America during the last century, and so it is now in Soviet central Asia. All in all it seems that never before has so much of the world's surface been occupied by so many people.

The population map for the beginning of the nineteenth century bears no resemblance to the present one, and the latter probably looks very different from that which future generations will see after the year 2000. However, through all the changing circumstances one can always see the three great and fundamental factors—natural conditions, economic conditions, and the events of history.

PART III

THE EVOLUTION OF THE POPULATION

At the conclusion of our study of the distribution of population over the globe, two particular facts were stressed, the worldwide intensification of peopling and the variations in the area occupied and in local densities. Each of these two facts corresponds with one aspect of the evolution of population: the first, with the natural increase which at the present time is causing a rise in total numbers at a rate never before attained; the second, with the continual migrations which are taking place on an ever-increasing scale and in a great variety of circumstances.

These two movements are not indeed unconnected, but like all human facts they are linked by their causes as well as by their consequences, and their different combinations give to different peoples their peculiar and complex characters.

It is difficult to be precise about the growth in world population because even in the recent past for a great part of the world only estimates were available. If, however, one accepts the conclusions of the experts who estimate that the world had 500 million people in 1650, 1,000 million in 1850, 2,000 million in 1940, and 4,000 million in 1975, one cannot but be struck by the accelerated rate of growth. The population doubled itself in two centuries prior to 1850, again in less than a century and at the present rate will double again in forty years. A frightening view indeed if one thinks of the future!

This accelerated rhythm is linked with a phenomenon to which the name 'demographic revolution' has been given, and which is undoubtedly one of the most important events in the modern world. In former times populations grew slowly or even stagnated, for after a long period in which births slightly exceeded deaths there would come a famine or an epidemic which, by destroying part of the population, would nullify the increase. In England, between 1200 and 1600, it has been estimated that such a crisis occurred about every fifteen years. In France, even in the nineteenth century, there were local famines in 1817, 1846, and 1847, epidemics of cholera in 1831–32, 1849 and 1854, 1859 and 1865, of influenza in 1870. In India in a more recent period for which there are statistics, it is estimated that the famines of 1891 and 1896, accompanied by plague, killed 5 million people, and the influenza epidemic of 1918–19, between 15 and 20 million.

This oscillating evolution really ceased in western Europe towards the end of the eighteenth century, as for the first time in history the number of deaths was regularly less than the number of births, thus permitting a regular rise in the growth-curve. It seems that Britain and Scandinavia were among the first countries in the world to record an almost constant excess of births over deaths and this was the beginning of the great movement which, as it spread all over the globe, has provoked the acceleration of demographic development.

CHAPTER FIVE

The Retreat of Death

In principle, life commences with birth and it would appear logical therefore to start with the birth rate. However, if it is a question of the evolution of the population and not just of demography, the fundamental fact is the decline of the death rate, for it is this which has caused the cessation for the first time of those oscillations in the balance of births and deaths and has created a positive credit balance; it is this also which determines the more or less vigorous expansion of those peoples amongst whom the birth rate, for the present at least, has remained merely constant.

The death rate

To assess the importance of death in a group of people, we use the death rate. This is calculated by dividing the number of deaths in a given year by the population in the same year and multiplying the result by 1,000 so as to avoid an excess of decimals. The calculation necessitates knowing the total population of the given area, which is obtained from the most recent census with an adjustment for the estimated annual increases; the number of deaths in a year is in general, in all countries, the subject of compulsory declaration. It is evident that the value of these figures, especially the second, is variable, depending on the quality of the statistical services of the country concerned. Thus for India in 1950 the deaths registered represented a rate of 16·1; the death rate calculated as a result of special enquiries was 27·4. In order to make worldwide comparisons, therefore, it is necessary to take great care.

A knowledge of the death rate, even as accurately as possible, is not enough, however, for there is often a difference between the male and female rates, and again appreciable differences in the rates for different age-groups; whilst the death rate, which is also in general related to the sanitation and general living conditions of the people, reflects the age-composition of the population and is powerfully influenced by the number of elderly people.

Let us take the example of the United States. In 1950, 1,452,454 deaths were recorded in a population which the census of the same year numbered at 150,697,361. This gives a death rate of

$$\frac{1,424,454 \times 1,000}{150,697,361} = 9{\cdot}6$$

Within the different age-groups the rate was 29·76 for infants under a year old, and without going through the whole gamut, only 1 in the 16–17 age group, 2 for the group aged 32–33, 10·3 for the 52–53s, 98·4 for the 80–81s, and 500 for those over 107 years old!

Though it is normal for the death rate to increase amongst the elderly, a particularly significant feature is the high proportion of infants under a year old who succumb, and this is called the *infant mortality rate*. This is calculated by dividing the number of infants of under one year who died in the course of a year by the number of live births recorded in the same year. Thus, in the United States in 1955, 106,903 infants died before reaching the age of one year and 4,047,295 live births were recorded, which gives a rate of

$$\frac{106,903 \times 1,000}{4,047,295} = 26{\cdot}4$$

One thing becomes immediately apparent: there is a certain correlation between a high general death rate and a high infant mortality rate.

The comparison is significant between the different types of people

General and Infantile Death Rate

Country	Year	General death rate	Infant mortality rate
Algeria	1954		
(Muslim population)		13·7	86
(European population)		8·8	48
United States	1974	9·4	16.7
(White)		9·2	14·8
(Non-white)		10	24·9
United Kingdom	1974	11·9	16
France	1974	10·7	14·1
Japan	1974	6·6	11·7

Source: *U.N.O. Demographic Yearbook.*

in Algeria and the United States, but anomalies begin to appear when we compare for example the death rates in the U.S., the U.K., France and Japan. In fact, we must take account of the other factor mentioned above, namely the proportion of elderly people.

The crude death rate is evidently a worthwhile figure in itself, because it records the proportion of people in a certain country or community who die each year. But if we wish to make a comparison between two countries with a different age structure and profoundly different social and sanitary conditions, we must have recourse to what is called a *standard mortality ratio*. We choose a type of population (usually that of Germany, England, France, Italy and Sweden, at the date of the nearest census to 1910); this population type has a certain age composition. We compare each age slice of this population type with the corresponding slice of the population under consideration and thus obtain a standard mortality ratio.

The interest of this will become apparent from some examples: in 1936 France had a death rate which was high in comparison with its neighbouring countries but this was not due to poor conditions in France but to the proportion of elderly people which at that time was the highest in the world; thus the crude death rate was 15·3, but the standard rate was only 12·2. At the same date Hungary, which had a much poorer standard of living, had a crude rate of 14·5 but a standard rate of 15.

As another example, the age structure of the various Départements of France is very different: Alpes Maritimes has many retired people ending their days in Mediterranean sunshine, but the sanitation is good and the standard of living high; thus in 1935–37, the crude death rate was 13·2 and the standard rate 10·3. By way of contrast, Calvados, the rich agricultural area of Normandy, is much addicted to alcoholism which provokes an unusually high male death rate; thus for the same years, the crude rate was 17·5 and the standard rate 20·7.

There are many other ways of appreciating the progress achieved by nations in combating death, for example figures of the average length of human life, the expectation of life at various ages, and so on. We shall return to this later.

The beginnings of the decline

It was in western Europe, and as far as one can judge from the scrappy contemporary data available, almost certainly in the north-western countries that the death rate first began to decline. For the whole of western Europe the mean death rate dropped from 30 per thousand at the beginning of the nineteenth century to 18 per thousand about 1900, and to 11 at the present day. The causes are to be found in a complexity of events which includes medical discoveries and the improvement of living standards. Europe had no precursor, and no help came from outside—in contrast to what now happens in many countries.

Before 1750 medical care, such as it was, had virtually no effect at all on the health of the population, but thanks to the great advancement of anatomical studies and to the introduction of anaesthetics at the beginning of the nineteenth century, and to the introduction of antiseptic surgery a little later, medical science became much more efficient and at the same time began to concern itself with the battle against epidemics and infectious diseases. After 1796, thanks to the researches of Jenner, vaccination against smallpox became widespread; this scourge had been responsible for 10 per cent of all deaths, and even for 30 per cent of those of children under four years.

But the rapidity and efficacy of medical progress became all the more effective as economic progress in the same period rendered its wider diffusion possible; the development of transport, of education, and the mixing of the population as a result of the industrial revolution, all favoured the spread of the medical discoveries. Then again the general progress of agriculture which accompanied and preceded these developments permitted an improvement in the general food supply. At the end of the Renaissance, the practice of fallow disappeared from Milan, Tuscany and Flanders, and by the early twentieth century it was almost non-existent in north-west Europe (only 5·2 per cent of the land surface in 1935). Yields increased; that of wheat from 7 quintals per hectare about 1800 to 20 quintals about 1940. The potato, always the poor man's food, was the staff of life in Ireland and in northern Germany during the nineteenth century, and the Irish famine might easily have been even more deadly if the precious tuber had not existed at all. The consumption of meat in Germany rose from 17 kg per person per annum in 1816 to 52 kg in 1912; that of sugar in France from 11 kg about 1880 to 21 kg about 1925. The progress of transport made possible the quick relief of distress due to local failure of the harvest.

Though the death rate has suffered a first setback, that is not to say that the improvement is final. The decline has not been uniform or even general, for the benefits derived from medical discoveries, from increased agricultural output and from a rising standard of living have to be set against difficulties due to the creation of a new world of industry and factories. The first phase of industrial and urban development is nearly always marked by a temporary rise in the death rate; it is not a case of a sharp rise in the curve, linked with exceptional occurrences such as an epidemic or a famine but of a fairly constant rise which reflects the profound misery of the proletariat, and the appearance of occupational diseases. This sort of thing happened in the United Kingdom between 1810 and 1830, and in Germany between 1840 and 1870. The hard conditions of labour, in which women and children were employed in heavy tasks and even in the mines, and the misery of the filthy hovels in which masses of people, drawn together by the rapid growth of industry, were herded, are responsible for this anomaly. At Manchester, in the working-class districts about 1840, four out of five children died before reaching the age of five years.

As the years pass, the situation gets better; laws protect the workers from exploitation; child labour and later that of women, is regulated; wages rise and the mortality graph curves definitely downwards. The dates at which this occurs are roughly as follows: in Sweden 1830, England, 1870, Germany 1880, France 1890.

The struggle had been long and severe. When one compares the situation of the west European, slowly pushing death backwards, with that of the countries which have been aided by European experience, the result is striking. In Great Britain, it took a century for the death rate to fall from 23·3 per thousand about 1850 to 11·6 in 1960. In Japan the same result has been achieved in thirty years—from 23 in 1920 to 11·6 in 1949.

After western Europe it is the countries with white population, all over the world, which have recorded a similar trend—Canada and the U.S.A., Australia and New Zealand; the rest of the world follows slowly.

Present trends

Having once begun, the trend cannot stop; it spreads thanks to medical advances and the action of those countries where it first appeared —which were the most advanced in the world. Certain discoveries like special vaccines for the worst endemic diseases, and antibiotics, have had astonishing results for they permit, in a few moments, the prevention or cure of diseases which have caused wholesale slaughter.

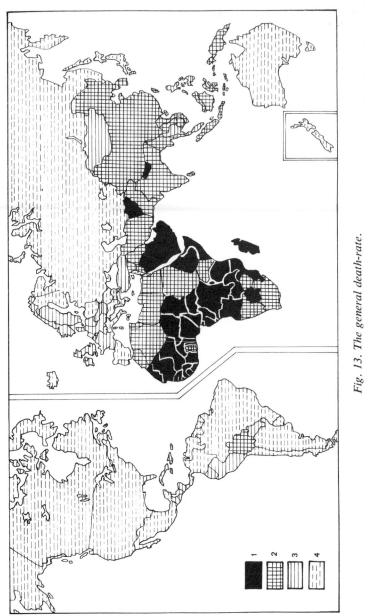

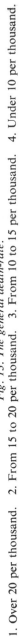

Fig. 13. The general death-rate.

1. Over 20 per thousand.   2. From 15 to 20 per thousand.   3. From 10 to 15 per thousand.   4. Under 10 per thousand.

When, as in many rural countries of Africa, Asia, and Latin America, there is but one doctor to 10,000 or even 100,000 people, he cannot pretend to give individual attention to the sick, but he can save thousands of lives with a single needle. There is thus in all countries a constant decline in the death rate, which accelerates as information travels faster, as better means of transport and communication become available, as technical and economic power increases and an international spirit of mutual aid creates new possibilities for the struggle against disease and death. An actual famine or epidemic occurring at this moment in a country whose frontiers are open and its territory accessible can be rapidly assuaged by an influx of help from every quarter of the globe. Thus every year the surplus grain harvest of the United States comes to the aid of countries which have suffered some natural calamity. On a smaller scale, France sends grain to African countries when the need arises; the U.S.S.R. does the same for its satellites.

Though progress is general and constant, it does not everywhere follow the same rhythm. Three groups of countries may be distinguished.

The countries in Group A are those which have had a low death rate for a long time; it is difficult to improve on these results and the

Decline in the Death Rate

	1938	1960	1974
Group A			
United Kingdom	11·8	11·5	12
U.S.A.	10·6	9·4	9·4
Australia	9·6	8·6	8·7
Group B			
Sri Lanka	21	9·1	7·7
U.S.S.R.	20	7	8·7
Japan	17·7	7·5	6·5
Group C			
India	23·7	—	16.7[1]
Nigeria	—	—	24.9[1]

Source: *U.N.O. Demographic Yearbook.*

[1] Estimate 1965–70.

death rate diminishes but very slowly indeed. In this group fall most of the countries of western Europe, Canada and the U.S.A., Australia, New Zealand. Some of them, owing to the increasing age of the population, even have a slight tendency to an increased rate—as in the case of Denmark, with 8·7 in 1955 and 10·2 in 1974.

The countries of Group B are those which have the most marked reduction. This is where important transformations have taken place in recent years. In Sri Lanka the vigorous campaign against malaria has completely altered the biological equilibrium. In the U.S.S.R. the efforts of the new regime have borne fruit—there was one doctor to 1,650 people in 1937 and one to 430 in 1975, and in one of the least favoured republics, Kazakhstan, one practitioner to 8,000 people in 1939 and one to 890 at the present time. Before the revolution, there were 150,000 cases of smallpox a year, but the disease had virtually disappeared by 1935, and similarly other diseases—scarlet fever, diphtheria, typhoid and syphilis—are almost conquered; tuberculosis cases have been reduced ten or fifteen times; an important part of the national budget is devoted to hospitals, maternity wards, crèches, propaganda for hygiene and the improvement of sanitation.

As for the third group, it includes those in which the effort made is still insufficient to overcome the hostility of the natural environment, the backward state of the people, and their poverty and lack of equipment. It is very difficult to get figures, for the official statistics were manifestly inadequate in the past and are incomplete at the present time; one can only refer to particular studies or to calculations made on the basis of the census. Included in this group are some of the tropical countries of America, Africa and south-east Asia. However, even in these areas much progress has been made in certain better-developed communities, and especially in the towns, though the rural masses remain largely untouched. This process is not new; it is but the first witness of a still more important evolution, which is being extended to these parts of the world also.

The extreme cases

The earliest estimates available for the United Kingdom, in the middle of the eighteenth century, give a mortality rate of at least 30 per thousand; this is in accord with statistical information for the beginning of this century from such countries as Chile and Mexico (about 32 per thousand), and we may suggest that what might be called the 'natural' rate, in the absence of major demographic accidents, was between 30 and 35 per thousand. It would appear that no large country in the world at the present time reaches such a high figure. Even studies of the worst cases suggest only 18 to 24 per thousand in 1975, and this for countries like India and certain parts of tropical Africa. In general, one may say that the intertropical regions still have rates of more than 18 per thousand, especially those in which, because of the preponderance of lowland and jungle, the natural conditions are least favourable. Even in these regions, as soon as mountains can counteract the pernicious effects of the low latitude, the rates would seem to drop to less than 18, as in the Andean states of Latin America.

A second great group of states has mortality rates generally below 12; these are essentially the temperate countries inhabited mostly by white races. Two varieties are distinguishable, the old countries of western Europe where the prolonged demographic evolution has resulted in a high proportion of elderly folk which gives a slightly higher mortality rate (about 10 to 12), whilst the vast 'new' territories of the U.S.S.R., Australia, North America and the Argentine have maintained till recently a higher birth rate and so a smaller proportion of elderly people, and thus have death rates as low as 7 to 10. The lowest death rates in the world are to be found in countries like Israel (7·3) and Japan (6·5), where at the same time there is a young population and—for varied reasons—a high level of services and education.

Lastly, between these two extremes, a third group includes those countries in course of development, where important minorities, as in South Africa, or masses of urban population as in Middle Eastern countries, have death rates much lower than the rest of the population. China, in so far as its demographic characteristics can be accurately observed, now seems to fall into this group, doubtless thanks to the drive for better health made during the last few years.

Calculations made for large areas of continents gave similar results (cf. p. 91): North America stands at the top of the list with a death rate of about 9 per thousand; then come the different European sectors, whilst at the bottom are south and south-east Asia and the African continent. The average rate for the whole world has been calculated at 18 per thousand for the period 1957–61, but it appears to be slightly diminishing year by year, and has now fallen to 13 (1965–74).

Reduction of infant mortality

We have already noted the significance of infant mortality in the general death rate from a quantitative standpoint, namely that any reduction in the former means a substantial reduction in the latter. The graph for Japan, a country in which the important and relatively recent demographic transformation has been the subject of good statistical analyses, illustrates well the close relationship between the two phenomena.

The saving of infants has also a qualitative significance for these are human lives which can develop and play their part instead of being snuffed out at the commencement. The economic aspects, however, are different from country to country. In the highly developed countries where the standard of life is high, and the demand for labour strong, every child is an economic investment which results in a growth in the potential of production—'with every mouth there is also a pair of hands'—and each infant saved has an economic value. In the underdeveloped countries, where conditions of life are precarious, where poverty and undernourishment dog the masses, the reduction of infant mortality is a medical success but a human and economic problem, temporarily at least, which must be accompanied by a revision of the demographic outlook, notably with regard to birth control, and by a reorganisation of the economic system so as to absorb the newcomers.

As with the general death rate, the figures for infant mortality are very varied, and change rapidly. In 1948, of the 148 countries for which the annual statistics of U.N.O. give a more or less reliable figure for infant mortality, one-third had a rate of over 100 per thousand. The highest figure was for the towns of Burma, where amongst 2 million people the infant mortality rate was 304 per thousand; others not far behind were the native population of Northern Rhodesia (Zambia) with 259, India (estimated) 185, Brazil 170, Greenland 161; Europe had some of the lowest figures, from 21 in Sweden to 120 in Yugoslavia.

In 1974 the list of countries contained 172 names, and only 20 per cent of them had an infant mortality rate of more than 100 per thousand. It may be assumed that the quality of the statistical information has been maintained or even improved in most cases. It is thus possible to discern real progress, but among the 20 per cent a few states still have rates of over 200 (e.g. Gabon 229, Niger 209),

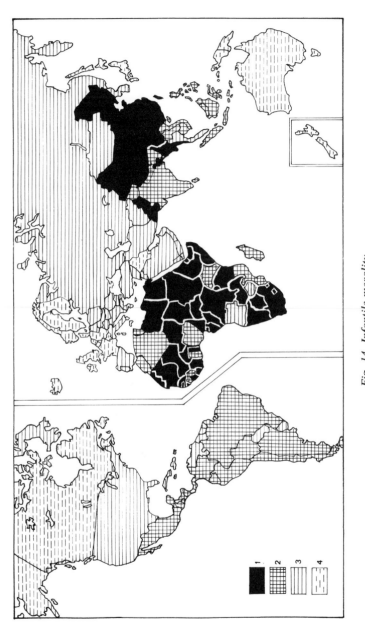

Fig. 14. Infantile morality.
1. Over 100 per thousand. 2. From 50 to 100 per thousand. 3. From 20 to 50 per thousand. 4. Under 20 per thousand.

whilst most of the rest fall between 100 and 150. The most favoured continent is Europe, where the lowest rate of all is 9·2 per thousand in Sweden, followed by Finland with 10·1 and the Netherlands with 11; but there are high rates in Portugal (38·4), Yugoslavia (40·4) and Albania (86·8). For the whole of north-west Europe the figure is under 16. In the U.S.S.R. the rate has fallen from 47 to 26·4 during the last twenty years.

In detail there are recognisable and striking differences between different races, for race is much bound up with the general standard and mode of life. Thus in the Republic of South Africa, the infant mortality rate is still 122 for the coloured population (black and half-caste) and 36 for the people of Asiatic origin, but it falls to 21 for the whites. In the United States the general rate has dropped to 16·5—though it was still 29 in 1950, with 27 for the whites and 45 for the non-whites; in some of the states the contrast is even more striking, for in North Dakota in 1955 it was between 24 (white) and 85·8 (black) and in New Mexico 38 and 87·3.

In the contrast between town and country, it seems that there are laws which differ widely according to the general nature of the civilisation and of the well-being of the people and the medical services. In the more advanced countries, the rates are almost identical (e.g. German Democratic Republic 17·6 in the towns and 17·9 in the rural areas; Finland, 12·4 and 13 respectively). If the overall standards are lower, the towns have a distinct advantage over the countryside (e.g. Israel, 19·7 in the towns, 30 in the rural areas; Japan, 11·7 and 14·9). In some countries, the rural rate is manifestly under-estimated because of incomplete registration of infant deaths (e.g. Salvador, 79·2 in towns, 52·6 in rural areas). In Brazil, in certain countries of Black Africa and of south-east Asia, local enquiries suggest that infant mortality in the rural areas may be double that in the towns, where there are better medical facilities (e.g. Liberia, 82 and 158).

In France, the parental home of deceased infants has been carefully recorded since 1951. Some very precise calculations for 1969 have given the following results: general infant mortality rate 20·2 per thousand, for rural communes 21·4, towns of 10,000 to 20,000 people 21·4, towns of 50,000 to 100,000, 19·9, Paris 13.5. In this case, infant mortality seems clearly to decrease with the quality of the sanitation and water supply on the one hand and the state of evolution of the population on the other.

In the United Kingdom, the infant mortality rate is 17.8 per thousand for the urban population and 15·1 for the rural; here, the sanitary conditions are good everywhere and the important factor is the concentration of the population in the industrial towns where infant mortality is higher. The converse is true for Romania, where the urban rate is 35.8 and the rural rate 42.5; in this case, where sanitary provision is not uniform, the towns are in a privileged position.

Among the other geographical aspects of infant mortality, two remain for consideration: they are *climatic influences* and the *economic-social class* of the family.

In a country like Brazil where there are strong climatic contrasts, associated it is true with contrasts of race and mode of life, it is worth noting that for the period 1948–50, the infant mortality rates were 243·6 for the district of Recife and 236·2 for Fortaleza, in the tropical area, but only 95 for the state of Rio Grande do Sul and 86 for the city of São Paulo—both of which are in more temperate latitudes.

Climatic influences affect young infants in two ways; heat favours all the intestinal maladies whilst cold affects the respiratory system. Studies have been made in France which show some interesting results: for the period 1947–50 a comparison of infant mortality during the summer months with the annual rate showed that the worst region was the hot zone of southern France, and especially the south-west, where humidity was added to heat. In contrast, the proportion of winter deaths was higher in general in the north and east, and in the alpine zone. In another investigation a graph of infant deaths by months of the year, at the beginning of this century and now, shows a strong preponderance of deaths from gastro-intestinal infections at the beginning of the century, whereas this maximum has now vanished since there is better supervision of milk quality and improved technical means of combating the inconveniences due to heat.

Naturally the success of the struggle varies with the *socio-economic environment* into which the infant is born, and the chances are better in more developed and wealthier classes. Various studies made in the United Kingdom, France, and the U.S.A. have made the measurement of differences possible. In France, for the period 1952–53, the average infant mortality rate was 36 per thousand, but the figures varied from 17 in the upper classes, 22 in the middle classes—prosperous tradesmen and professional people—to 45 amongst the agricultural workers and 54 amongst the labourers. Thus, the probability of surviving the first year of life is sensibly greater for the child of an industrialist, a lawyer or a doctor than for the child of a labourer. These differences diminish, however, as the state of the economy and the general standard of living improve. A similar enquiry in France in 1959–60 into the infant mortality rate in relation to socio-economic classes, showed that the overall rate was reduced to 27·4 per thousand, and the variation from 16 in the case of the upper classes to 32 for agricultural workers and 40·5 for labourers.

Moreover, the influence of the geographical environment varies within the first year of life according to the lapse of time since birth. Doctors and statisticians recognise an important distinction between the first month and the eleven which follow. During the first month, the dominant causes of death are linked with physiology and the circumstances of the accouchement, i.e. they are endogenetic. It seems that there is a strong correlation in particular, between the methods of accouchement and death during the first few days. Calculations made for the different départements of France, relating the infant death rate during the first ten days with the local medical facilities suggest disturbing coincidences. Thus, for the Département of Seine-et-Oise:

Infant mortality and accouchement in Seine-et-Oise

	1947	1948	1949	1950
Mortality rate in first ten days	14	14·2	12·4	9·8
Percentage of accouchements in hospitals	48·6	49·2	56·4	70·7

Source: INSEE.

The mortality during the first month represents a variable percentage of the total, according to the level of the total itself (even if one takes account of the fact that the registration of still-births is not the same for all countries); it represents a higher proportion of the total mortality in countries where the general rate is low, as the following table suggests:

Infant Mortality Rates

Country	one year	under 1 month
Egypt (1950-53)	133·4	20
Egypt (1971)	103·3	17·6
Japan (1950–53)	53·9	27
Japan (1971)	12·4	8·2
U.S.A. (1950–53)	28·4	19·9
U.S.A. (1970)	20·1	15·1
England and Wales (1950–53)	28·5	18·2
England and Wales (1972)	17·2	11·5
Sweden (1950–53)	20·3	14·6
Sweden (1972)	10·8	8·7

Source: *U.N.O. Demographic Yearbook*, 1957, 1974.

This is due to the fact that the very nature of its causes makes it difficult for infant mortality to fall below a certain level.

On the contrary, during the course of the next eleven months, exogenetic causes predominate, and most of these are linked with the environment, infectious diseases and alimentary troubles becoming preponderent. In France, it is reckoned that almost half the deaths during this period are due to social conditions, in particular to the defects of housing and their consequences. Thus a massive reduction appears to be possible. Take the example of Japan, where infant mortality fell from 61·7 in 1948 to 11·3 in 1975; the number of deaths in the first week after birth remained almost constant, but the number in the first month dropped from 28·2 to 7·2 per thousand, and that of the next eleven months fell dramatically, from 33·5 to 4·3. If there were adequate statistics for countries where the rates are much higher, the same striking result would doubtless be obtained.

One demographic statistician is prepared to regard as due to geographical or other exogenetic causes a proportion of the infant deaths equal to all those occurring in the last eleven months plus one-quarter of those in the first month; thus, for an infant mortality of 25·5 per thousand, as in England and Wales in 1954, the proportion ascribed to exogenetic causes, that is, for the most part available, would have been 12·1 per thousand. The present figures for Sweden,

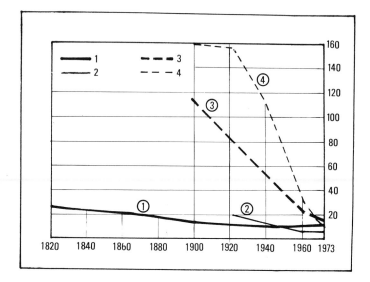

Fig. 15. General and infantile death rates in the U.K. and Japan.
General death-rate: 1. in the U.K. and 2. in Japan. Infantile death-
rate 3. in the U.K. and 4. in Japan. Rates per thousand, given on
vertical scale.

Norway, Netherlands, Japan and Iceland are thus very close to the
utmost limit that could be attained.

Once having survived the first year, a child's chances of survival are
considerably greater. However, certain customs may render him
vulnerable for a rather longer period, for example in black Africa at
the time of weaning; the disappearance of maternal milk and the
absence of any dairy products in substitution thereof, brings about
the deficiency disease known as 'kwashiorkor' which attacks children
at any age between six months and six years, and is most frequent in
two- and three-year-olds. This disease is characterised by a reddening
of the hair and skin, by retarded growth, the infiltration of fat,
oedema of the stomach and cirrhosis of the liver; it often ends in
death or in gravely impaired health. Another dangerous moment is
when the nursling leaves its mother's back, for it is then very susceptible to cold.

The number of children dying between one and four years of age,
compared with the infant mortality rate, is significant:

Ratio of Number of Child Deaths (one to four years) to Number of Infant Deaths (under one year)

Country	Year	Ratio (%)	Year 1971–2
United Kingdom	1959	14·4	18·5
Canada	1959	15·2	21·2
South Africa (whites)	1958	21·4	19·6
South Africa (non-whites)	1958	51·7	41·2
Chile	1957	26	16·2
Japan	1959	34	31·5
Nigeria (Lagos)	1959	93	66·4
India[1]	1959	105	89·5

[1] Data for a part of India only.

Source: *U.N.O. Demographic Yearbook*, 1960, 1974.

It may thus be estimated that in a great number of countries, in Africa, in South America, in India and doubtless in other south-east Asian countries as well, almost half the children die before reaching fifteen years of age. In the developed countries such as those of western Europe this proportion falls to about 5 per cent. Thus the larger part of humanity has still great progress to make, not only as regards infant mortality, but as regards the loss of young life in general.

Causes of death
As with infant mortality, so with the general mortality rate, the causes of death have varied with the passage of time and are spatially very diverse; the changes constitute one of the typical aspects of demographic evolution and one of the most favourable elements in the development of populations. In effect, thanks to the almost continuous chain of medical discoveries, the spread of education, the improvement of sanitation, and the growth in many parts of the world of substantial centres from which improvements may radiate, many enemies of humanity are in retreat almost to the point of disappearance.

We have come to distinguish two series of factors responsible for death, the exogenetic and the endogenetic. The former are essentially the result of the environmental influence: they comprise all the infectious, pulmonary and digestive diseases, which are linked with microbes, with climate, food supply and poor conditions of life. We have already shown that there are certain natural conditions like excessive cold, humid heat and sharp temperature changes, which directly or indirectly have adverse effects on the human body. Such factors exercise their maximum effect in countries where the material and technical aspects of civilisation are weak and have not been able

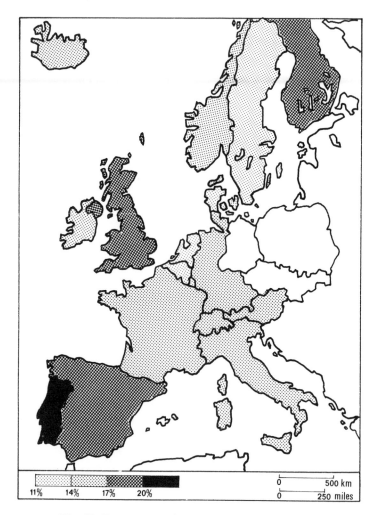

Fig. 16. Exogenetic and endogenetic causes of death.
The proportion of deaths due to exogenetic causes, by countries.

to weaken, let alone neutralise, the injurious effects of the environment. On the contrary the endogenetic factors are essentially biological; in this case the causes of death are either congenital or are due to a rapid alteration in bodily functioning. Infant mortality in the first ten days, cancer and diseases of the circulatory system fall within this category.

Historically, a country with a long demographic evolution will pass from a preponderance of the exogenic factors to an almost complete dominance of the endogenetic, as the following figures for the United Kingdom show:

U.K. Principal Causes of Death (per thousand deaths)

In 1848–72			In 1947		
Infectious diseases		321	Circulatory System		386
Tuberculosis	146		Heart disease	217	
Scarlet Fever	57		Cancer		149
Typhus	38		Infectious diseases		71
Respiratory diseases		148	Tuberculosis	50	
Bronchitis	66		Respiratory diseases		91
Pneumonia	57		Bronchitis	35	
Nervous System		129	Pneumonia	46	
Digestive System		83	Nervous System		76
Enteritis	47		Digestive System		45
Circulatory System		53			

In the mid-nineteenth century one person in three in the United Kingdom died from infectious diseases; today scarcely one in fifteen, and recent progress has been rapid because of the development of stronger and stronger antibiotics. Tuberculosis, classed with the infectious diseases, is in fast retreat; the respiratory forms of this disease have fallen by 66 per cent, other forms by 85 per cent—though it is worth noting that lung-tuberculosis remains the most important killer of adolescents and adults, causing one-quarter of all deaths between ages ten and fifty-five. Swedish and Finnish statistics show the same situation. On the other hand, amongst the endogenic factors, cancer is taking a more and more important place, and deaths from this cause have multiplied proportionally fifteen times. It is noteworthy, however, that the part played by cancer appears to increase as others decrease, since it occurs mainly in people above a certain age so that the number of fatalities grows appreciably as the human life-span is extended; also, of course, the diagnosis of it has made great progress. The consequences of this evolutionary course are striking: in 1947 in England and Wales there were 515,591 deaths; if the general death rate and the living conditions had been as they were in the mid-nineteenth century, the number would have been 1,105,964. Thus 600,000 human lives had been saved by the decline in the death rate, the result mainly of a decrease in the exogenic causes. The same tendencies are continuing, for in 1970, amongst the causes of death in the United Kingdom, diseases of the circulatory system had risen to 453 per thousand, and cancer to 202; whilst deaths from infectious diseases amounted to 69 per thousand, and diseases of the respiratory system 135 (an increase possibly related to urban pollution, for although the Clean Air Act and technological changes in industry have almost abolished the smoke problem, the vast increase in the density of motor traffic in towns has greatly magnified pollution from exhaust fumes); diseases of the digestive system caused only 13 per thousand deaths, but accidents had risen to 12 per thousand.

It is extremely difficult to make comparisons between countries in respect of the causes of death, for usually in those countries where health conditions are at their worst, not only is there no certainty that all deaths are registered but for the most part the causes are unknown. And in the better developed countries themselves it is also difficult because of the differences in records; in the United Kingdom the doctor makes a report on the cause of death, in France a single word may suffice, whilst in many countries an elderly person's death is simply recorded as due to 'senility', whether there is another cause or not. The comparisons made below must therefore be treated with great reserve. We have tried to compare the causes of death in a country with a high mortality rate and in another, Israel, which has one of the lowest death rates in the world, with a country of recent and rapid demographic progress (Japan) for which reasonable statistics are available, and one (the U.S.A.) in which a low death rate is a phenomenon of long standing.

The analysis for countries in the first group is extremely difficult because the causes of death are only declared in an approximate fashion and in any case they pertain only to part of the population.

In Egypt, in 1970, with an overall death rate of 14·4 per thousand, 34 per cent of deaths resulted from diseases of the digestive system and 11 per cent from pulmonary diseases. In Lagos, the capital of Nigeria, with a 1970 death rate of 24·9, infectious diseases represented 17·1 per cent, respiratory diseases 16·3 and digestive troubles 11·1 per cent; but only 2·5 per cent from cancer and 5·8 per cent from circulatory disorders. The following figures for the total coloured population of South Africa, calculated in 1958 and 1969, show both the general nature of the mortality causation and a slow but significant rate of change:

Union of South Africa, 1958 and 1969: Deaths of Coloured Population

Diseases	Percentage of deaths		
	1958		1969
Infectious diseases	11·7 ⎫		
Pulmonary diseases	14·5 ⎬ 49·2		47
Digestive diseases	23 ⎭		
Cancer	5·9 ⎫		
Circulatory system	18·9 ⎬ 24·8		25·4
Accidents	4		

Source: *U.N.O. Demographic Yearbook*, 1960, 1972.

It is apparent that the three typically exogenetic groups (infectious diseases including tuberculosis, pulmonary and digestive diseases) cause half the total deaths, or double the number of those caused by typically endogenetic diseases such as cancer and circulatory disorders.

The second type is that of a country in which the death rate has improved rapidly, and Japan is taken because it has a good statistical service. Between 1947 and 1959, the general death rate fell by one-half and the causes became reversed: exogenetic causes represented more than twice the endogenetic in 1947 and only 40 per cent of them in 1959. Deaths from tuberculosis in particular have diminished, falling in the proportion of 5 to 1 for the respiratory forms and 10 to 1 for other forms. In the same period the number of accidents doubled. The figures for 1970 confirm the trend: with a very low overall death rate of 6·6 per thousand, 13·3 per cent of deaths were recorded from exogenetic causes and 51 per cent from endogenetic causes. The increases in cancer and heart disease are spectacular.

Japan: Causes of Death 1947 and 1970 (percentages)

Diseases	1947 (death rate 14·6 per thousand)		1970 (death rate 6·6 per thousand)	
Infectious diseases	20·4		3·4	
Pulmonary diseases	15·3	} 51·6	6·5	} 13·3
Digestive diseases	15·9		3·4	
Cancer	4·9		17·6	
Circulatory system	13·8	} 18·7	40·4	} 58·0
Accidents	3·4		3·0	

Source: *U.N.O. Demographic Yearbook*, 1960, 1972.

Lastly there is a third group of countries with a low death rate. Our two examples are the United States, in which the death rate has been practically stationary for a long time, and Israel which owing to its peculiar circumstances of recent immigration, especially of adults and children, has one of the lowest death rates of any country in the world. The calculations show that exogenetic mortality is reduced to less than 10 per cent, though cancer and the many forms of disturbance of the circulatory system retain important places.

	United States 1970 death rate 9·4 per thousand		Israel 1970 death rate 7·2 per thousand	
Infectious diseases	0·8		2	
Pulmonary diseases	4·8	} 8·2	4·2	} 8·1
Digestive diseases	2·6		2·9	
Cancer	17·5		17·1	
Circulatory system	48·7	} 69	42·6	} 62·9
Accidents	2·8		2·2	

Source: *U.N.O. Demographic Yearbook*, 1960, 1972.

It is the countries of western Europe, with the United States, which have the highest proportion of endogenetic mortality—80 per cent in Sweden, 72 per cent in the United Kingdom; in the latter case almost two-thirds of the endogenetic causes are concerned with the functioning of the circulatory system, but among people of over sixty-five, one in three dies of cardiac trouble though the proportion is only one in seven between ages twenty-five and forty-four. As with cancer, one can discern in this group of diseases the undoubted influence of the prolongation of the life-span and the ageing of the population.

Such comparisons as these are interesting not only from the point of view of theoretical study but also because they point the way towards a further reduction in the death rate, particularly in the less favoured countries.

The increasing life span

The lowering of the death rate, particularly at the lower end of the age scale, results in an increase in the average length of human life. In times past, even in western countries, an octogenarian was an exception and a sexagenarian by no means common; at the present day there are so many people of such ages that to die before sixty is almost a disgrace! What was the exception has become the rule. In France, during the hundred years since 1851 the number of people aged over sixty, increased by 59 per cent, that of the over-seventies by 10 per cent, and of the octogenarians by 141 per cent. The average age at death, calculated from the records of a little village in the département of Nord, increased from 26 years about 1720, to 33 years about 1796, 38 years in 1820, 52 years at the end of the nineteenth century, and 57 years on the eve of the second World War. This is the sort of thing that has happened in the past, and is still happening, in the world at large on a much vaster scale.

This sort of progress is generally measured by statistics which give the 'expectation of life'; this, calculated at birth, is obviously equal to the average length of human life. Unfortunately, as with mortality statistics, comparative data are very difficult to obtain, both in time and space but chiefly in time.

On account of the numerous reservations which hamper the interpretation of the statistics, we shall content ourselves with suggesting a division of the world into three groups of countries. The first group has an expectation of life of less than 45 years; it consists mainly of equatorial and tropical Africa, and also perhaps India where the estimates give values between 40 and 45 years. In the second group the expectation is between 45 and 60 years, and here we find most of Latin America, in particular Argentina and Chile for which there are reasonable data, south-east Asia, the northern and southern ends of Africa (Egypt and the coloured population of South Africa which appear to have figures slightly in excess of 50), and (with averages of over 50) the countries of eastern and Mediterranean Europe. The third group has an expectation of more than 65 years; it comprises mainly the countries of white civilisation, together with states which have made rapid recent progress, and in which, for profound reasons as in Japan, or from accidental causes as in Sri Lanka, the demographic conditions have enormously improved. Also included are the

Progress in the Expectation of Life at Birth
(Years)

Country and Date	Men	Women
Sri Lanka 1920–22	32·7	30·7
1946	43·9	41·6
1967	64·8	66·9
Japan C. 1900	43·9	44·8
1947	50	53·9
1972	70·5	75·9
France C. 1910	48·5	52·4
C. 1930	54·3	59
1971	68·5	76·1
United Kingdom C. 1910	51·5	55·3
C. 1930	58·7	62·9
1970	67·8	73·8
United States C. 1910	49·8	53·2
C. 1930	57·7	61
1972	67·4	75·2

C = Census.

Source, *U.N.O. Demographic Yearbook*, 1957, 1974.

U.S.S.R., where the figure rose from 42 (for men only) in 1926–27 to 65 in 1970–71. Among these favoured nations certain may have at present an expectation of over 70 years, averaged for both sexes; such are Canada and the United States, Australia, New Zealand, United Kingdom, the Scandinavian countries, France, Israel, and at the very top of the list, the Netherlands.

This situation results from a continuous evolution which has accelerated remarkably since the last war, with the discovery of means of combating the infectious diseases (antibiotics and the conquest of malaria). The rise in the curve is just as remarkable in developed regions such as France, as in countries like Sri Lanka where malaria was the endemic scourge. Even in the least favoured countries, as we have already said, the advantage of these new drugs is that they enable mass treatment to be given which can utterly transform the health of the whole population, instead of merely saving lives in carefully selected individual cases. This transformation is of the utmost importance at the present stage in the evolution of human societies.

In a large part of the world, infant mortality remains at a high level; but having rounded this dangerous headland, the survivors have much better prospects before them, for there is no doubt, as has often been suggested, that the intensity of child mortality represents in fact a process of natural selection:

Expectation of Life

Country and date	At birth	At age 15	At age 50
Sri Lanka 1946 men	43·9	45·3	19·7
women	41·6	42·9	20·2
1954 men	60·3	55.6	24·5
women	59·4	54·8	25
1967 men	64·8	55·8	24·8
women	66·9	57·7	26·2
Netherlands 1953–55 men	71	58·5	25·7
women	73·9	60·8	27·5
1972 men	71	57.3	24.5
women	76·8	63	29·4

Source: *U.N.O. Demographic Yearbook*, 1957, 1974.

The example of Sri Lanka in 1946, which may be paralleled by Japan some years ago, and by other countries of the same type, shows that the poorer the demographic conditions, the better is the expectation of life at age fifteen than at birth. A young Indian, if he is fortunate enough to reach his fifteenth year, has as long a life still before him as the newly-born infant. The case of a youngster from one of the more developed countries like the Netherlands, shows that the adolescent European (or one from other countries of the same type) is much less proportionally favoured.

A classification by countries, however, is much too succinct; other factors enter into the picture, linked with what we might call the 'way of life'. Statistics for the Republic of South Africa show profound differences between the different ethnic groups—white, Asiatic, black, and coloured. The same is true for the United States, where in 1955, the expectation of life at birth was 67·3 years for white men, and only 61·2 for negro men (and 73·6 for white women with 65·9 for black women).

Within a single country appreciable differences may be recorded, for one reason or another. Thus, in France, it would appear, perhaps paradoxically, that the Paris conurbation is in the most favoured position, despite the constant complaints of its citizens about the conditions in which they live—simply because of the excellence of the services and the opportunities for using them. But in addition to such circumstances, climate, the nature of occupations, and the socio-economic classification of the population, may play a part: amongst the large cities, the maximum life-span of both males and females is found in the capitals of the rural south, whilst the lowest occurs in the mining and industrial cities of the north:

Average male expectation of life			
Maximum		*Minimum*	
Montpellier	70·3	Béthune	63·1
Limoges	70·0	Lens	63·2
Toulouse	70·0	Roubaix	63·3
		Denain	63·4

Average female expectation of life			
Maximum		*Minimum*	
Cannes	77·0	Roubaix	71·2
Pau	77·0	Lille	71·7
Montpellier	76·9	Denain	71·9
Limoges	76·8	Valenciennes	72·2
		Dunkerque	72·2

The differences in the mortality rate which result from the standard of living also have their repercussions on the average length of life, but certain additional factors are involved such as the nature of the occupations and the quality of the health services. Thus coal miners, their lungs corroded by silicosis, die relatively young, while, in France, railway locomotive drivers, carefully chosen on the basis of their physical aptitudes, and under strict medical care throughout their period of service, retire at 50, and thereafter have a longevity greater than that of most other French men, generally passing 80 years. Conversely, wealthier people, harassed by business worries and over weight through excess of eating and drinking, die prematurely. In human geography there are no rules which are without exceptions.

Finally, in the two tables given above, one fact is strikingly obvious, and that is the very special way women are affected by death.

Feminine mortality

Before discussing the peculiarities of the feminine mortality rate, it is as well to note the doubtful character of many statistics. For in many countries, girls are considered as of secondary importance and the records for them are less complete than for the males, especially as regards births and deaths of babies and children. Despite the difficulties however, it is fairly clear that there are important differences in the way death affects males and females.

It is well known that at the moment of conception, as well as at birth, there is an excess of males over females, but the boys' organism being more delicate, their infant mortality rate is higher and equilibrium is rapidly re-established.

The detailed comparison of mortality rates by age-groups permits us to divide female life into three stages:

Childhood. Whatever the demographic evolution of a given country may have been, it always happens that infant mortality is higher—by 10 to 25 per cent—amongst boys than amongst girls; during the years of infancy the rates become uniform and the rhythm becomes the same for both sexes.

Infant mortality, Girls and Boys (rates per thousand)
(1970–72)

Country	Girls	Boys
Israel	20	22·6
U.S.A.	17·6	22·5
Sweden	8·9	12·7
Japan	10·9	13·8
Guatemala	80·5	93·4

Source: *U.N.O. Demographic Yearbook*, 1974.

The reproductive period. During the course of the second period of female life, differences appear between two large groups of countries. Those with good conditions of life have a female death rate noticeably inferior to the masculine rate, and the difference is sometimes striking, as in France:

Adult Mortality in France (1972) (per thousand)

Age group	Male	Female
15–19	1·28	0·56
20–24	1·8	0·56
25–29	1·58	0·68
30–34	1·91	0·92
35–39	2·71	1·35
40–44	4·33	2·08
45–49	6·64	3·11

Source. I.N.S.E.E.

This anomaly is linked with alcoholism which produces an excessive death rate in men. Cirrhosis of the liver caused the death, in 1970, of more than 17,000 men, representing 3·6 per cent of all male deaths; the women on the other hand were only affected half as much. Of all the countries which publish the causes of death, France stands unhappily at the head of the list in this respect, followed closely by Portugal.

In the second group of countries, those in which conditions of health are still poor, it is the women between fifteen and fifty who die sooner than the men; the risks of maternity are clearly responsible for this. Amongst the Muslims indeed the lot of a woman in travail is compared to that of a warrior going into battle. In black Africa, a woman in labour is considered impure, and she gives birth alone or aided by the loathsome attentions of some old crone who is more of a danger than a help to both mother and child. The proportion of women who die in childbirth in the hospitals of these countries is very high, for only desperate cases are taken there, and often after hours of suffering and long journeys by jungle paths under very trying conditions. Let us look again at the figures for Sri Lanka:

Adult Mortality in Sri Lanka, 1952, Male and Female

Age group	Male	Female
15–20	7·6	12·4
20–30	11	21·7
30–40	16:6	28·2
40–50	25·8	28·7

In this year (1952) almost 2,000 women (out of a total of 95,298 deaths and for 313,352 births) died from complications arising in pregnancy or in childbirth; this represents about one-quarter of all the female deaths between the ages of 25 and 44. It is only right to add that great progress has been made, but the same dissymmetry is still to be found in certain countries, for example Malaysia, Pakistan, Peru, and doubtless other states or particularly ill-favoured parts thereof, for which we have no reliable statistics.

Senescence. Lastly during the third period of female life, we find again a general tendency for females to live much longer than males, and we need only look back at the tables of expectation to confirm this. Thus at the present time, in certain countries of black Africa, such as Nigeria, Niger and Haute-Volta, and in south-east Asia (Pakistan) female life expectation is lower than that of males right up to the age of 60. But such cases are becoming less common. In the United Kingdom, at 50, a man has only 23 more years to look forward to, whereas a woman may hope for more than 28 years. This is reflected in the age structure of the population, and thus it happens that in demographically mature countries the proportion of females to males increases as the age groups rise and this is shown in the 'population pyramid', as we shall see.

The role of social inequality in death rates

Amongst the great causes of differentiation in both general and infant death rates, we have mentioned the role of social factors. This expression covers the 'way of life', which is not only bound up with the financial position of the individuals but also with their level of education and their customs, that is, just those elements which in detail escape all general classification and would require a series of case studies to obtain valid comparisons.

We have to consider not only the rise in the average standard of living, in the level of wages that permits a greater number to have a better food supply and a more comfortable existence. The evolution of modern societies which put man in the forefront of their pre-occupations, upsets the traditional free play of riches and poverty. Thus, in those countries enjoying 'social security', the worker may receive as much care as the more fortunate individual, and the famous gynaecologist who receives a handsome fee for delivering the child of a celebrity finds the most humble women in his hospital. Furthermore, the building of modern, spacious housing estates for the working classes, and new towns planted in the midst of green spaces, changes the conditions of life and gives to the less fortunate the possibility of a healthy dwelling without being tied to the old and sordid quarters where rents are cheaper.

These transformations are coming about gradually in many parts of the world. In the socialist countries, they are part of the fundamental conception of the regime and they accompany, as far as is possible, not only the creation of the new industrial society but also the revolution in the countryside. Communist China, which can scarcely feed its population and uses only a few ounces of steel per inhabitant, boasts of its hospital and crèche building, and of its accelerated training of first aid doctors. The proportion of the national budget devoted to 'social questions' is remarkably high in all the states in this group. In the more advanced countries of the west, social measures have largely and progressively penetrated the traditional ways of life and the New Zealand formula 'security from the cradle to the grave' could be taken as a slogan by most of the countries of western Europe, North America, and Australia. Finally, in the remainder of the world, ideas of the same kind are arising but they spread slowly and sporadically.

Historically we may distinguish three stages: in the *first*, in the absence of efficient medical services, death knocked alike at the doors of rich and poor; this was probably the case all over the world until the middle of the eighteenth century, In a *second intermediate stage*, medical advances had begun to be capable of exercising a tangible effect, and the rich people benefited much more rapidly and deeply, and their death rate dropped well below the average; and since, in western Europe, this stage coincided with the development of industry, the hard conditions of life of the workers and of the masses crowding into the towns reinforced the inequality. In France it is estimated that the period of maximum inequality in the death rate was the second half of the nineteenth century:

Evolution of Death rate in Paris (per thousand)

Area	1817	1850
Rich quarters	24·9	18·2
Middle-class areas	27·3	25·1
Poor districts	36·5	33·7

Source: E. Vedrenne-Villeneuve, *Population*, 1961, p. 698.

In the United Kingdom, at York, in 1840 the average age at death was 48–56 for the gentry and 23·8 for the workers.

There follows the *third stage*: improvements in the general conditions of life accompany more and more effective social legislation, and inequality of the classes tends to diminish and becomes blurred. In Paris, the relation between the death rate in the poor quarters and in the wealthy districts could be reckoned at 1·85 about 1850, 1·42 in 1891 and 1·26 in 1946. At Amsterdam, in the new working-class districts, the death rate is practically the same as in the fashionable quarters. In the United Kingdom, a study of the mortality figures for England and Wales for 1950 gave results which lead to similar conclusions. The authors distinguish five social categories—(1) upper classes; (ii) middle classes, shopkeepers, farmers and certain employees; (iii) craftsmen, foremen, skilled workers, and certain other employees; (iv) fishermen, miners, semi-skilled workers; (v) labourers. The evolution of the death rate in these five classes shows a noticeable relative lowering in the case of the second, fourth and fifth, and on the contrary a rise in the first and third. In 1921–23 the death rate in the lower classes was 52 per cent higher than in the upper classes, and one could assume that one death in three was due to social factors. At present the most favoured group is the second, and for persons aged over sixty-five, it appears that the fifth class had the lowest death rate. The author concluded that 'social inequality in death rates still exists amongst children, but disappears in old age' —which was certainly not the case thirty years ago. To explain this evolution we must recall the distinction already made between endogenetic and exogenetic causes. The latter play a much more important role amongst children, whilst beyond a certain age the endogenetic causes predominate.

Death Rate of Married Men aged 20–64, England and Wales
(mean index = 100)

	Social Classes				
	1	*2*	*3*	*4*	*5*
1921–23	82	94	95	101	125
1950	97	86	102	94	118

Source: L. Tabah, *Population*, 1955, p. 62.

The better-off ones can protect themselves more efficiently against environmental diseases and this explains their slight advantage at the adult age; but on the other hand there is little protection against the wear and tear of the organism or its malfunctioning. The analysis of the causes of death amongst the five classes distinguished above confirms this point of view; deaths from pulmonary tuberculosis, syphilis, cancer of the stomach, pneumonia, bronchitis, and miscellaneous accidents rise from the first to the fifth category; the reverse is true of

PLATE 1. *Recife, Brazil: market near the port*

PLATE 2. *Nile Delta: irrigation canal, pyramids in distance*

PLATE 3. *Futa Jalon, Guinea: the road to the village*

PLATE 4. *Coast of north-east Brazil: fishermen repairing their* jongades, *light-weight raft-boats*

PLATE 5. *Fadioute, Senegal: fishing village raised on piles in the lagoon*

PLATE 6. *North-east Brazil: women washing clothes on the banks of the river São Francisco, near Remanso (Bahia state)*

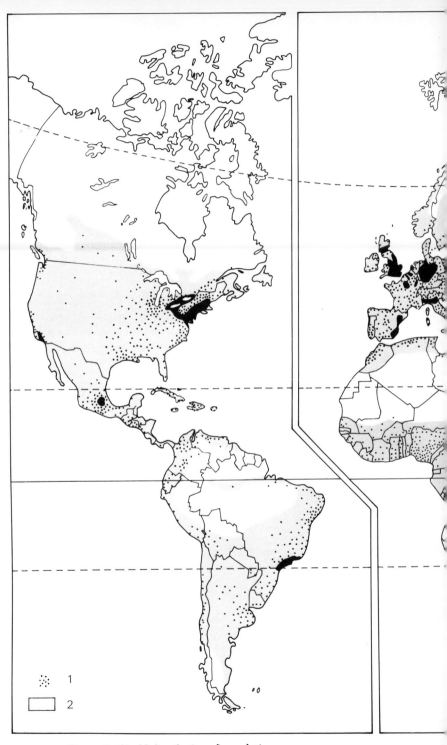

PLATE 7. *World distribution of population*

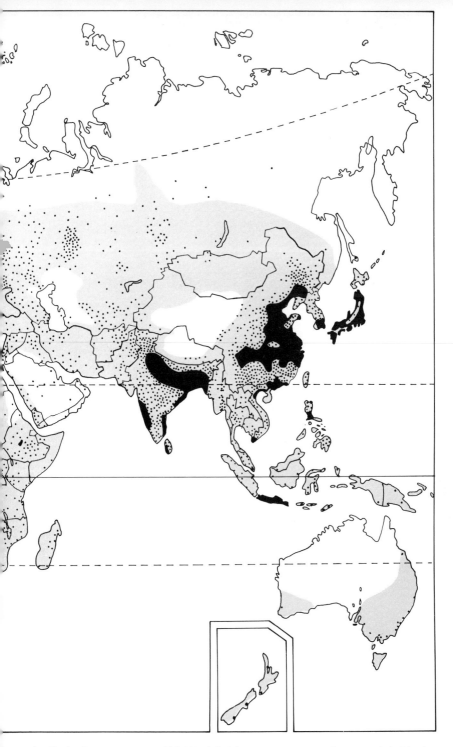

1. Each dot represents 500,000 inhabitants. 2. Areas almost uninhabited.
Equatorial scale approximately 1:110 million.

PLATE 8. *Family Planning promotion by bus, India.*

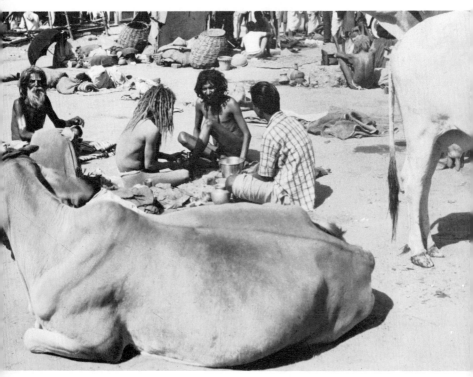

PLATE 9. *Calcutta: sacred cattle and holy men*

PLATE 10. *Nomads and peasants in Thessaly, Greece*

PLATE 11. *Natives of Ouvea, in the Loyalty archipelago (New Caledonia)*

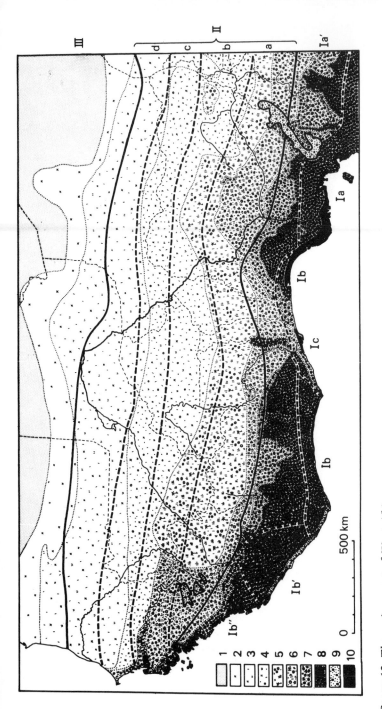

PLATE 12. *The environment of West Africa*

VEGETATION: 1. Desert. 2. Semi-desert. 3. Steppe with spiny bushes and short grass. 4. Low savanna. 5. High savanna with trees, palms and tall grass. 6. High savanna (moister) with open woodland. 7. Mixed savanna and forest. 8. Dense rain-forest at low and moderate altitudes. 9. Mountain vegetation types. 10. Mangroves.

Ib. Tropical with 2 short dry seasons
Ib'. Hot tropical with short (3 months) dry season
Ib". Hot tropical with moderate (4 months) dry season
Ic. Tropical with two well-marked wet seasons
IIa. Sub-tropical with marked wet season
IIb. Sub-tropical
Ic. Semi-desert with marked tropical characteristics

cancer of the prostate, of the kidneys, of the bladder, leucaemia, thrombosis, and diabetes. The study also shows that social factors remain important in explaining differences in infant mortality which is more than twice as high amongst the children of class (5) than of class (1).

Other more recent studies confirm these observations. In the United States, in 1960, the mortality index for men aged 25 to 64 was 113 for individuals having no more than elementary education, 81 for university graduates; in relation to income, the index was 151 for those earning under $2,000 in 1959 and 84 for those earning over $10,000; and, resulting from a combination of education and income, the index for the professional and upper classes was 80, for working classes 137. These inequalities are also combined with those for race—the overall index for whites was 92, and for blacks 178. Similar conclusions regarding the importance of cultural levels in relation to the death rate emerged from a French enquiry in 1973: this showed that, at the age of 35, male life expectation varied from a maximum of a further 40·8 years for school teachers, and 40·3 for the professions and administrative personnel, to a minimum of 33·5 for various categories of workers and labourers.

The conclusion that can be drawn from these observations is two-fold. In the more advanced countries, there is progress towards a diminution in the role of social inequality in death rates; ideally one would expect the virtual disappearance of this factor as the struggle against the exogenetic causes of death becomes increasingly efficient, general, and independent of wealth. In the second place, a stage of development like this has only been reached in very small parts of the world; a larger portion is striving for it, including Europe, North America, Australia, New Zealand and the communist countries. But the greater part of the world and the vast majority of mankind is still only in the second stage of development, in which medical progress reaches only a small part of the population, generally the most wealthy or those who happen to be located near to a doctor, a hospital or a dispensary, whilst the mass of the people are untouched except by general or occasional measures, such as a vaccination campaign or an itinerant medical mission.

Urbanisation and mortality

The development of towns being one of the principal characteristics of the present evolution of population distribution, it is particularly important to analyse the influence of this movement on demographic rhythms. Unfortunately we are cruelly handicapped, for it is impossible to rely on the all too infrequent statistics. There are in fact two sources of error: the presence of a medical service, which is particularly dense in the towns, produces an influx of patients and swells the mortality figures when the real locality of residence is not given; and the existence of a much more efficient registration service in the towns whilst demographic facts in the country districts are under-recorded. These two sources of error both lead to the same result, the inflation of the mortality statistics for the towns. For most countries therefore the documentation must be handled with great care.

Individually, for the countryman who migrates to the town, the adaptation is not always easy; in the United States it has been noticed that he is much more vulnerable to certain diseases such as influenza and other microbe-borne infections; at the other extreme, in black Africa, deficiency diseases appear in the uprooted jungle-dweller by reason of the derangement of his traditional feeding habits—for the new townsman tends to imitate the diet of the whites, but can only buy the cheapest food, especially bread, a policy of 'full stomach at low cost'. A study made at Bahia, in north-eastern Brazil, showed an almost complete disappearance of milk and a reduction by half in vegetables and fruit, in the diet of recent urban immigrants. Conversely, water is of better quality, and the possibilities of medical care are more numerous and nearer at hand. If one further remembers the execrable living conditions of the shanty-towns, the 'favellas', the ancient crumbling houses in the older quarters, the promiscuity and often the overcrowding, and the mixture of arrivals from all parts of the country, one can imagine that death is very close indeed, especially if poverty is excessive or if the occupation of the uprooted man is an unhealthy one. Tuberculosis and alcoholism help to multiply the evil effects.

For a long time there must have been an alarming debit balance. At the time of the industrial development of western Europe, the slums of the growing towns were veritable child cemeteries; eye-witness accounts of Manchester and Lille agree on this point. We have already noted the temporary rise in the overall death rate which characterised the nineteenth-century phase of industrialisation, in Germany as well as in Britain. Contemporary experience in the towns of developing countries is similar. In the towns of the Gold

Coast, thirty years ago, the death rate was three times higher amongst the newly-arrived immigrants than amongst the existing urban population, and many more returned to die in their villages; men between fifteen and forty-five were particularly hard hit. Amongst the working population of the shanty towns of Calcutta or Bombay, the situation would be even worse. At a time when the official infant mortality rate for India was 198, figures of 348 were quoted for the textile city of Ahmedabad, and even 666 for Bombay. Amongst the children of mothers who worked up to the last minute the mortality reached 485 per thousand, and amongst the families living in one room, the appalling figure of 828 per thousand was calculated. In India too, only 16 per cent of the towns have a satisfactory water supply; tuberculosis is rife: between 20 and 35 per cent of the rural population suffering from the disease and 80 to 90 per cent of the poorer people in the towns, with 7 per cent acute cases in the Bengal towns but only 0·6 per cent in the rural areas. Centres of pilgrimages and great fairs, which gather the multitudes together, are well known as centres for the propagation of epidemics.

After the lapse of time, however, the situation may change; the uprooted country folk can adapt themselves; if the immigration has not been too great or too continuous, the town organisation can improve, particularly if a developed centre already exists, and, for reasons of self-preservation as well as from altruistic motives, the environment can be cleaned up and a more human welcome given to the newcomers. Such has been the case in the areas of white colonisation in Africa. Technical and medical progress have been able to improve matters, and more recently to alter the whole situation. The example of Freetown is a good one: a systematic improvement of sanitation since 1946 and the massive use of insecticides since 1952, combined with the treatment of malaria and the distribution of preventive medicines in the schools, with a series of vaccinations against smallpox and yellow fever since 1953, and inoculation against sleeping sickness. The results are clear: splenic indices have dropped from 70 or 80 per cent just after the war to about 25 per cent in 1954. Freetown is no longer the 'white man's grave'; true, it has not yet become a black paradise, but the improvement is very noticeable.

Another example of this sort of development can be seen in the great Brazilian cities. When for the whole of the country the admitted general death rate was about 20 per thousand, in the eight largest cities it fell to 16·7, but there were important differences between the individual cities. Thus São Paulo, the economic metropolis and the richest city, which has most employment and pays the highest wages, a plateau city of the interior enjoying a healthy climate and good medical facilities, had a rate of 11·5; Rio de Janeiro, the former capital and the second industrial city, situated on the coast in a less favoured climate and with a much more mixed population, had 16·4 and occupied second place. A glance at the causes of death in these two cities shows for example that deaths from tuberculosis were two-and-a-half times more frequent in Rio than in São Paulo. Lastly, the record of mortality for cities like Recife and Fortaleza—about 27 per thousand—reminds us that these are the cities which attract the miserable immigrants from the dry zone of the north-east; their employment opportunities are few and the wages low, and their situation, with land and sea closely interwoven and a very hot climate, not such as to provide an environment conducive to good health.

In the developing countries it seems that the towns must be first killers and then saviours. Of course, certain cities have for a long time acted as medical centres, not only for cures but also for the spread of hygiene and knowledge of countermeasures against illness. The death rate in rural areas in the United States apparently surpassed that of the towns between 1900 and 1930. In any case, with all the reservations that must be made when using these statistics, one may still note that in countries which, at the time, were neither of advanced development nor underdeveloped, there are odd inversions; in Yugoslavia for example, the general death rate in 1950 was 13·2 per thousand (perhaps a low figure), whilst in Belgrade it was 8·6, in Ljubljana 9·8 and in Zagreb 9·1; the other large towns had higher rates. In Egypt, the general rate was then estimated at 25 per thousand, and the records show 21·7 at Alexandria and 22 at Cairo. In Brazil, the city of São Paulo has a lower death rate than the surrounding State, and the same is true at Bahia. In the republic of Guinea, an accurate study made in 1955 found that the proportion of the total population aged between 15 and 24 was 583 per thousand in the country but 615 at Conakry, and that the infant mortality was 202 in the country and 142 in the capital, with the expectation of life 30–31 years in the interior and 35–36 in Conakry. The situation in Guinea is typical of the intermediate stage of medical equipment and social life. Finally, in France, in 1969 the infant mortality rate was higher in the rural communes, diminishing in the towns in proportion to their size. It would seem that there are here plenty of opportunities for research.

Lastly comes the third stage of the development, the best understood, characterised by the classic opposition of town and country. Mortality is higher in the urban centres because progress has rendered the whole area, whether of town or country, more homogeneous from the point of view of sanitation, and other factors come into play. American sociologists have endeavoured to disentangle the factors which favour the countryside, and they suggest five: (i) the lower density of population in the country which is important in the spread of infectious diseases; (ii) the more solid structure of the rural family and the higher degree of maternal care; (iii) the open-air life and physical activity which are good for the body; (iv) the untroubled spirit; (v) the better adaptation of the human organism to a country life in which for so long it evolved whereas the artificial life of the towns is, so to speak, alien to it. In England and Wales in 1972, for example, urban mortality was 12·3 and rural mortality only 11·1 per thousand.

Some examples taken from various states of the U.S.A. (Virginia, Georgia, Mississippi) point to the same conclusions. And yet even there one finds traces of the second stage. The detailed analysis of mortality in Virginia showed that, especially among the negroes, the death rate was higher in small towns, that is those that have all the inconvenience of agglomeration without a complete medical and social service.

Mortality in Virginia (1940) (per thousand)

	White	*Black*
Rural areas	9·2	14·8
Towns, 2,500–10,000	11·5	18·8
Towns, 10,000–100,000	9·9	17·3
Towns, over 100,000	10·4	16

Source: T. Lynn Smith, *The Sociology of Urban Life*, p. 264.

We find the same phenomenon in the figures of infant mortality for a region such as the north of France where this scourge attains high rates in relation to the national average, and where the inadequate medical facilities have been the object of severe criticism. The worst affected towns are again the small ones, mainly the large over-grown villages and the small mining towns where sociological condi-tions are poor.

Infant Mortality in Northern France (*1953*) (per thousand)

Rural areas	53·2
Towns, under 10,000	58·4
Towns, 10–50,000	57·6
Towns, over 50,000	49·2

Source: *Atlas du Nord de la France*, plate XI by R. Nistri.

The correlations between urbanisation and mortality thus appear to be both badly known and extremely variable.

Problems of the decline in mortality

The struggle against death, which has not ceased since the beginning of human existence, has thus entered a new phase during the last two centuries; after so many centuries of groping efforts, it has become really efficient, and its results have spread over ever-widening terri-tories with the lapse of years. The struggle is never-ending, takes place everywhere and is crowned with more or less success; it repre-sents Europe's finest gift to the rest of the world.

If, however, these successes may be claimed as a victory, they are themselves responsible for a situation which poses many and grave problems. To prevent men from dying is not always to be able to preserve all their faculties. Doctors can save a human being by an operation or by strong medicines, but may leave him with a much reduced life, perhaps even no more than a vegetative existence. Is it worth while to prolong indefinitely the life of an apparently empty carcass? Must we tenaciously nurse hopelessly abnormal children, or stand by indefinitely to preserve the health of idiots? These are questions that may seem harsh, but they are sometimes dramatically solved by those who have most love for the victims. Many tragedies thus arise, and euthanasia has its protagonists.

The growth in the number of elderly people must also be the object of considerable thought. The psychology and material welfare of these people are the object of studies and special measures in the most advanced countries, in which old people already form a large proportion of the population. We shall return to this matter later.

Lastly, the reduction in infant mortality, the happiest possible event in itself, has as a consequence, especially in certain poor and under-nourished countries, the rapid growth in the number of mouths to feed, and so, with stagnant resource development, the increase of poverty.

The conquest of death should thus not be considered by itself but in relation to the whole psychological and economic evolution of human society.

CHAPTER SIX

Variations in the Birth Rate

In contrast with death, against which man can only put up a defence, birth depends essentially on human initiative.

The birth rate. The simplest and most commonly used method of evaluating the birth rate is to calculate the number of births per thousand inhabitants. This is done by dividing the number of births in a given year by the population living in the same territory during that year. Thus, in the U.S.A. in 1950, 3,554,149 births were registered amongst a census population of 150,697,361:

$$\frac{3,554,149 \times 1000}{150,697,361} = 23 \cdot 6$$

This figure, like many other demographic figures, is liable to certain more or less serious errors. If the year in question lies between two censuses, the total population must be estimated and the calculation is that much less precise. Also, one must be certain that the number of births has been correctly declared—and in many countries the data are incomplete; even in the U.S.A. probably 2 or 3 per cent of all births go unregistered. In many other countries the situation is even less satisfactory: in north-eastern Amazonia (Brazil), a family may take advantage of a move or an encounter with a census officer to declare the birth of several children at once, and one may find in some districts a variation of 500 or 1,000 per cent from one year to another merely because there has been an administrative check. In many Muslim countries, and in the Far East, where female children were for long of little value, the disproportion between the numbers of male and female births registered leads to the conclusion that many girl babies were either not registered or were suppressed. In China in the 1930s, there was an estimated birth rate of 37 per thousand, whereas in the north-eastern part, occupied by the Japanese whose control was much stricter, the figure was greater than this by one-quarter.

Though the birth rate has the advantage of being easily calculated and understood, one must guard against its apparent precision. But this is not all. True, it is interesting to know the proportion of births in a given population, and for geographers in particular this is useful information. But for demographers, or indeed for anyone who attempts to appreciate the vitality of a people, the crude birth rate is insufficient because it fails to take account of the age- and sex-composition of the population; thus a country with a high proportion of elderly people may appear to have a feeble vitality whereas in actual fact the adults of reproductive age may be more prolific than those of another country in which the average age of the population is lower. A colony on the pioneer fringe, in which women are few in comparison with men, may have a low birth rate, but the few women may well have very many children.

The first method of allowing for these anomalies is to calculate a standardised birth rate by relating the actual composition of the population to an idealised model, and multiplying the crude birth rate by the coefficient thus obtained. In 1935, the crude birth rate in France was 15·3, and the standardised rate 16·3. In the U.S.A. in 1940, the crude birth rates of the white population were 16·8 in the towns and 18·3 in the country districts, but the rectified figures were respectively 15·8 and 19·5.

Fertility rate. Another method, relying on real facts rather than on a mere mathematical device, is the calculation of a fertility rate, for example by relating the number of children under five years of age to the number of women of reproductive age (15 to 44, or 15 to 49, or 20 to 44, according to the various authorities). In the U.S.A., for the whole population, the result was 419 per thousand women aged twenty to forty-four in 1940, and 552 in 1950; for the black population only, 706 in 1950.

This calculation can be made from the census data and it is possible even for countries with relatively poor records. It allows both the age composition and the sex composition of the population to be taken into account, but of course it can only be performed for the period of five years preceding a census.

A comparison of crude birth and fertility rates is significant: thus for France, the mean crude birth rate for the year 1974 was 15·2, whilst in Hungary for the same year it was 17·8; but the fertility rate in France was 61·6, that in Hungary only 51·9. French women of reproductive age thus had more children than Hungarian women, but the French population included a much larger proportion of elderly people.[1]

Reproduction rate. Starting as before from the number of births, we can also calculate a reproduction rate which may be defined as the average number of female babies born per thousand women during their reproductive period. This figure is clearly not influenced by the age composition of the population. For the U.S.A. it has varied from 1,101 before the last war to 1,443 in 1946; for England and Wales from 850 to 1,210—figures which demonstrate the general rise in the number of births just after the end of the war. In eastern Europe, the ratio was almost always under one during the years 1930–40, and it rose above one almost everywhere after 1945. These figures give some idea of the possibility of the replacement of one generation by another —but they are available for very few countries.

Physiological birth rate. The use of these various statistical devices reveals considerable variations in the intensity of reproduction. One might expect that a normal population, with no Malthusian checks to its growth, would have a birth rate of more than 60 per thousand. This indeed was almost the rhythm that could be distinguished in eastern Europe before the industrial revolution, and in French Canada (over 60 per thousand at the end of the eighteenth century and still 50 per thousand in the mid-nineteenth century) where families of thirty children were not unknown. But now, according to the most recent estimates, the rates even in the most fecund parts of the Third World are from 40 to 60 per cent below the possible maximum.

THE 'NATURAL' BIRTH RATE

Race

The teeming masses of the Far East, the wide open spaces of black Africa—these are two examples frequently quoted which suggest an opposition between the prolific yellow races and the more moderate

---

[1] One should obviously not compare these two types of figures without caution. Thus T. Lynn Smith in his *Fundamentals of Population Study* gives for France in 1946 a population of 28 children under 5 per 100 women aged 15 to 49 (this was due to the small number of births during the period of the war: mean birth rate 1942-46, 16·6 per thousand), and he takes into account the birth rate in 1946, which, at 21 per thousand, was the highest recorded for half a century. The comparison is of little significance.

reproductive capacity of the blacks. The facts are indisputable, but are they the result of customs, habits, different natural environments or merely of different racial capacities? Rather than widely separated examples like this, let us take racial groups living side by side and if possible in the same natural conditions and at the same stage of psychological and economic evolution. In the population crucible that is Brazil, we find the following number of children born to 100 women: 311·2 in the case of the whites, 331·9 for the 'coloureds', 301·9 for the blacks, and 313·1 for the yellow (Japanese). Also in Latin America, Hawaii's census records 2,185 children per thousand married white women, and 2,710 per thousand coloured women; in Trinidad, a study made of women over forty-five showed that the Asiatic women had an average of 5·36 children each, while the blacks and mulattoes had only 3·45. In South Africa, the birth rate has been estimated at 38 per thousand for the blacks (Bantu), 35 to 40 for the Asiatics (Indians) 42 to 47 for coloured people, and 23·6 for the whites.

Thus, amongst the peoples that one might regard as having a very primitive birth rate, there appears to be a rough classification of fertility; the mixtures (mestizos, mulattoes) are usually at the head, followed by the Asiatics who are almost always remarkably prolific; the blacks are much less fertile and sometimes even less so than the whites. Detailed studies of very small groups in Bahia (Brazil) seem to confirm this impression.

It is very difficult to lay much store by these fragmentary considerations, which are rendered even more uncertain by reason of the imperfections of racial classification which have been referred to above (p. 20). Furthermore, almost throughout the world, whenever two different races are side by side, they are seen to be at different stages of evolution, and the variations in fecundity may well be due to quite other than racial considerations. Thus, in the U.S.A. the blacks are appreciably more prolific than the whites; in 1950, there were 467 children under five per thousand white women aged fifteen to forty-four, and 513 per thousand black women; even if one takes smaller and more homogeneous groups like the agriculturalists of the South, the proportion of children under five is higher by a quarter among the blacks than among the whites. But it is evident that other factors than merely racial may be involved, such as standard and mode of living, and education. The South, where the difference of fecundity is most marked, is the very region where the rural black population is most numerous, most dense and least highly evolved.

Climate

Human sexual life instinctively follows the rhythm of nature. In countries with strong seasonal contrasts, the arrival of spring is accompanied by a paroxysm of sexual activity; the frenzy which overtakes the Eskimo at the reappearance of the sun has often been described. The monthly curve of births in the rural countries of Western Europe usually showed, in former times, a maximum at the beginning of the year, resulting from conceptions which had taken place in the previous spring. Conversely, particularly cold winters, or influenza epidemics, show up even now as dips in the curve, nine months later.

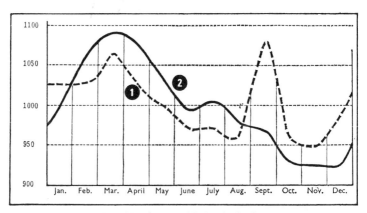

Fig. 17. The monthly birth-rhythm.
Average number of births per month, about 1900, in Sweden (1) and France (2).

Outside such seasonal or occasional influences, one may well enquire whether climate in general, through its influence on the human organism, plays a part in fecundity. It is a matter for discussion whether the particularly feeble reproductive capacity of all the peoples of circumpolar latitudes is due to the rigours of low temperature or rather to the long absence of light. This is the only positive example; elsewhere, in all latitudes there are peoples living side by side having very different behaviour.

Diet

Food supply does not depend only on the possibilities offered by the natural environment, but also on the standard of living. Its influence on fertility is a matter for controversy. Recent experiments on animals seem to show that a high protein intake induces many cases of sterility; the birth rate falls progressively as the consumption of protein-rich foods such as meat, eggs and milk increases; on the contrary—and this is the theory brilliantly sustained by Josué de Castro in his famous book *The Geography of Hunger*—a high fertility rate is characteristic of the poorest peoples and those most seriously undernourished. However, impoverished food supply has other consequences also, for it results in the great weakness of the women-folk and so is responsible for many miscarriages.

Be this as it may, the consumption of rice seems to have important demographic consequences. This remarkable cereal, so tolerant of the conditions of soil and climate which are offered to it, and producing two or two-and-a-half times as much grain per acre as wheat, has permitted an incredible overcrowding amongst the rice-eaters of the Far East. Rice is not only the cereal which seems to permit the maximum number of people to avoid starvation on the smallest space; deficient as it is in protein, it may provide women with a diet which predisposes them to fertility; furthermore, it can be consumed by very young infants either as a gruel or as a pulp, enabling them to survive, and thus to be weaned early so that the mother is ready to conceive again. The Asiatic woman often gives birth once a year, and this the African woman rarely does.

Health

Though there is no parallelism between the general state of health of individuals and their capability of reproduction—for the most miserable and under-nourished people are often more prolific than the more vigorous and well-nourished—there are certain correlations. The development of epidemics, favoured by bad hygienic conditions, may result in partial or complete sterility; the ravages produced by the wide dissemination of venereal diseases in Africa have often been quoted as bearing a heavy responsibility for the widespread sterility which results, in some parts of black Africa, in between one-quarter and one-half of all the married women never becoming pregnant.

Modern treatment in particular of syphilis has produced good results, and 'enfants de la piqûre' as the North Africans call them (literally, children resulting from a hypodermic injection which has cured the parents of the disease) have multiplied in recent years. But medical action also has indirect consequences: for instance, quinine which was formerly used as a protective against malaria, also possesses abortive powers; the transformation of the natural environment and the suppression of this form of medicine have resulted in a marked rise in the birth rate. In Sri Lanka for example the birth rate in the formerly malarial irrigated paddy districts rose from 37·4 in 1945–47 to 50·4 between 1950 and 1952; in the same years, in the tea and rubber plantation districts, which had never been so unhealthy, the birth rate has remained stationary at about 41 per thousand.

The part played by the general improvement in health has also another quite indirect effect on the birth rate. In 1800, in western Europe, a family which had six children might expect to rear three of them; in 1914, five would survive, and in 1960, 5·92. The virtual certainty of parents being able to rear all their children has led them naturally to adapt the number of births to the required size of family.

Population structure

Another element weighs directly and heavily on the birth rate; this is the composition of the population by age and sex. It is migrations which determine the most rapid and profound variations in demographic structure: thus the displacement of male workers into the towns and the factories leaves the countryside peopled mainly by women, children, and old people, while inflating the male population of the attractive areas. In Africa there are many examples: Algerians who cross the Mediterranean to work in France represent one adult male in seven (and even one in two in parts of the mountains of Kabylia); negroes who go to try their luck in more or less distant towns (in Guinea, a study made in 1955 found 149 men aged fifteen to forty-five amongst 1,000 inhabitants in the Futa Jalon highlands and 319 in Conakry).

In other parts of the world, the encouragement of migrations towards the pioneer fringes or new towns, and the settlement of the workers of great enterprises in special housing estates, have the opposite effect of creating new islands of population containing many adults of both sexes and often young couples, and the birth rate in such communities is high. Amongst the groups of European population living in the black states of tropical Africa, the birth rate was generally above 30 per thousand, or more than 50 per cent higher than in the European country of origin (e.g. French in Dakar 34 per thousand in 1956; Belgians in Ruanda-Urundi 34 to 40 per thousand about 1950–55, British in Nyasaland 39·4 per thousand in 1958).

Religious prescription

All the great religions favour family development and are in general opposed to most forms of contraception. Communities which are profoundly religious therefore have high birth rates. In this respect the Muslims take pride of place, because they belong generally to the less technically advanced countries and religious prescriptions remain very strong in a traditional society where the forces of disruption are as yet very weak. Even when Muslims and Hindus are both present in the same area, it is the former who have the higher rate: Kingsley Davis noted this in India, and more recent work in Trinidad confirms it, for here the Muslims have a fecundity 11 per cent higher than the Hindus. In predominantly Muslim countries the figures are very high. But whilst certain countries remain strictly traditionalist (Saudi Arabia 50 per thousand, Pakistan 50·9, Algeria 47·1, in 1970) in others the rate is sagging (Egypt 48 in 1956 and 35·4 in 1973, with Tunisia 35·8 in the same year). In former Palestine, figures of 52–53 per thousand were suggested for the Muslims, and in the Iranian plains perhaps over 50 per thousand. However, in Syria the country districts have a birth rate of 45 per thousand whilst Damascus has only 29·1 per thousand, and perhaps here is the beginning of a new factor of differentiation. In Cyprus, the fecundity of Turkish Muslim women and orthodox Christian women has been compared; living in similar conditions, the numbers of infants per female are almost equal—5·2 for the Turkish women, 5·3 for the Christians: in fact, orthodox Christians obey the same rules of family development as Catholics.

Within western societies, the Catholics are more prolific than all the other groups—Protestants, Jews, agnostics—whatever the degree of material and economic evolution of the groups concerned. The Canadian example is classic; the deeply religious Catholic French community, essentially rural, has a birth rate one-third higher than that of the British, who are mainly Protestant and urban. In Quebec, between 1926 and 1950, the birth rate was 28·2 per thousand; in Ontario, the British stronghold, it was 20 per thousand for the same period, and in British Columbia 17·8. In the United States, a study of Indianapolis showed that Catholic fecundity was 11 per cent higher than that of Protestants and 57 per cent higher than that of Jews. In the Netherlands, in 1938, there were 165 children per thousand married women under fifty years of age among the Catholics, 113 among the Protestants and 79 among the Jews. One could multiply these examples; but it is worth adding another established fact which results from detailed studies such as that covering religious practice in France. This is that even among the Catholics we must distinguish between those for whom their religion really constitutes a way of life, and those for whom it is merely an outward expression; only the former retain the high birth rate, as the Breton and Flanders regions bear witness.

Traditional customs

Finally, there are several traditional customs which have undoubted repercussions on the birth rate; they, too, are generally linked with religious beliefs or prescriptions.

One of the most important is the actual concept of marriage—monogamy or polygamy? The Muslim religion and African tradition admit polygamy, which generally has an unfavourable influence on the birth rate, for in the first place the polygamous male monopolises for his own benefit several females; generally, the richer and older he is, the more wives he has, so that among certain black peoples the poorer young men cannot find a wife at all. Furthermore, plurality favours the dissipation of sexual effort and diminishes the fecundity of the wives, especially if there is no rule of cohabitation in rotation. There are some picturesque examples: a sultan with 600 wives but only 100 children; another, in former Togoland, with 50 wives and only 19 descendants, or a head-man with 30 wives and only 5 children. Among the Mossi, in a village with a population of 700, 54 polygamous men had 147 wives but there were 50 celibates aged twenty-two or over; in another example from the same people, 1,096 polygamous males with 2,906 wives had only 2,995 children whilst in the neighbouring Catholic mission station there were 926 monogamous couples with 1,905 children. In other areas, in the Cameroon, the adult–child ratio for two communities, one polygamous and the other monogamous, was 2·18 in favour of the latter.

Some other facts must be noted, however. First, the consequence of polygamy are less baneful when, as in Guinea, there is no favourite wife but a regular succession of cohabitation; secondly we must distinguish between various types of polygamy, the simultaneous form just referred to, and the 'successive' type, more common in white Africa, in which a man may change wives two or three times during his life; in this case the first wife at least will have a more or less normal number of children. Finally, polygamy is tending to diminish, partly by reason of religious and psychological evolution, more generally from purely economic causes; in Africa, as elsewhere, the more society evolves, the more expensive do wives become. In the traditional society, the extra wife is often a supplementary agricultural labourer: she cultivates the soil, keeps house and often feeds her own children; in the towns the family equilibrium is upset. Nevertheless, in black Africa and in Madagascar polygamists still seem to represent between one-fifth and one-third of all the men, though in general they each have an average of only two or three wives. In lower Togo and in Dahomey, monogamy predominates; thus 57 per cent of the Likouala people of the Middle Congo, 60 per cent of the Guineans, 54 per cent of the people of Cotonou are monogamous, and in Dakar the census records only 20·5 per cent of polygamists. There is an ascertained correlation between the development of monogamy and the growth of education and the exercise of responsible functions; at the other end of the scale, the proportion of monogamists is also very high amongst the poorest people.

The existence of polygamy is in part determined by other customs which themselves have strong and direct influences on the birth rate, such as the frequent forbidding of sexual intercourse during the whole period of pregnancy and breast-feeding—for the African mother frequently suckles her child for two or three years. In any case this custom of prolonged suckling diminishes the possibility of fertilisation, but if it is accompanied by prohibition of intercourse, the result is absolute, and many African women only have a child every three or four years.

THE 'CONTROLLED' BIRTH RATE

In addition to the primeval factors in the birth rate—natural environment, biological make-up and traditional customs and taboos—there is another fundamental one, which is the human will. It is this which permits individuals to escape from the elemental laws of instinct, and families to adjust the number of children to their circumstances or their desires. This action is itself determined by several external circumstances which may act in different ways. Thus one passes from what may be termed a 'natural' birth rate to another form, less spontaneous, the 'voluntary' or 'controlled' birth rate.

In actual fact, human choice is not entirely free; it is oriented by complex motives, moral, intellectual, economic, social and political.

But having submitted more or less consciously to this or that influence, the individual takes the appropriate action to achieve the desired end.

The development of education

There is a very close correlation between the duration and importance of the period of schooling and the size of families: the further education is advanced, the smaller the number of children, and that in countries of very different socio-economic levels. In the United States, the number of children per female, aged forty-five to fifty-four varies from 1·86 in the case of women who had at least four years at a university, to 3·06 for those who simply had the ordinary schooling lasting seven or eight years, and to 4·82 for those who had no schooling at all. In Trinidad and in Puerto Rico, only two years of elementary schooling are sufficient to cause a lowering in the figure, but then further such schooling has little effect; a new fall comes amongst those who have had secondary education.

This development of education acts in several ways: it multiplies the preoccupations and attractions of the individual, and it gives him at the same time knowledge and new ambitions and changes his attitude with regard to family responsibilities.

The primacy of the individual

The whole trend of contemporary western civilisation is towards the exaltation of the individual, in emancipating him from traditional ideas, and in caring for his individual development.

Man is no longer merely a link in a family chain which must at all costs perpetuate and preserve or increase the inherited wealth and status; he is no longer held captive by more or less outmoded customs, or the passive slave of traditional beliefs. He submits no longer, he chooses. France, where the eighteenth-century philosophers asserted this human liberty, and where the Revolution of 1789, shaking the very foundations of the past, consecrated the liberation of every citizen, was also the first country in the world to experience a diminution in the birth rate.

The diminishing strength of religious sentiment also plays a part in this evolution. Even though the faith remains, the submission of the individual is less strict, and in order to avoid internal crises to which this opposition may give rise the religions themselves have been adapted and rendered more supple. Catholicism, for example, admits individual choice (in family matters) for valid reasons and permits its realisation by certain natural methods.

Similarly, the development of the rôle of women has accentuated the tendency for smaller families. Woman is naturally more subject to malthusian tendencies than man: childbirth puts her to the test, and she is often scared of it; such fear existed in 300 wives out of 1,000 interrogated in the United States, and it might suffice to provoke 10 per cent of the cases of sterility. Moreover, the working woman who finds herself with two heavy burdens, her domestic chores and her professional activity, does not wish to add to her family. An enquiry in Paris in 1957 showed a fecundity index of 2·03 for women in employment and 3·36 for those who did not work. The inequality persists even if family size is reduced: in France in 1968 the number of children per working married woman aged 35 to 39 was 1·46, compared with 2·16 for the same category but with no employment. Such a difference is not confined to advanced countries; in Trinidad, the women who are simply housewives have an average of 7·39 children each, the skilled female workers 3·17. The total numbers are different but the proportions are similar.

Lastly, the children themselves are no longer just collections of interchangeable beings, reared without care and contributing their quota to the family budget at the earliest possible age. They are less numerous, more precious, better cared for and more expensive; and the laws which prohibit child labour and are continually lengthening the period of compulsory schooling lay ever heavier financial burdens on parents and on society as a whole. Psychological and economic arguments mingle here to produce the same result.

Welfare

The pursuit of welfare is in opposition to fecundity not only because a child is a worry, an 'adventure', to use Sieburg's expression, which may well disrupt the daily domestic harmony, but also because it is the cause of expense which will subdivide the family income.

There is often a close correlation between family income and the number of children. In the United States, an enquiry based on monthly rents showed two children per woman aged forty-five or over, in the case of rents of over 50 dollars, and 4·76 children in the case of rents less than 5 dollars, with a regular progression between these two extremes. In England and Wales and in France, studies on the basis of socio-professional categories (i.e. taking account both of income and the nature of the employment) have led to the same conclusion: the smallest families are found amongst the non-manual workers of the middle class, for example 'black-coated workers' in commerce, who have a relatively low income and a bourgeois standard of living. One may compare this conclusion with the remark based on the study of Indianapolis, in the U.S.A., that the limitation of the family is at its strictest where the difference between the actual and the desired standard of life is greatest.

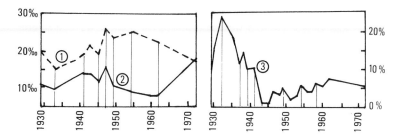

Fig. 18. Marriages, births and economic prosperity in the U.S.A.
1. Birth-rate.   2. Marriage-rate.   3. Unemployment rate.

The poorest people, possessing little and being poorly educated, have but few ambitions either for themselves or for their descendants, and so are the most prolific. In France, there are 4·1 children per woman aged forty-five or over, amongst the agricultural labourers, and 3·99 amongst the industrial labourers. The representatives of the middle class, on the other hand, though they may not possess very much, always desire to improve their lot and to prepare a better future for their children; their hopes are encouraged by this 'social capillarity' which nowadays characterises all advanced societies. Thus this group has the smallest fecundity—2·64 for commercial employees, 2·69 for the 'middle classes'. Lastly, the well-to-do, with large incomes and occupying a social position which they can hope to assure for their children, are less strictly malthusian, with 2·94 for the 'upper classes' and 3·26 amongst the professional groups. In England and Wales it is also found that the greatest fecundity is reached amongst the labouring and unskilled worker classes, followed by agricultural workers, while the lowest rate is found amongst office workers and the administrative classes.

All these conclusions relate to countries which are fully developed and have reached a kind of socio-demographic equilibrium. It should be noted however that when, in any country, the change begins to occur from a 'natural' to a 'voluntary' birth rate, it commences amongst the richest and most educated classes and only gradually seeps down to the masses.

Fluctuations in income also have their effects on the size of families. In the past, one attempted to correlate fluctuations in the price of wheat or other commodities, that is, the abundance of the harvest, with the number of births in the following year. Certain correlations do exist, though they are not precise and are difficult to interpret. It seems that a short period of prosperity may favour the growth of families, whilst a general and regular rise in the standard of living provokes first a flattening of the curve and then a slight diminution in the number of births. The individual gets accustomed to his well-being, and always wants more. The progress of technical civilisation which enables him to amuse himself, to have a car, to travel, creates many diversions which distract him from the more prosaic and exacting attractions of family life.

The onset of an economic crisis, accompanied by large-scale unemployment, such as occurred in most of the world's great countries in the early 1930s, profoundly affects the birth rate. In the United States, the rate fell from 20·1 per thousand for the period 1925–29 to 17·4 per thousand for the period of 1930–39, whilst it rose again to 19·9 with the war of 1940–44. In the same way the profound economic malaise which affected little Austria, so maimed after the first World War, had very striking effect; in 1936 the crisis was at its height and unemployment had even reached the administrative classes, and in 1937 the birth rate reached its nadir at 12·8 per thousand; in 1938 the 'Anschluss' which integrated Austria's economy with that of Germany, provoked an economic revival, and in 1939 the birth rate, stimulated also by the encouragements to procreation offered by the Third Reich, reached 20·7 per thousand.

There is thus something of a contradiction apparent between the behaviour of individuals and that of large groups; the less advanced peoples of the world, and the poorest individuals within a group, have most children, but when economic difficulties strike a whole group, the group has a tendency to restrict its reproductive rhythm. In fact, however, it is only in advanced societies, which are capable of appreciating the situation and of exercising some controls over their reactions, that one gets such a reduction. On the contrary in the poorer and less advanced countries, the increase in numbers accentuates the poverty, and this in turn often causes an increase in the birth rate; Josué de Castro has painted this picture in agonising terms with respect to parts of Brazil, India and the Far East.

Economic causes have undeniable consequences on the rhythm of births, but we must also examine closely several allied factors such as education, mode of life, residence, and so on, in relation to the type of society in which they occur.

Residence

It is a commonplace to say that the countryside is more prolific than the town, and all the statistics seem to confirm this view.

In Germany, in 1939, 28·1 per cent of the families dwelling in towns of over 100,000 inhabitants had no children at all, whilst only 8·1 per cent had families of five or more; for localities having fewer than 2,000 inhabitants, the percentages were 13·5 and 21·2. In Argentina, it has been estimated that the number of children under five years for each 100 women aged between fifteen and forty-four was twice as high in the rural districts as in the towns (52·9 as against 24·8 in 1947). In the United States, detailed figures show an absolute correlation between residence and fecundity:

Fecundity according to place of residence
(Number of children per 1000 married women over 45)

Towns of over 3 million people	2,228
Towns of 1 to 3 million	2,367
Towns of 250,000 to 1 million	2,410
Towns of less than 250,000	2,619
Small towns of over 25,000	2,899
Small towns of less than 25,000	2,800
Rural population, non-farming	3,069
Rural population, farming	3,910

The same phenomenon is found in France, where, in 1967–69, the net reproduction rate was 1·26 for the entire country, but 1·05 for the Paris conurbation, 1·22 for cities of over 200,000 inhabitants, 1·30 for towns of 50–100,000, and 1·35 for the rural communes.

Furthermore, in the U.S. study referred to above, it became apparent that fecundity increases as one moves from the centre of a town: thus, in the cities with over 3 million inhabitants the number of children under five per thousand women aged fifteen to forty-five ranges from 404 in the central districts to 491 in the suburbs, and the difference is the same for the black as for the white population.

The same phenomenon is found in general wherever adequate statistics are available: thus in Brazil 54·2 per cent of all the women living in towns had children, and 60·1 per cent of all those living in the country districts. Moreover, each urban mother had fewer children on average than her rural counterpart: the percentage of live-born children per 100 women aged fifteen and over is 447·9 in the towns and 563·6 in the rural areas, with the suburban areas half-way between, with 503·7. This is the same story as in the United States.

The conclusion seems inescapable that towns have fewer children than the countryside. The reasons are not far to seek. In towns a child is a heavier burden, needing more looking after in a small space; houses are smaller, the cost of living higher, and entertainments are more numerous. All these factors lead to the same result, that town life is less propitious for family development than country life, whilst in the suburbs there are intermediate conditions which conform to the general pattern of centrifugal increase.

Political intervention

All the factors hitherto discussed have more or less direct repercussions on the birth rate, but it may happen that the demographic situation in a country is such that the responsible authorities decide, within the limits of their powers, to influence the population curve in one direction or another.

The attitude of governments towards the population curve may take one of four forms: (i) indifference, which was the general rule before the development of public awareness of demographic problems and which still persists in countries where the resources appear sufficiently adapted to the needs of the population; (ii) a desire to increase the population, either for reasons of international power politics, as was the case with the totalitarian regimes (Germany, Italy, Japan) before the second World War, or to supply manpower for the opening up of vast new territories, rich and under-populated, as in the Soviet Union after 1935 for the development of Asiatic

Russia, or in the effort to people empty Australia; (iii) an effort to maintain the birth rate in order to avoid dangerous disequilibria in the age-pyramid (see p. 166) due to an ageing population (cf. the family policy of France, maintained and reinforced, since 1939); (iv) a desire to find a way of hindering the population growth, if the country's productive capacity is insufficient and especially if the growth is so rapid that it renders almost illusory all the efforts and investments made to increase the standard of life—as is at present the case in India, Pakistan and as was the case until recently in Japan.

Government action is more likely to be successful if it is directed towards an advanced people, capable of adopting more or less complicated methods of birth control.

Birth control

Human action to limit the number of children may be effected in three different ways: it may be preventive, parallel or corrective. In the first case the individuals run no risk, by sheer abstinence; in the second, by mechanical or chemical means they prevent the sexual act from achieving its purpose; in the third, conception having occurred, they eliminate either the foetus before birth (abortion) or the child after birth (infanticide).

Even in former times, people were often concerned, either from economic or social motives (such as the desire not to over-divide the inheritance) to limit their families. In France for example there were delayed marriages, and it was the custom for the younger sons of large families and for daughters also, to enter the religious life or to remain celibate. In Japan, the *samurai* were not allowed to marry before the age of thirty; in India, widows were not allowed to remarry; even amongst married couples complete continence might be practised when the family was judged to be sufficiently large. But these were heroic remedies, to which married couples would frequently add the practice of abortion and especially of infanticide. In Japan and China the elimination of unwanted children, especially girls, was very widespread. The combination of such methods enabled a country like Japan to maintain an almost stable population, around 30 million, for some 250 years.

At the present day, however, the size of families in advanced countries is controlled by what we have referred to as 'parallel' human action: in the course of a normal sex life the means are introduced which eliminate the consequences. Some of these are called 'natural' and are admitted even by the Catholic church: such is the famous Ogino method, of periodic continence related to the feminine physiological cycle. Others are artificial, intervening in various ways to avoid conception. These contraceptive processes are often combined, in the same communities, with the post-conception corrective which is abortion.

The perfecting of a contraceptive pill and the rapid spread of its use have upset the traditional pattern of population growth. It is now possible to speak of an absolute control of the freedom to conceive. The diffusion of this method began in the most developed countries, contributing in the United States and Canada to a dramatic fall in the number of births. In 1968, a study involving more than 7 million persons showed that only 6·5 per cent used the pill, whereas 29 per cent used intra-uterine contraceptives, 29·7 per cent sterilisation and 35 per cent the old-fashioned methods. At the present time, various enquiries tend to show that about half the women contacted use the pill, the spread of which is far more rapid than that of all the other contraceptive techniques (India 1 per cent only, but Bangladesh 34 per cent, Uganda 80 per cent, Iran and Brazil 95).

Bearing in mind that the right of abortion has been legalised in many countries during recent years including, in 1947, even France, for long antagonistic towards it, and Italy, despite Papal opposition, in 1975, it is clear that the subject of 'family planning' is becoming ever more important in modern society. For some countries it represents freedom of choice for the individual, for others it is a vital necessity. Thus in India, in 1956, there were but 147 centres for family planning advice and the supply of contraceptives; but by 1961 there were 4,165 and by 1969, 28,848. The communist countries, including China, all the great industrial nations, and a large part of the Third World now allow or even encourage the practice of 'birth control'. In a recent list of seventy-nine states of the Third World, only thirteen had no policy for population control (Report on Population, *Family Planning*, October 1975).

THE EVOLUTION OF THE BIRTH RATE

The above factors play different roles in different parts of the world, in different regions within a state, in different communities within groups, and even in different individuals. However, through this apparent anarchy one can discern general trends. The most striking fact is the diminution of the birth rate: there are fewer and fewer countries in the world with excessively high rates, and even in the most prolific countries the overall rate is generally lower than the maximum; in all countries which are still demographically evolving, the proportion of the population which practises voluntary family limitation is increasing. All countries, however, are not progressing in the same rhythm and the growth-curve sometimes shows reversed trends and other curious kinks. Several types of evolution may be distinguished.

Normal evolution

In those countries in which the death rate has fallen regularly for a long time, a slow adjustment has been made and the birth rate has also fallen, though somewhat later than the death rate. Such is the case in north-western Europe.

In England, the birth rate was 37·3 per thousand about 1800, 32·6 about 1850, 29·9 about 1900, 16·3 about 1930 and 15·5 about 1950. This is the adaptation of family development to general progress: side by side with it goes the decline in the death rate, material and intellectual progress and the rising standard of living. The curve has not a perfect regularity, for it reflects several stages in progress. The birth rate rose slowly, responding to the changes in socio-economic equilibrium due to the development of industry and towns, between 1850 and 1880; it rose sharply after each of the two world wars—it was 19·8 per thousand in 1946–47—after which it declined somewhat to stabilise itself at 16–17 per thousand until 1971. Since more than three-quarters of the couples married between 1940 and 1949 practiced some form of contraception, one might have expected this level to be maintained; but in fact the rate has fallen still further to 12·4 in 1975. Where will it stop?

To this type of evolution illustrated by the United Kingdom one might add the birth rate curves of the Scandinavian countries, of Ireland, and of France and Germany; each of these countries had a slightly different rhythm, more precocious in France and Ireland, rather slower in Germany, with minor fluctuations.

Accelerated evolution

In some other countries, a similar pattern of the evolution of the birth rate occurs as in North-West Europe, only it has proceeded more slowly, retarded by tradition and general backwardness, but nevertheless with a marked tendency to a lowering of the rate. In this category are the countries of the Mediterranean and eastern Europe. The Catholic tradition, the mainly rural economy and sometimes, as in Italy for example, a Fascist policy in favour of large families, have militated against a very drastic reduction in the birth rate.

Conditions have changed since the last war, through the upheaval suffered by so many people and the acceleration of economic progress, especially in the countries of eastern Europe and even in Italy; so that the decline in the birth rate has suddenly become more pronounced. Thus the rate in Italy has dropped from 30 per thousand in 1920–24 to 15·7 in 1974, a figure almost equal to that for France, which Italy surpassed by 60 per cent before the war; in Hungary the rate has fallen from 30·2 in 1920–24 to 14·7 in 1970, and in Bulgaria from 39·6 to 16·3 per thousand.

In other parts of the world for which adequate data are available, a typical example which merits attention is provided by Japan, where the rate was 35 per thousand in 1920–24, 19·4 in 1955 and 17 in 1962. This is the best national example of a systematic policy of reducing the birth rate, and it is worth analysing in more detail.

The population of Japan, which had been stable at about 30 million for some 250 years up to 1868, took a great upsurge after this date, reaching 45 million by 1900, 65 million by 1930 and 95 million in 1960, thanks to a birth rate which has remained almost constant at over 31 per thousand from 1872 to about 1950. A slight regression had been noticed between 1920 and 1937, however, of exactly the same order as that which England had experienced between 1876 and 1893, and this might have been construed as the beginning of birth control. But the Government, which had not ceased since 1920 to assert its approval of a high birth rate, took measures in 1941 which favoured large families. The plan was to reach 100 million by 1960 so as to have surplus population available for conquering and occupying parts of eastern Asia and its island fringe. The war dashed these ambitious projects and threw the programme out of gear; the colonies were lost, and 6·2 million Japanese were repatriated there from between 1945 and 1949. As a consequence, the land occupied per family fell from 0·99 hectare in 1938 to 0·74 hectare in 1950, whilst the numbers of unemployed rose from 240,000 in 1948 to 700,000 in 1955. Confronted by this dramatic change in fortune, the government decided on a voluntary reduction of the birth rate which, carried out at an increasing pace, would in the course of a few decades reduce the total population. The eugenic laws of 1948 and 1949 advocated contraception, authorised the sale of contraceptives and encouraged publicity relating thereto, and also legalised abortion and even sterilisation, with the consent merely of the attendant doctor. In the first stage of this programme, which lasted until 1952–53, and rather longer in the outlying parts of the Japanese archipelago, the people made for the easiest way—abortion—for this required no particular precautions or special instructions. In the second stage, thanks to propaganda, education and the widespread diffusion of contraceptives, the number of abortions diminished, as the number of couples practising more or less systematic contraception increased. In one of the mining regions, in 1948, the birth rate was 42·9 per thousand, and one abortion had been registered; in 1952–53, the figures were 33·5 per thousand and 63 per thousand respectively, whilst in 1954–55, after the creation of a committee for the spread of contraception, they were 14·4 and 49, i.e. a reversal of the abortion trend. In 1957–58 the progress continued, and the figures were 5·4 per thousand and 28 per thousand. However, the total number of abortions remains high. It rose from 246,000 in 1949 to the record level of 1,100,000 about 1955, and remains at around 750,000 a year. Under these circumstances the birth rate has fallen markedly, from 30·1 during the years 1945–49 to 19·4 in 1955 and 17·1 in 1960; though since that date it has recovered slightly to just over 18 per thousand. Indeed, responsible Japanese have become concerned at the risks that could accompany a too rapid fall in population, for since 1956 the net reproduction rate has been less than 1; complaints are beginning to be heard of the lack of sufficient working population and the increased cost of maintaining the elderly. Thus, the bold Japanese experiment—which in any case had been strongly criticised—enters a new and modified phase. And even though almost the entire female population of reproductive age practices birth control, official pressure to limit the size of families at all costs is becoming much less urgent.

The same trend is apparent in Eastern Europe where during the last dozen years or so, certain measures have been taken to raise the birth-rate—for example, by limiting abortions, giving aid to mothers with more than one child, improving the system of maternity leave and childbirth assistance. In some countries the birth rate has risen— to 18·4 in Hungary, in 1975, and in Czechoslavakia from 15·9 in 1970 to 19·5 in 1975. But Eastern Germany has remained unaffected by this recovery, and its birth rate continues to decline (to 10·6 in 1975).

Inverted evolution

The curve of the birth rate, having fallen to a more or less low level, may rise again, not merely temporarily as after a war or an economic crisis, but steadily for a long period, and this is not just an accident. Such an upsurge was undoubtedly produced during the nineteenth century, as far as we are able to see from the available statistics, at the time of the economic transformation of the north-west European countries. As we have already noted in the case of the United Kingdom, the mixing of the population, urban promiscuity, the regular wages of the workers, and child labour, all favoured early marriages and the multiplication of children. The same phenomenon is happening at the present time, though in very different circumstances and for diverse reasons.

In a country with a high birth rate, a rapid rise may occur following a medical discovery which provokes an improvement of health and in consequence a reduction in certain types of sterility. We have already cited the case of certain communities in Sri Lanka which were formerly a prey to malaria. One could also no doubt, if the statistics were available, find the same thing in the rural areas of Africa or Latin America, which have been recently affected by the widespread application of vaccines and antibiotics. In these cases, naturally, the change in the curve is only temporary and will soon be compensated by the general tendency for a recession.

But the same phenomenon is also observable in countries where the birth rate had already reached a low level, as in the United States and in France.

In the *United States*, upsetting all the forecasts, the birth rate has risen in pronounced fashion and not merely temporarily, from 17·4 between 1930 and 1939 to more than 24 per thousand between 1950 and 1960. The rise in the number of children has been most pronounced amongst those groups in which the fall in the birth rate had been most severe. The rural folk, who formerly had many children, are having fewer and fewer; on the contrary, the workers, the middle classes, the town-dwellers, and particularly those who are leaving the congested city centres for the sprawling garden-suburbs which are developing, seemingly without end, all round American cities, are having larger families. What was the cause of this unexpected trend?

Specialists have considered the problem and have come to the conclusion that the reasons are both sociological and psychological. In the first place the proportion of marriages has increased whilst the average age has fallen—27 per cent of males between the ages of 25 and 40 were married, in 1940, but 51 per cent in 1950 and 59·8 per cent in 1971. Then there was the sense of relief at the end of the war, the feeling of economic prosperity and well-being, and perhaps a twinge of conscience concerning the need to maintain vitality in the face of the growing power of the Soviet Union. In any case the enquiries revealed changes in feminine mentality more favourable to slightly larger families. However, though all these possible causes still exist, the birth rate has begun to fall rapidly: still above 21 per thousand in 1964, it has fallen progressively to 14·8 in 1975 and the trend is continuing. In explanation, the success of the pill is offered, and the growth amongst young people of an expressed discontent with the society in which they live.

We have laid stress on this American example, but it may be noted that other large countries relatively recently populated by white races show the same features: in Canada, Australia, New Zealand, the birth rate rose about 30 per cent between the prewar years and 1946, and was maintained at this level until the end of the 1960s. In all these countries, we may talk of a voluntary increase in the birth rate, due partly to economic needs and partly (as in the case of Australia) to a growing consciousness of strategic responsibilities. All these countries have very low densities (Canada 1·8 persons per square kilometre, Australia 1·3 and New Zealand 8·8), and at the same time an enormous potential wealth. In Australia, as in New Zealand, there is a lack of manpower, and government policy is to encourage demographic development. Nevertheless, the birth rate has declined since 1970—Canada 15·4 in 1974, with Australia and New Zealand each 18·4.

France provides a quite different example. In this country the birth rate diminished earlier and more pronouncedly than in any other country of the world, and it was the only country to have fallen to 20 per thousand by the beginning of the twentieth century. The reasons for this premature evolution have been much discussed; it seems that one can see in it a consequence of the Revolution of 1789 which, psychologically and socially, made the Frenchman a creature in advance of the times, free from a strict attachment to the dogmas of the *ancien régime* (religion, monarchy, family), and before whom,

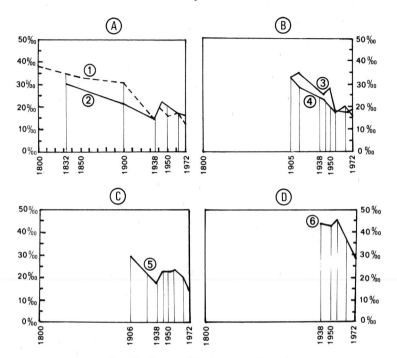

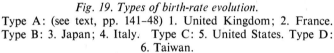

Fig. 19. Types of birth-rate evolution.
Type A: (see text, pp. 141–48) 1. United Kingdom; 2. France.
Type B: 3. Japan; 4. Italy. Type C: 5. United States. Type D:
6. Taiwan.

thanks to the suppression of the privileged social classes, opened a
future full of possibilities. Individuals thus controlled the size of
their families in accordance with their personal preferences, taking
account of their desire for well-being and their ambitions for their
own and their children's future. The spirit which dominated France
in the nineteenth century was that of the bourgeoisie, more devoted
to thrifty foresight and the amassing of wealth than to following the
promptings of instinct or generosity; the country did not experience
the great industrial developments which upset other European
countries like Germany and the United Kingdom. All this explains,
no doubt, the anomalous evolution of the French birth rate up to the
eve of the second World War, when, between 1935 and 1939, it was
only 15·1 per thousand.

Since the war the French rate has been higher, at 18 per thousand,

and this result has been achieved thanks to a policy of family encouragement which had its origin in 1938 and has been continually improved and perfected by each successive government which has controlled France's destinies since that date. Expert opinion is that this legislation has been most efficient as a means of encouraging a higher birth rate in a society where contraception, though officially ignored, was the general rule, and where the tradition of family limitation is deeply rooted.

What are these measures?

The psychological conditioning is very discreet; it is mainly effected through schools and by such expressions of family love as the 'Feast of Mothers' (or 'Mothers' Day'). But the most effective influences are the financial ones, which have also a psychological aspect; thus parents receive a certain sum of money at the time of the birth of a child. Amongst other measures, one might mention the progressive reduction in taxation according to the number of children, the special tax on single persons and on childless couples, the bounty paid to husbands whose wives do not go out to work, and the monthly allowances paid to families with more than two children.

These policies have not hindered the reduction in the number of large families and have had no retarding influence on the general evolution of the birth rate; but they have favoured a certain recovery amongst the most malthusian families. The number of couples having one child has risen by 2 per cent, but for those with two children the rise is 22 per cent; for three children, 6 per cent; and for four, there is a reduction of 2 per cent with a continuing reduction for larger families.

The interest of the French example was to show the powerful effect of an official policy of encouraging family expansion even in a country where the custom of family limitation was more deeply rooted than in any other nation in the world. In this country too, however, the success of this policy was only temporary, and since the end of the 1960s a regular fall in the birth rate has been recorded, to a mere 14·1 per thousand in 1975. New legislation, while retaining the general attitude towards the family, has permitted the sale of contraceptives and has even authorised abortion under certain conditions. Still, the French birth rate remains slightly higher than in other countries of western and northern Europe, including West Germany, where the rate was only 9·7 per thousand in 1975.

Early symptoms of evolution

Lastly, it seems that in most of the countries inhabited by the coloured peoples of Asia, Africa and Latin America, despite the uncertainty of earlier figures and the sketchy character of more recent statistics, a recession in the birth rate has begun to appear. It is true that in many of these countries the present figures are higher than those of the past, as in Brazil, Mexico, and most of the republics of Central and South America, but it is the improvement of a still incomplete registration which is responsible for this apparent anomaly.

From restricted areas where the statistical services introduced by foreign powers have been of higher quality, some significant figures emerge: thus in Taiwan the birth rate fell from 45·9 per thousand in 1950–54 to 23 per thousand in 1974–5, and in Puerto Rico, where it has been established that 86·5 per cent of the births were registered in 1940 and 95·9 per cent in 1950, the birth rate has dropped from 39 per thousand in 1940 to 36·6 in 1950–54, to 32 per thousand in 1958–60, and to 23·3 in 1974.

It is not even certain that the regression is proportionally as important in all this group of countries; it is very possible that in certain Latin American countries like Peru, Venezuela and Colombia, in certain Muslim countries of North Africa and the Middle East, and in many parts of black Africa, the number of births in relation to the population has scarcely yet begun to diminish. Local studies have pointed in this direction, but they are too fragmentary to lead to a general conclusion.

The mechanism of evolution

In fact, it is unprecedented that within a single fairly large country, or even within a fairly large community, the birth rates should be strictly uniform. Nevertheless one can almost always distinguish two groups.

The first group to adopt the practice of family limitation is small in numbers, made up of the most advanced individuals, the richest and most educated, who generally live in the towns; their example is followed by an ever-increasing section of the population. Thus in France at the end of the nineteenth century, the towns and their environs already had very low birth rates, whilst the more remote countryside, such as Brittany, the mountainous regions and the areas more closely bound by tradition, particularly those influenced by catholicism, still retained very high rates. But half-way through the twentieth century a peculiar trend is discernible, for the birth rate has risen in the towns and in the countrysides formerly most affected by low rates, whilst the remote regions, formerly the most prolific, show a regular decrease. This study of the fecundity of French marriages has thus linked up with more general studies on the same theme in western European countries. After a secular recession, there has been a slight tendency to recovery in fecundity during the last twenty-five years, and this phenomenon brings to light the existence of two classes of people, a 'backward' group that continues its downward trend, and a 'forward' group, now more numerous, that, having reached its minimum rate some years ago, now has a tendency to increase its numbers of children. This, then, is the evolution characteristic of the most advanced countries.

On the contrary, in backward countries it is the second group, the poor and ignorant masses, who form the great majority; they are mainly rural, or else part of the mass of manual workers in towns, who have only recently abandoned the tilling of the soil. These masses are only slowly and sporadically influenced by birth control, except where governments have stepped in with a propaganda campaign. Even in the latter case, as in India, for example, the political effort has had but meagre results.

BIRTH RATES IN THE MODERN WORLD

Extremes

The demographic annual of the United Nations gives official birth rate data for almost the whole world, but as the footnotes and commentaries point out, these data are incomplete or uncertain for many countries. Many of the figures are calculated only from a fraction of the population which has been more closely examined, and this fraction generally consists of the population of one or more large cities and cannot therefore be very representative. Thus for Ghana the birth rate is given as 46·6, but this figure is calculated for a zone in which registration is compulsory, comprising 153 places with 35 per cent of the total population. In Brazil the rate of 30 per thousand is given for Rio de Janeiro and the state capitals, though the rate calculated from the whole census is 38 per thousand. In most African countries only the European birth rate is available. In some cases the statisticians try to rectify the results obtained from these fragmentary sources by using data from the general census or from sample studies. In the world as a whole, the highest birth rates are still above 50 per thousand, as in Angola, Madagascar, Niger, Rwanda, Togo, Afghanistan, Pakistan and Yemen.

The greatest uncertainties are generally present in those high birth rates which characterise the most backward and most prolific countries, so that it is among these high rates that there is the most risk of error. We may surmise that the highest rates are around 50 per thousand.

In the case of the lowest rates, the data are generally more exact, for in these cases the most advanced countries are concerned, with the best statistical services. The record would appear to be held by West Germany, with a rate lower than 10 per thousand, but most European countries have rates not far above this minimum.

Between these two extremes there is a wide range of values, but it is possible to group countries in several classes, those with birth rates lower than 20 per thousand, those with between 20 and 30, and those with more than 30 per thousand (See Plate 24).

Countries with birth rate under 20 per thousand

Within this group are all the countries in which the mass of the population practises family limitation. Here are the majority of European countries, with but few exceptions; outside Europe, all the large white countries (Canada, U.S.A., Australia, New Zealand, U.S.S.R.), together with Japan, come into this category. But although the present result in all cases may be the same, the progress towards it shows certain differences.

In western and northern Europe, family limitation began to develop over a century ago in a section of the population, and it has gradually spread throughout. The birth rate has, so to speak, become uniform, with little difference between different parts of the territory or between country and town. In the United Kingdom the mean rate is 12·7 per thousand for the last two years; it only varies from 13·4 per thousand in England and Wales to 18·9 in northern Ireland, with Scotland in between at 13·8 per thousand. The same fact has been established by selecting sample figures to characterise the birth rates in different regions. Thus in 1939 the rates for south Wales, Northumberland, and Durham, largely mining regions, were higher than those for the greatest agricultural region in the country, East Anglia; in 1947, except for London, which had a much lower rate than anywhere else, the rates for the great industrial cities like Liverpool and the Merseyside conurbation, Newcastle and the Tyneside conurbation, were higher than those of the surrounding countryside. So far as the uniformity of rate in different social classes is concerned, it has been noticed that since 1940 a slight rise in the rate has occurred amongst non-manual workers, and the differences are becoming blurred. The story is much the same in Switzerland.

The world's record would appear to be held by the two Germanies, in which the Democratic Republic had a rate of 10·4 in 1975 and the Federal Republic 9·7. The rate had been artificially boosted by the policy and power of nazism before the war (it was 19·7 in 1938), but it has since declined regularly to its present low level which is hardly sufficient to sustain the following generations. Sweden, which formerly held the low record, seems now to have stabilised at a rate of about 13 per thousand, roughly the same as Austria, Belgium, Netherlands and Switzerland. All those countries which experienced a surge in the birth rate after the war, to a level higher than that of the pre-war years, have been victims of this recent decline.

Amongst the countries of Central Europe, Czechoslovakia may be grouped in this first class; its low birth rate before the war was due to the Czech part of the territory, which had evolved in similar fashion to its western neighbours.

A second group amongst the 'under-twenties' had, before the war, a relatively high rate; it contains the Mediterranean peninsulas of Italy and Greece, almost all eastern Europe except Poland, and also Japan. The maintenance of demographic vitality was due to the predominance of rural life and to strong traditions, particularly the influence of religion.

The typical countries are Italy (23·8 in 1938 and 15·7 in 1975), Greece (26·1 and 15·6 respectively), Bulgaria (22·8 and 17·6); in Hungary, the rate had already declined rapidly after the first World War (19·9 in 1938), but after maintaining a slightly higher level until 1956 (about 20 per thousand), it plunged catastrophically after the political uprising, and was only 14·6 in 1960; but it recovered to 18·4 in 1975. In fact, the countries of Eastern Europe form a sub-group in which, as we have seen, the governments, after a period of *laissez-faire*, have revived policies of family aid that have resulted, since the end of the 1960s, in a stabilisation of the birth rate or even a slight increase, except in East Germany (in 1975, Poland 19, Czechoslovakia 19·5). In the U.S.S.R. itself, where the rate had dropped to 17·4 in 1970, a slight rise is suggested by the latest estimates. Finally, there remain within this group certain European countries in which the birth rate is around 20 per thousand—Spain 18.2, Portugal 19.3, Yugoslavia 18·1, Iceland 20·4, Romania 20·3.

Outside Europe, Japan, whose demographic evolution we have already analysed, can be placed in this group.

As a whole, all the countries in this second group have sharply reduced the number of children, but the movement is much less natural, progressive and widespread than in those of the first group, and it is in most cases the result of official policy—legislation as in Japan, the de-christianisation of the east European countries, the legal dissemination of contraceptive information and the legislation of abortion. There are therefore very strong contrasts within these countries. In Italy, for example, Trieste, the Piedmont, Tuscany, Friuli and Venezia Julia have rates below 13 whilst Campania, Sardinia, Apulia, Basilicata and Calabria are above 24 per thousand.

Finally, there is a third group, comprising the large states that during the last two centuries have received masses of European immigrants; these states have recently regained the birth rate level of under 20 per thousand that they had already reached before the second World War. We have already noted the example of the United States; but the same phenomenon is present in Canada, where the rate has fallen from 28.2 per thousand in 1955 to 15·4 in 1975, and in Australia and New Zealand with 18·4. In these countries there is neither official policy, nor the menace of over-population, nor the incidence of poverty to explain the decline.

Birth rates between 20 and 30 per thousand

In this group are classed all those countries in which there is partial family limitation; but the rates vary widely and we should be in error in regarding them as all of one type.

In the first category we may put the countries in which family limitation is making progress, but is not yet universal. In Europe, only Ireland belongs to this group (22·3 in 1975). Outside Europe, its white extensions in South America—Argentina and Uruguay, are on the same road.

The second category comprises small communities which exist within fundamentally different and often hostile groups, and in which there is some demographic pressure. As a state, Israel is a good example; its overall birth rate fluctuates around 27 per thousand, but it is obvious that the population is heterogeneous, and one-third of it is of African and Asiatic origin, with a fecundity twice that of the European and American stock. In the same group one may classify the colonies of Europeans living in the midst of other peoples— Arabs, Blacks and Asiatics; their birth rate is commonly around 25 per thousand (as with the whites in South Africa and Rhodesia); such colonies are composed of younger folk than those of the home countries from which they sprang, and they often enjoy more favourable conditions and a better standard of life.

In this category there appears to be little recent variation in the birth rate, whilst the first category shows a constant diminution. Only those countries in the first category, therefore, are likely without much delay to join the ranks of those having a birth rate lower than 20 per thousand.

Birth rates above 30 per thousand

All the other regions of the world, that is almost the whole of Africa, southern and eastern Asia, and a large part of Latin America, have birth rates greater than 30 per thousand. But we have already noted the lack of certainty in the data available for those very countries which are the world's greatest baby factories. Most of them must have rates greater than 35 per thousand, and probably about 40 per thousand, but how can they be appraised? In these countries, the mass of the people are condemned by ignorance or inability to leave their number of children to nature. However, it cannot be denied that local evolutions have begun to take place. In Brazil, the overall birth rate is 37·8 per thousand, but it is probably more than 40 per thousand in the poorest parts of the north-east (where under-registration is considerable), some 30 per thousand in the more advanced states of São Paulo and Rio Grande do Sul, and only 25 in the district of Rio de Janeiro. Another evidence is that the family of a manual worker is 40 per cent larger than that of a non-manual worker. Further, studies in Bengal have shown that the fecundity of rural women is 28 per cent higher than that of women living in Calcutta, and within the city the women of highest economic and social status are the least productive of children.

It is reasonable to suppose therefore that in future years there will be a progressive lowering of the birth rate in this group as a whole. The movement will certainly be more rapid in these states which have a responsible government and fixed economic objectives. China, to which the experts attributed a birth rate of 33 per thousand in 1970, has set in motion a whole suite of policies designed to limit population growth. Since the expectation of life grew from 40 years in 1959 to 60 years in 1973, whilst infant mortality fell from 100 to 20 per thousand in the cities between the same dates, it was clearly necessary to combat the excess of births. In 1963, the aim was to limit the growth to 1 per cent in the towns and 2 per cent in the countryside, but this target has not been achieved. However, in the industrial cities, and in particular in Pekin, the birth rate has fallen from 43·4 per thousand in 1963 to 17·8 in 1972. In the Shanghai area, 70 per cent of the women of reproductive age use contraceptives, and the pill has been available since 1964. Voluntary sterilisation is common after the birth of the second or third child. Further, later marriages are encouraged (at 25 for females and 28 for males, in the villages). Abortion is available on demand, but contraception is preferred. It may be expected that with a programme like this, the Chinese birth rate will sink well below 30 per thousand. One cannot say the same, however, for most of the other countries that have an excessive birth rate, because of the backwardness of their mainly rural populations.

CHAPTER SEVEN

Natural Population Growth and its Consequences

Decline in the death rate, evolution of the birth rate: the combination of these two variables has varied consequences, above all for the rhythm of growth of populations.

NATURAL GROWTH

In almost all countries of the world, the annual number of births exceeds the number of deaths. In the United Kingdom, in 1974, 738,714 births were registered and 667,400 deaths, giving an excess of 71,314. These figures represent a birth rate of 12·4 and a death rate of 11·9 per thousand, resulting in a natural increase of 0·5 per thousand. For Japan the figures are 18·8 and 6·9, giving an increase of 11·9; for Salvador they are 40·1 and 8, an annual increase of 32·1 per thousand. The population growth, due solely to the natural factors of birth and death, thus appears to be very variable from one country to another and often within a single country. We have already emphasised indeed, the wide scatter of values of both birth rates and death rates in different parts of the world. A multitude of combinations is thus possible; almost every country has its own particular rhythm of growth, and even if at the present moment two countries appear, from their official statistics, to have similar rates, it is but rarely that they will have arrived at this point by the same declension.

Moreover, for some countries we can calculate the demographic development with great precision from the known birth and death rates, but it is clear that for other countries the risk of errors will be considerable since both variables are of doubtful accuracy. Nevertheless we may attempt to divide the countries of the world into a number of types.

1. *Primitive types*
Here we are dealing with populations which have at the same time a high birth rate and a high death rate—a veritable squandering of human life, for although births are very numerous, the infant mor-

tality rate is of the order of 200 per thousand and more than half the children die before reaching the age of fifteen. But it is for such peoples that we have the least reliable statistics, and it is difficult to say whether such figures still apply to entire states. Certain of the Andean countries, like Bolivia, some interior areas of black Africa, and certain parts of south-east Asia probably still fall into this group. Population growth is very small since the birth rate only slightly exceeds the death rate, and accidents such as epidemics and famine were, at least until recent years, relatively frequent.

These last bastions of pre-industrial revolution civilisation are in a situation similar to that of Europe 200 years ago. They include the most isolated and backward peoples in the world, numbering probably no more than 100 million; and the numbers remaining in this primitive condition are rapidly decreasing as medical science comes to their aid and reduces the death rate.

2. The 'youthful' stage

This type includes the most vigorously growing populations in the world, in which the birth rate is much greater than the death rate; three stages in this evolution maybe distinguished.

The Guatemalan type. Here the birth rate remains very high whilst the death rate has already begun to decline; in Guatemala, the figures are 43·4 per thousand for births and 15·4 for deaths, giving a natural increase of 28 per thousand. One may indeed characterise this type as having a growth rate of between 20 and 30 per thousand. It probably includes almost all the countries of Africa, the Middle East, and eastern Asia, as well as several moderately advanced countries of Latin America (Cuba, Honduras, Argentina, Colombia and Paraguay; the growth rates, however, have been calculated from the most recent censuses and not from the birth and death rates which are unusable figures in these cases).

These are the countries which will experience the greatest increases in population in the near future, for the decline in the death rate has already begun and may still accelerate whereas most of the countries concerned have a 'natural' birth rate that no influence, political or otherwise, has so far attempted to hinder. And they may represent between one-half and two-thirds of the world's present population. Included amongst them are still countries like India, Pakistan and Bangladesh.

The Thailand type is an extreme variant of the preceding type, in which the birth rate is still very high but the death rate has fallen more markedly (42·8 and 10·4 per thousand); the natural growth rate is thus the highest in the world, between 25 and 35 per thousand (actually 32·4 per thousand in Thailand). In such regions the population may well double in less than a quarter of a century. This situation is a stage through which most of the countries classed as 'Guatemalan-type' will pass; and the world is thus faced with an alarming increase, without such energetic countermeasures as have been taken by Japan.

The Thailand type is not very widespread since it requires very special conditions, namely a population which has retained a natural birth rate, but thanks to medical and health services generally provided from outside sources, has materially reduced its death rate. Included in it are some small areas and countries in which western influence has predominated, as in Sri Lanka, which has trebled its population between 1900 and 1960, and Puerto Rico. Some Latin American countries are also approaching this stage if one may believe the figures calculated from the most recent census data— 33·7 per thousand in Venezuela, 30·7 in Peru, 34·3 in Mexico, 28·3 in Brazil and 29·6 in Panama. Rates of increase such as this apply to somewhat more than 100 million of the world's people.

The Chile type. In this case, the birth rate has already fallen slowly and the death rate has been attacked with vigour and is now quite low: in Chile the birth rate is 27 per thousand and the death rate 8·4, giving a natural growth rate of 19·4 per thousand. We may include in this type all those countries having a natural growth rate of between 15 and 20. Fifteen years or so ago, this group included almost all the major countries of white civilisation outside Europe, but in these countries the demographic situation has evolved still further and has now reached a stage of maturity. The category now includes only a small number of countries, such as Israel (birth rate 27·6, death rate 7.3, natural growth 20·3). China has a similar growth rate, but made up from somewhat different figures—birth rate 33·1, death rate 15·3, growth rate 17·8. The inclusion of China in this group gives it a total of some 900 millions, and the natural growth rate is equal to the present average for the whole world (19 per thousand).

3. *The mature stage—reduced birth rate type*

This group includes countries whose demographic evolution is more advanced. The birth rate is already low and the death rate has been reduced to its minimum. Most of the examples are developed contries with a white population; it is possible, however, to distinguish different stages of evolution.

The most dynamic group includes countries such as Argentina, Uruguay and New Zealand, in which the natural growth rate reaches or exceeds 12 per thousand (e.g. Argentina, birth rate 21·9, death rate 9·5, growth rate 12·4). Next, there are several countries that have only recently reached the mature stage, through a marked fall in the birth rate; they occupy a middle position, and the question of demographic renewal is not yet a cause for concern. The Soviet Union (growth rate 8 per thousand), Canada (8·3), and in Europe, Yugoslavia, Spain and Poland, all countries with a natural growth rate of between 8 and 12 per thousand, are included in this group.

At a lower level of growth is the United States, with 5·6 per thousand. But by reason of a birth rate which remained high until about 1970, the effects of the recent fall are not yet fraught with grave consequences. On the contrary, in those countries in which the birth rate had been declining for a long time, as in France (growth rate 4·8 per thousand), Denmark (4·2) and Sweden (3) the demographic stagnation is accompanied by an increase in the numbers of elderly people.

The most unfavourably placed of all are the countries which in recent years have had a negative population balance-sheet: notably the two Germanies, where the birth rate is the lowest in the world and the death rate relatively high. West Germany has recorded an annual loss of 3·1 per thousand, whilst the Democratic Republic has a negative balance of 1·6. Already Austria and Belgium are on the verge of such a situation, and they could soon be followed by the United Kingdom and Sweden.

One might envisage that ultimately most countries will attain this state of demographic maturity. Already their number is increasing appreciably; twenty years ago they includes 400 million individuals, a total that has now perhaps reached 1 billion, or one-quarter of the world's population.

The general growth of population

All the three groups of countries outlined above are thus participating in the general growth of the world's population. Exceptions are rare —small communities like the Fuegians, certain tribes in black Africa and Oceania, the aborigines of French Guiana and perhaps a few ethnic minorities in the interior of China, are declining at the moment as a result of the disruption of their normal life through economic changes or the destruction of their normal biological environment. The normal rhythm of growth has never before reached such a pitch. Statistics prove it—even allowing for the growth of properly censused territories as against those for which previous estimates of population were always too low. In 1850, the estimated world population was 1,000 million; in 1940, it had reached 2,000 million; in 1950, 2,497 million; by 1961, 3,000 million, and 4,000 million in 1976. The pace of growth is now about 72 million a year, that is, the population of a France and a Czechoslovakia is added to the world every year; estimates of the increase give a growth rate of about 19 per thousand.

The rhythm is accelerating rapidly, moreover, and the statisticians of the United Nations, taking into account local circumstances and the diversity of possible trends, forecast more than 6,000 million by the year 2000.

Obviously such predictions are disputable. The great unknown at the moment is China, which may give rise to vital errors; for this great country holds more than one-fifth of the world's population, and the annual growth rate is only estimated. Further, it is almost impossible to predict with any certainty what will be the demographic trend of three-quarters of the world's population during the next few decades. Though one may certainly envisage a rapid and considerable reduction in the death rate, it is very difficult to predict the same for the birth rate, which is influenced by so many factors, individual and collective, natural and volitional. However, it is almost impossible to conceive of an expansion of the Japanese experiment on any large scale, and it is thus most unlikely that the global population will not attain the forecast figures, at least during the next twenty or thirty years.

Regional differences
Within this flow of the human tide, all sections of the globe do not play equal parts. A tabulation of growth rates shows a distinct grouping.

Thus, of the world's 72 million increase in 1975, Asia, having 56·7 per cent of the total population, gained 64 per cent, and its proportion is constantly increasing. Asia is a continent with already high population densities, apart from the south-west, and its death rate is still the highest in the world—so that considerable progress is likely

Growth of population

	Mean annual increase Rate %		Percentage of world	
	1950–60	*1970–73*	*1950*	*1975*
World	1·7	2·1	100	100
Africa	1·9	2·7	8·7	10·1
Americas	2·1	1·9	13·2	14·1
North	1·8	0·9		
Central	2·7	3·3		
South	2·3	2·4		
Asia	1·8	2·1	54·6	56·7
South West	2·5	2·9		
South	1·8	2·5		
South East	2·1	2·7		
East	1·8	1·8		
Europe	0·8	0·6	15·6	12·1
North West	0·7	0·4		
Central	0·8	0·6		
South	0·9	0·7		
U.S.S.R.	1·7	0·9	7·1	6·5
Oceania	2·4	2·0	0·5	0·5

Source: Various United Nations publications.

N.B.: The figures are for total increase, that is natural increase plus migration. The differences are positive (2 per thousand) for North America, 8 per thousand for Oceania, and negative (1 per thousand) for Asia and Europe.

during the years to come and the Asiatic masses will bear heavily on the world's destiny. The only exception is provided by Japan.

Africa is the continent with the highest growth rate (27 per thousand) but the density is still low. America, with over 20 per thousand, gains each year one in seven of the world's new inhabitants. But there is an importance difference between North America, the relative importance of which is tending to diminish, and Latin America which is expanding rapidly. However, the total population of the Americas is only 14 per cent of the world's total, and the densities are low, so that the continent can support a large increase without internal stresses and without imperilling international equilibrium. The Latin American birth rates of about 29 per thousand also foreshadow a large margin of growth in the years to come, and the exaggeration of the disequilibrium which already exists between the Anglo-Saxon peoples of the North and the Latino-Indian peoples south of the Rio Grande.

The U.S.S.R., in which the growth rate was high, has vast spaces and low densities which will enable it to absorb very large increases. However, its demographic rhythm is such that there has been a lowering in the natural growth rate during the last few years, for if the death rate has almost reached a minimum, the birth rate has decreased too.

The natural growth rate in Oceania is very high, but it affects a very small population; moreover, since in the above Table the growth rates are calculated on the basis of the global increases between 1970 and 1973, the figure quoted is an exaggeration, for there is some immigration flow, especially into Australia, and the real natural growth is more like 14 per thousand.

There remains Europe, and its part in the total growth is small. Its overall growth rate is only 6 per thousand. The European story is long and complex, and may not yet be at an end; in the nineteenth and early twentieth centuries, the European growth was proportionally much more rapid than that of the rest of the world; but between the two world wars the growth rate fell to 7·1 per thousand. After the last war it had shown a tendency to rise slightly, but now the decline is general in the whole of Europe. Two facts are certain, first, that the European peoples are no longer destined for a great expansion, and secondly that the part they play is decreasing and will continue to decrease during the next decades; furthermore, bearing in mind the high densities already present in most European countries, a larger growth rate is neither necessary nor desirable.

Regional disparity within countries

Outside these great continental or semi-continental groupings, it must be pointed out that there are many detailed variations. We may take two examples, Italy and the United States.

As regards *Italy*, we have several times underlined the demographic differences between the population of the Po plain and that of the south. In northern Italy, the natural growth rate is only 3·2 per thousand, but in Central Italy, it is 5·9 and in southern Italy and in the towns it is 13·6 per thousand. Indeed, in the Piedmont province of Pavia, deaths are actually more numerous than births; in Liguria the figures are similar. In these northern regions, richer and more advanced, family limitation has been the custom for a long time and the age composition of the population is less favourable than in southern Italy, so that the death rate is a little higher (10·9 as against 9·2). On the contrary, in Sardinia, Sicily, Calabria, Basilicata, Apulia, and Campania, natural growth represents two-thirds of the number of births. In Campania, 110,000 births are registered as against 38,000 deaths; in Sicily 105,000 and 40,000 respectively. In these southern regions the birth rate is just beginning to fall, while better medical and social services have already caused a sharp improvement in the general standard of health.

In the *United States*, there are also strong regional contrasts, produced in much the same way as in Italy; though the death rate in the various States varies only from 6·3 to 10·9 (1974), the birth rate shows much greater contrasts, varying from 11·9 per thousand to 25·5 per thousand. This being so, the natural growth rate varies from 2·4 in the States of Pennsylvania and Massachusetts to 19·2 in Utah, or eight times as high. Thus side by side we find States with very different demographic rhythms. In the east are the oldest most industrialised and most urbanised States, resembling the rhythm of old Europe, as the following table shows:

States with the lowest natural growth rates

State	Natural growth Rate	Percentage of population that is urban
New York	3·2	89·3
Rhode Island	2·5	90·0
Massachusetts	4·4	97·1
Connecticut	3·4	92·5
New Jersey	2·8	94·2
Pennsylvania	2·4	81·2

Source: U.S.A. census.

At the opposite extreme, the States with the highest rates are found in the South, where the negro population in the east and Spanish/ Indian in the west are very prolific, in the agricultural states in the centre, such as the Dakotas, and in the central part of the western mountain and plateau region, which is the home of the Mormons.

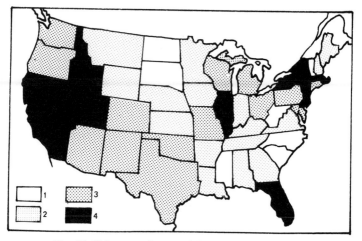

Fig. 20 Urban population of the United States, 1974.

By states. 1. Less than 50 per cent. urban.   2. 50 to 65 per cent.
3. 65 to 80 per cent.   4. Over 80 per cent.

Each of the three states that hold record growth rates may illustrate one of these three types: New Mexico, with a rate of 11·8 per thousand and a high proportion of 'Mexicans', Mississippi with 9 per thousand (and having 37 per cent of negroes in its population), and Utah, with 19·2 per thousand, one of the two main strongholds of the Mormon communities.

This strong differentiation of population growth rates may have, within countries, similar consequences to those we have outlined for the world as a whole; it is the least advanced regions and peoples that have the highest rates of growth, and we are witnessing a disproportionate increase of the most prolific elements, which at the same time are often the least favoured sections of the nation. In the United States, the proportion of Negroes in the total population rose from 8·4 per cent in 1930 to 11·1 in 1974, in South Africa, between 1970 and 1975, the European population increased annually by 8·4 per cent, the coloured by 26·2 and the Asiatic by 15·3 (the figures for the black population are unreliable). In New Zealand, the proportion of Maoris to Europeans, which was 6·3 per cent in 1955, reached 8·8 in 1971 and looks like rising to 15 per cent at the end of the century if the two groups maintain their present birth rates.

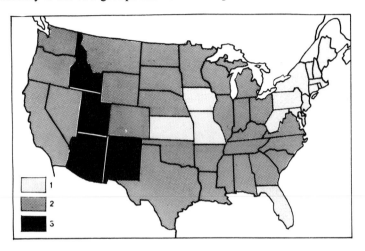

Fig. 21. Natural population growth by states in the U.S.A., 1974.

1. Less than 5 per cent.   2. 5 to 10 per cent.   3. Over 10 per cent.

An immense field of study lies open here—in the consequences that such variations may have on the psychological, sociological and economic evolution of different countries.

Age composition of populations

Another consequence of the nature, volume and variation of the natural growth rate is the age structure of the population.

A community with a high birth rate and poor health conditions, in which therefore the span of human life is but short, has a high proportion of juveniles and very few old people. On the contrary, a country which has had a low birth rate for some time, together with a high standard of living and good welfare services, will have relatively few juveniles and many elderly people. All kinds of intermediate combinations are possible.

Naturally there are other factors also which may help to determine the age composition: persistent emigration, for example, is a very

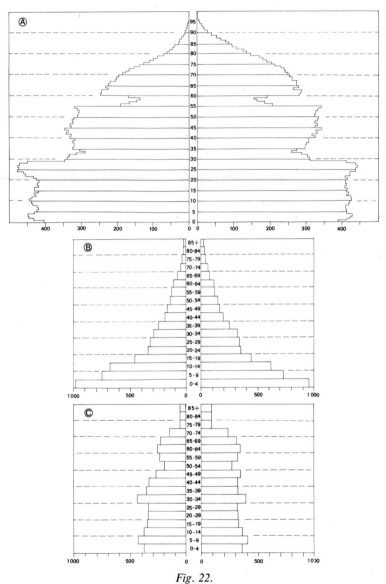

Fig. 22.

A.   *Age pyramid for France, as at 1 January 1975.*
B.   *Age pyramid for Algeria (15,270,000 population in 1972).*
C.   *Age pyramid for German Federal Republic (incl. West Berlin)*
        (61,674,000 in 1972).
   Males to the left, females to the right. Numbers in thousands.

important one, the consequences of which we shall examine later. Before going further, however, we may offer a classification based on the above considerations of natural growth.

The age-composition of a population may be expressed graphically either by age pyramids or triangular diagrams.

The age-pyramid. This is constructed either by using the actual numbers of males and females in each age-group (generally taking five-year intervals), or by using percentages representing the proportion of individuals in each age-group within the total population.

Such a diagram shows immediately all the major and minor incidents in the demographic evolution: thus the age-pyramid for France shows the high proportion of old people resulting from the long period of falling birth rate (18 per cent over 60 years of age), the appreciable growth of the under-15 age-groups, resulting from the rise in the birth rate after the second World War (32 per cent under 20 years of age), and deep indentations which result from the two world wars (1·5 million killed, and about 1·7 million unborn children during the 1914–18 war, 600,000 killed and 300,000 unborn children during the hostilities of 1939–45). The losses during the first war were mostly of young men, and this results in a more pronounced deficiency than one would normally expect in the over-66 age groups; on the other hand, the low birth rate during the war years had its repercussion twenty years later, between 1934 and 1938, in the *classes creuses*—literally, the 'hollow generation'. During the second war the 600,000 deaths comprised only 100,000 military personnel, and the remainder being deportees and those who died in concentration camps, or during air raids or of malnutrition, that is, individuals from all sections of the population, from the youngest to the oldest; the demographic result is thus more generalised.

Triangular diagrams. These are graphs constructed on three axes of an equilateral triangle. Each country is thus only represented by a dot placed in a position corresponding to the proportion of children, adults and old people. This is a much more generalised representation than the age-pyramid, but its advantage is that it permits ready comparisons between a whole series of countries, each of which is shown by a dot within the same triangle (Fig. 23).

The different categories

Populations are often divided into three groups, the children, who may be either under 15 or under 20 according to the statistics, the

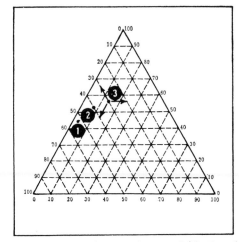

Fig. 23. Triangular population diagram for Brazil (1) *United States* (2) *and France* (3).

Percentages of 'under-20', on left, of '20 to 65 years', on right, and of 'over-65' along base.

adults and the elderly folk for whom a lower limit may be either 60 or 65. We shall take 20 and 60 as the limits.

Calculations made for all countries of the world for which age composition statistics exist show that the number of 'under-twenties' varies between extreme values of 28·7 per cent in Sweden and 30·1 per cent in East Germany, and 53 per cent in the Philippines and in Brazil —the higher figures thus being twice the lower. An even greater difference is found between countries if one takes the proportion of 'over-60s'; the figures are around 3·3 per cent for Brazil, Venezuela, Thailand, and Mozambique and 19·5 per cent in Belgium, 19·1 in Great Britain—a 1 : 6 variation.

In general, the countries which have the most children had the fewest old people, and one may hazard the following three-fold grouping:

The west-European type. Here the proportion of 'under-20s' is generally below 30 per cent and of the 'over-60s' around 19 per cent. England and Wales may be taken as typical of this category, with 30·6 per cent juveniles and 19·2 per cent elderly people. It is a type which is at the moment but feebly represented in the world as a whole, in this extreme form, but parts of Europe and of the white populations outside Europe are trending towards it.

The United States type. Here the 'under-20s' form 35–40 per cent of the population, and the 'over-60s' between 8 and 14 per cent. In the U.S.A. there are 37 per cent in the first group and 14·3 per cent in the second, the middle section of adults thus amounting to half the total population. Most of the white populations outside Europe fall into this class—Australia, New Zealand, Argentina, Canada. The U.S.S.R. with 37 per cent and 11·8 per cent respectively, also belongs, as do most of the countries of eastern Europe, and Japan.

The Brazilian type. The abundance of children and the almost complete absence of old people characterise this third group. In Brazil there are 53 per cent in the 'under-20s' class and only 5 per cent over 60. The percentage of juveniles is generally over 40 or even 45, whilst the elderly form only 4 to 8 per cent of the population. Almost the whole of Latin America, except Argentina and Uruguay, falls into this class, as do Africa and Asia. This class contains the greatest number of countries, and those with the greatest densities of population. Evolutionary progress is slow, owing to the maintenance of the high birth rate, and to the low standard of health and well-being which hinder the prolongation of the human life-span.

It is in this third group that the proportion of adults is lowest, since it is less than half and may be even only 40 per cent of the total; under such circumstances progress is particularly difficult and the burden on the relatively small number of workers is especially heavy.

CONCLUSION

The foregoing discussion leads us to several general conclusions. The prime fact is the fantastic growth of world population; the annual growth rate continues itself to grow: it was 0·8 per cent during the first part of the twentieth century, 1·8 between 1950 and 1960, 1·9 at present, whilst the most recent forecasts are for a growth rate of 2 per cent between 1975 and 1985. At this rate there will be 5 billion human beings in 1985 and 6·5 billions by the year 2000.

This demographic explosion has not been experienced everywhere with the same violence. An increasing divergence has occurred between the developed and the developing countries, and the population of the latter, which may develop a growth rate of 2·4 per cent during the next few years, will grow from 2,537 millions in 1970

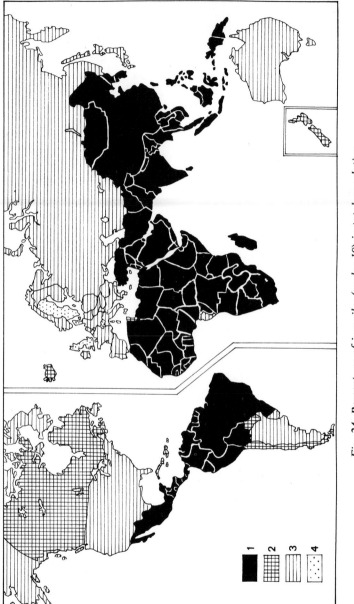

Fig. 24. Percentage of juveniles (under 19) in total population.
1. Over 50 per cent.   2. 40 to 50 per cent.   3. 30 to 40 per cent.   4. Under 30 per cent.

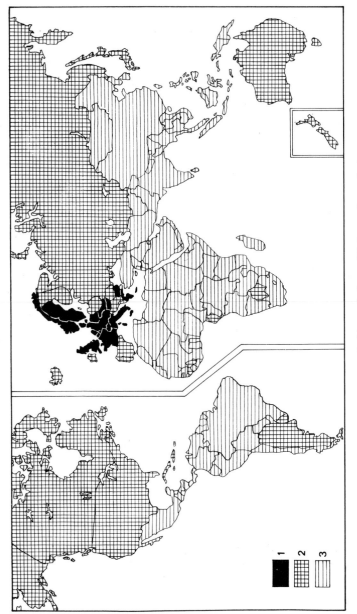

Fig. 25. Percentage of old people (over 65) in total population
1. Over 10 per cent.   2. 5 to 10 per cent.   3. Under 5 per cent.

to 5,030 millions in 2000; thus, with an overall world increase of 77 per cent between 1970 and 2000, the developed countries will grow by 26 per cent and the developing countries by 99 per cent. The most massive increase will be in southern Asia, from the Philippines and Indonesia to the Mediterranean coasts of Lebanon and Turkey; the one-third of the world's population now living here will have swollen to 40 per cent by the end of the century. On the other hand eastern Asia (China and Japan), although experiencing a large growth in absolute numbers, will see its relative importance decline. The most rapid increase will be in Africa, where the experts estimate a growth rate of 3 per cent by 1985, giving an expansion of $2\frac{1}{2}$ times between the late 1970s and the end of the century. Tropical Latin America, which at present tops the growth rate league, will slow down during the next few years. As for Europe and North America, their population will only grow but slightly.

If we calculate the proportion of the population that does not earn its own living by the formula

$$\frac{\text{Under 15s} + \text{Over 65s}}{\text{Number of adults}}$$

we see that it is 55 in 1975, and it should be maintained at this level. But in the developing countries it is 80 at present and will only decrease very slowly until 1990, after which it may decline more rapidly—but only if the anticipated fall in fecundity takes place. This disparity is most impropitious for economic development.

PART IV

POPULATION MOVEMENTS

Man is a mobile creature, capable of enquiring, susceptible to suggestion, and endowed with imagination and initiative. This explains why, having conceived the notion that his wants might be satisfied elsewhere, he may decide not merely on going there but also on the means by which his project can be achieved.

This movement of people, which can be traced far back into prehistory, has gone on unceasingly for thousands of years, and the present distribution of man over the earth's surface owes much to it. Without getting lost in the detail of the great currents of human migration, one can distinguish several fundamental themes. First is the role of the Asiatic centre of diffusion; from here great westward invasions were propagated into Europe, from here eastward movements first peopled the Americas, whilst south-westward movements infiltrated into Africa and the Mediterranean basin. Secondly, the role of Europe as a relay station: until the discovery of the New World its western end was simply a cul-de-sac in which the waves of conquering invaders from the east, the north and the south-east petered out, but when the Atlantic was opened up by the discovery of the Americas its shores provided the jumping-off point for millions of migrants destined for the new lands. Thirdly, the Americas appear as a magnetic crucible, having attracted Asians as well as Europeans, and having drawn also from Africa. Fourthly, Africa has had a passive role; many times invaded by progressive waves that probably came from the north-east, then pillaged of its manpower and later colonised, it is now becoming itself again. Finally Australia, which may in ancient times have contributed to the peopling of the southern part of South America, has now itself become the recipient of European immigrants.

It is true that most of these great movements are things of the past, but they have left such obvious traces on the modern inhabitants and their civilisations that it is necessary to give them more than a passing glance. The racial complexity of certain parts of the world, to which reference has already been made, has its origin in these migrations.

The major types of migrations

Numerous ways could be suggested of classifying the diverse and complex movements, in order to build up a complete picture, and various names have been suggested to define the different types of mobility. But here we propose a very simple division, taking first long-distance or international migration, secondly movements on a smaller scale, within individual countries, and thirdly the oscillatory migrations which embrace all those movements in which the migrant does not abandon his place of abode but returns to it more or less periodically.

CHAPTER EIGHT

International Migrations

Under this heading we include all those movements involving the crossing of one or more frontiers, not merely between adjacent states but often from one continent to another. Distances, however, are not what matters: a Ukrainian who moves to Vladivostok traverses a much greater mileage than a Pole who goes to seek work in France, but he remains within the same political unit.

International migrations are distinguished first in our classification because their statistical evaluation is easy, at least in theory. As they cross each political boundary, the migrants leave traces of their passage in the records of the frontier posts on both sides of the line. But it must be noted that such statistical records have not always existed, and even now they are sometimes misleading; for example, the figures given in Germany for Germans leaving their country for Argentina do not agree with those published by the Argentine government for the same persons; and other similar examples might be given. We should not, however, give way to undue pessimism on this account; statistics do exist.

Secondly, international migrations are distinguished because of the complex difficulties created not merely by the actual removal but also by the relations between the newcomers and the existing inhabitants. True, it is not all plain sailing even for a Breton seeking work in Paris or for a dweller in Oklahoma trying his luck in California, but at least the language and the national sentiment are the same; but the foreigner who arrives in a new country has none of these advantages.

Permanent migration

A complete break with the homeland and a plunge into the heart of an entirely new environment are not accomplished without difficulty, for the delicate problems of assimiliation are added to the uprooting. Often, the emigrant does not know that he will never see his native land again; unforeseen circumstances, either good or bad, may keep him away. But in any case, on arrival he faces some very severe tests. There is a wide variety of possible circumstances.

Almost invariably, particularly in modern times, the emigrant does not go in complete isolation towards the unknown. Perchance he has friends, from his own village or region, who have preceded him and have given him information; or maybe he is migrating with a whole group, which will create in the new country a little island of the old. The case of the Polish colonies in northern France is well known. The Poles came between 1920 and 1930 to work in the coal mines, bringing with them their families, their priests and their school-teachers; they maintained their language, their religion, their newspapers, their feast-days and their folklore, and in 1939 they were still almost completely unassimilated; most of them hoped eventually to return to Poland with sufficient savings to take over the family farmlands. Then came the war, the nature of which led them to throw in their lot with France; and the changed political circumstances in their native lands after the war led most of them, despite the call of the Polish government to return, to become French; their sons did service with the French army, their children attended French schools; even their Polish language was abandoned, and the segregation of twenty years was ended. Opinion has it that in a few more years assimilation will be complete.

As other examples one could quote the villages with German names in southern Brazil and northern Argentina, where German is still spoken and they eat locally-produced sauerkraut and sausage; or the Italian villages which produce the best wines in Brazil; or the Swiss dairying communities which are found both in eastern United States and in the temperate lands of South America.

The wider the differences between homeland and land of adoption, the greater the difficulties. In the United States, amongst the immigrant groups, only 10 per cent of the Italians—Latin, Catholic and not speaking English—married American wives, whereas 42 per cent of the British immigrants' did so, at the beginning of the century. These difficulties of assimilation have provoked reactions on the part of the receiving country, and are the cause of the restrictive practices initiated by the U.S. Government when the Mediterranean and Slav contingents began to overwhelm the older immigrant waves which were mainly British and northern European. In 1921, the first of the 'quota' laws fixed the permitted annual admissions at 3 per cent of the population of each country as represented in the United States at the 1910 census; a second and more severe law was promulgated in 1924, and this pushed the basic census back to 1890—at which date the preponderance of the Anglo-Saxon element was not in question— and the proportion was reduced to 2 per cent.

Thus the problem of assimilation bears equally on the migrants and on the receiving country, particularly when the latter is wide open and the immigrants numerous.

Temporary emigration

Many emigrants cannot make up their minds to abandon completely their native land; urged by necessity, they go for a more or less prolonged period to a country that will permit them to earn a living, and if possible accumulate sufficient money for their return, then, with the profits of their labours they go back to their native village, where, by reason of the low standard of living, they become senior citizens of some affluence. In Sicily, in southern Italy, in Greece, and in other parts of south-eastern Europe like Albania or Bulgaria one is shown the houses of these 'Americans' who are ending their days peacefully after their labours on the other side of the Atlantic. The Japanese too practised this sort of migration before the war. It is particularly evident in South America: thus, in the Argentine, between 1910 and 1950, out of a total of 14,159,876 immigrants, only 2,318,422 stayed permanently. Many Basques from southern France and northern Spain, for example, are temporary immigrants.

In this case, clearly, the question of assimilation retreats into the background; but it often happens that children born during the period of 'exile' remain in the place of their birth and become good citizens of the new country. Thus the emigration becomes permanent in the second generation.

Somewhat similar are the temporary migrations of much shorter duration, for example of Algerians to France. This is a case of peasants exiling themselves for a few years only, in order to help the family remaining at home, or to earn money to buy a piece of land, or simply to get the wherewithal to marry. Some 350,000 Algerians work in France, that is 5 per cent of the Muslim Algerian population, or more than one adult man in ten. Most of these workers come from the mountain districts, particularly Kabylia; they are young men with no technical skill. They go across to France for perhaps eighteen months to three years and then return home, sometimes for good, sometimes to set off six months later for another spell. About 70 per cent of them are labourers, employed on constructional work, in the mines or in agriculture. For them, with but few exceptions, the question of assimilation does not arise, neither is there much change of occupational status. They put down no roots in France, and leave few traces behind them; only 10 per cent are married to or living with a European woman and only 2 per cent have their families with them.

This type of temporary migration exemplified by the Algerians in France is an extreme case; it might be matched by that of those Mexicans who cross over into the United States. Both are exceptional cases of international migration, which cannot be considered in the same class as simple seasonal migrations.

The changing character of international migration

In earlier times, to abandon one's homeland and emigrate to a far-off country was an adventure fraught with grave dangers. The exiles, often very poor, made lengthy journeys on the deck or in the hold of a wretched vessel. Of the starving Irish who quitted their country in the famine of 1845, 6 per cent died at sea, and counting also those who died soon after arrival, one in five of these unhappy creatures failed to make a home on the welcoming continent.

After the trials of the voyage came those of adaptation—to an unfamiliar climate, to conditions of nourishment and health for which the body was unprepared, and to precarious economic circumstances; and the consequences were often disastrous. The movement of people from the temperate lands to the tropics proved to be particularly ill-fated: in Brazil in 1873-74, of 1,800 Germans installed in the cacao plantations of Bahia, 100 died almost at once and there were 738 deaths in all; in British West Africa (the 'white man's grave') the death rate amongst Europeans at the end of the nineteenth century was 76 per thousand—but as a result of the war against malaria and yellow fever it had dropped to 8 per thousand in 1936–38. Even in Algeria, much closer to the temperate lands, the death rate was 234 per thousand at Marengo in 1849, as a result of malaria, hardships, and epidemics, whilst at Fondouk half the European population was wiped out in 1845.

As time went on conditions improved; communications became easier, and the transfer of news quicker and more certain. It was possible to know what happened to the emigrants. After the announcement of a successful establishment, whole village populations from the Swiss or Italian Alps would pour out, a few at a time, to the other side of the ocean. The 'penny post' concession, in the early Victorian period, did much to favour emigration, by enabling the departed son to send news cheaply to his family. Moreover, new arrivals would quickly discover small colonies of their compatriots already installed, and so there grew up the Irish, Jewish and Italian quarters of New York, and the German 'colonies' of the Middle West.

Lastly, and more recently, the spontaneous character of these international migrations has tended to disappear; they have become regulated and sponsored. The policy of the United States, which has made the frontier a barrier, as much against Europeans as against Asiatics, had already given a foretaste of this sort of negative regulation. In Europe agreements in very precise terms were signed between different governments, as between those of Poland and France, or Italy and France, to arrange for the migration of workers. In this respect however the palm belongs to Australia, which has the most elaborate immigration policy of any country in the world.

In Australia they are much concerned to select immigants of a certain origin: the preference is for Anglo-Saxons or strictly northern Europeans; they are also concerned about the age, status and physical and intellectual qualities of the intending immigrant. In order to integrate him completely with the Australian community, they take him in hand from the moment of selection: he at once receives instruction in the English language (should this be necessary), is taken care of during the voyage, and has his new life carefully explained to him; on arrival he is sent to a special centre where he is given technical and spiritual guidance, and during his first two years he is carefully watched to see that he makes progress in the language and gets a job to earn his living. After two years he is considered to be a true Australian, and is allowed his freedom in his new country.

Such is the measure of progress in these matters during the last hundred years.

Population transfers

Side by side with these movements which, however controlled and regimented they may be, are still spontaneous, the world has witnessed other displacements of a different and compulsory kind, forced upon one set of people by another.

In the past, the slave trade and the forced movement of labour are the most tragic examples. From 1442 onwards, the Portuguese sought blacks from Africa to satisfy the labour requirements of the Iberian peninsula, but from 1517 the hunt was intensified in order to furnish the Americas with slaves, and from 1620 the English became the great Negro-hunters, and having established their famous (or infamous) 'triangular trade', began to sap the manpower of the coastal regions of tropical West Africa. This trade, though officially abolished in 1807, continued in fact until after 1850. One can only guess at the yearly number of victims: perhaps 75,000 by 1790, more than 130,000 by 1830. And how much additional loss of life for every cargo that reached its destination! The case has been cited of ten villages, numbering 2,000 souls, destroyed in order to obtain 20 women. And at least 15 per cent of the victims would die during transportation. In East Africa it was the Arab and Hindu slave-traders who raided especially to get women, children and eunuchs for the harems of the Middle East; in this direction, often four-fifths of the human cargo died en route. It has been estimated that some 20 million Africans were thus deported to the west, and 10 to 15 million to the east. Africa is probably still paying for these frightful ravages and this inhuman traffic.

Wars and international disagreements have also produced migrations, sometimes voluntary, sometimes forced. Concerning ourselves only with the comparatively recent past, we may recall the voluntary evacuation of part of the population of Alsace-Lorraine after the 1870 war, from the territory annexed by the Germans; some of the evacuees went into France, some to Algeria. Then there was the compulsory exchange of populations, after the 1923 Treaty of Lausanne, between 1 million Greeks living in the coastal towns of Asia, who were returned to Greece, and 300,000 Turks from Europe who took their place. More recently, after the second World War, it was the Germans who, harassed on all sides—for the aggressive nationalism of the German minorities had set all European nations against them — gathered together within the German frontiers—or rather, within the West German frontiers. In 1956, some 15·5 million persons were registered as refugees of German nationality, within Germany; 11·2 million of them were in the Federal Republic and in West Berlin and there were even some in Austria. In 1950 the number of refugees represented 19·8 per cent of the population of the Federal Republic but the proportions rose to 32·6 per cent in Lower Saxony, 23·6 per cent in Bavaria, and 20·6 per cent in Hesse. Only the most westerly provinces, close to the French frontier, were relatively unaffected by this demographic deluge. At first the difficulties were many, both economic and psychological, but the re-adaptation of the refugees has proceeded apace, and at the present time almost all the new arrivals—who were at first, much younger than the indigenous population (34·5 per cent under twenty and 11 per cent over sixty, as against 32·1 per cent and 13·3 per cent respectively)—have found employment within the booming German economy, which in 1958 was even suffering from shortage of manpower. The refugees included those expelled from Poland, Czechoslovakia, Hungary, Rumania, and from the Soviet-controlled Eastern Zone (including East Berlin).

Another influx, of much more varied provenance this time, has gathered within the frontiers of the new state of Israel, created on 16 May, 1948, on the cessation of the British mandate, and surrounded by hostile Arab states. The decree of free immigration from the very beginning intensified a movement which had been going on, more or less illegally, since the end of the nineteenth century. In 1946 there were 583,327 Jews in Palestine of whom 450,000, mainly from Germany, Poland and Rumania, had entered during the twenty-eight years of the British mandate. Since 1948, 1,500,000 immigrants have arrived, but the provenance has changed, partly because the Jewish communities of Central Europe were decimated by the Nazis or had already fled, and partly because certain Arab states in Asia and North Africa have practised a policy of systematic expulsion or at least persecution of their Jewish minorities. In these circumstances, the new arrivals during the 1950s came mainly from Asia, particularly Iraq (three-fifths of the immigrants in 1951) and from North African territories (89 per cent of the immigrants in 1958); conversely, during the same period (actually 1948-75), 190,000 people left Israel, most of them Jews, mostly recent immigrants but a few older ones as well, and almost all destined for America.

As a last example, the independence of India (18 July 1947) and the partition of Pakistan provoked the transfer of more than 17 million people; in 1957, there were 8·4 million refugees in Pakistan and 8·85 million in India, or 10 per cent of the Pakistan population and 2 per cent of that of India.

It has been estimated that the migrations of the last twenty-five years, bound up with the second World War and the nationalist movements which followed it, constitute the greatest population movement of all time—perhaps 100 million people have been involved.

Asiatic emigration

Many groups of people from within the vast continent of Asia have quitted their homelands for other parts of the globe in the past, and the movement undoubtedly continues. The habit of emigrating, however, is not universal but seems to affect certain peoples, particularly those whose habitat is in naturally favoured areas, that is, close to a sea coast. Among the 'expansionist' peoples of Asia are the Chinese, Japanese, Indians and the Syrians and Lebanese.

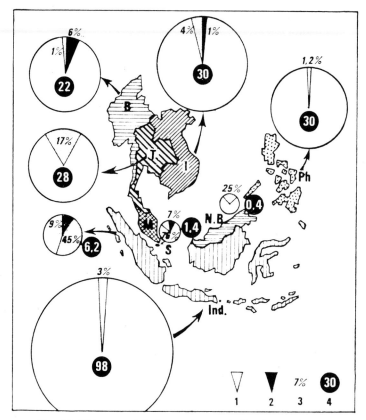

Fig. 26. Chinese and Indian emigrants in South-east Asia.

1. Chinese. 2. Hindus. 3. Percentage of Chinese or Hindus in total population of country. 4. Population total in millions. B. Burma; I. Viet-Nam; Ph. Philippines; T. Thailand; M. Malaya; S. Singapore; Ind. Indonesia; N.B. North Borneo (Sabah).

A map of the peoples of south-east Asia, that cross-roads on the edge of the continent, shows very well the general importance of Chinese expansion, and the more localised penetration of Indians. The demography of Singapore is characteristic: only 200 or 300 people lived in the marshes of the island in 1819 when the first British settler, Sir Stamford Raffles arrived; six months later, there were 5,000 Chinese traders and in six years, side by side with the British, they made Singapore the greatest commercial centre in south-east Asia. At the present time 76 per cent of the 2,235,000 people who dwell in Singapore are of Chinese origin and 7 per cent from the Indian sub-continent.

The *Chinese* have not thrust out many tentacles of colonisation outside south-east Asia, though one finds small groups of Chinese traders in almost all the great cities, particularly New York, London and San Francisco, and the Chinese *restaurateurs* have spread the cult of Chinese cooking from one end of the world to the other. At one time they appeared to be establishing quite a foothold in the United States, as a source of cheap labour, but the competition which they thus provided led to the laws of 1868 and 1882, which barred their entry. The trading propensities of the Chinese are well known, and Chinese merchants practically dominate the commerce of all the countries to the south of China. They represent 40 per cent of the population of Malaya, 10 per cent of that of Thailand, and between 2 per cent and 4 per cent of that of all the others (Indonesia, Philippines, Viet-Nam, Burma). During the periods of European colonisation they formed groups of profit-taking intermediaries or middlemen between the masses of the rural population and the small European minorities; and since the change in the political status of the former colonies and the transformation within China itself they have succeeded in maintaining themselves, for their function in local trading appears to be indispensable. At first they set up in a small way, men only, in a small quarter of a town; then, assured of an all but complete monopoly of certain traffics, they later bring their wives and develop family life in a position of security.

This same almost indispensable role of petty trader characterises the small groups of *Syrian* and *Lebanese* colonists, especially in the towns of black Africa; they are grocers or owners of small shacks in which they sell miscellaneous wares such as tinned food, cloth, petrol, even glass beads which they barter amongst the native traders. They function as virtually unavoidable middlemen; their success is assured by reason of their ready adaptability, their disregard for harsh living conditions, even in the remote interior, by the absence of native competition and by the fact that the Europeans, who prefer greater comforts, are preoccupied with administration and other less parasitical tasks.

The spread of *Indians* through the world is due to quite other causes; they are found in many countries formerly under British rule. The English transplanted them in order to make good the lack of local labour supplies: thus they were settled in South Africa where the bulk of them are to be found within a belt 129 km long and 56 km wide, to the north and south of Durban; they form 12·5 per cent of the population of Natal. Introduced between 1860 and 1911, they numbered a little over 120,000 at the beginning of the century and about 700,000 at the present time; a large proportion are concentrated in the city of Durban itself, and more than two-thirds of them are town-dwellers. One-fifth are Hindus and almost all the remainder Muslims. The same kind of policy ('indentured labour') was responsible from 1905 onwards for introducing Tamils from Madras Presidency into Malayan rubber plantations; at the present time 11 per cent of the Malayan population is of Indian origin. Guyana and the former British West Indies have drawn on the same Indian sources and they now have many small groups numbering about half a million people in all.

Much more active and daring was the policy of expansion which lay behind *Japanese* emigration. Confined within their archipelago and deeply convinced of their own superiority which was to give them pre-eminence in the Far East and perhaps even further afield, the Japanese for a long time conceived systematic emigration as part of their national policy. Emigration was in any case a matter of necessity by reason of the over-population of the islands, but it did not appeal to the popular taste and for long was actually prohibited by law. It began about 1885 and went hand in hand with the development of Japanese imperialism. In fact, it was never completely free, and the government always exercised a strict control over the emigrants, selecting them before departure and constraining them afterwards to remain in groups from which devotion to the mother country would never be absent. Young men emigrants obtained wives from the homeland, unknown and chosen from photographs, and with these they founded families. Within modest limits, the currents of emigration flowed in two directions: one led to the American continent, whither the first Japanese departed as labourers under contract, about 1885, to become established in Hawaii, in the United States and in Canada, and also, after the Mexican commercial treaty of 1888, in Latin America, particularly in Peru and Brazil; the other to the adjacent Asiatic mainland and islands, where the imperial Japanese flag was beginning to fly.

The movement towards the Americas lasted rather longer in the South than in the North, but it finally came up against some obstacles. As early as 1907 the United States took restrictive measures to protect itself against what was regarded as yellow infiltration; this had the effect, from 1908, of diverting the flow towards Latin America, where solid blocks of 'professional' emigrants, all agriculturalists, established themselves in Peru and Brazil, and grew rapidly. In the latter country there were 34,000 Japanese in 1920 and 225,000 in 1943—but this was still a small proportion of the total population. In Asia, the colonists who went to the conquered Asiatic territories, which were already overpopulated, were naturally reluctant to do manual work alongside other yellow peoples, and were all 'black-coated workers' or traders. In all, on the eve of the war, there were some 1·8 million Japanese in Korea, Manchuria and Formosa; at the same time there must have been 1·2 million others resident abroad, about half of them on the American continent. The highest number of departures was recorded in 1933, when 27,000 persons left but 14,000 returned. The end of the second World War provoked the wholesale return of these expatriates, some 6·3 million in all, of whom half were civilians and half military personnel, but the two-way traffic has resumed very slowly since then, particularly with South America, especially in Brazil (600,000).

In total, then, the vast continent of Asia, which contains more than one-half of the world's population, has not until now shed many of its inhabitants: 20 million Chinese, 10 million Indians, 3 or 4 million Japanese—that is about the total share of Asia in the great migrations which have taken place during the late nineteenth century and the first half of the twentieth.

The European Tide

It is otherwise with Europe. This small continent, situated at the extremity of the Old World, has more than any other part of the world generated the great migratory movements of the last 150 years. At least 50 and perhaps 60 million people have participated in the great outflow and more than half of these have gone to North America. It has been calculated that this exodus represents, from 1846 to 1932, an annual total of 3 per thousand of the European population.

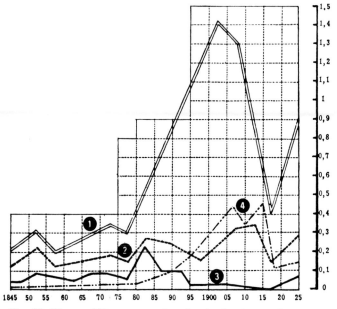

Fig. 27. Waves of European emigration in the nineteenth century.

1. Total European emigrants.   2. British.   3. German.   4. Italian (in millions). (From M. Reinhard and A. Armengaud, 'Histoire générale de la population mondiale').

The movement was not of course new; it followed the slow infiltration of French, English, Dutch, Portuguese and Spaniards which had been taking place since the sixteenth century into the West Indies and the coastlands of the Americas, South Africa and India. But the sudden intensification coincided with the demographic expansion of Europe, the sharp rise in population, the development of means of transport and of an economic prosperity which, while creating satisfaction also gave rise to other needs and encouraged men to seek elsewhere what they could not find at home.

The story of emigration can be divided into several chapters. The first wave crossed the Atlantic about 1850–55, the second towards 1875, the third between 1885 and 1890, the fourth, and far the most important, between 1905 and 1913, the fifth about 1925, and the sixth immediately after the second World War. The greatest number of emigrants in any one year left the European shores in 1913; it comprised 1,527,000 persons, including 565,000 Italians, 389,000 British, 206,000 Spanish, 194,000 Austrians. North-west Europe was the first part of the continent to send its sons across the ocean and these countries have contributed the greatest numbers, some 25 million in all—from the British Isles, Scandinavia, Belgium and the Netherlands. Emigration from the British Isles alone represents two-thirds of the figure, and of these 65 per cent went to the United States, 15 per cent to Canada, 5 per cent to Australia and 5 per cent to South Africa.

As the nineteenth century wore on, other countries began to participate more actively in the emigration movement. Seven million Germans altogether left home in the first great exodus between 1878 and 1892 and in the further rushes after the two world wars of the twentieth century, which left Germany bruised and impoverished; 10 million Italians emigrated, mostly after 1885—42 per cent to the U.S.A., 21 per cent to Brazil, 20 per cent to the Argentine, and 10 per cent to France—but many of them returned to end their days in their homeland. Since the beginning of the twentieth century the countries of central and eastern Europe have joined the assault on the new lands—20 million from Austria-Hungary, 3 million from the Iberian peninsula, 700,000 Greeks, as well as Russians and Poles.

A simple enumeration of the number of emigrants gives, of course, an inadequate idea of the impact of the European population on the world—for they have bred abundantly. Take the case of Ireland, which is typical. During the past 100 years 6 million Irish have left their country—but there are now 16 million Irish scattered outside their native isle, of whom 50 per cent are in the U.S.A. and more than 12 per cent in the United Kingdom. A brief glance at today's world is sufficient to reveal the extraordinary significance of this European mobility. What would now be the population of the American and Australian continents if the waves of European emigrants had not been directed to their shores?

Since the end of the second World War—a period which we might perhaps name 'the finite world', the world known, administratively occupied and politically controlled in all its parts—European emigration has slackened appreciably. The United States, as we have seen, has imposed systematic barriers; most countries of the world impose conditions as to the numbers and quality of immigrants, and only a few countries are in fact ready to absorb newcomers, e.g. Canada, Australia and Uruguay. Even there, however, it is no longer a case of uncontrolled immigrants integrating themselves as best they may into the national economy, but of individuals whose integration under the best conditions is carefully supervised and whose numbers are therefore carefully limited. The Australian example, quoted above (p. 179) is significant in this respect.

Since the end of the second World War about 9 million Europeans must have left their continent. The average has been about 700,000 a year and the highest number left round about 1950. At the present time the exodus seems more or less stabilised at about half a million a year—though it must be remarked that the whole of eastern Europe is absent from the published figures. Italy alone furnishes about one-fifth of this number, with Spain and the Netherlands about equal at 8 or 9 per cent; West Germany follows with 6 per cent; but the prize undoubtedly goes to the United Kingdom, where emigration has re-started with renewed vigour to produce 28 per cent of the total, the largest number from any European country. Thus north-west Europe has re-gained the supremacy which it had in the middle of the nineteenth century, with 41·5 per cent of the total number of emigrants, southern Europe holding the second place with 37·7 per cent and central Europe the third with 20·8 per cent. Of these emigrants, the great majority are still making for the Americas (71 per cent, of which 44 per cent to North America and 27 per cent to South America); 6 per cent have gone to Africa, 5 per cent to Asia and 18 per cent to Oceania. It is very noticeable how persistently cultural and particularly language affinities influence the direction of emigration—the Anglo-Saxon people go mainly to North America and Australia, as do the central Europeans, whilst the Mediterranean people go mainly to Latin America (of the Italians 57 per cent and of the Spanish 70 per cent including 42 per cent to the Argentine and 27 per cent to Venezuela).

The attraction of Europe

At the same time as all this emigration, since the end of the second World War, we have to notice a current of immigration into Europe, to the extent of $2\frac{1}{2}$ million people. Most of these, no doubt, are persons who emigrated some time ago and are now returning to their native land. This is particularly the case with the Italians, for example, amongst whom this custom is very common; and indeed the net balance of migration in recent years has been only one quarter of the recorded number of emigrants. There is also another factor at work, however, for detailed studies have shown that certain European countries have a considerable attraction for immigrants.

Some of these centres of attraction have functioned thus for some time, but at first only within the continent. The French case is well known: at the end of the first World War, suffering from a long period of low birth rate and from the tragic consequences of the loss of so many young men during the war, France welcomed large numbers of Poles and Italians to fill the gaps in the ranks of the working population, especially in mining, agriculture and building. Between 1920 and 1931, 1,920,000 foreigners entered France, of whom one-third were Italian, 32 per cent Polish, as well as Belgians and Spanish. In 1931 the proportion of foreigners in France reached its maximum of 7 per cent, or 2,891,000 persons. The economic crises of the 'thirties' and the slowing-down of French expansion, followed by the second World War, put a stop to this influx and even provoked some movement in the opposite direction, but after 1945 the call went out again, rather differently oriented this time, so as to include, as well as Europeans (mainly Italians and Spaniards), a large number of northern Africans, particularly Algerians. This is the first example of a European country tapping an extra-European reservoir of unskilled labour.

This movement has developed to such an extent that by 1975 it involved 4 million foreigners, or 7·7 per cent of the entire population. At the same time the range of nationalities has widened: 720,000 from Common Market countries, including 573,000 from Italy; then 812,000 Portuguese, 606,000 Spaniards, 103,000 Poles and 86,000 Yugoslavs; outside Europe most of the recruitment is from Algeria (846,000) following an agreement between the two governments, with 270,000 from Morocco, 149,000 from Tunisia; there are also Turks, Greeks, and some from French-speaking territories of Black Africa. But the vast majority of the foreign population is from 'Mediterranean' countries.

The situation in the United Kingdom is also remarkable. It has been estimated that there are now 2,500,000 non-natives here, comprising rather more than 900,000 Commonwealth citizens (200,000 West Indians, 180,000 Australians, New Zealanders, Canadians and South Africans, and 600,000 Asiatics), about 700,000 from Eire, and 400,000 foreigners including 100,000 Poles, 100,000 Italians and

150,000 Germans. A few days' residence in London is very instructive: one can eat in a host of Italian, Hungarian, Greek and Chinese restaurants: the hotel chambermaid may be Jamaican, the receptionist a New Zealander. The case of the West Indians has become notorious because of the occasional racial disturbances which have occurred in Nottingham, Birmingham and in parts of London; 40 per cent of them are in the Greater London area and 30 per cent in the Midlands. Many have been recruited into public services such as transport, hospitals and road works, and into the lower grades of hotel service. Some London services even have their own employment agency in Barbados.

The most important reason for this flow of immigrants into Europe is undoubtedly the need for certain types of labour; but there is another, found in France and in the United Kingdom alike, by reason of the former extent of the colonial empires of these two states. This is the large influx of young people from the former colonial territories; having been instructed in the language of the colonial power they now seek in its universities and technical institutes the further education which will enable them to take part in the running of their native country. Obviously such immigration is of a very temporary character, but it figures in the official statistics and is clearly useful in fostering the spread of European influence.

Though the events of the last few years have not altered the position of France, which has for long been characterised by the influx of immigrants, they have appreciably modified the situation in the United Kingdom, which we may briefly analyse. After having been the pioneer in the mass migration of Europeans to other continents, Great Britain functioned as a relay station at the end of the last century, admitting hundreds of thousands of Irish and at the same time sending its citizens out to the ends of the European world in North America, South Africa and Australia. Between the two wars there was but slack movement either way, but from 1931 onwards immigration began to exceed emigration, and in the forty years 1931–71 the excess of immigrants exceeded 2 million. In 1960, 130,000 British left the Kingdom, and 175,000 entered it, and in 1973 the immigration was estimated at 200,000, one-half of them from the Commonwealth countries. This influx became so obvious, and from some points of view so disquieting, that a law of November 1961, reinforced in 1968 and 1971, gave the government power to exercise control over immigration from the Commonwealth, the colonies and

Eire. The immigration of foreigners was in any case already closely controlled. It is indeed an extraordinary turn of fortune that Britain, of all countries, should have a problem of immigration.

We may also cite the case of Switzerland, where a large part of the economy is dependent on the presence of more than 1 million foreigners, or 18 per cent of the total population, amongst them a preponderance of Italians and Spaniards. This has led the government to adopt a restrictive policy which resulted, in 1975, in the anticipated dismissals and retirements and in the departure of 110,000 foreigners. Germany too has had recourse in recent years to the employment of migratory foreigners, who now represent 4 per cent of the population, and include 511,000 Turks, 475,000 Yugoslavs, 476,000 Italians, as well as Greeks, Spaniards and others.

In the light of these examples, we may well speculate on the demographic future of western Europe. Perhaps its destiny will be to draw to itself, on the one hand, either temporarily by reason of their profession or more permanently because of the attractiveness of life (artists, authors, journalists and others who come to live in London or Paris), some part of the present or future elite of many countries, and on the other hand, by reason of its high standard of living and the preferences of its people, a mass of labour to undertake the rough work in mining, building and agriculture, and the unattractive, poorly-paid jobs in domestic and public service. Conversely, some of its children, highly educated both in techniques and in culture, will feel themselves confined in a continent already well-equipped, densely peopled and steeped in tradition, and will prefer to seek elsewhere the space, the possibility of carrying out new plans, and the struggles and responsibilites of the pioneer that the old continent can no longer offer.

CHAPTER NINE

National Migrations

There are other migrants who do not cross international frontiers but are content with movement within their own country. It is much more difficult in such cases to assess the importance of the migratory movements and to trace them accurately. Only those countries which maintain a dossier for each citizen can have any exact idea of the successive removals of an individual and so could reconstruct, if need be, the general trends with their direction and terminal points. In some other countries where the census information is accurate and detailed, documents are published periodically which enable one to take stock of the situation, but in most cases such documents are only available every tenth year. In the intervals one can only make estimates or take samples. Other documents could be utilised, such as registers of electors or the lists compiled by agricultural benefit societies or other social security organisations, but such lists often give no more than the birthplace of the individual, and his present and previous address, so that there are often many links missing in the chain. Moreover, the abstraction and classification of such data requires mechanical methods and much skill and time in interpretation. Lastly, in many countries even the censuses themselves are incomplete; insufficient information about change of residence is asked for, and the replies are often inadequate. Under these circumstances one can only make sample studies, or estimates derived from one administrative department or another. At a pinch one could also get an approximate answer by a calculation based on the total population of any area: the natural growth subtracted from the total growth should indicate the proportion of the total growth due to inward (or outward) migration; and if this is done for increasingly smaller and smaller areas, a general pattern of movement will emerge.

General mobility

The study of migration within a country is the more intricate, in that it is not concerned merely with definite movements from one place to another, but with a whole series of complex movements. There is no state, however small, that has not experienced this fluidity of human movement. True, it is apparent in varying degrees, but the extreme cases are well known. The great instability of the Slavs, always ready to change their location, is proverbial; it creates considerable problems of economic organisation. Some people have seen in this trait the influence of the vast Eurasian plains, in which there are no physical features to suggest a permanent abode, and of the ancient custom of building wooden villages which, being so often burnt, provided no permanent fixture to hold the inhabitants.

In the United States the general mobility is just as much in evidence: at least one-fifth of the population moves in any one year and this rhythm of migration has been maintained almost unchanged for a century. Between 30 and 33 million people have changed their residence each year since the last war, and of these 5 million have crossed a state boundary. Before trying to unravel the lines of movement which make up this mobility, we should note that, here again, it is linked first with large expanses of physically uniform terrain, uncut by political boundaries, and secondly with an immigrant population which, concerned in the early stages with the pioneer development of new lands, has turned, after the colonising period, to the search for greater prosperity and a higher standard of living. There are even many who could be called 'professional' migrants— these are the 'hobos', generally unmarried, who number several hundred thousand and who range widely and continually, seeking one kind of a job after another.

In Western Germany, mobility reaches 6·2 per cent; it is most active over the shortest distances; 71 per cent of the removals are within a single *Land* and 29 per cent from one *Land* to another.

This general mobility corresponds in part, perhaps, to a predisposition which affects certain groups; undoubtedly it is more common amongst certain peoples, and within communities, amongst certain individuals, particularly those who like to take risks and those who love change for its own sake. A study has been made of the new arrivals in California, the state which lies furthest from the cradle of the Union and most remote from the shores of Europe, and yet is at present witnessing the most dynamic population growth. This showed that a large proportion had already failed in their first attempt to settle elsewhere, and many more had been in trouble with the police; in other words, they were not passive people. On the contrary, the 'poor whites' of the south-east are those who find themselves incapable of a readjustment, or of doing anything or going anywhere different—and the community tramples on them pitilessly. Within this general mobility there are also the more vigorous impulses and recognisable trends of movement, and for every one 'hobo' there are at least ten serious migrants for whom removal is a real necessity, such as officials, members of the public services or private businesses, and managers of branch establishments.

The major trends

This need to move is a response to what one might call the internal 'organisation' of the country in question. Depending on the stage of economic and demographic evolution reached, this organisation or development assumes different forms, both as regards the rural community itself and as regards the relations between country and town. It may happen at different stages in the general social evolution, and has in its turn its different stages, which may well exist side by side.

The lessons of history teach us that the development of rural settlement proceeds in three stages, first a progressive conquest, secondly, after the lapse of time, and in certain circumstances, a withdrawal, and thirdly and lastly a reoccupation. The relations between town and country are of infinite variety, however, and it is also possible to distinguish a phase of concentration and a subsequent period of reflux, or rather, of diffusion. In addition to this spatial classification there are other aspects to be considered, such as the volume and continuity of the movements, their parallelism or interference, and whether they are spontaneous and individual in character, or directed and collective.

A description of all the possible movements is beyond our scope; we merely propose to reveal the most striking and typical among them by a few characteristic examples, and to indicate the parts of the world in which their action is mainly observable.

MIGRATIONS IN RURAL AREAS

The conquest of new territories

When men are compelled to increase the extent of the lands which they occupy, either because of increasing numbers or increasing needs, they seek new territory wherever they can find it. If space is limited, and the best lands are already occupied, they go up into the mountains, or string out into remoter valleys. It was this kind of movement, in thirteenth-century Europe, which forced the mountaineers of the western Alps to cultivate higher and higher slopes; the same urge which made the early colonists of New England, continually increased in numbers by new arrivals and blocked in their westward expansion by the relief of the land and by Indians, infiltrate far into the interior valleys in what is now the north-eastern corner of the United States. In the plains, man turned to the reclamation of low-lying marshlands, and the Dutch, who became specialists in this work, were very much in demand for similar tasks in Poland, in Flanders and in the Vendée of western France, where there were coastal marshes to be conquered.

Such relatively small and hazardous conquests of terrain took place within a Europe already well peopled. On the contrary, in the new countries there were large chunks of continents on which the waves of immigrants could spend their force, surmounting huge physical obstacles and encountering only sporadically the previous occupants. In *North America* the picture of the pioneer fringe moving progressively westwards across the vast expanse of the Middle West is an impressive one. To the thirteen original states were added between 1783 and 1820 the seven states east of the Mississippi, plus Louisiana; between 1820and 1860 were added the remaining states bordering the Great Lakes and those covering the central plains. By 1850, 45 per cent of the inhabitants of the United States were located west of the Appalachians. The construction of transcontinental railways, and the accompanying grants of land, led to the creation of more new states and the penetration of colonisation to the Pacific coast; except for California and Oregon, already constituted as states around 1856–60, the remainder of western U.S.A. was not subdivided until after 1860. In 1910 the population of the Rocky Mountains and Pacific coast states was double what it was in 1860. Accompanying this spread of colonisation there were modifications of farming methods and of crops; the average size of land grants doubled between 1909 and 1916, for the dryness of the west compelled dry-farming and extensive grazing, whilst the great flour-milling centres followed the westward movement of cereal growing from Rochester in 1850 to Chicago and St Louis by 1890 and to St Paul, Minneapolis and Omaha at the present time. The population 'centre of gravity' lay east of Baltimore in 1790; by 1890 it was west of Cincinnati, and in 1960 it lay in central Illinois—noticeably moving along the same parallel of latitude. In

Canada, there has been a similar development of the economy of the
central plains and the progressive movement of people westwards;
but at the present time the trend is rather towards the north-east and
north-west, and it is the forest and cold zones that are submitting to
modern colonisation.

In *Latin America*, the best known example is the pioneer fringe of
São Paulo, where the spread of the agricultural conquest was linked
with unrestrained speculation in coffee. This culture, which exhausts
the soil and leads to devastating erosion, pushed the 'fazendeiros'
steadily westwards. Starting at Campinas about 1850, the plantations
have now gone beyond the limits of São Paulo state and have invaded northern Parana and southern Minas Geraes. New colonists
as well as migrants from the north-east of Brazil have taken part in
this conquest; more than 2 million immigrants entered the state of
São Paulo between 1870 and 1952, and round about the turn of the
century this same state was absorbing between one-half and two-
thirds of all the new immigrants into Brazil, whilst the number of
coffee bushes planted trebled in a few years. Few regions of South
America have experienced such a parallel expansion of population
and agriculture, but something of the same sort has occurred in
Antioquia (Colombia), in the central valley of Chile, in several fertile
valleys in southern Argentina, in the cotton plantations in northern
Argentina, and in recent colonisation of lower California (Mexico).
At the present time Brazil is trying to create new pioneer fringes; the
deforestation and creation of new cacao plantations in southern
Bahia, the development of new plantations around Brasilia and of
roads giving access thereto, and also the construction of great
highways across the Amazonian forest, with accompanying colonisation, are noteworthy examples.

In *Asia* the onward thrusts of colonisation are important. Even
Japan has had its pioneer fringe in the interior of its very restricted
islands, and rural migrations have taken place from the grossly over-
populated south-west towards the north-east where some utilisable
land was still available. The centre of gravity of the population has
moved from east of Kyoto in 1898 to a point in the north of Gifu pre-
fecture in 1947. The ultimate phase of this movement is the occupation of Hokkaido, which for centuries, had remained as the domain
of the Ainus, who were hostile to Japanese colonists. About 1800,
Hokkaido contained 20,000 Ainus and 30,000 Japanese; towards the
end of the nineteenth century there were still scarcely 60,000 colonists

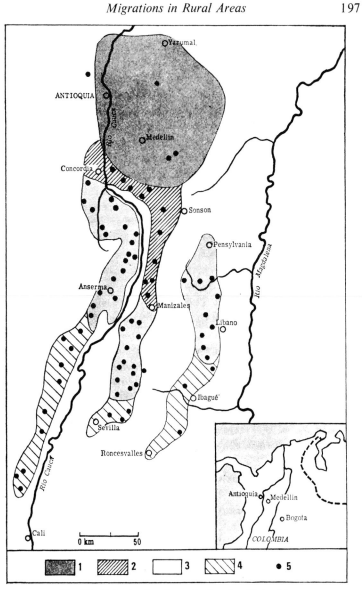

Fig. 28. Colonisation from Antioquian Colombia.

1. Limit of colonised area about 1790.   2. Area occupied between 1795 and 1850.   3. Area occupied 1850 to 1900.   4. Area occupied since 1900.   5. Black dots are locations of Antioquian colonial settlements.

and those mostly in the south-west, nearest to the Japanese mainland. But military colonisation, accompanied by a systematic exploration of resources, began in 1875, and the construction of a railway system aided economic progress, so that in 1901 the island had one million inhabitants and at the present day has nearly 5 million. Government projects aim at 6 million. There are still important areas of colonisable land, but the tractor-worked fields, the meadows and the apple orchards, confound the Japanese peasant, accustomed to swarming over rice-fields, and it has taken the years of misery following the second World War to stimulate the migratory movement once more.

In the heart of the great Asiatic continent, Central Asia is the field of conquest of the two great giants, the Soviets in Asiatic Russia and the Chinese on the fringes of their vast domain. In the Soviet Union there have been many pioneer fringes since the Revolution, for the area of land cultivated rose from 291 million acres in 1913 to 370 million in 1940, and by now may have reached 500 million acres. There has been expansion northwards into the European forest zone, and in central Asia the movement has been outwards from the black earth belt, to the north by deforestation and to the south by irrigation of the semi-arid lands. The greatest extension has been in the Kazakhstan republic, where the area of cultivated land increased by 412 per cent between 1913 and 1955; in this republic too there was the greatest population increase—51·4 per cent between 1940 and 1960. This conquest of central Asia is as much a technical as a human victory: between 1861 and 1913 the area sown in Siberia increased from 25 to 37 million acres thanks to 4 million new inhabitants, but in 1954–55, 75 million acres were cleared by powerful equipment operated by 550,000 trained workers.

There has not been the same kind of progress in the fringe territories of China. Chinese emigration into Manchuria began in the eighteenth century, preceded and accompanied by military operations for the protection of the colonists on the plain. On this north-eastern fringe the attraction was opium, not gold as elsewhere in the world. Progress was slow, and until 1925 scarcely 125,000 immigrants a year settled in the area; but between 1926 and 1928 the figure rose to half a million. Then pressure from the Russians, naturally anxious at such massive colonisation, the troubles of the war and the Japanese occupation, and infiltration from Korea, succeeded in paralysing the Chinese advance; but the colonisation has now been resumed under the new regime—a colonisation, as in the U.S.S.R., officially organised and directed, and paid for out of the public purse. So now the population, which in 1910 was only 15 million, is over 50 million and, of these 90 per cent are Chinese and only 2 per cent indigenous Manchus.

Similarly, in the neighbouring territory of inner Mongolia, the Chinese have been extending their peaceful penetration into the interior provinces of Si-Kiang and Tibet. It is all very systematic, and there are three types of migrants, workers, specialists and colonists; the first two prepare the basic necessities, especially communications, and the third cultivate the land. Travel expenses fall on the government, which also provides housing for the new arrivals. The colonists are mostly poor peasants from the most over-populated provinces (Hopei, Shantung); they are joined by the whole armies of young pioneers recruited from all regions and races of China, who help with the work of clearance and cultivation.

All these developments are of the recent past or are still in progress; they are continually increasing the area occupied by mankind. They take place over vast expanses, hitherto unoccupied or but sparsely peopled, and they have attracted millions of individuals drawn from many countries and sometimes over great distances; the fields of Ukraine and White Russia have contributed their quota to the peopling of Soviet Central Asia, and the Chinese deltas and river-lands have furnished colonists for the high semi-desert plateaus of the remote interior. Similarly there is a daily stream of migrants from the famine-ridden areas of north-east Brazil to the temperate south or the promised land of the unoccupied west. But in all such cases the peasant, though he may change his latitude, his culture and his tools, remains a peasant, tied to the land. It is simply a vast expansion of the rural way of life.

Similar phenomena, but on a much more limited scale, are found in small and densely-peopled countries. Here also the urge has been to reclaim unfertile ground, whilst the over-populated areas provide the new colonists. The marshy littoral and deltaic plains of Italy, thanks to complete reclamation, have become the seat of a new and intense colonisation. Thus, in the Maremma, 300,000 people have been settled, coming from the Po plain, the Adriatic coast, the mountains of Abruzzi and even from Sicily; the mountains of central Italy have exported their excess population to the shores of the Gulf of Taranto and the mountains of Sicily and Sardinia have peopled the reclaimed coastal plains of those islands. In North Africa a new peasantry has been installed in the alluvial plains as a result of river control; and the Egyptians have considerably increased the size of their oases after the completion of the new high dam across the Nile. In Israel, irrigation canals have enabled villages to be built even in the Negeb desert. In tropical Africa, there are plans for the creation of rice-fields on the Guinea coast and in the interior riverine lands; each increase means a few dozen or a few hundred more families transplanted to reap the new harvest. One could go on multiplying such examples.

Usually the transplantation, whether spontaneous or directed, brings some amelioration in the lot of the migrant, even though the journey and the initial stages may have been tough. The newly-cleared land allocated to him will be much larger than he had before, the dwelling more modern and more comfortable (though he may have to wait for it and there are still pioneer camps under canvas in Central Asia and Israel and hutments in the Brazilian pioneer fringe). But there is still the uprooting, and the home-sickness, so strong and painful amongst rural people; and there is much need for adaptation to the new environment.

In the present world, it is more often a question of development based on previous occupation rather than spreading out over vast expanses of fertile, empty land as was the case a hundred years ago when the American pioneers moved westwards. In the twentieth century 'conquest' has been achieved by a succession of technical victories which have enabled the empty spaces to be filled up, either, on the European model, by occupying the last tiny pieces of a continent already completely peopled, or in the Latin-American fashion, by the spreading of a thin skin of occupation from the coastal population clusters towards the still empty frontier zones of the interior. The extension of the habitable globe is now very limited; it proceeds by slow steps at the expense of the frozen wastes of the north, and by occasional bursts in the deserts or on the edge of the great forest belts.

The intensity of the effort expended in the development of new land is proportional to the extent of the need and the availability of immigrants, that is to say, the demographic pressure within the country in question. The U.S.S.R. is tenaciously striving to find new cereal-growing lands and to people them; the United States too, after subsidising its farmers to leave good soil fallow in order to avoid over-production. is now encouraging them to produce a surplus for export. Thus rural colonisation is still a living theme in the U.S.S.R., in China, in Africa, and Latin America; it is a thing of the past in Europe and the United States where there are merely transfers from one place to another.

Movements of withdrawal

In some areas the rural population is actually leaving the land. The regions most affected by this are the least hospitable, those whose occupation was only effected as a matter of necessity when population pressure made it essential to use every little corner of land, or—which comes to the same thing—when the poverty of the returns rendered essential the use of the largest possible area in order to get an adequate harvest.

Mountain areas are the first to be affected by this withdrawal, and this generalisation applies all over the globe. One can see it happening in southern China, where several mountain tribes from Yunnan have moved down to grow cotton in the neighbouring valleys (thereby tripling their income), and at the foot of the Andes in Colombia and Venezuela, where improvements in the Piedmont areas have permitted an appreciable agrarian colonisation by mountaineers from the upper valleys. In the United States, since the second half of the nineteenth century, the isolated interior valleys of New England have witnessed the abandonment of farms by a rural population tempted by the wide open spaces to the west or the industrial cities of the south. Depopulation is even affecting certain parts of the Rockies where, however, the numbers were never very great.

But it is in Europe that the abandonment of the mountains has been most marked, for it was in the European mountain areas that the growth of population in the course of centuries has been greater. A relief which was not repellent, and a situation in the heart of an old and densely-peopled continent, had favoured the establishment of farms, hamlets and valleys up to quite high altitudes. Often the mountain-dweller could only survive by having associations with the neighbouring plains; perhaps he would take his flocks down to winter pastures, or perhaps he migrated for part of the year to add to his income by hiring out his labour to the plains farmers or by acting as temporary chimney-sweep, charcoal burner or chestnut-man—and incidentally bringing a picturesque element into the winter life of the towns. With the development of modern economy such expedients became insufficient, and it is by abandoning the mountains, much against his will, that the high-altitude farmer has sought the remedy for his distress. Depopulation has been most rapid in countries where economic development has been most advanced. Thus in England, 1811 may be reckoned as the starting point, and the movement accelerated after 1861, and is still going on. In France it is the 1841 census that shows the greatest populations in the Alps and Central Massif. In Austria and Italy the growth of mountain population went on right up to the end of the nineteenth century and even into the twentieth; the exodus from the Apennines and the Dinaric Alps scarcely began until after 1920, and in the mountains at the extreme south of the Iberian peninsula and of southern Italy, whether continental or insular, the increasing control over slopes, the new terraces that one sees south of Naples, and the glaring white villages

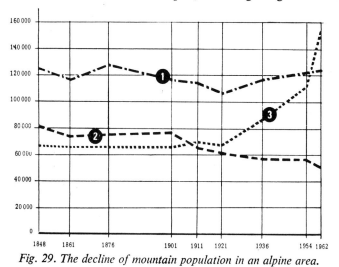

Fig. 29. The decline of mountain population in an alpine area.
1. Population of foreland. 2. Population of mountains. 3. Population of major valleys (From P. Guichonnet in *Rev. de géographie alpine.* 1963.)

at 3,000 ft on the flanks of the Sierra Nevada, show that these regions are still full of vitality.

The movement can be translated into figures: about 50 per cent of the population of the French Alps has left within the last hundred years, and actually more than 60 per cent in Bauges and the Briançon region; the Cevennes have lost almost three-quarters of their inhabitants since the beginning of the present century, and the Scottish Highlands have lost nearly one-half. This of course is reflected in the landscape, in abandoned terraces, waste lands within the dry-stone walls which were once field boundaries, and ruined villages. In the poorest and most isolated districts, even the almost complete depopulation has not permitted those who remain to find a new economic equilibrium; the withdrawal will only cease with the death of the last survivor. On the other hand, in lower valleys, richer and more accessible, an improved economy has been developed, often by the use of other resources; thus in the northern French Alps, tourism and industry have helped to restore part of the rural population.

Mountains are not the only areas to be affected by depopulation; in many countries the cultivated plains show the same thing. Indeed statistics show that the rural proportion of the total population is diminishing the world over. But we must distinguish between very prolific countries in which migration diminishes the proportion without lowering the actual total of the rural population, and those countries with but little population growth, in which the withdrawals are of long standing and result in an actual dimunition in the numbers of rural dwellers so great that it is sometimes spoken of as a veritable rural exodus or 'flight from the countryside'. Poor and remote areas are especially affected, but so also are those served by good transport media, for the temptation which is daily present ends by being too great, thus favouring migration.

The rural dwellers who abandon their fields turn either to the towns —and we shall examine their case later on—or to other rural areas. In the old countries of Europe, the peasants generally quit the over-populated rural areas—over-populated, that is, bearing in mind the technical possibilities of land use and the financial requirements of the present generation. Those who go are generally the younger ones, aged twenty to twenty-five, and most of them go to the towns and to other occupations. In the new lands, the attraction of new crops, or new clearings, and the general expansion of rural colonisation can also cause extensive rural migration even though conditions in the originating area do not really require it.

Movements of re-occupation

It may happen that, after a cycle of occupation which ends with abandonment, the evolution of a rural area may begin all over again. A new cycle may begin, a reconquest of the agricultural area. This new phase is generally less spontaneous than the earlier one; it may be due either to large landowners being desirous of rehabilitating their lands and introducing more careful exploitation, or to the enterprise of public bodies which, within the framework of a more or less consistent policy of land reclamation, are engaged in preventing the extinction of abandoned areas.

We have already referred to the ravages wrought by the westward movement of the São Paulo coffee belt, leaving behind it exhausted soils and abandoned farms; now, as a result of a determined effort of private recolonisation, a new wave of coffee culture has commenced, in the same areas, founded this time on soil-conserving methods, and bringing with it a new stratum of population. In France, a large fertile area in the centre of the Aquitaine Basin has been largely abandoned by its inhabitants; this happened for the first time towards the end of the nineteenth century, and more or less spontaneously the gaps were filled by peasants from the Central Massif and Brittany; the second recession was after the first World War, when as a result of the cruel losses suffered therein by the adult male population, whole villages found themselves peopled only by women, children and old folk. To remedy this situation, Italian colonists under contract were installed in new villages, with their own school-teachers and their own priests, amongst the French population. The second World War brought this experiment to ruin and left the land abandoned again; and a third phase of recolonisation has now started, largely by the transfer of peasants from Brittany, whose own holdings in their native villages were too small to be economic, and who accepted the much larger farms offered by the Ministry of Agriculture in Aquitaine. These Bretons are generally couples aged forty to forty-five, with several grown-up children, who could not possibly live on the income from their small-holdings and who were prepared to 'exile' themselves; the departure is especially distressing for the women-folk, who leave behind their relatives and their buried forbears. However, such rural migrations or transfers have assumed some importance in recent years, and the same sort of thing has occurred with Bretons being moved to the south-eastern part of the Paris Basin, which was also under-peopled in relation to its productive capacity. More recently still, yet another wave of rehabilitation is taking place in Aquitaine, by repatriates from North Africa, first from Morocco and then from Algeria; these enterprising landowners who ran big modern farms on the other side of the Mediterranean have bought large tracts of land and may well transform the rural landscape of these areas, whose economic viability has been precarious.

Sometimes there is a longer interval between the first period of settlement and the second; such is the case in Syria, in the region around Homs, where the peasants are extending their fields in areas which were once irrigated by the Roman colonists; when digging the soil they come across traces in the form of water intakes and canals, and they are making use of them again.

Thus the sudden departures and the long migrations of rural people, as well as the less perceptible trudging which carries them over shorter distances, help to modify the equilibrium of the countryside. They are movements very difficult to define with statistical precision, which go here and there within a complex world of their own, without the bursting energy and precision of destination of movements from the country to the town.

URBANISATION

This is the most powerful movement of modern times; it began a century and a half ago, and with the growth of transport media it has reached almost overwhelming proportions during the last hundred years. It has boiled up and swelled, and far from being arrested, it is being amplified as time goes on. Large cities are becoming gigantic, and new centres are being created everywhere (see Plate 29).

There seems to be no limit to the rising proportion of town-dwellers; it has reached 87 per cent in Belgium, 86 per cent in Australia, 73·5 per cent in the United States. In France it rose from 46·4 per cent in 1921 to 70 per cent in 1968, and in the U.S.S.R. from 17·9 per cent in 1926 to 60 per cent in 1975; in South Africa, from 25·1 in 1921 to 48 in 1971, and in Japan from 21·7 in 1925 to 52 per cent in 1970. On the contrary, the growth is relatively insignificant in countries already highly urbanised; in England and Wales the percentage of town-dwellers was already 77 per cent in 1901, and it had only risen to 80.7 per cent by 1961.

Attraction of new industrial areas

The first movement of this kind was directly due to the transformation of modern technical civilisation which began with the Industrial Revolution of the late eighteenth century, with its exploitation of coal-fields and development of machines which concentrated into factories the work formerly done by dozens of scattered craftsmen. Large cities did of course already exist—we can discuss their growth later on—but now it was a case of many local centres attracting labour from the surrounding countryside, thus leading to the clusters of small and specialised towns, each with its agglomeration of workers' houses, that characterise the settlement pattern of the older European industrial areas. The initial attraction due to proximity was reinforced by the development of modern means of transport, and migrants came from further afield. The more important towns stood out from the network of settlements, and the whole assemblage constituted an area of high population density which one might almost call an urban rash. Such is the northern French coal-field, in Nord and Pas-de-Calais, where there are over a hundred places with over 3,000 inhabitants and thirty towns with over 10,000, all within an area 120 km long and 11 to 16 km wide; the average density is over 1,000 to the square kilometre. And yet before 1780 there was nothing to distinguish this area from the surrounding agricultural districts.

These industrial zones no longer grow only by attracting labour from rural areas within the same country; they go further afield, beyond the political frontiers. Thus the Ruhr gets miners even from southern Italy. They are also characterised by considerable transfers of labour, for example the migratory metal-workers, miners and building workers in Western Germany, or the miners from the closed collieries of the Cevennes who were moved to the iron mines of Lorraine.

Such zones characterise all the world's great industrialised countries; they are generally associated with two different types of industries, first those based on mineral fields with a scattering of mines and of industries based thereon, and secondly those which were established before the modern period of intense concentration, such as the traditionally scattered textile industries, e.g. of Lancashire and Yorkshire, and southern New England.

In new countries the same phenomenon is in course of development: the mining and metallurgical districts of central India and of China are having wide repercussions on the surrounding rural areas, the more so since mechanisation is in an embryonic state. In the Damodar coal basin, the population increased by 117 per cent in fifteen years, as against a mere 57 per cent increase in the surrounding regions. In the mining areas of Africa it is the same; on the Jos plateau in Nigeria the tin mines, exploited since 1905, have attracted a large population including 44 per cent from outside the district. So the migratory movements which took place in Europe in the early nineteenth century are being repeated a century and a half later.

We may contrast with this attraction by widespread industry the temporary recruitment which is necessary for great public works. Even in well-developed countries, the construction, for example, of a great dam needs the concentration of considerable manpower for a certain period; the Donzère-Mondragon scheme on the Rhone required 5,000 men for five years, and a small town had to be built to accommodate them. In France the greater part of this temporary labour is recruited from amongst the mobile workers of North Africa and Italy. In India, where such construction is still done using men and women as beasts of burden to carry stone, etc. the labour requirements are even greater; the employees usually come from the adjacent areas, but often, after the job is finished, do not go back to their fields, and having been once uprooted, migrate to other construction works or seek new employment in some town. Such a transformation of whole areas into gigantic workshops—a phenomenon particularly characteristic of present-day China—contributes a great deal towards the de-ruralisation of the population.

Urban concentration

Within the different countries of the world and throughout history, complex organisations have developed to carry on certain vital economic functions, and very few countries have been without them. Central Africa is almost alone in its lack of any spontaneous urban life worthy of the name. Great cities existed even in ancient times, despite the absence of mass transport media, and though we can only guess at their populations, better known examples of later date give some idea of the size attained by certain urban agglomerations before the railway age. Thus Paris had 498,000 inhabitants at the time of Louis XIV, and 518,000 in the reign of Napoleon I; during a century it had changed little, but fifty years later, in 1860, it passed the million mark (the first French railway dates from 1835). During the same period London, which had little more than half a million inhabitants at the end of the seventeenth century, grew, within the present County limits, to 959,300 in 1801, and the urban area reached 2,362,000 at the census of 1861.

It is thus from the first half of the nineteenth century that we can date the great extension of urbanisation; and we may note at once that its roots lay in the absorption of a large part of the excess rural population. Of themselves, the urban agglomerations have but a slow natural growth, and the greater part of their development is due to the continuing influx of migrants from the rural areas. In Brazil, between 1940 and 1950, the growth of the eight major cities was 12 per cent by natural excess of births over deaths, and 28·7 per cent by migration; for the lesser towns, down to a limit of 5,000 inhabitants, the figures were 18·2 and 17·3 per cent respectively. During the years 1950–65, Greater Paris has grown at a rate twice that of the remainder of France, half by excess of births and half by immigration. In West Germany, the communes with less than 2,000 people have lost 16·7 per cent of their population by emigration, whilst the towns of more than 100,000 inhabitants gained 8·7 per cent by immigration; the currents of migration are directed more towards some areas than others, and whereas the Rhine-Palatinate area gained 20·4 per cent, Hamburg gained only 3·9 per cent.

These migrations have gone on to such an extent that the proportion of urban population is now over four-fifths in England and Wales, in Belgium, Iceland, Sweden, New Zealand, Australia, Israel and Denmark, and more than three-quarters in Venezuela, U.S.A., Canada, Chile, Netherlands, East Germany and Austria. Even within a single country, however, the urban growth is not uniform in all classes of towns. Disregarding exceptional cases which may be due to particular favouring circumstances of longer or shorter duration, we may point out several general features.

The very great cities, after considerable growth on their own, become surrounded by larger and larger agglomerations. The 'urban region' of New York now contains 16,207,000 inhabitants, and has increased by 3 million in the last thirty years; that of Tokyo has 11,161,000 people and, despite the serious effects of the war, a growth of 4 million during the same period; Greater London has more than 10 million and the 'Paris district' almost 10. Moscow and Shanghai, within their city boundaries, already have 7,051,000 and 10,700,000 inhabitants respectively. And one could go on adding such monstrosities as Los Angeles, whose urban zone incorporates 8,351,000 people, an increase of 156 per cent since 1940.

Side by side with these giants there is a host of medium-sized towns. If we consider only those with over 100,000 inhabitants and for which there are reasonably satisfactory statistics, we can estimate their number throughout the world as 2,900. But this total is growing at an amazing speed: in the United States there were 68 such towns in 1920 and 245 in 1970, in France 15 and 53 respectively, and in Brazil 6 in 1920, 11 in 1940 and 87 in 1970. Parallel with this growth in numbers is their increasing importance relative to the national population; in Brazil, during the period named above, the proportion of people living in towns of over 100,000 rose from 8·7 to 30·2 per cent; in the Soviet Union, between 1926 and 1973, the increase was from 31 towns of over 100,000, representing 6·5 per cent of the total population, to 238 towns and 34 per cent.

In the older countries, the towns which are now growing have all existed for centuries, sometimes as cities, but sometimes also merely as large villages which undergo spectacular expansion. It also happens that certain elements in the old pattern remain untouched by modern growth, and one can find small provincial towns, celebrated perhaps for a short period of history, which now sleep peacefully around their old castle. But in the newer countries where wide open spaces have but recently been occupied and resources developed (e.g. in the colonized areas where a new external administration had been established), streams of migrants from many directions have converged to create new artificial nuclei of urban life in a few short years.

The astonishing development of new large towns in the U.S.S.R. referred to above contains many examples of this kind, such as Komsomolsk, on the Amur, created in 1932 and now with a population of 234,000. In each mining area, amongst the huge industrial plants and the newly reclaimed lands, new towns are developing day by day. It is in Kazakhstan, the region where the opening up of new lands has been most extensive, that urban life has also developed to the greatest extent, for the urban population has grown from 8·4 per cent in 1926 to 58 per cent at the present time, and the capital city, Alma-Ata, from 45,000 to 813,000 inhabitants. Urban development within the U.S.S.R. has been greatest in Asia, but it is the countryside of the west, traditionally rural, that has supplied the migrants. This movement is not only recent, for in the Tsarist period voluntary or forced migration to Siberia, Turkestan and Kazakhstan was already established. Between 1906 and 1909, more than 5,000 colonists a year made the journey, and another 200,000 up to 1913. In 1860, Siberia had 3 million European inhabitants, in 1941, 9,500,000. The Soviets have stepped up this eastward movement; between 1925 and 1929, agrarian reform uprooted 1,100,000 peasants from European Russia, of whom 22 per cent were from the Ukraine, 16 per cent from the central black-earth belt, 15 per cent from the Middle Volga, 15 per cent from White Russia and 11 per cent from the western regions. Between 1925 and 1939, some 5 to 7 million were transferred, more or less voluntarily, over the same eastward routes, and strategic and technical developments during and after the war have strengthened this flow. According to the 1970 Census, European Russians have swarmed east of the Urals, so that they now form 30 per cent of the population of the Kirghiz Republic and 43 per cent of that of Kazakhia. Between 1939 and 1970, the population of White Russia only increased by 4 per cent, and that of Ukraine by 21 per cent, while the whole U.S.S.R. increased by 32·3 per cent, eastern Siberia by 40 per cent and Central Asia and the Far East by even greater proportions. It is in this last region, on the eastern edges of Soviet territory, where colonisation has been most complete, that one finds the highest percentage of urban population (80 per cent) and 90 per cent of the inhabitants of these new towns have been transplanted from the towns and countryside of European Russia to the Pacific coast.

The intense urbanisation of the Soviet Far East is not peculiar to that area. It is a phenomenon common to all areas recently colonised by advanced Europeans. It is noteworthy that the proportion of urban population in Australia is almost as high (80·8 per cent) as in the United Kingdom; and in California, which represents the greatest area of modern colonisation in the U.S.A., since its population more than doubled between 1940 and 1960, the urban proportion is 93 per cent. It is towards the great cities of California that the waves of immigrants converge, whether they be farmers uprooted from the central plains by climatic accidents or unwise land speculation, or enterprising town-dwellers from the central and eastern states attracted by the dynamic economy of the Pacific coast.

Another good example of the powerful attraction exercised by these new urban nuclei is Brasilia, the new capital of Brazil, towards which the mad rush of men and women from all parts of the country is of epic proportions. Here there were 6,000 inhabitants at the end of 1956, and three years later, ten times as many. By 1976 there were 700,000—and twenty years previously the whole area was completely empty! Arriving on foot, by lorry, through forest and steppe, along endless tracks, people from all corners of Brazil have come to live in their new capital; true, 23 per cent of them are from the state of Goiaz, and about 20 per cent from neighbouring Minas Geraes, but one-quarter are from the remote and neglected north-east and the remainder from all over the country, even from the prosperous São Paulo region. The attractive power of towns is clearly not always proportional to their economic potentialities, and paradoxically one could almost say that they were more alluring if they are situated in neglected or poverty-stricken regions, even though their façades simply hide another form of misery. Thus Recife, on the edge of the dry and famine-ridden north-eastern area, is the Brazilian city which owes most of its growth (actually 75·8 per cent) to migration; and it expanded by 140 per cent between 1940 and 1960. Its neighbour, Salvador, which has a similar pattern of growth and which gained 240,000 extra inhabitants in the last ten years, could only provide 5,000 new industrial jobs during that period.

In the same way, the inhabitants of the inhospitable Apennines quit their villages in large numbers (375,000 between 1952 and 1958) for the neighbouring towns of southern Italy which are quite incapable of offering them employment, since the inhabitants of these same towns migrate either abroad or to the industrial cities of northern Italy.

The reader will retain, from the preceding pages, some impression of the power of fascination which towns exercise over the rural population and over the inhabitants of smaller towns. Individual migrations often consist of successive removals, from the countryside to the small neighbouring town and from thence to the local metropolis. In the United Sates migrations from town to town are actually one-and-a-half times as numerous as those from rural areas to towns. At Kisangani, in Zaire, only one-third of the new arrivals are first-stage migrants, and they mostly, especially the women, have someone to go to.

The example of three French towns illustrates the variability of this process of urban recruitment. *Arras* is a centre of historic importance but is now somewhat static; it is the centre of a rich agricultural district but just outside the main northern industrial area. It has less than 40,000 inhabitants, of whom only 27·5 per cent were born there, but two-thirds of whom came from the *département*, that is from the surrounding district; the rest came mainly from the densely populated industrial regions of Nord and Seine, and altogether nine-tenths of the inhabitants were born within less than 100 km of Arras. *Le Mans*, a major town of western France, is in the throes of considerable demographic and industrial expansion. It has 184,800 inhabitants more than three-quarters of whom were born outside the town;

half the immigrants are from the Sarthe *département* but recruitment has come from all the *départements* within a radius of 200 km, and also from Seine. In the case of the great metropolis, *Paris*, the recruitment is much more diverse: 45 per cent of the inhabitants are Parisian by birth and 44 per cent provincial, but the remaining 11 per cent came from beyond the French frontier. Of the migrants from the French provinces, most come, naturally enough, from the *département* of Seine-et-Oise which encircles the city (76·2 per thousand), but

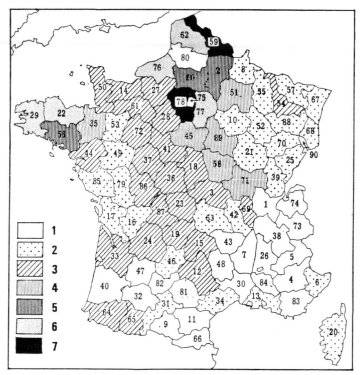

Fig. 30. Origins of the population of Paris.

Numbers per thousand of the population of the *départements* of Seine originating in the various *départements* of France, in 1954.

1. Less than 5 per thousand.   2. 5 to 10.   3. 10 to 15.   4. 15 to 20.
5. 20 to 25.   6. 25 to 35.   7. More than 35 per thousand. The figures which help to identify each *département* are those used for vehicle registration.

(From 'Paris 1960', issued to mark the centenary of the Statistical Society of Paris.)

quite distant *départements* come next on the list, like Nord (250 km distant, with 43·1 per thousand), Seine Maritime (also 250 km distant, with 29·6 per thousand) and the *départements* of Brittany (500 km distant, with 75 per thousand). All the *départements* of France, in fact, except those of the far south-west and south-east, have large contingents within the capital city.

Urban de-concentration

We may well ask what limit there is to the attractive power exercised by towns over individual men and women. Looking at the crude figures, it would seem to be infinite, but if we pause to examine the matter in detail we may be drawn towards two conclusions, one statistical and the other spatial.

A scrutiny of statistical information for the interior subdivisions of a great city shows one main characteristic, that the central zone tends to remain stable or to become depopulated whilst the total population continues to grow. This is indeed a general rule throughout the world. The matter becomes clearer when we draw our second conclusion, for if the growth figures are mapped, we see at once that population growth takes place in concentric belts and the older and larger the original nucleus, the further out are the growth rings.

London provides a remarkable example of both these trends. The depopulation of the centre began as early as the nineteenth century, and the 'City' housed 128,129 people in 1801, 50,569 in 1851, 10,999 in 1931 and only 4,771 in 1961. All the central districts are affected, and even London County itself ceased to grow after 1931, and has in fact suffered a decline of 20 per cent, for to the normal outflow was added the wartime destruction; on the contrary, the outer ring is still in full growth, but getting further and further from the city—and even the area known as 'Greater London' lost 0·21 per cent between 1951 and 1961. The zone of greatest growth is now outside the limits of Greater London, and nine out of the ten English counties with the greatest population growth between 1931 and 1961 are located within commuting distance of London; the growth in these counties was actually 20 per cent in the decade 1951–61. What does this sort of thing mean? Simply that people are being pushed out from the centre of great cities by congestion, overcrowding, less healthy conditions and the competition of other types of building—administrative, commercial and industrial; on the other hand, improved transport facilities and the taste for a quiet suburban residence have encouraged citizens to spread out into the country around the great cities—a spread which has its consequence, of course, in the daily journey to work, which we shall study later on.

Let us note simply that this reversal of urban concentration may lead to an almost infinite extension of the world's great conurbations, which extend their tentacles along the lines of rail and road transport. The countryside is invaded, step by step, by a gigantic collection of building lots, and agricultural land is swallowed up. In the United Kingdom, whose citizens have an irrepressible urge to have an individual house and garden, the situation is indeed frightening. It has been estimated that to house all the urban population in this fashion would necessitate the sacrifice of an area equal to 10 per cent of all the existing cultivated land, and that at the end of the operation one-sixth of the English Lowland would be covered with houses—for most people naturally have no wish to go and live in the mountains or other inhospitable areas.

This spreading-out of urban areas is the result of a twofold migratory movement, on the one hand, of newcomers who install themselves in the peripheral zones where they find living cheaper and the conditions not too different from those in their home area, and on the other hand, and in much greater numbers (as has been shown by enquiries in the Paris region), of town-dwellers who move out from the dark, overcrowded and often unhealthy houses of the inner zones to modern dwellings on the outskirts. These latter are generally families with children, who have outgrown their tiny apartments in the centre of the city, and are happy enough to have more space, even at the price of being further out. Numerous other examples could be cited of this 'inverse migration'. In the United States, out of 6·9 million white migrants into suburban areas between 1940 and 1950, 3·3 million came from the inner zones of towns and 3·6 from rural areas.

It often happens that, outside the great cities, domestic building takes place in the territory of rural districts, and the inhabitants are thus classed in the census as 'rural'. It is this fact which explains the considerable differences that one finds between the numbers classed as farmers or farm-workers and the total rural population. This distinction is carefully made in the statistics of the U.S.A. Between 1960 and 1970 there occurred a veritable explosion of suburbs, which now contain more people than the city centres or the rural zones, and are still expanding rapidly:

	1958	*1970*
	(per cent)	
Urban population	61·2	73·5
Rural population, total	38·8	26·5
Rural population, non-agricultural	27·0	22·8
Rural population, agricultural	11·8	3·7

1958 from D. J. Bogue, *The population of the United States*, p. 27; 1970 from U.S. Census.

The decade 1950–60 thus broke all records for 'suburbanisation', that is, in the American sense, the overflow of people outside the zones hitherto defined as 'urban'.

The phenomenon of de-concentration can also take on another aspect, that is, of ordered and controlled migrations such as those developed of late in Great Britain, in which groups of people from particular localities, rather than individual families, are moved into the 'New Towns' or into 'Expanded Towns' (provincial towns that have agreed, more or less willingly, to accept the 'overspill' from the great cities). Both types are employed simultaneously in the process of de-congestion; Glasgow for example has the New Towns of East Kilbride and Cumbernauld, situated some 20 to 25 km from the city and capable of taking 100–150,000 people, and also thirty-two other Scottish towns which have agreed to accept its surplus population; these latter are situated all over Scotland, from Inverness to Berwick. The 'overspill'—voluntary migrants in an epoch when everything is planned—has been re-housed in new quarters and found work in specially constructed local factories. Thus, according to the plan for de-congestion, 300,000 people, or nearly one-third of Glasgow's population, have taken part in these migrations. The same solution has been applied to the problem of London and certain other great cities (Birmingham, Liverpool, Manchester). In a slightly different form it is found also in the policy of 'industrial decentralisation' which has been operating in the Paris region since 1950. It has even spread as far as Shanghai, a city much preoccupied with inner congestion and rural immigration; here a systematic de-concentration is envisaged, with the withdrawal of part of the inhabitants into the peripheral zones.

Thus, in sum, the congestion of people in cities, having reached its limit, is followed by a paroxysmal eruption, and some of the urban dwellers return to the countryside—but under very different conditions.

Migration of retired people.

At the end of their active working life, many people seek, for their declining years, a more peaceful environment, better economic conditions and a less rigorous climate than those of the localities in which they were obliged to live whilst earning their living. This is essentially the idea of people living in the economically rich countries, and it is only opposed by the desire not to break with the familiar round and not to go too far from the grown-up children who have settled nearby. However, even in poor and underdeveloped countries there are retired army officers and pensioned officials who return to the place of their birth.

In France, where so many city-dwellers have strong and recent connections with their birth-place, it is often towards this, be it village or small town, that they turn for their retirement. Thus in the French statistics one finds that in many provincial areas there is a large proportion of people from the Paris region; this is the case with the Central Massif and Brittany and many other *départements* within a wide radius of the capital; this apparent anomaly has no other origin. It is accompanied by the presence, in certain areas, of retired peoples' villas or converted family houses. More generally, however, it is the climatically favoured areas that attract old people; in the United Kingdom the whole of southern England, but especially the coasts of Kent and Sussex, Devon and Cornwall, fulfil this role; in the United States it is Florida which appears in this respect to be an annex of the great cities of the east, whereas more distant California is subject to a rather less intense pressure. In France, the Côte d'Azur is an international retreat where wealthy retired people from almost every country in central and northern Europe have gathered, as well as many French people, mostly Parisians.

Population movements and economic evolution

Having reviewed in turn most of the various forms of migration or uni-directional movement, both within the international sphere and in the more restricted but equally varied medium of individual countries, we may put forward two conclusions.

The first is that the greatest, most widespread and most complex movements originate in countries where deep changes of any kind affect the lives of men. In a traditionally rural society, the individuals move but little and their displacements are mainly guided by a vague urge towards the town. In communities that are better-informed or disturbed by economic transformation, more important movements begin, with precise but often contradictory objects; no one is completely satisfied and settled, and often the government itself organises systematic compensatory movements to counteract past or present voluntary migration. One movement brings others in its train. Witness the case of western Germany, where a migration rate of 5·2 per cent for the indigenous population compares with 9·2 per cent for the refugees, that is those who have already suffered one uprooting.

The second is that migrations create much greater upheavals in human life when the migrants come from countries with primitive economies where material contrasts are great. In the nineteenth century a migrant across the ocean faced an often tragic adventure, but nowadays more often than not he simply fits into a pre-existing pattern. In new countries where progress is rapid, the rural dwellers abandon their fields for the newly-cleared areas or the growing towns, as in the U.S.S.R. In old-established countries, migration is mostly between similar environments; in the U.S.A. 32·5 per cent of the removals are from one town to another and only 6·8 per cent represent transfers of agriculturists to the towns. In other words, in more advanced countries, though migration may still involve large numbers, it generally involves no change in the fundamental mode of life.

It is therefore very difficult to describe in a few pages all the complex migratory movements, which vary so much from one country to another, and the few examples quoted in this chapter can only give but a slight idea of this inexhaustible variety.

CHAPTER TEN

The Causes and Consequences of Migration

Whether migration takes place over long distances or short, whether it involves a few hundred or several millions of individuals, it ends in all cases by transforming both the area of origin and the area of reception, and sometimes also by modifying not only the migrants' way of life but also their very metabolism and their mentality. It is indeed not without some profound motive that a human being can undertake such an adventure, and through the many currents of migration that we have attempted to trace, certain common incentives can be discerned.

THE CAUSES OF MIGRATION

At the commencement of a study of the causes of migration, one word—'dissatisfaction'—might almost be a sufficient explanation, for it is this which leads people to seek something else, and often it is no more than a hankering after something new, the vagueness of which is part of its attraction. Many are the people who would never have migrated had they known more clearly what was waiting for them at the end of the road!

In studies of migration the accent has generally been placed on the incentive provided by dissatisfaction with one's economic lot, and indeed most writers would regard this as the essential motivation. It seems, however, difficult to accept such a categorical assertion, for psychological factors play a considerable and often vital part, and in any case, even in a decision urged by precise economic facts, one finds also some other aspect, of which the subject was perhaps himself barely conscious, but which played its part at the final moment of choice. We should not of course try to isolate these two factors, economic and psychological, but on the contrary should be at some pains to show their intimate interpenetration.

Absolute poverty

The prime cause of migration is absolute poverty, from which man flees, driven by the simple urge to survive. In such circumstances a sudden accident which upsets an already precarious equilibrium has much greater and more rapid effect than perpetual gnawing hunger, which dulls the spirit of reaction. One can speak of adaptation to poverty, and many underdeveloped countries are at this stage, but it is not possible to speak of adaptation to a famine or to an epidemic.

The tragic history of Ireland in the mid-nineteenth century illustrates both cases perfectly. Two series of events brought an insupportable surfeit of poverty to a population which had been growing since 1770 and which lived extremely frugally, at subsistence level, on milk and potatoes. In 1793, an electoral law induced the large landowners to subdivide their lands into very small parcels in order to increase the number of their political supporters; this was followed in 1829 by a reform which quintupled the value of land required per elector, and thus provoked the eviction of many small tenants, who had no alternative but to become miserable day-labourers or else to swell the ranks of the beggars or make the first moves towards emigration. It was into this situation of barely concealed poverty that the second event, the potato blight of 1845, irrupted. By depriving the island of its essential food, this created a frightful famine, with 750,000 recorded deaths; and the non-arrival of any outside help prompted the survivors to rush for the ports to seek any boat which would take them elsewhere. Some went to neighbouring Great Britain, others to far-off United States, which looked aghast at these armies of grey and starving spectres; one out of six of these emigrants died at sea or soon after their arrival.

The remarkable thing about the Irish emigration, however, is that after its paroxysmal beginning resulting from the tragic circumstances which affected the island, it did not cease when a more stable economic equilibrium was re-established, but has continued with greater or less intensity right up to the present day; this is perhaps a good example of movements which were initially prompted by purely economic causes but have gone on for psychological motives.

One can trace to the same cause of absolute poverty many of the present-day migrations in Africa, in Latin America and in Asia. A study made recently of immigrants newly arrived in Salvador, in north-eastern Brazil, showed the state of despair that afflicted them. In reply to the question 'Why did you come here?' the reply in four-fifths of the cases was 'I had no work'. The annual and seasonal curves of the intensity of immigration into the cities of north-eastern

Brazil show an upward trend in dry years, when the whole north-east, being even more inhospitable than usual, is evacuated, and entire families are found sleeping in the streets of Recife, chased there by the spectre of famine; and also, during each year, at the time of the dry season when agricultural unemployment is widespread and the gap between harvests is difficult to fill for those who have no credit balance.

Regarding this state of absolute poverty, then, one can draw two conclusions, first that the slightest aggravation can trigger off migration, and secondly that the only brakes on a more general movement of emigration are the apathy and acceptance of misery which characterise most communities in this condition. The passive resignation of the Indians of the High Andes, which has struck all observers, is a trait found, more or less marked, in many other peoples.

The destruction of the established economic equilibrium

Of quite a different type are the migrations which have uprooted Europeans for more than a century, carrying them either across the oceans to the New World or causing them to abandon their fields for the towns or for other regions. An economic equilibrium was already established in Europe at the beginning of this period, based upon agriculture and rural crafts. It was the development of factory industry and of new means of transport that upset this equilibrium, which had engendered a certain distribution of population.

Here, too, the vagaries of agrarian legislation enter into the picture, such as the many enclosure Acts which affected certain parts of the United Kingdom, and especially the enclosure of common lands in 1801; these aggravated the lot of the poor peasant, who was forced to face ruin and the abandonment of his land. Thus was constituted a rural proletariat, uprooted and ready to seek a new life either in the towns or abroad. Two other contemporary events also had their repercussions on a society already severely shaken. The first was the end of the period of artificial prosperity which had accompanied the Napoleonic wars, and the second was the Industrial Revolution, roughly between 1760 and 1830 (during which period the population doubled, the production of coal and iron quadrupled, and the consumption of raw cotton rose from 8,000 to 100,000 tons). To the dispossessed peasants were added the ruined artisans, and by the end of Victoria's reign the only village craftsman left was the blacksmith. Under these circumstances all those who could do so cleared out;

and they were not the poor and incompetent, but those who were worth 'from £200 to £2,000', that is, a large proportion of those whose means of livelihood had been destroyed by the revolution.

Something similar happened in the Alpine valleys and in the textile-working countryside of Picardy, in France; the craftsmen, ruined by the competition of the industrial products emanating from the newly established factories, which attracted a hitherto scattered manpower from the countryside to the towns, were the first to quit their native villages. Later, the introduction of mechanisation into farming displaced agricultural workers, who found themselves superfluous. So rural depopulation proceeded by stages, corresponding first to the disappearance of the village craftsmen and then to the replacement of an increasing number of farm labourers by machines. Finally, in the evolution of the European countryside there has come the necessity for raising the standard of living in parallel with that of the town workers; a new transformation has begun, with the regrouping of holdings to produce economically viable farms, and this displacement of small proprietors has produced yet another contingent of rural migrants. This is especially noticeable in France, by reason of the survival there until recent years of a very large peasant class.

Other examples can be quoted of breaks in the equilibrium of modern economic systems, which are followed by new waves of emigration. When the soils of the United States 'dust bowl' were blown away by the wind, and banks and syndicates bought up immense areas of land, the ruined and dispossessed farmers of Oklahoma and Arkansas evacuated themselves to the orchards, the irrigated lands, and the cities of the new 'promised land' of California. The lack of vitality in the traditional industries of New England, and especially in the outmoded textile mills, has provoked the departure of 150,000 industrial workers since the end of the war, despite recent efforts to develop new and active industries.

In India, the demographic upsurge of recent years has created an unbearable over-population of rural areas, and many have therefore quitted the villages, notably the Brahmans, who are the ground landlords. In the environs of Madras, one-quarter of the families of the village of Dusi were Brahmans, but these represented two-fifths of the emigrants. This shows once again that it is not always the poorest and most depressed classes who migrate, but on the contrary those who have the ability to adapt and convert themselves to new circumstances.

Repulsive and attractive forces

This is the second aspect of migration: a cause of departure is not in itself sufficient, there must also be something to attract the emigrants. This factor of attraction may be real or imaginary, and it is here again that the economic and psychological aspects mingle; the appeal of the town may correspond to a reality, meaning less arduous labour, more regular wages and an improved living standard—but it often happens that this is simply a mirage, and the real thing is simply another form of struggle against poverty.

However, these 'positive causes of migration', as we may term them, are not absent; the waves of prosperity within the expanding economy of the United States in the nineteeth century are reflected accurately by the waves of immigrant Europeans. The curve is a series of successively higher peaks separated by deep troughs: the first peak, in the 'fifties, corresponds to the expansion of the railway network and the opening up of the western territories which provoked Abraham Lincoln's celebrated reply 'Uncle Sam has a farm for each one of you'; the prosperity which followed the Civil War, and the years of well-being that ensued, correspond to a second peak about 1871–72; between 1873 and 1879, on the other hand, the numerous bankruptcies and the fall in prices amounting to 30 per cent in agriculture and 50 per cent in industry (due largely to the entry of Ukrainian and Australian wheat into the European market in competition with American exports) caused much unemployment, and the curve falls. It rises again from 1879–80, and immigration reached a maximum between 1887 and 1893; a veritable tidal wave broke on all the cities of the east coast as well as on San Francisco and even on New Orleans despite the bad reputation of its climate. Another downward curve corresponds to the financial crisis at the end of the century, and this is followed by a last massive rise in 1902–3. The great expansion of the United States deprived Europe of 38 million persons in 111 years, an average of 345,000 a year; and in the same period the U.S. national revenue quadrupled.

The discovery of new resources also attracts the migratory masses, and has in some instances played a major part in the peopling of vast areas. Thus the exploitation of coal in the nineteenth century was responsible for creating the greatest European areas of high density, and the discovery of gold helped to people western United States after having stimulated the Spanish penetration and colonisation of

Latin America, whilst almost at the same time the same metal created nuclei of population in south-western Australia and was responsible for the great urban development of the 'gold triangle' of South Africa. Much more recently oil has succeeded in attracting and immobilising the nomads of the Arabian desert around towns which have sprung up in the sand, and those of the Sahara desert around the new oases which have been developed from deep-seated water supplies revealed by the oil borings.

Clearly, the attraction of profit is a powerful incentive to migration, but there are others also—a more agreeable job, a more welcoming environment, a more satisfactory way of life. When the South Wales miner quitted his valley, when the textile worker abandoned the drab monotony of his Lancashire town, to move to Greater London, it was all these things that he sought. The wages that he was already earning were adequate for his needs, but they were lower than he could get in mechanical or electrical engineering, in the food industry or in the printing trade. In the United States, where the farming population is already much reduced, the drift to the towns slackens when the unemployment figures rise above 5 per cent; there was even a return to the land in 1932 and in 1945, and on the other hand frantic rural depopulation during the war and in 1951–52 at the time of the Korean affair and the re-armament programme. The same kind of motives affect the French workers who converge on the metropolitan region, for under the zonal wage-rate system workers are paid more for equal work in the large cities, owing to the higher cost of living therein.

Here lies one of the possible means of influencing migration in accordance with the regional needs: substantial advantages in the form of higher wages, better housing, bonuses and favourable contracts.

Psychological motives

There are some migrations, however, which owe nothing to the desire for gain; the search for political or religious freedom, accompanied sometimes by the need for self-preservation in the face of persecution, has been responsible for mass exoduses which were quite contrary to the economic interests of the migrants. When the 'Pilgrim Fathers' sailed across the Atlantic in the *Mayflower*, they were more concerned with the preservation of their faith than with the conquest of a new world. In the same way the Jews who fled from Nazi Germany before the war abandoned comfortable economic situations to install themselves clandestinely in a country which did not belong to them, and they did not know that they were saving their own lives and preparing the way for a new State which in time would serve as a rallying ground for Jews from both east and west.

Political totalitarianism, when it menaces the consciences and the lives of individuals, is also a cause of migration: one and three-quarter million Russians fled from their homeland at the time of the Bolshevik revolution, and many hundreds of thousands of Spanish republicans have fled from Franco Spain. Having abandoned everything, they have all simply sought asylum in a land where they can speak and act freely; and many former members of the Russian Tsarist aristocracy are now to be found living very humbly indeed.

There is another psychological motivation that is less tragic, and that is the appeal of the group. It has been observed that migrants from a village, from a town, a region or a country, will often encourage one another in the act of migrating and re-form as a group at the end of the journey, Hence the various 'quarters'—Chinese, Negro, Irish, Italian—that one finds in many large cities, especially in the United States. When the news from the departed son or friend is good, the migratory movement spreads and many more individuals follow for no other reason than the fellow-feelings which unite families or friends, or simply the example provided by the first one to leave the traditional home.

In this respect we must also remember the influences exercised by the availability of information, and of knowledge acquired either through teaching or through contacts with the outside world. Compulsory military service has depopulated many a French countryside, for the young rural recruit is called to the town at an age when he has no family responsibility and no land holding to tie him to his birthplace, and he is very strongly attracted by urban life.

Finally, an enthusiasm for something new, for new tasks to undertake, is a sentiment which animates many of those who venture to migrate. There is a 'pioneer spirit' which seeks not merely a higher living standard, but also difficulties to conquer, natural obstacles to overcome, new enterprises to develop. An extreme case is provided by the pioneer farmers who clear the edge of the Canadian forest, only to yield the farm thus created to someone else whilst they go further on to perform the same task all over again.

The means of migration

In all migratory movements, means of transport play an essential part. Indeed, one might say that the great surge of migration coincided with the development of railways—though the role of these, as of roads, is a very complex one.

The opening of a railway or of a new road in an old country has often led, in the early stages, to the migration of some of the people living in the area traversed—as in the case of mountain valleys rendered more accessible by the new means of communication. At a later period, on the other hand, the railway appears to act as a line of attraction, and to lead to the regrouping of the population who remain; towns served attract the local rural people, villages with stations become more alive than those further away, and specialisation in agricultural products may be stimulated or even made possible where it did not exist (e.g. the collecting of fresh milk, vegetables and fruit, the long distance transport of perishables to large towns, etc.); and always the population pattern shows larger groupings and higher densities along the axes and around the crossing points of the routes.

In new countries, the peopling is often dependent on the construction of railways advancing into the wilderness; thus was it with the great transcontinental lines of the United States, where the building of the railways was accompanied by land grants to the new colonists; and the trans-Siberian was similarly followed by a narrow ribbon of population. Many towns indeed owe their creation to the development of means of transport in the nineteenth and twentieth centuries, and their population to the routes which converge upon them, drawing people from the rural areas both near and far. The scale of urban growth is often proportional to the importance of the railway line which crosses the town: thus in the middle of the nineteenth century Alençon and Le Mans were roughly the same size, but the latter gave passage to the main line from Paris to Brittany and is now two and half times larger than its rival which is less well served. Another feature which is often distinguishable is the local attraction of a railway station on the low ground, serving an old town situated on a hilltop; the new quarters gain in importance, by reason of better accessibility, over the old centre.

The availability of transport has a psychological as well as a material role in the migratory movement. During the last century, the railways, by facilitating easier travel between town and country, contributed to the dissemination of knowledge to the rural masses and thus, by putting temptation in their way, helped to increase the migratory flow.

The obligations of organised life

In the modern state, many factors impose the necessity for migration upon quite a large proportion of the population. Thus, in the United States in 1949, 40·2 per cent of the members of the armed forces, 22·8 per cent of the mining engineers and 21·1 per cent of the hospital nurses lived in a different county from that of their birth.

It is difficult to imagine Civil Servants working out their whole career in one place. Many classes of employees in both public and private sectors of the economy are required periodically to change their place of employment; and this happens not merely through promotions but also for the convenience of the employee himself, who may seek reunion with his family, a better climate or a more interesting job.

On the other hand, a national development programme, both in countries with a free capitalist economy and in communist states, can only be carried out with the help of more or less voluntary migration, oriented and guided by motives far above the level of the individual. In the free world, those who agree to migrate must be persuaded of the advantages which will thus accrue to them. Opposition is sometimes deeply rooted and uncompromising: for example, in the Central Massif of France the government wished to drop the exploitation of the small and unprofitable coal basins, but came up against implacable opposition from the local miners. Under authoritarian political regimes, opposition of this kind is not tolerated: in the U.S.S.R. in the Stalin era recourse was had to deportation in order to ensure the clearance and peopling of certain of the eastern territories.

THE CONSEQUENCES OF MIGRATION

The mixing of peoples as a result of migrations has many and varied effects, and one could go on describing them endlessly. Here we shall endeavour to classify them into several groups.

Consequences in space and in numbers

These are the best known and the most striking, and at the same time the most relevant to the geographer. They fall into two complementary series: (i) the reception areas absorb people hungrily, the towns expand, the countryside fills up and new lands are opened up; statistics record the changes in number, and the map shows the modifications in distribution, the increased densities; (ii) conversely, the source areas see their population diminishing, their towns vegetating, their countryside emptying and their fields going to waste.

On the international scale, a striking contrast exists between two extreme cases, those of the United States and Ireland since the first third of the nineteenth century. In 1819 the United States had 5,800,000 inhabitants, at the beginning of the twentieth century 76 million, and in 1975 212,300,000. This prodigious growth is due in very large measure to the influx of immigrants which reached its maximum at the turn of the century; between 1880 and 1900, 9 million European settlers arrived, and between 1900 and 1910, the greatest influx of all, no less than 8,800,000 new arrivals. The role of immigration in the population growth has been evaluated as follows:

Decade	*Natural growth*	*Immigration*
	(per cent)	
1870–80	71·5	28·5
1880–90	57·1	42·9
1890–1900	68·5	31·5
1900–10	58·2	41·8
1910–20	64·4	35·6
1920–30	77·6	22·4
1930–40	94·1	5·9
1940–50	94·6	5·4

As the United States filled up, so Europe lost part of its population: between 1820 and 1943, 7 per cent of the population of Switzerland, 11 per cent of that of Italy (but 30 per cent of that of Sicily and Campania and 46 per cent of that of Basilicata and the Abruzzis) crossed the Atlantic. But Ireland stands as an even better witness of this mass migration from Europe. See following page.

The United States received three-fifths of the Irish emigrants in the nineteenth century—an excellent example of the complementary character of the outward and inward movements mentioned above. Later (between 1900 and 1924), the Irish sought a place mainly in the Dominions, and since 1931 England has received about 80 per cent of the emigrants.

Percentage variation[1]

Decade	Ireland
1841–51	−19·5
1851–61	−11·5
1861–71	− 6·5
1871–81	− 4·6
1881–91	− 8·8
1891–1901	− 5·1
1901–11	− 1·6
1911–26	− 3·4
1926–37	− 0·5
1937–47	+ 2
1970–74[2]	+ 4·4

[1] T. W. Freeman, *Ireland*, p. 120.
[2] *Demographic Yearbook*, 1974.

Another instance of those complementary changes is provided by the vast movement of urbanisation which during the last hundred years has been upsetting the world's population distribution, is affecting more and more countries and is obviously not yet at an end. The inflation of the town-dwelling population has as its corollary the depopulation of the countryside, and in some cases severe disequilibrium now exists.

In France, between 1846 and 1946, the national population total increased from 35,400,000 to 40,300,000, an increase of 4,900,000. During the same period, the Paris region gained 4,600,000 inhabitants, and one might roughly say that the whole demographic increase was absorbed by the one capital city. Under these circumstances the other French towns have not had a sufficient influx and the urban hierarchy is thus in disequilibrium with an overwhelming metropolis and an almost complete absence of other great cities. On the contrary, in more prolific countries in which the general increase has been more considerable, as in the United Kingdom, the phenomenal growth of the London conurbation has not hindered the development of several other 'millionaire' cities; it is true, however, that the English countryside has been emptied to a much greater extent than the French.

Demographic consequences

These, like the numerical consequences of migration, reveal themselves at once, and are traceable not only in statistics but even in the character of the population, at both ends of the line. The sex ratio may be disturbed to a greater or less extent, and the age pyramid may assume strange shapes.

In general it may be said that men are more prone to migration than women, and it is not uncommon for the departure zones to become depopulated of their menfolk, or at least of the young men, whilst the reception areas have an unfortunate lack of women. This anomaly has always been noticeable in the early stages of great far-flung migratory movements, and it has often been the cause of mixed marriages; thus the first Iberians who settled in Latin America willingly chose partners from among the indigenous population before the supply of women sent out from Europe—'the best merchandise that could be imported into the islands'—put a brake on cross-breeding. The Indians in South Africa, and the Chinese in south-east Asia, were almost entirely male communities before the arrival of women of their own race from the home country, and the white men who colonised parts of Asia and Africa in the nineteenth century were almost always unaccompanied.

In the United States, during the period of maximum immigration, there was always a great majority of males—129·2 men to 100 women in 1910; amongst some immigrant groups the disproportion was even higher—189·8 for the Chinese and 296·8 for the Philippinos in 1950, and 392·8 for the Indians in 1940. Thus until 1950 there were always more men than women, but since that date the situation has become reversed and there were only 97·9 men to 100 women in 1960, a response to the slackening of immigration and a variation in the composition of the immigrants in recent years with the influx of fiancées and young wartime brides between 1941 and 1950, during which period there were only 68 male immigrants for 100 female.

Differences are equally distinguishable within a country, between town and countryside. But the anomalies are not the same, varying with the stage of technical and economic evolution. In the least developed countrysides, as in Africa, it is the men who go off, more or less for good, leaving their women in the village. The crops are therefore ill tended, whilst in the towns, the scarcity of the female element puts a price on it and leads to bad habits. Divorces multiply; prostitution is rampant and becomes a profitable trade.

Amongst the Negroes of African towns like Brazzaville, men dominate very slightly amongst the adult population, children are relatively few and old people almost non-existent. More than one-third of the women reach the end of their reproductive period without having had a child and the number of births per wife is much inferior to the rate required for simple regeneration. In the mining and forest camps, the situation is even more serious and there are often two or three times as many men as women. In general, the newer the town or other settlement, the greater the disproportion of the sexes.

At this stage we may perhaps formulate another proposition: the greater the importance of a town and the greater, therefore, the change imposed on ways of life, the fewer are the women who migrate to it. In India, in 1931, there were 120 men to 100 women in towns of 50–100,000 inhabitants and 161 in the large cities with over half a million. In 1951, there were 175 men to 100 women in Calcutta, 163 in Howrah and 130 at Ahmedabad, and all the great commercial and industrial towns showed similar inequalities.

In more advanced societies, conditions are generally different; both men and women leave the countryside, and many villages are left peopled only by those who consider themselves too old to leave. There is thus not the same disequilibrium in the sex ratio between the departure and reception areas. It may even happen in extreme cases that it is the young women who refuse to remain tied to the land. They prefer, as in Ireland, or in certain parts of France, to enter domestic service in a town or to emigrate. The young men in the countryside can only marry below their own station. Young Irishwomen will cross the ocean in search of a very problematic future rather than stay tied to the family farm. A similar phenomenon is to be found amongst the Europeans of Latin America, in that the women leave the countryside more willingly than the men.

These migratory peculiarities, added to the fact that most of the migrants are relatively young, have their effect on the age structure. A comparison of numerous statistics suggests the conclusion that in migrations of the 'economic' type, more than half the individuals who go to seek their fortune elsewhere are under the age of thirty, with one-third actually between twenty and thirty; but the proportions are sometimes higher than this.

An accumulation of adults is thus characteristic of reception areas; but the situation becomes inversed after the exodus in the source-areas, and in the United States in 1950 there were 63·8 per cent of

Proportion of Migrants (age at time of emigration)

	Under 30 years	20–30 years
	(per cent)	
Italians in the Paris region	77	53
Poles in northern France	80	46
Immigrants in interior U.S.A.	59	29
Immigrants into Poto-Poto (Africa)	86	?
Immigrants into Salvador (Brazil)	?	36

persons aged eighteen to sixty-five in the towns and only 53 per cent amongst the agricultural population.

Even here, however, there are variations, for when the urbanisation movement is in full swing and the towns burst with new arrivals every day, the proportion of young adults is very much higher; and when the migratory waves slacken, the average age of the adult population rises. Again we can get statistical confirmation from the excellent data available over long periods in the United States. In the period 1900–20 each decade saw the proportion of the urban population rising by about 5 or 6 per cent; in 1910 the towns contained 59·2 per cent of the population aged between 20 and 65, but the proportion of individuals between 20 and 30 years old was much greater than that of those aged 45–65. During recent decades, however, (since 1940) the towns having had their fill, the urban growth is but 2 per cent per decade (if one retains the earlier definition of what is urban); in the towns, the population comprises 61·1 per cent of persons aged 20–65, but the representatives of the 45–65 age group are much more numerous than the 20–30 group.

Age composition of United States towns (per cent)[1]

	(years)					
	0–4	5–19	20–29	30–44	45–64	over 65
1910	9·9	26·8	20·9	23·1	15·2	4·0
1950	10·1	20·5	16·7	23·0	21·4	8·2

[1] J. Bogue, *The Population of the United States*, p. 103.

In countries where urban expansion is now accelerating, the influx of young adults is very noticeable. As examples may be quoted the recently created new towns which have been started from scratch in the pioneer zones of Asiatic Russia, in which the proportion of adults is greater than 60 per cent. Other equally striking examples are to be found in countries where modernisation is in progress; their towns are developing at an increasing pace: Dakar held 112,547 inhabitants in 1941 and 230,887 in 1955, and the number of Europeans doubled between these two dates, whilst the African population (200,780) more than doubled. In both racial groups some two-fifths were aged between 20 and 40 in 1955, and as much as 45 or 46 per cent in the unplanned suburban growths which have recently appeared on the roads converging on the town, whilst the average corresponding figure for the agricultural population is hardly 30 per cent.

In Guinea, where a detailed investigation was made in 1955, the same contrasts appear. Conakry is attracting people from the interior, especially men from the overpopulated Futa Djalon highlands, and a comparison of the figures is very striking: there are children, women and old people in the mountains, and adult men in the town.

In Durban, which had a population of 591,000 in 1956, after a growth of 24 per cent since 1951, the proportion of Asiatics (mainly locally born) was only 28 per cent for the 20–40 age group, whereas for the Negroes, whose influx was mainly responsible for the urban expansion, the figure for the same age group was 55 per cent.

Age distribution of population in Guinea (per thousand)[1]

Age groups	Futa Djalon			Conakry		
	Male	*Female*	*Total*	*Male*	*Female*	*Total*
Under 15	219	231	450	159	183	342
15–45	149	241	390	319	253	572
Over 45	76	84	160	54	32	86
	444	556	1,000	532	468	1,000

[1] *Enquête de Guinée*, 1955.

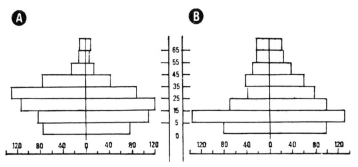

Fig. 31. Age-pyramids for Conakry (A) and Futa Jalon (B).

Males to the left of the central line, females to the right. Vertical scale of age-groups; horizontal scale, proportion per thousand of the total population.

These demographic consequences of migration, moreover, have their after-affects as well, for as the migratory movements wax and wane, so both the sex ratio and the age composition of the population fluctuate. A rapid growth in urban population corresponds to an accumulation of adults, with men more numerous at first and then a slow recovery of equilibrium between the sexes; after a certain time the balance is redressed for many of the adult women will be producing children in abundance. As an example, among the working classes of Milan and Turin, there are only 1 or 2 per cent of 'native' families having six or more children, but the proportion rises to 10 per cent amongst the immigrants from central and southern Italy.

One could indeed speak of 'cycles' in the demographic consequences of migration.

Biological consequences

There are yet further consequences of mass migration which are reflected in the demographic character of populations. The transplanted individuals are subjected to unaccustomed contacts; they find themselves in new conditions of life, and often in a *milieu* very different from that of their homeland. Some consequences of this upset are beneficial, for the uprooting of rural people breaks up the old communities, favours mixing of all kinds and destroys the risks of consanguinity which are prejudicial to the health of their descendants. Research work in this field has shown the parallelism that exists between the sclerosis of social structures and the high proportion of marriages between first cousins—between 7 and 20 per cent in Japan, India, Israel and Brazil, but only 0·5 to 2 per cent in European countries and 0·05 per cent in the United States. In the three provinces of northern Italy which are both mountainous and industrial (Como, Varese and Milan) the percentage of consanguineous marriages fell from 6·17 for the period 1903–23 to 1·85 for 1933–53, and at the end of this period the city of Milan by itself had a percentage of only 0·98, though the figure was two and half times greater in the rest of the province.

Conversely, adaptation to a new way of life is not always easy; new arrivals from the countryside into the towns suffer from lack of air and space, from noxious fumes and dust, and from changes in diet. The incidence of respiratory diseases amongst the country-folk who migrate to the large industrial cities of the temperate zone, or amongst the Mediterranean people working in the mines of the humid and foggy regions of northern France is much higher than amongst the 'natives' or others already long since acclimatised. And we know only too well what hecatombs of Europeans were the first establishments in tropical and equatorial Africa and America, and what devastating ravages are suffered by the Andean Indians, accustomed to their high plateaus and dry climate, when they are forced to descend to the unhealthy humidity of the equatorial coastlands. Some races have not indeed been able to survive the complete upsetting of their ancestral mode of life, like the Indians of the Antilles or of the north-east coast of South America, who were transported by the Iberian conquerors in the sixteenth century for forced labour in the mines or on the plantations. More recently, the compulsory immobilisation of the nomadic Kazakhs in Asiatic Russia and their installation in the towns or on the arable lands has been followed by the disappearance of many of these people.

Another cause which may play a part in altering the health of individuals affected by migratory movements is the destruction of the equilibrium of their pathogenic complexes. The contact of the white man with the Fuegians has caused among the latter the spread of pulmonary diseases, hitherto unknown amongst these people, and they have been literally decimated. And what of the effects of improved transport and the subsequent multiplication of migratory movements on the people of Africa? The intensity of movement between one region and another has favoured the upsetting of the pathological balance of the African, and many diseases, formerly endemic and relatively inoffensive, have become active and deadly. The arrival of new germs or the mixing of vectors of different origin provoked a sharp recrudescence of malaria in the twentieth century— in Madagascar in the 1900s, in Ruanda-Urundi and in Kenya between 1920 and 1940, and in Sierra Leone in the 1930s.

The migratory journeys cf greater or less extent and regularity made by numerous populations who are still nomadic, by workers called to the mines and plantations, and by pilgrims, all help to multiply the effects of malaria and to increase the fever-ridden areas whilst hindering any general programme to counteract this scourge. Similarly there were recent extensions of sleeping-sickness, in Cameroon about 1920, and in the Gambia, where the number of cases quadrupled between 1911 and 1939.

At the present time, new methods of attack, and inurement to the new conditions, have enabled the situation to be stabilised. But the health control organisation which exists at the entrances to almost all countries, the precautions that are taken in India with regard to arrivals from Africa, in order to guard against the introduction of yellow fever, and the suspicion which surrounds anyone who has set foot in Africa before arriving in Brazil, all show that the risk is still there and that it is not underestimated.

The problems of contact

People differ in many ways, and those who find themselves transplanted into a new environment very different from their homeland may become involved in conflicts of a general and collective kind— racial, linguistic, etc.—or more individually in matters of religion or politics.

Racial contacts, in whatever sense one understands the term 'race', are often difficult. If tropical South America, with the most motley collection of peoples in the world, has often been quoted as an example of harmonious relations between diverse races, it is not only because the original contacts were made a very long time ago, but also because cross-breeding has produced every kind of intermediate variety. However, even in such an apparently ideal situation one cannot help noticing the tendency for modern colonists to cling together—like Italians and Germans in the south, and the Japanese— and also the economic segregation which in fact exists, especially in the north-east where the Negro population, if not systematically pushed into the background, is usually confined to the underprivileged social classes. However, it must be added that the exceptional success of this human marketplace is largely due to colonisation by Latin peoples, who are much more resilient in their relations with other races than are the Anglo-Saxons.

Most of the white colonisations during the last three or four centuries provide examples of more or less acute problems of racial contact; South Africa is an extreme case, in which, having failed to resolve the difficult problem of living together, they have come eventually to envisage a policy of complete separation—'apartheid'—which economically is no solution at all for the small number of whites undoubtedly need the labour of the much larger number of blacks. In Australia and New Zealand, the absence of such difficulties is due to the very small number of aboriginals; but in New Zealand especially there is some apprehension for the future, for the health measures imposed upon the Maoris, who numbered only 80,000 at the time of the British arrival and no more than 40,000 at the beginning of the twentieth century, have had such good results that there are now 230,000 of them, and if their birth rate is maintained at its present level they will constitute 20 per cent of the New Zealand population by A.D. 2000. Already there are some signs of a changed attitude of mind in the relations between the two races, and the whites in particular are becoming more and more opposed to mixed marriages (which were frequent in the early days when there were few white women). On the other hand, the Maoris are leaving their reserves and establishing themselves in the towns, where they are obliged to take the roughest jobs and live in crowded and sordid lodgings; naturally they feel persecuted.

Finally, in the United States, the black and white problem is very far from being solved, especially in the Southern States where the Negroes form over one-quarter of the total population and as much as 37 per cent in Mississippi.

Oppositions much more delicately shaded than black *versus* white may also occur at times. A good example is provided by Guinea, where side by side are the Soussons people of the coastal plain and the Peuls of the neighbouring Futa Djalon highlands. The latter, unable to eke out a living in their mountain environment, go down to the coast to find work, but there is rivalry and hostility between the two groups, and fights are not uncommon, sometimes ending in murder. After such affairs the Peuls retreat to the shelter of their mountains. The effects of this antipathy are so well known that, in connection with the works for harnessing the river Konkoure, prepared by French engineers, a sociological study came to the conclusion that the inhabitants of the villages to be flooded would have to be rehoused in separate communities according to which racial group they belonged to. Here is a case of traditional antagonism surviving and maintaining its aggressive vigour at the present time.

Linguistic differences also cause difficulties. Even peoples that have lived side by side for a long time, like the French and English in Canada, and the Boers and English in South Africa, jealously preserve their identity, in which the essential element is language. In Canada, though individuals of British origin formed only 49·7 per cent of the population in 1941, 57 per cent of the inhabitants recognised English as their mother tongue and almost four-fifths spoke it, for this is almost a necessity in getting a job or occupying a position of any importance. About half the migrants from Netherlands, Germany and Scandinavia take up English immediately, and the use of English is fostered also by the persistence of a strong current of immigration from the British Isles—whereas French grows only by the immigration of Belgians and Italians.

For many migrants, the abandonment of the mother tongue does not happen until the second generation, especially amongst the women, who remain at home whilst their husbands are forced to adopt the new language at work. However, when the immigrants arrive in groups, they may preserve their national language—as did the Polish families who arrived in France in the 1920s. It has needed twenty-five years, another great war, and a changed political regime in Poland to secure the assimilation of these people and their decision to remain permanently in France. In some parts of Brazil and Argentina, Italian and even German are more spoken than the national language.

Conversely, the colonial migrations which have spread cultural influences have had an opposite effect; they have introduced European languages into vast territories where they have become the most convenient means of communication. In Guinea, for example, the national leaders make their speeches in French and not in their native tongue, in order to avoid offending the susceptibilities of the other ethnic groups who dwell in the country!

Religious differences often accompany ethnic or linguistic diversity, and migratory movements may result in the juxtaposition of people professing different faiths, like the Catholic French in Canada alongside the many Protestant British sects. On the other hand they may cause the adherents of one faith to flee from the contamination or persecution of others; thus the Mormons sought seclusion in the mountains of Utah and the Mozabites in the desert, whilst the Jews have fled from countries where they had lived for centuries, and the Palestinian Arabs have taken themselves into exile in Jordan.

Other aspects of contact

All these great conflicts are the result especially of long-distance international migrations. However, other frictions may develop even within the confines of a single state. Thus, the planned decentralisation of urban population and industry involves the transfer of industrial workers, usually socialist in their politics, into small suburban or provincial towns which are very conservative, and this may change not merely the local atmosphere but the electoral majority, and some residential areas have protested very strongly against such an upsetting invasion.

A final sociological consequence of migrations is that each individual seeks to recreate something of the atmosphere of the place that he has left behind, and it is in this way that civilisation is enriched, by the many contributions from all the various folk who ultimately find themselves living together within the same frontiers or in the same place. In this respect the cosmopolitan atmosphere of the great cities, with their societies, churches, libraries and restaurants in declared connection with a multiplicity of races and nationalities, is but a caricature of what is happening elsewhere more profoundly but perhaps less visibly.

To sum up, in the face of all the difficulties that are presented by the contact of individuals drawn from widely separated horizons, two attitudes are possible: first adaptation, which is inevitable for the isolated individual who finds himself lost in the crowd, unnoticed and with little power of resistance, and secondly, on the contrary, the struggle against assimilation which takes place through the formation of a group, and the attempt to recreate something of the original *milieu* in the midst of the new environment. The latter tendency may in fact become so serious, like a tumour in the body of the adopted country, as to provoke reaction against it, either legally (as by immigration restrictions in many countries of the world, including the United States and more recently, in Europe, the United Kingdom; such laws are aimed particularly against certain categories of people judged to be less adaptable on account of their different civilisation, for example the Latin races in the Anglo-Saxon world), or by collective manifestations of resistance or discontent on the part of the main body of the people, whose national sentiments are shocked by the attitude of the newcomers.

Financial aspects

Movements of people naturally entail movements of capital, and there are other financial repercussions, direct and indirect.

It was estimated in 1879 that each immigrant augmented the value of United States territory by $400; the price of land increased with each wave of immigrants; it is easy to gauge the colossal enrichment for which 46 million new arrivals from across the Atlantic were responsible. And to this intrinsic value must be added the actual cash that the immigrants brought with them—averaging $50 per person in the United States at the end of the nineteenth century, $138 in Canada between 1900 and 1915. All told, immigrants must have brought to the United States, directly or indirectly, some $18,000,000,000—a very handsome dowry from old Europe to its overseas child! Similarly, each immigrant brought £15 into Australia between 1914 and 1920 and £30 between 1928 and 1931.

Contrariwise, we must remember that the immigrants do not immediately forget their homeland, and many are very faithful to their relatives left behind. Statistics for the United States tell us that on the eve of the first World War, Italian immigrants were sending home four times as much per individual as English immigrants, and Greeks ten times as much as Germans. No wonder that Uncle Sam found the immigrants from southern and eastern Europe, coming from much poorer countries than the earlier waves from northern and central Europe, much less desirable! But the flow continues; Italian receipts from emigrants total half as much as the income from tourists (and at the beginning of the century these two sources of income, at that time equal, covered half the adverse balance of trade); in Greece, the contributions of emigrants amount to almost as much as the combined revenues of the tourist trade and shipping. The sums remitted by Algerians working in France were as great, in 1955, as the entire Algerian agricultural wage bill.

It is also a fact that migrations are costly, though it is impossible to evaluate this precisely. During the last century, when they were spontaneous, it was the cost in human life and suffering that were most noticeable, and the price was paid by the many who died or encountered insuperable difficulties of adaptation.

In modern times the wastage of human life is much less, but the monetary cost is continually rising. Quite apart from the cost of transport, which may weigh heavily on the budget of those countries, like Australia, which themselves pay the fares of their immigrants, the establishment of the new arrivals requires land and equipment, and the price of these is highest in the most advanced regions and countries.

In France, it has been calculated that each rural family that moves into a large town costs the State at least 20,000 francs in supplementary urban services such as schools, hospitals, transport, refuse-disposal. Moreover, the cost of public services is 2·2 times as great per inhabitant and per year in the *département* of Seine (i.e. Paris) than the average for the whole of France. Conversely, in the rural areas from which the migrants come, the schools are almost empty, the rail services hardly used, and to these costs must be added the economic and social disequilibrium which are difficult to redress: one can hardly close the village school even though the number of pupils falls by half, for those who remain still have the right to education, and it is the same for trade, transport and local administration.

Certain migrations are even more expensive because they are entirely paid for by the authorities; the example of Australian policy towards immigrants has already been quoted. Another example is that of the Breton families who agreed to quit their tiny and uneconomic small-holdings and take up farms in the middle of the Aquitaine Basin or in the south-eastern part of the Paris Basin; in their case the Ministry of Agriculture bore the expense of removal and of re-establishment on much larger and better appointed farms. In most countries with a state controlled economy, the public purse bears the cost of such transfers.

Economic repercussions

There is another economic aspect to migrations, other than the financial one, and that is the economic effect on the areas which lie at both ends of the movement. The dispersal areas are unquestionably penalised; they lose their most active elements, the young men and women, or at least the most enterprising among them. And this happens precisely when these young people have been provided with all that was necessary for their growth and education. Such areas thus lose the fruits of their investments and are subject to a relative impoverishment at the same time as they lose part of their potential labour force. To avoid this sort of thing, an English statesman went so far as to propose, immediately after the last war, the emigration of a whole slice of the population, such as a complete town all at once, to the Dominions, in order to avoid this problem of young individuals going off alone.

However, such departures may have beneficial consequences, for if they are not too numerous and leave behind sufficient active elements, it is possible for a reorganisation of the community to take place, on a sounder basis and with a higher standard of living. In the countryside, underemployment disappears, and at a later stage the farmers increase the size of their holdings; in industrial areas, unemployment is abolished. Such effects have been described in certain parts of southern Italy which have been relieved of their surplus population. The most prosperous parts of rural France, like the fertile plains in the central Paris Basin, have for the same reason experienced an increase in the size of farms and in the level of individual incomes.

On the other hand, mass emigration leads to the decay or at least the stagnation of the area affected. Many French villages in the southern Alps and Central Massif have been virtually extinguished by an exodus amounting to between 50 and 70 per cent of the population since the middle of the nineteenth century; only the old folks remain, and neither marriage nor birth is registered; the school has been closed, the houses crumble one by one and the farmlands, dry and poor it is true, are progressively abandoned. In cases where the young men migrate temporarily, the working of the soil is left to the women, children and old people, whose labour is insufficient to improve it and even to maintain it in good condition; in certain parts of Kabylia, in Algeria, one man out of two is living in France, and half of these are aged between twenty and thirty-four; in the highlands of Guinea, some villages have lost four-fifths of their men and such improvement of agriculture as the natural environment renders possible is in fact impracticable. In Nigeria, the valley of the Zanfara and other areas are unexploited for lack of manpower; the young people prefer to seek temporary employment far away in southern Nigeria or in Ghana, for this gives them greater prestige and provides them with a cash income to buy a wife—which they could not do if they stayed on the parental hearth.

It thus seems that there is a certain threshold of vitality in a community, and if emigration causes the population to fall below this critical limit, all possibility of organisation and transformation disappears and the region is condemned. The threshold is more easily reached if the local population is sparse and the appeal from outside is great: for the truth of this statement, contrast the evolution of the poor mountain districts of France (sparse population, considerable attraction of neighbouring plains and towns) with that of physically

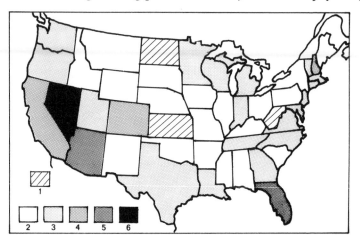

Fig. 32. Population changes in the United States, 1960–70.
1. Decrease.   2–6. Increase: 2. Under 10 per cent;   3. 10 to 20 per cent;   4. 20 to 35 per cent;   5. 35 to 70 per cent;   6. Over 70 per cent.

similar regions in Italy (densely peopled, and demographic saturation of the whole country). Likewise, in New England, the people least favoured by their natural environment migrate to the central and western parts of the continent or to the great industrial cities of the east; the states of Maine and Vermont, between 1940 and 1970, only increased their population by 15·8 per cent and 28·4 per cent respectively, whilst the whole United States increased by 46·7 per cent; thus the increase in these two pioneer states of New England is even less than the natural growth rate, obviously indicating consideranle emigration. In Canada, between 1941 and 1951, the province of Quebec, peopled by the prolific French and with an essentially rural economy, increased by 22 per cent, whilst the whole of the Dominion increased by only 18 per cent (1941–51). Since that time the situation has altered, for the French birth rate has appreciably diminished and the large flow of immigrants has gone mainly to the English-speaking provinces. Such differences in local evolution are typical of the general conditions prevailing in each of the two great states of the North American continent.

On the contrary, many reception areas are overtaken by a growing stream of population which has cost them nothing, which is ready to work, and which is spontaneously drawn towards the growing points;

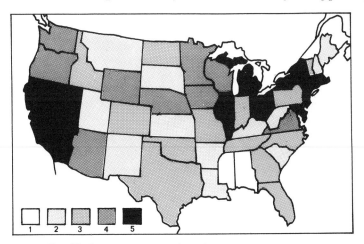

Fig. 33. Income 'per capita' in the United States, 1975.
Income *per capita*: 1. $2,500–$3,000.   2. $3,000 to $3,500.   3. $3,500 to $4,000.   4. $4,000 to $4,500.   5. Over $4,500.

this is an asset from which dynamically expanding countries have drawn much profit.

In North America, in Australia, and elsewhere, each wave of experienced Europeans, ingenious and dogged, offered new possibilities—farmers to open up new land, workers to man new factories, inventors to fulfil new requirements. Even now a glance at a list of scientists or university professors in the United States will show how much is owed to the German Jewish influx which began in 1935. In Europe, the demographic growth of the great metropolises, such as London and Paris, is doubled in effect by the huge growth in industrial or 'tertiary' potential provided by the migrants, and it is difficult to say which of these two movements encourages the other. Greater Paris grew at more than double the pace of the rest of France between 1946 and 1954, but the demands for planning permission for new buildings, between 1946 and 1950, actually represented 35 to 40 per cent of the national total.

At the opposite extreme, certain migrations due to absolute poverty can have most disastrous effects, for they constitute an economic sur-charge on the reception area which is almost impossible to bear under conditions which hold out no conceivable hope of being able to offer employment to the invading hordes. Such is the case in the towns of all the underdeveloped countries, towns which are being invaded by poverty-stricken inhabitants of the countryside, unskilled, and often driven by hunger or despair. Indians sleep and die of hunger in the streets of Bombay, and the inhabitants of all the shanty towns of Africa and Latin America overwhelm the cities and upset the national economic equilibrium to no purpose.

Countries with a diversified regional economy exhibit within their own frontiers this double aspect of internal migration, beneficent on the one hand and overwhelming on the other; thus São Paulo grows both in prosperity and in the size of its population, whereas in the cities of the north-east, like Recife and Salvador, these two elements are completely dissociated; in Italy, Milan and Turin dip to their own advantage into the manpower reserves of the South and the islands, whilst Palermo and even Naples are almost suffocated by the influx.

A consideration of the *quality* of the migrants is also important: there is no common measure between the expatriate of north-western Europe or even a farmer from France or Germany, who migrates to the town in his own country, and the illiterate, half-starved peasant who quits his native hovel. The importance of the migrations from Europe lies not merely in their bulk but also in their quality. When a Welsh miner or a Rhenish cultivator leaves for the United States, he is a master rather than an apprentice. He gives as much as he gets. If the State of São Paulo stands at the head in the Brazilian economy, is it not because it has received more than 2 million immigrants since 1870, of whom almost half have been Italians, representing one-sixth of its population? At the present time the inflow from other parts of Brazil is four times as high as the entry from abroad, but the current of immigration continues to flow—and it includes many technicians and other specialists who help to keep progress moving.

Thus the economic consequences of spontaneous migration appear to be most favourable (*a*) in countries with an active and advanced

PLATE 13. *The market at Labbe, Guinea*

PLATE 14. *The cattle market at Feira de Santa Anna, Bahia, Brazil*

PLATE 15. *The Lofoten Islands: settlement clings precariously to the rocks*

PLATE 16. Trulli *at Alberobello, Apulia, Italy*

PLATE 17. *Nomad encampment in Morocco*

PLATE 18. *Senegal: Peul village in the Serer country*

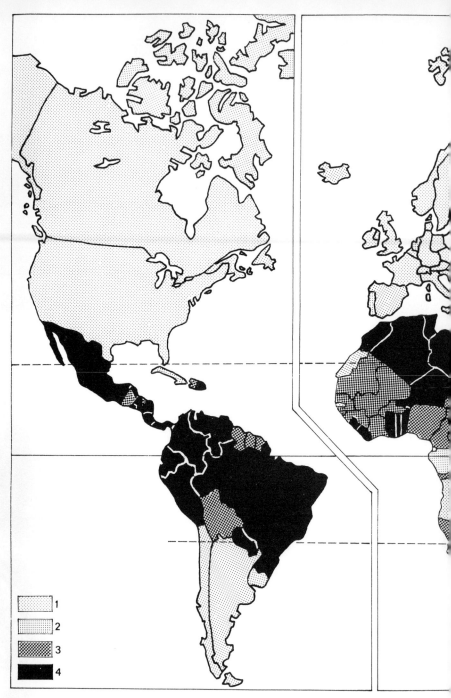

PLATE 19. *Natural population growth by Countries*
1. Under 10 per cent.   2. 10 to 20 per cent.   3. 20 to 25 per cent.   4. Over 25 per cent.

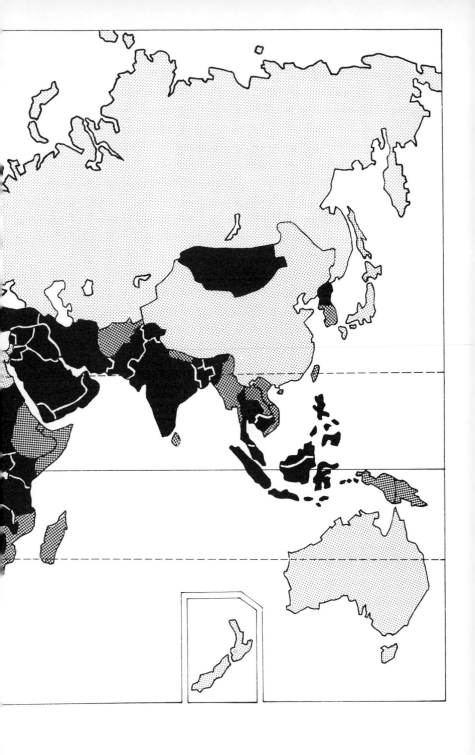

PLATE 20. *Sudan: woman pounding millet*

PLATE 21. *Benares: ablutions in the sacred river Ganges, in winter*

PLATE 22. *Havsa, Turkey: village market place*

PLATE 23. *Urbanism in the automobile age: the car park at a shopping centre on Long Island, New York*

economy, and (*b*) when the immigrants themselves come from developed countries. It was this combination that not only created the prosperity of those extensions of European civilisation but also contributed towards modernising the exploitation of Europe itself, changing the traditional equilibrium and economic structure. On the contrary, in less well developed countries, migrations can create serious disequilibrium. Here also there is a threshold; below it, poverty is added to poverty, but above it, thanks to the existence of some favourable elements, either human or natural (mineral or agricultural resources, means of transport, new technical developments, or new politico-social regime) upon which all depends, the influx of people creates a more intense activity and a greater prosperity.

The economic perspective in directed migration
Many of the drawbacks noted above can be avoided by directed migration; the liberty of the subject is lost but society gains in efficiency. In theory the risks of disequilibrium between the areas at either end of the migratory stream should disappear. The co-ordination of the movements eliminates the possibility of local demographic bulges, either temporary or permanent, and thus also their immediate consequences (unemployment, underemployment, lowered individual income, recruitment of underpaid labour) and their more serious after-effects (economic crisis, deficiency diseases caused by undernourishment, social discontent leading to rioting and violence). It also eliminates the economic bottle-necks due to temporary shortage of labour in districts with expanding industries, and all their accompanying evils (pushing up of wage rates, instability of a labour force which is the subject of strong competition, and interruption of production schedules).

Such migration is much more expensive for the State, and that means for the general public, but it offers much less scope—and risk—to those who take part in it. It is perforce limited by the absorptive capacity of the local environment.

The Australian case can be studied with precision: the number of immigrants was 200,000 a year in 1948–49, 300,000 in 1950 and in 1953; after the latter year the contingent was reduced to 100,000 a year, a figure which represents the maximum that Australia can absorb into its economy whilst not only preserving a high standard of living for its people but also guaranteeing jobs and adequate wages for the newcomers from overseas. The burden is indeed enormous, for it represents a 20 per cent addition to the population in little more than ten years; and 60 per cent of the immigrants are 'assisted', that is cared for by the Australian government from the moment of departure from their homeland. The retardation after 1953 had the effect of doubling the number of employment vacancies, especially in mining, shipbuilding and the food industries—which shows that even controlled immigration does not always produce an exact balance of resources and needs.

In communist countries, where the dictates of high authority are often the cause of migratory movements, it also happens that the adjustment is not quite perfect. At the present time the U.S.S.R. is running into difficulties over the provision of an adequate labour force for industry: agriculture, indispensable for the maintenance of the country's food supply, continues to retain a very high proportion of workers. Despite this the development of Soviet Asia must be credited to the vast displacements of mankind in which the present political regime, by constraint of one sort or another, has played the leading role.

The advantage of not relying on individual or popular inspiration in the choice of locality and the mode of travel is evident enough. In the case of international migration, we have already noted that negative formulae such as quotas or prohibitions can play their part, the same as positive regulations like directed or voluntary recruitment; in many cases agreements between governments have become the means of control (as between the Italian government, for example, and those of France, Switzerland and Germany). Within a country, control and regulation are much more difficult, for although in communist or dictatorial states there is no regard for individual liberty, this is certainly not so in the democracies. We have already noted the way in which appeal is made to the interests of the individual. A policy like that of industrial decentralisation in France favours counter currents of migration, giving the advantage to provincial regions, hitherto neglected and rather isolated, at the expense of the traditional industrial zones such as the northern coalfield and the environs of Paris and Lyon. In this case, planning resorts to economic incentives in order to put a brake on the normal migratory movements. Somewhat similar is the policy pursued in the 'Development Areas' of the United Kingdom, notably North-East England and South Wales, of renewing the economic potential, arresting the outward movement of population and creating new zones of prosperity.

The special circumstances of post-war migration

These currents of movement fall into neither of the two classes just examined; they were not spontaneous and they were made under constraint; they affected considerable numbers and all classes of people, and they happened under conditions of almost total economic and political disorganisation. They also had important economic consequences of which we must take note.

Let us consider first the transfers of population in Europe after 1945. In those countries where the extent of the changes brought about by the war was considerable, as in Poland and Czechoslovakia, the unfavourable consequences were keenly felt; whole regions had to be entirely repopulated, as in western Poland and the Sudentenland, by people transferred from the eastern zones, or even repatriated from Soviet territory. Such transfers were accomplished at an enormous cost in reconstruction and re-equipment. Then again, Slovakian and Polish peasants from the east were directed to areas where industry had been proponderant, and so the general lack of labour in such areas was accentuated by a lack of skilled operatives; it was necessary to rebuild a body of professional know-how and, even so, the newcomers were much inferior to those whom the war had caused to flee.

Furthermore, hampered by their desire for industrial manpower, these countries have been led to diminish too rapidly their agricultural population, and this has resulted in underproduction of food crops, a problem not yet fully solved. In the industrial sphere, their development has been characterised by the low quality of the labour force and low level of productivity, and also by shortage of capital which has affected certain industries such as mining, textiles and some of the chemical industries. And finally, the elimination of the Jewish minorities has resulted in a shortage of professional men, especially in Poland.

Conversely, the two Germanies, but especially the Federal Republic, have received large influxes of displaced persons. Until 1950, this undoubtedly weighed heavily on the economy, through unemployment and the diversion of resources to help refugees, which would otherwise have been employed in investments designed to increase output. But dire necessity at last gave a crack of the whip to the economy: the pressure of labour on the market developed production and stimulated consumption. Moreover, the abundance of labour kept wage rates low and this favoured exports and so in fact contributed to the expansion. Although at the beginning the burden on West Germany was very heavy, it has probably in the long run hastened the country's economic recovery. As for the refugees themselves, their status is lower than that of the autochthonous population; their wages are lower, and their occupations largely within the least favoured categories (agriculture, building, domestic service, mining); their numbers include many wage-earners (as opposed to salaried staff) and a high proportion of manual labourers; their housing conditions are noticeably inferior.

A second example is provided by Israel where the proportion of the population gainfully employed rose by 90 per cent between November 1948 and June 1957. Thanks to this influx, the cultivated area increased by 125 per cent and the area of irrigated land more than quadrupled; the numbers employed in industry rose by 60 per cent and the production of hydro-electricity more than trebled. Even this economic expansion, however, could not entirely take care of the flood of newcomers, and the percentage gainfully occupied fell from 43·9 in 1948 to 35·1 in 1957; it was estimated that 10 per cent of the available labour force could not be employed and that 20 per cent were only partly occupied. Female employment has diminished in order to make way for men, and the proportion employed in agriculture has risen from 12·1 to 15·6 per cent—the absorptive capacity of agriculture being higher at this level of employment than that of industry. Moreover, this state of affairs has been accompanied by a considerable adverse balance of foreign trade; between 1950 and 1955 exports scarcely paid for one-fifth of the imports, and the proportion at present is about one-half. It is obvious that Israel could never have hoped even partially to assimilate such a rising tide of immigrants if the state had had to rely on its own resources, without the massive aid which has been forthcoming from other countries and from powerful Jewish organisations all over the world, especially in the United States; and the need for such assistance will long continue to be felt, especially with the burden of military expenditure.

Thus the considerable and often savage transfers of population resulting from military events have repercussions which amplify those of ordinary migratory movements.

Social and professional changes

This is not the place to examine in detail the occupational structure of populations, but all the same we must point out that migrations influence this structure by associating vertical movements across the economic stratification with the horizontal movements of geographical displacement.

Spatial mobility is often indeed accompanied by professional mobility. Those who accept uprooting also admit the possibility of a change of occupation. What matters to them above all is either to improve their economic situation if they have been driven out by poverty, or simply to find some means of earning a living if they have emigrated for political or psychological reasons. Thus it frequently happens that the migrant does not take up his former occupation when he moves. Though many rural folk do nothing but change from one piece of land to another, retaining their deeply-ingrained peasant mentality even though they increase the size of their holding and adopt new methods, for the most part they achieve an economic and social promotion. Such is the case with the 'colons' who have abandoned the overpopulated hills of southern Europe for small or large farms in South America, with the peasants from central and northern Europe who have carved out farms for themselves during the opening up of new lands in North America, and with the 'colonials' who have cast aside their European mediocrity to become plantation-owners overseas.

The great modern phenomena of industrialisation and urbanisation have created just as profound modifications in the activities of people as in their distribution. When the countryside empties, it is usually the urban factories which benefit, and the peasant class is the chief victim of migrations from one end of the world to the other. When the Algerians go to work in France, or the southern Italians in the Belgian and German coalmines, when the Negroes of southern United States leave the cotton fields for the great northern manufacturing cities, when the poor country-folk from the Brazilian hinterland, or the African peasants, are drawn by the urban mirage into the great cities, it is always the peasant class which recedes in the face of an increase in workmen, employees, domestic servants and shopkeepers.

An important study of all the immigrants into France between 1920 and 1930 provides evidence of this tendency. See following page.

The change of occupation is not always as simple as a mere transfer from something elementary to something more advanced. It may happen that the migrant, changing his country or merely his natural environment, finds it advantageous to take a backward step and

Occupation before emigration[1]	Italian workers in Paris region	Polish miners in N. France
	per cent	
Working farmers	10	14
Agricultural labourers	13	27
Miners	0	36
Artisans and labourers	53	23
Others	24	
	100	100
Occupation after emigration		
Miners	0	76
Unskilled or skilled workers	89	0
Foremen and overseers	11	0
Others	0	24

[1] A. Girard et J. Stoetzel, *Français et Immigrés*. Cahiers I.N.E.D. Nos. 19 et 20. 1953–54.

return to agriculture; thus, of the Italian farmers established in the agricultural areas of south-western France, some 15 per cent were not in agriculture before their emigration. But a sample study has revealed the reasons for their 'reconversion': all were attracted from the moment of arrival by the impression of well-being and freedom that they found in rural France, by the absence of social segregation and by the possibility of obtaining a holding large enough to enable them to live in comfort. Of the families studied, 16 per cent were owner-occupiers of their farms, 6 per cent were part-owners, 65 per cent were share-croppers or tenant farmers, and only 13 per cent were agricultural labourers—though 40 per cent of them entered this last category when they arrived in France.

Within the compass of international migrations it is generally impossible to appreciate statistically the changes of occupation that occur; but within the bounds of a single country it is easy enough to see the diminution in the numbers earning their living on the land and the growing tide of urbanisation.

Agriculture and urbanisation in the U.S.A.
(per cent)

	1900	1920	1940	1960[1]	1970
Urban population	39·7	51·2	56·5	70	73·5
Active agricultural population	32·9	25·6	19·8	9	3·7

[1] There was a change of definition after the census of 1950; under the old definition the 1960 figure would have been about 66 per cent. *U.S. Statistical Abstract and Census.*

It is in the countries which are economically most advanced, and in which the different sectors of activity are most sharply defined, that the alterations in the occupational structure are the most real and the most important. Thus when a Breton peasant takes a job in an automobile factory in France, or when a mid-west farmer signs on at an aircraft works in Los Angeles or becomes an insurance agent in Chicago, the change of occupation is irrefutable. But when an unemployed and landless agricultural worker from north-eastern Brazil tries to avoid dying of hunger in Recife and ends up by peddling cigarettes or bits of sugar-cane, one can hardly talk of a 'professional migration': it is just one form of misery replacing another.

Consequences of migration: the balance-sheet
The importance of migrations is obviously very considerable. They play a part just like natural growth, in the distribution, evolution and composition of human communities. But they also permit the correction of those natural growths which are excessive or maladjusted. Even if they are disordered, they represent a spontaneous human attempt at better adaptation to the economic possibilities which the world offers, and when they are controlled or even compulsory, they offer the means of matching population to resources, of transforming the occupation-structure, of developing human relationships, and as a result, of properly managing both land and production. And finally, we should not neglect the role of migratory threads in the progress of the complex web of civilisation.

CHAPTER ELEVEN

Rhythmic Migrations : Seasonal and Daily Movements

Certain migratory movements are distinct from those already discussed, in that they obey a kind of rhythm and do not involve the complete uprooting of the people involved. It is often as difficult to describe them precisely as to evaluate them statistically, and they are by no means easy to represent cartographically. They may be inspired by different incentives, but in all cases man is seeking something that he lacks on the spot, whether it be relaxation, work or simply the means of survival. By reason of their characteristic feature, which is a to and fro motion like the swing of a pendulum, they may perhaps be called 'oscillatory migrations'.

Long-period oscillations are usually seasonal, short-period ones daily; in both cases they represent an adaptation of man to circumstances of climate or of space which are not uniform. They may be a response to the requirements of work, or merely the pleasurable employment of leisure. Their very diversity makes it necessary to distinguish several types.

MIGRATIONS FOR WORK

The alternation of the seasons, the very succession of day and night, present changing aspects and conditions for human activity. The utilisation of these opposing possibilities necessitates movements of varying amplitude and character.

Seasonal migration

Nomadism. At the head of this class comes the migrations of nomads. The real nomads, those who wander over the desert at random, following haphazard rain showers or other favourable circumstances, hardly come within the definition of seasonal migration, but equally one cannot include them as either permanent or temporary migrants. Theirs is a state of perpetual wandering.

The region in which this•type of nomadism is best represented is the Middle East, more precisely the Arabian desert and its northward extensions into Iraq, Jordan and Syria, Between 3 and 4 million individuals wander endlessly within this area, scorning political frontiers. It is estimated that there are still 420,000 Bedouins in Syria, perhaps 3 million in the vast territory of Arabia, and one million in Iraq and Jordan.

Dwelling in a tent, jealous of his freedom, and prizing his camels more than anything else in the world, this true nomad is a member of a restricted and narrow community; he lives in the heart of the desert, accompanied only by a herd of camels. His movements are irregular and variable, following the chance occurrence of rainstorms which are reported by professional watchers, called Sleyb. However, it is rare for them not to have a few brief points where they stay for longer periods: wells, marked with the tribal sign, or small oases whose occupants pay them *khawa*, a kind of friendship tribute in the form of part of the crop harvest. It is the bottoms of wadis where slight moisture favours a little vegetation, as well as the wells and oases, that most attract the Bedouins and form their assembly points and foci of attraction. In Arabia, the Nejd, already dotted with sedentary settlements between Hayil and Riadh, is frequented by at least half the country's nomads; to the north, in Iraq and Syria, the Maamoura region serves as the pasture ground for several tribes; the famous region of the Al Sirhâne wells, extending from Jordan to the Nejd, is a gathering-ground for tribes of camel-men who come from as far afield as Syria.

The *Sahara* is another vast area which still contains more than a million and half nomads.

The great camel-men of the north-west, the Requibats, may be taken as an example of genuine old-fashioned nomadism that survives in all its vitality; their wanderings extend over distances from 300 to 1,000 km within Morocco and the western Algerian Sahara, and depend on the extreme variability of the rainfall. Those who possess nothing but camels are the most audacious in their wanderings; other groups are rendered less mobile by flocks of sheep. By tradition the Requibats used to buy provisions and cloth in the Moroccan markets of Goulimine, where also they would sell their animals, wool and salt; temporary difficulties are hindering their movements into south-eastern Algeria. A higher standard of living is coming to these people; more flour, tea and sugar are being bought, and some of the

Nomadic peoples of the Sahara (thousands)

Territory	Arabs	Tuaregs or Berbers	Toubous	Total
Morocco	14	6	—	20
Algerian Sahara	126	9	—	135
Tunisia	3	—	—	3
Libya	250	3	2	255
Chad	83	—	195	278
Niger	4	264	3	271
Sudan	34	196	—	230
Mauritania	400	—	—	400
	912	478	200	1,592

men earn a living as labourers or in the army, which adds to the total resources.

The west, south and east of the Sahara are also occupied by people that one could really call nomads. The Ahaggar, the oldest of the Tuareg groups of Hoggar, comprises 12 per cent of nobles, one-third slaves and the rest dependent tenants. The slaves wander with the flocks, seeking pastures at distances of up to 1,000 km to the south, whilst the women and children, and the men if they can, remain in tented camps with the goats and donkeys. To the profits from their animals they add an income from caravan transport, from salt, of which the administration grants them a monopoly and which they exchange for millet after a journey of 1,300 to 1,600 km, and from wheat, cultivated by the tenant farmers, which they barter for dates. This economy, however, is becoming more and more precarious, for the resources are diminishing; the economic value of the animals is almost nil, camel caravans are being displaced by lorries, the cultivators, encouraged by the state, are staking out their own gardens and refusing to pay tribute, and wild game is becoming rare; meanwhile, the needs are becoming greater and the shops of Tamanrasset exercise an irresistible fascination.

All in all, the situation of nomadic peoples is seen to be precarious; the penetration of civilisation, of governmental control and of means of transport tends to reduce more and more the space available to the tribes, and so hardly favours the retention of this mode of life, which, though it had its noble aspects and demanded much of its followers, is becoming more and more reduced to simple pastoralism for which the economic circumstances are very unfavourable. Finally, demographic growth is at such a rate, in some groups, that numerous nomads must of necessity abandon their tribe and adopt other modes of life. The discovery of oil in the depths of the harshest desert and the development of modern techniques of irrigation, are powerful attractive forces.

Semi-nomadism. Through many transitional types one comes to another sort of nomadism which is associated either with a fixed point, such as an oasis, and vast surrounding grazing grounds, or with two regions which offer sharply differentiated climatic characteristics.

The most characteristic forms of semi-nomadism are found in the northern Sahara. Here, on the desert fringe, are enacted to and fro movements, much more pronounced in the past, and now generally hindered by the development of agricultural colonisation, and regulated as to dates, areas and grazing grounds. In this region which borders on North Africa, French rule has caused nomadism to pass from being a dominant and tyrannical way of life to being a mere relic, adapted only to certain peoples and well-defined areas. Limited in its extent by the spread of cultivation and by changes in the law of property, closely confined in time by the dates of the harvest, and rendered easier by the creation of wells and halting-places along the migration tracks, it has been reduced to modest proportions. In a climate such as this, between 2 and 10 ha are needed for each sheep or goat, and the problems arising from contact with sedentary cultivators are not always easy to solve.

In the west of the Libyan desert, there are about 95,000 nomads and 50,000 settled people; seasonal migrations take place between the fertile, cultivated areas of Jebel in the west and of Sirte in the east, and the oasis of Fezzan in the interior. In the north, a small sedentary white population practises cereal culture and the gathering of olives, and defends itself vigorously against the encroachment of the nomads; in the south, on the other hand, is a coloured sedentary population three times as numerous as the nomads—these are the former slaves who till the soil on behalf of their masters. The tribes move between these two poles of attraction, but almost always they have some village to which they are attached, either in the north or in the south, and in which a part of the population remains all the year whilst the flocks and the men go from pasture to pasture. The nomads are not merely pastoralists; they are also the middlemen of trade and commerce between the north and the south. They provide cattle, vegetable oil and cereals, especially wheat, to the settled population of Fezzan, in exchange for dates. Within a set-up such as this, all kinds of transitional stages are possible between nomadic and sedentary life, and differences are sometimes found even within a single tribe.

By way of contrast, the Rebaia of Souf may be taken as an example of semi-nomadism in an almost perfect state of preservation. They possess small individual herds of camels, sheep and goats; they are a coherent group, well-balanced, in which semi-nomadism is an ancient tradition; that is probably why they have so far resisted the attraction of sedentary life. They spend two to four months in autumn in the palm plantations, harvesting dates, then from December to February, the tribes scatter in search of pastures, some going north to the Nemencha mountains, others south to the Erg; the cattle graze *acheb*[1] and give abundant milk, and then, about May, they all return to the oases.

As in the case of the real nomads, the improvement of transport, the exploitation of petroleum and the development of public works and irrigation, and lastly the military operations of the last few years which have caused many to lose their cattle, have all conspired to provoke the adoption of a settled existence. At Ouargla, for example, half the former nomad population has now settled down. Some traces of the old life are retained in the new, for the women of the former nomads continue to take part in tilling the soil, which is something sedentary women never do; and the new village is laid out just as the old tent encampments were—the tent solidifies into a hut, and then into a house, but still on the site of the old tent; so that the houses are in line and spaced out, completely different in arrangement from the cramped and overpopulated *ksars*.

We may well ask whether this transformation of the nomadic life is not in fact a backward step. The standard of life and the dietary habits of the nomad are certainly superior to those of the settled cultivator, and furthermore the migratory movements represent the best possible means of utilising the resources of a certain type of environment. Perhaps it would be better to conserve and improve the migra-

[1] *acheb*: a plant which grows in the desert.

tions rather than to suppress them. But the northern edge of the Sahara is not the only region where such phenomena are to be found.

In *East Africa*, the migratory currents of nomadism are still flowing. They begin in Cyrenaica, where colonisation has made its effects felt much less severely than in North Africa where desert or semi-desert conditions are much more extensive. In the Sudan, it is officially estimated that 15 per cent of the population still deserve to be classed as nomads, but other studies have suggested that a more realistic figure would be 40 per cent; they are mostly Nilotic tribes, in the area south

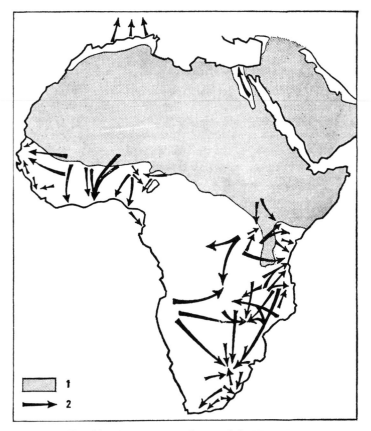

Fig. 34. Migrations in Africa and the Near East.
1. Zone of nomadism.   2. Migrations in search of work.

of latitude 12°N. They live in permanent villages in the wet season during which they grow crops and pasture their cattle around the village; then at the end of the rains, in December, they lead the cattle further away but still return each night to the village. In January and February as the drought intensifies, the herds are taken to the banks of marshes or rivers; the whole tribe follows the cattle, except for the old folk and some children who remain in the village; distances travelled may be considerable, and there are no fixed itineraries—but nevertheless the Census classifies many of these tribes as sedentary. On the contrary, the Arab tribes who inhabit the provinces of Darfur, Kordofan, Kassala and Blue Nile are registered as true nomads. Their life is bound up with the migrations of their herds; they dwell in tents and may shift their camp by twenty miles a day. In the wet season they are in the north, moving south at the beginning of the dry season, when they may get as far as the upper Nile valley.

In the new republic of Somalia, created in 1960, probably three-quarters of the population are nomads, whose only concern is to find pasture and water for their flocks and herds, regardless of national and international frontiers. In general, these movements are from north to south and back again, alternating with the wet and dry seasons. In the north, in the depths of the dry season, most of the tribes and herds are concentrated in the vicinity of permanent water-holes, but with the arrival of the first rains in April they disperse towards the Haud plateau, an undulating area between 600 and 1,200 m in elevation where there are irregular and sometimes heavy rains. When the decision to move off is taken, the tribe may cover as much as a hundred miles in sixty hours. In southern Somalia the migratory movements are shorter and more regular and are somewhat akin to transhumance. In other East African countries the proportion of nomads is much smaller.

In the *Middle East*, sheep-rearing peoples practise a restricted form of migration; they live near to cultivated areas and only move in order to find pasture for their flocks before returning. The development of mechanical transport has made it possible to associate the traditional wide-ranging shepherding with the possession of a fixed resting-place from which the flocks are taken by lorry to the grazing grounds. Thus, on the periphery of the zones of traditional nomadism a sedentary life is beginning to develop, in contact with the area of settled cultivation; the rhythm is of three to five months' winter sojourn in one place, and then migrations for the rest of the year.

These new-type nomads join in friendly agreements with the neighbouring sedentary people, either for the common grazing of certain numbers of animals or for the making of *samné*, a popular kind of butter made from sheep's milk.

Everywhere else in the world we can witness similar trends towards the transformation and disappearance of nomadism; if the herds still migrate, they do so under the care of a few specialised herdsmen, and the majority of the former nomadic populations are becoming sedentary. This has been the result of colonisation in the southern Sahara and in the Sudan, of Soviet or Chinese action in Central Asia and of the systematic organisation of herding in Lapland.

Transhumance and the pastoral life of mountain areas. The same kind of evolution has made itself felt in the smaller and more regular migratory movements of the same type, in which the flocks and herds make use in turn of different levels in the relief of the land, which become accessible at different seasons. These movements have existed for a long time, in great strength, in all parts of the world which offer such contrasts. In mountain areas, it is the progressive warming-up and snowmelt, later and later at higher altitudes, that is the key to the movement. The severity of the winter cold prevents living at high altitudes, and the lateness of spring growth on the alpine pastures forces the peasant to devise the alternative solution of withdrawing to the valley and sheltering the animals in stables during the winter months.

All the European mountain areas were once the scene of similar seasonal movements, and the ascent to the alps was the great event at the end of the spring—from the fringes of the Aquitaine basin and the Ebro basin to the high plateaux of the central Pyrenees, from the plains of the Rhone valley, from Piedmont and Lombardy and from the lower valleys of Switzerland and Austria into the alpine pastures of neighbouring mountains, and from the plains to the mountains of the Balkan peninsula. Entire villages would take part in the migration; the priest, the mayor and the schoolmaster would go with the families and the animals. Hutments at intervals up the mountain flanks still bear witness to the stages by which, during the course of the year, these collective movements or *remues* were undertaken. The depopulation of the mountains, together with the development of cultivation in the plains and lower valleys and the partial abandonment of the alps, have caused the decline or even the disappearance of these village migrations. If the herds do continue to move, they are grouped under the care of a few specialist herdsmen, whilst the bulk of the population remains in the valley.

In Africa, an investigation made in 1936 noted that 36·6 per cent of the Saharan population were nomads but that 75·7 per cent of the population of the high plains and Saharan Atlas followed the rhythm of movement of their flocks. It was the same around the mountains of Central Asia and Asia Minor, between the Parana plains and the neighbouring high plateaux of southern Brazil, and between the valleys and the 2,000 m Ethiopian plateau.

Agriculture and seasonal migrations. Even cultivated regions do not demand an equal labour force at all times of the year. The winter is the dead season, but the fields come alive again in the spring, needing much care during the whole of the vegetative period and a large amount of additional labour at harvest time. So long as machines were inadequate to replace human labour, the least populated areas, and also the richest areas, thrust deeply in their search for all kinds of labour into regions, both near and far, which had a population surplus. With the accelerated progress of mechanisation, a sort of hierarchy develops amongst rural areas, which is a function of the industrial and technical status of the country in which they lie. Thus in the most advanced countries like the United States, the seasonal movement of agricultural labour is restricted to the harvesting of fragile crops—of which the number is diminishing year by year (witness the development first of cotton-picking machinery, then beet harvesters and now machines for harvesting salad crops). In moderately advanced countries, such as France, wheat and other cereal crops are almost entirely mechanised, though crops like sugar-beet still need a good deal of careful hand labour. In the least developed countries, all the work is manual and there are no machines at all.

The attraction of temporary labour was once exercised over great distances, even as far as taking advantage of the seasonal inversion of the two hemispheres. Italians would sometimes embark in the autumn to help with the Argentine harvest and then with their earnings they were ready to return to their own fields when summer came back to Europe. This, however, was an extreme and rare case.

Much more often it is the excess population which seeks work and wages elsewhere. The Paris Basin and the northern region of France formerly were powerful centres of attraction; the growing of sugar beet, very extravagant in its labour demands, both for the numerous cultivations and dressings during the period of growth and for the lifting, was the great consumer. Between 1920 and 1940, besides Bretons and people from the Central Massif, Belgians, Poles and Italians came in whole trainloads to the French arable lands; at the present time much more machinery is being used, but there are still some 40,000 seasonal labourers coming from Italy, Spain and Algeria.

Other kinds of cultivation or activities connected with agriculture also demand an influx of labour which in France could only be supplied from outside its frontiers—such as rice-cultivation in the Camargue, the wine-harvest in the Midi and especially in Languedoc, flax-retting, hop-picking and work in the sugar factories of the north. In recent years these seasonal migrations have diminished as a result of mechanisation (beet-lifters, grape-harvesters, etc.) and of the rise in agricultural wages. They may still involve 125,000 people each year, 90 per cent being agricultural workers. Most of them are Spaniards, who have taken the place of the Italians and Belgians who used to arrive before the last war; Portuguese have appeared on the scene since 1970, and also North Africans, notably Moroccans. Women make up about one-third of the total labour force.

In countries with higher overall population densities it is unnecessary to seek foreign seasonal labour; thus in Italy the Lombardy rice-fields at the periods of weeding and of planting-out attract tens of thousands of workers (over 40,000 in the single district of Lomellina in Pavia province, which is one of the main centres of Italian rice. growing); one half of these men and women, mostly young and unmarried, come in from neighbouring parts of the Plain, the rest from Venezia and form the South.

In the United States, the main region demanding seasonal labour is California; the workers move according to the rhythm of the harvests, living in camps with their families for the whole of the year. Many Mexicans take part in this journeying, which may extend over 3,000 km. It begins in January with the lettuce harvest in the Imperial Valley, and then, as the year advances, the workers move north, gathering on the way the citrus fruits of southern California and the vegetables of the Los Angeles area; some go further north to the vineyards of Fresno, where they harvest the grapes in the early autumn. Midwinter, the dead season, allows them to return south to begin the cycle over again. Other workers come from the great central plains of the United States; they too begin in the Imperial Valley and go thence to the peach orchards of the Sacramento valley, then returning south to cope with such of the cotton harvest as has not been dealt with by the increasing number of machines.

In Africa, the concentration of certain crop harvests necessitates large additional labour supplies, for the local population densities are generally low and there is little mechanisation. This is the case with groundnuts in Senegal, with cocoa in Ghana and Western Nigeria, and with cotton in Sudan. The migratory movements are generally from the north, where the population is too dense for the marginal agricultural conditions, towards the south where general development is more advanced and the agricultural possibilities are greater. Hitherto, the migrant labourers wore themselves out with long journeys on foot; nowadays lorries plough along the rutted tracks, making transport quicker and easier. The Mossi from the north of Upper Volta Republic take part in the cocoa-bean harvest in Ashanti, in south-western Ghana. Between one-quarter and one-half of the adult male population of north-western Nigeria leave their homeland every year during the dry season, and they stay away for up to six months; thus they ease the pressure on the food reserves of their own villages and return from the south with money and new ideas—and sometimes perhaps they do not return at all! In the Sudan it is the cereal-growers of the central region who, in the off season, from January to April, go to help with the cotton picking; here they mingle with members of nomad tribes who have also been recruited for the harvest.

These seasonal migrants all have the same idea: the essential object is to save as much as possible so as to be able to take a lump sum back home; they live at their place of work under insanitary and overcrowded conditions; they are often lodged by their employer in camps or barracks, and if food is not included, they eat very little. Frequently, at the end of it all, they allow themselves to be won over to the new environment, and especially if they are unmarried, they become genuine immigrants.

Other examples of seasonal migration. Some other activities also, by reason of special circumstances related to the seasonal rhythm, experience alternations of feverish animation and slackness, which are accompanied by the concentration and dispersal of the labour force.

Certain industries conform to these alternations by reason either of the nature of their raw material like the sugar-beet factories which only work from November to March, and mountain sawmills which cease when snow shrouds the forests—or of the irregular nature of their power supplies—like industries served by hydro-electricity. In the northern French Alps, the output of electricity is much greater during the summer than when the mountains are frost-bound; these cheap and abundant kilowatts are utilised by moderate-sized industries (e.g. carbide, explosives, aluminium) which employ North Africans. These workers arrive at the end of the spring, when the dry season in their own country puts an end to agriculture, and return in autumn for the olive harvest; mainly Kabyles, but also some Moroccans, they number between two and three thousand, and they live in hutments. There are also some others who work as labourers on public works and other constructional jobs in the mountains, making a total of about 5,000. Before the war, they were joined by a few Italians, but the latter have almost disappeared from this type of migration.

In Norway the same fluctuation in power supplies is apparent. In Luxembourg and in Germany, thousands of Italians go to work in building and quarrying: in the former, regulations require their departure by 15 December at the latest, and they must not come back until the following February or March. Switzerland, however, holds the record for seasonal employment with 250,000 a year, of whom nine-tenths are Italians.

Finally, there are towns with a seasonal rhythm—taking the word 'season' in another sense; they come to life in the spring and retire in the autumn, and demand the services of a whole suite of temporary employees such as tradesmen, hotel workers, musicians. When Vichy closes its doors, many of the specialists who have served the spa depart for Paris or Cannes; similarly there is an exchange of workers between Paris and the Basque coast.

Naturally there is little in common between this last example and the case of industry or agriculture. Seasonal migrants into these are often poor and unhappy people who have few resources; the seasonal migrations provide them with the means of survival or at least give them ready cash for the purchase of necessities; the others, however, receive salaries appropriate to their skills and appear as a privileged class, enjoying permanently, thanks to their migration, the most favourable circumstances.

Another solution is to encourage complementary seasonal movements. In England, for example, some of the larger seaside resorts have set themselves up as 'conference' centres (e.g. Blackpool, Scarborough, Brighton, Eastbourne, Torquay, Bournemouth and Hastings). By having these large gatherings in the off season they can retain their hotel staffs and help to pay their way throughout the year.

Daily movements

Whilst seasonal labour migrations are on the decline almost every-where, daily movements are increasing continually, both in number and in distance; these two facts are but two expressions of the influence of technical progress on human life and activity. Modern methods of transport are favouring what has become an economic necessity, namely the concentration of the means of production and the growth of towns.

Definition of 'to and fro' movement. When a large factory or group of factories exists in a certain quarter of a city, or even in a small town, it attracts a number of people, and the same thing happens with a concentration of business houses and offices. It is rare for residences to be located in sufficient numbers, close to the centres of attraction so that the daily journey to work is negligible. Indeed, in the modern world, all labour in industry, commerce, services and such other occupation in specialised premises involves the participants in a certain amount of travel, and for this pendular movement between place of residence and place of work we may use the American term (now also in common English usage) 'commuting'. It is impossible to get precise information for the whole of this tide of workers which flows in many directions and often moves on foot. Recognising that in fact there is an enormous number of persons involved in this daily or even twice-daily movement, we may restrict the use of the term 'commuting' to movements which have three characteristics, an appreciable length, the use of some mechanical means of transport, and some degree of convergence.

Distance is a fundamental criterion both with regard to space relationships and to administrative areas. Thus the inhabitants of a town who work in two or three local factories are outside our definition, whereas those who come in from the neighbouring villages may be classed as commuters. In the interior of a great city or even of a small town, there may be a daily 'swarming' of people; they come in from the periphery and converge on the 'central business district', and so, even if their journey is not very long, it crosses an administrative boundary, that of the borough or commune. This daily movement is thus capable of being recorded and mapped; the 'swarming' congests the roads at certain hours, and is an expression of the divorce of the home and the shop, office or factory.

With the improvement of transport, the commuting distance lengthens. In Germany, in 1960, an example was quoted of a Bavarian porcelain factory, some of whose workers made a daily return journey totalling 140 km. In Italy, 15,000 people travel daily from Bergamo province to Milan. In the Belgian coalfields, 1,640 miners have a daily journey of more than 100 km (about half of them live in the Kempenland and half in southern Belgium). In Germany, 350 miners have journeys of more than 100 km. In France, it has been estimated that the average time spent by a Paris commuter using public transport is 1 hour 20 minutes a day. The area within which the centre of Chicago acts as a magnet extends to more than 50 km from the city; a community like Park Forest, 42 km from the city centre, consists largely of commuters. Around London, the commuting range spreads up to 120 km or more, including the whole of the Kent and Sussex coastal area. It is evident that the existence of fast main-line expresses, of limited-stop suburban services, and of motorways, will permit localities quite far afield to have better links with the metropolis than places which are closer but only have inferior or slow services. Experience at Los Angeles has shown that the same car can travel 220 km in 165 minutes on a motorway ('thru' way') but only 200 km in 380 minutes on ordinary roads.

In general, zones of recruitment are star-shaped, with more or less numerous arms following the lines of movement. But there are exceptions, for some industries organise their own workers' transport using their own coaches or hiring vehicles from a firm which specialises in this form of transport. In such cases the commuting zone may be determined by special factors which may have nothing to do with the general availability of transport services. Thus textile firms in Lille recruit a large part of their labour force from amongst the young women from the Pas-de-Calais coalfield, a distance of 30 to 40 km from the mills; private coaches ensure the regular daily transport of these workers, and a commuting map would show a large spot of colour outside the ordinary star-shape of the normal suburban zone of recruitment.

Commuting distances increase with the power of the centre of attraction: in the Parisian region, only 18·2 per cent of the active population works near home, and the rest travel an average of 6 km from the suburbs or 4 km from localities within the city. In the whole of France, 45·8 per cent of the active population works more or less on the spot, and provincial towns with from 10,000 to 150,000

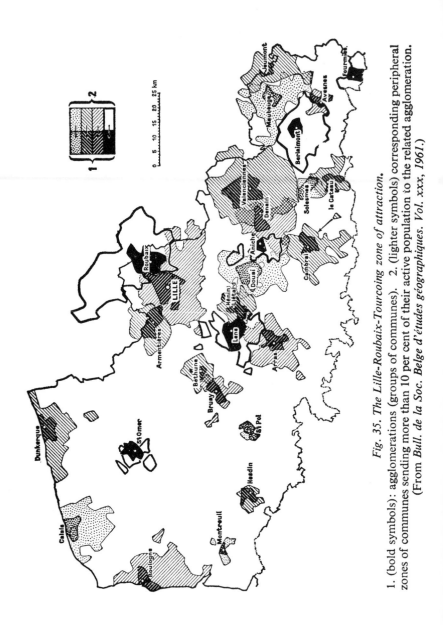

Fig. 35. The Lille-Roubaix-Tourcoing zone of attraction.

1. (bold symbols): agglomerations (groups of communes). 2. (lighter symbols) corresponding peripheral zones of communes sending more than 10 per cent of their active population to the related agglomeration.
(From *Bull. de la Soc. Belge d'études géographiques. Vol. xxx, 1961.*)

inhabitants do not generally attract labour from further than 2 km.

Reasons for the development of commuting. In 1901, there were about 100,000 workers in the Paris region who crossed a departmental boundary in the course of their daily journey to work; in 1921 there were 309,000 and in 1954 the figure had reached 1,025,000, and it has risen further in recent years. Reasons are not lacking for this expansion, and they include improved transport facilities, lack of foresight and organisation by the responsible authorities, and personal preferences.

The multiplication of transport facilities is the fundamental basis. To take again the example of Paris, in 1900 the first *Métro* line, which had just opened, carried 620 million passengers; in 1959 the *Métro* system carried 2,350 million. Between these two dates the speed of suburban trains has practically doubled, but within the city the speed of movement is if anything on the decline. By using the improved facilities the inhabitant of the Paris region, who a century ago made one journey a week, now makes more than one every day. The needs are growing more rapidly, however, than the possibility of satisfying them, and at the rush hours, whilst the number of places available per 1,000 inhabitants has quintupled, the number of actual journeys has increased ninefold. Indeed it is not the growth of facilities that has conditioned the daily movement, but rather the reverse.

We must seek other causes and first amongst these is the absence of a co-ordinated policy for the relation of dwelling-places to workplaces. We may say that in almost all the western countries, the surge of industrial development was followed only after a long delay by plans for town development. Though in mining areas or in new industrial towns, workers' dwellings (called 'cités ouvrières' in France) have been built close to the pithead or factory, the same thing has not happened in many old towns which have been overtaken by the industrial revolution and are now growing immoderately in the rhythm of modern urban expansion. However, during the last thirty years both Germany and the United Kingdom have begun to take seriously the problems of urban growth, and the communist countries are also preoccupied with the creation of balanced communities; the reconstruction of a city like Warsaw has been carried out by the careful location of industrial zones, business quarters and residential areas. But it is difficult (save in a case like that of Warsaw) to make a clean sweep of the past, and it is only in the British 'New Towns', which are

still of but modest dimensions, that spacing has been carefully calculated to absolve the workers from the necessity for too long and
too frequent journeyings. Similar efforts have also been made of late
in the Paris region, to bring residence and employment together;
here the creation of new towns, complete with dwellings, employment
opportunities and recreational facilities will, it is hoped, help to
reduce the volume of daily commuting.

Urban growth and housing policies being what they have been, individual factors are also important. Employers have often located
their factories so as to count on attracting labour from within a
certain perimeter: thus the French millowners of Roubaix and Tourcoing, in the nineteenth century, placed their factories as close as
possible to the Belgian frontier so as to attract labour from that
country. The location and development of the great Peugeot automobile factory in the small town of Montbéliard could only be
effected by drawing largely on the surrounding rural areas, and the
same process has contributed to the growth of Philips at Eindhoven,
who draw a quarter of their workers from the countryside, including
young Belgian girls who spend nearly five hours a day in a coach travelling to and from work.

Finally, the employee himself chooses, or is forced to choose his
dwelling-place with several considerations in mind. If there is a housing shortage, he lives where he can, often far from his work, and
many daily journeys are thus simply the result of the lack of planning
or of any coherent policy for matching housing and employment.
Other factors also play their part, such as a sentimental attraction to
birthplace or a familiar locality, the financial advantage of using an
inherited rent-free property even though it be far from the centre of
attraction. Rent is indeed a very important item; other things being
equal, it decreases with distance from the city centre, so that it is often
the poorest, unskilled and least well paid workers who have the longest journeys. However, there are variations, for the inner zone of the
city may be old, congested and occupied largely by industrial and
business premises; in this case the better-off folk move out and install
themselves in high-class residential areas, which are away from the
dust and smoke carried by the prevailing winds and have more space
and vegetation. The 'West End' of London corresponds to western
Paris. It is possible to distinguish three more or less concentric belts
around the centre of a city. As a rule, the first ring, surrounding the
central business district, is moderately or even poorly peopled; it is

usually known as the 'zone of deterioration'; the second ring contains the first suburbs, where quarters of different classes may jostle, depending on relief, aspect and the nature and density of the transport network; the outer ring extends towards the periphery, getting more and more diffuse, with the price of land, and so the rents, decreasing with distance from the city—inversely to the cost of transport, unfortunately.

The question of expense is not the only consideration, for individual taste also enters the picture. Some people cannot bear to leave the friendly congestion of the city; others prefer the peace and quiet of a semi-rural abode. An enquiry made in Chicago in 1956 produced the following result: 81 per cent of the people interrogated preferred to live away from the city because of the greater ease of raising a family, 77 per cent found the whole round of life more agreeable in suburbia. It is a fact that the number of children is much higher in the outer suburbs, which are especially the domain of young couples.

Lastly, the choice of employment also exerts an influence, for the wage-earner often prefers to leave his village or small town to seek work in the large city or metropolis, where wages are higher and opportunities more varied; the wage differential enables him to pay his fare and to have a more interesting job. In the same way, technicians and other specialists can only find appropriate employment in certain places or certain types of enterprise; and all these possibilities or necessities of choice have but one result, to compel people to undertake numerous journeys to work.

Different types of daily travellers. The simplest case is that of the rural dweller who has not yet been uprooted. He lives on a farm, the resources of which are insufficient, and engages in some other activity whilst continuing to make use of his land. All kinds of transitional stages are possible, from the man who only works in the factory during the winter when the land is idle, to the son or daughter who continues to live on the family farm but takes no part in the agricultural activities.

In the United States this kind of thing is widespread; in 1970, it was estimated that about 50 per cent of all farms could be classified in one or other of two categories, residential or part-time. In both cases the farmer has other resources at his disposal; a 'part-time' farmer is one who works for 100 days or more outside his farm, usually in an urban occupation. All the major agricultural regions of the United States figure in these statistics, except for the most rural of all, namely the corn belt, the Wisconsin–Minnesota dairy zone and the vast expanse of the Great Plains.

In France, those who engage in this double activity are known as 'worker-peasants'; they are very numerous around all the great cities and industrial regions. In the Alps, they are estimated to number between 20 and 25 per cent of the industrial employees (18 per cent in the paper factories; 33 per cent in the lime and cement industries, 35 per cent in heavy industries and 50 per cent in the mines and quarries). In summer, their numbers diminish and those who continue to work in the factories are exhausted by their farm work, so that they are given less arduous tasks such as maintenance work and overlooking—jobs which need the activity of mind rather than body. Their number is increasing with the decline of cultivation and the increase of cattle-rearing, and they are particularly numerous in the poorest and most mountainous areas. One of the inconveniences of this type of labour force is the frequency of absenteeism. Frequently this double employment is but a temporary stage, ending after a longer or shorter period in a complete uprooting and a migration to the town.

A second type comprises those who, being already artisans or workers, are drawn by the higher wages and more attractive jobs which are offered in the more important centres or in new industries situated at some distance from their traditional locations. In the United Kingdom, the 'industrial estates', agglomerations of modern and varied industries established in the older industrial districts which had been in a state of economic decline and stagnation (for example, certain coal-fields and textile areas), or in the vicinity of under-industrialised cities (like Edinburgh) have acted as centres of attraction for a large part of the population that was already in employment. As an example, the Treforest estate in South Wales has eighty factories making plastics, glass, polishes, dyestuffs, electrical wires and cables and other apparatus, chemical products, shoes, etc.; it employs 10,000 people, gathered from amongst the former miners and steel-workers of the coal-field; of these employees, 90 per cent make a daily journey to work of up to 20 km. Another example is the Peugeot factory at Montbéliard which has attracted many of the former watch- and clock-makers of the northern Jura; here the concentration of the motor industry, demanding a daily journey to work from the villages, is killing the traditional local crafts.

In a somewhat similar category come the wives and daughters of miners or workers in heavy industry, for whom the local industries can find no employment; they willingly travel to neighbouring towns with a more varied industrial structure, which may have more to offer. Thus the young women from the western end of the northern French coal-field are attracted to the textile industry of Lille; in South Wales the creation of new industrial centres has enabled 25 per cent of the women to find employment, and it is the same in north-east England, where there are thirty-five new industrial estates and the 'New Town' of Peterlee, where a woollen mill employs a quite different type of labour from the surrounding coal-field.

Two other classes of daily migrants result from the general pheno-menon of urbanisation and the expansion of great cities. Indeed, a study of the composition of the population newly established in the suburbs of large American cities between 1940 and 1950 showed that just over one-half of the new arrivals came direct from outside, set-ting up home on the periphery of expanding towns, whilst the other half resulted from the overspill of people from the town centre towards the outer suburbs. These two categories can therefore be dis-tinguished; first the new inhabitants coming from the countryside or from other towns—and amongst these the proportion of adults is very high (77 per cent between fifteen and forty-five years of age); they constitute a considerable source of labour placed at the disposi-tion of the urban industries, and their proportion of commuters is therefore high; secondly, those who choose to leave the centre for the suburbs, generally, because of the large size of their families (only 25 per cent between fifteen and forty-five years of age, and 41 per cent under ten years old)—and in this group it is the heads of families who continue to seek employment in the town centre.

In the opposite sense there are what might be called 'inverse commuters'; they live in the town centre and are drawn to factories set up in the suburbs or in a small neighbouring town. Their com-muting movements do not get mixed up with the great centripetal movements which draw all the workers almost at the same time to the same sector of the city, and are thus easier, even though often more complex: they escape the rush-hour crowds, but at the same time they do not benefit by the special transport arrangements which are made for the masses. Their situation is generally due to some excep-tional circumstances such as the removal of a factory or the creation of a new one; thus the great IBM company when it established its new works at Essonnes south of Paris, took with it about one-third of its former workers who were resident in the inner zones of the metropolis, and it was obliged to provide special coach services for those who did not have their own cars.

A last type to be added to this list is small in numbers but interesting in character: it comprises the 'high class' commuters (business men, administrators, intellectuals) whose research work or need for personal contacts requires certain residential conditions and who either live in the capital or other large city though their work may lie in a distant and less important place, or conversely live in a highly specialised locality and commute to the centre of their business activities. Such a centre of special activities, in relation to the great cities of eastern U.S.A., is Princeton. In south-east England the term 'stockbroker belt' has been coined for the series of villages and small towns, about 50–70 km from London, which have been invaded by wealthy business-men such as stockbrokers, managing directors, etc.

The main commuting zones. Those areas of the world which are most developed, industrially and technically, are also those in which daily commuting is best developed. All the great economic metropolises exercise a powerful attraction for labour supplies, but in addition there are large areas—the great industrial conurbations—in which the daily movements are inextricably interlaced, converging on several centres which compete for man-power. Such movements are a characteristic feature of the life of the region, but they are difficult to analyse in the absence of documentation sufficiently precise and accurate, and they pose difficult problems of cartographic representation. We must be content to simplify and generalise.

Western Europe includes many important regions characterised by the daily journey to work—in the United Kingdom, Germany, France, Belgium, Netherlands, Switzerland and northern Italy—in which many millions of people are involved. The amplitude of such movements is due to the development of great industrial regions, to the density of the population and to the multiplicity of urban centres.

In Western Germany, according to the census of 1950, 3,200,000 persons found employment outside the commune in which they resided. It was the towns of 10 to 15,000 inhabitants which, proportionately to their total employment roll, attracted the greatest number of workers from outside.

An investigation made in 1959, in the same country, showed that in northern Westphalia, 19·4 per cent of the commuters worked in

Daily journey to work in Western Germany, 1950

	Per cent of total number of communes	Per cent of outward-moving workers	Per cent of inward-moving workers
Communes with under 500 inhabitants	40	14·5	1·5
Communes, 500–5,000	—	33·0	—
244 largest communes	10	—	52·0
of which 46 largest cities			28·0

Source: J. Schiefer: *Marché du travail européen*, pp. 54 ff.

Cologne, 16·4 per cent in Dusseldorf and 16·6 per cent in Neuss-Grevenbroich. In the whole of the Rhineland a daily journey to work is the general rule, and the whole country has become divided into a series of overlapping dormitories, tributary to the large towns and cities. The daily journey commonly takes one hour. The phenomenon is still on the increase: it actually involves one-quarter of the work-force, without counting intra-urban movements; in some areas the figures are even higher, for example 31 per cent in Rhineland, 46·5 per cent in the Saar, and even 65 per cent at Ludwigshafen.

In a general way the same thing happens in the smaller countries like Switzerland, Belgium and Netherlands where short distances stimulate those movements of a 'suburban' type. In Belgium, 40 per cent of the working population is employed outside the commune of residence, in the Netherlands 15 per cent and in Switzerland 13 per cent. Of all the communes in Belgium, only three per cent have more than nine-tenths of the active population working on the spot. A map of the spheres of influence of towns with over 20,000 inhabitants shows a large star-shaped symbol for Brussels, whose influence is only counteracted on the periphery by the attraction of certain second-rate cities, Antwerp and Mechelen in the north, Alost, Gent and Renaix on the west, the coal-field towns and Namur on the south and Louvain, Tirlemont and Liège to the east. The Brussels commuters have a journey which averages almost 30 km, but 12 per cent of them come from more than 50 km away; the capital's zone of attraction covers 14 per cent of the entire country, and its labour force is 6 per cent of the national population. Some 47 per cent of the commuters are 'black-coated workers' and 53 per cent artisans of

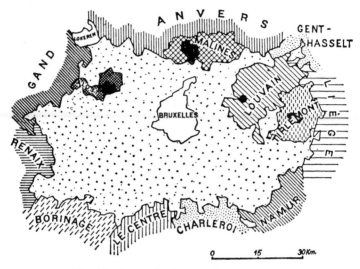

Fig. 36. Zones of influence of Belgian towns.
The unshaded area in the centre is the Brussels agglomeration.

various kinds; the Walloons, coming from a less overpopulated and more industrialised area, are mostly of the former class but from Flanders, where the surplus of rural population is more acute, come workers of all kinds including unskilled labourers.

In *France*, the daily journey to work is most in evidence around Paris, where more than 2 million individuals work outside their commune of residence. Of these, 720,000 move daily into Paris, where they make up 33·2 per cent of the capital's working population; 64 per cent of the commuters come from the three *départements* of the inner suburban zone. Within Paris, the *arrondissements* which form the centre of urban activity (1st, 2nd, 3rd, 4th, 8th and 9th) have more than four-fifths of their employees coming in from elsewhere. Outside the Paris region the greatest commuting area is in the north, where the density of the urban mesh and the multiplicity of industries produce a situation similar to that of the Ruhr.

In the *United Kingdom*, the great daily tidal flow of commuters within the London Basin is extending further and further out from the metropolis. Even the Channel coast towns like Brighton send their daily contingent to the capital. With this incessant growth of the commuting zone, it is not surprising that nine out of the ten English counties with the greatest population increase between 1931 and 1961 were within commuting distance of London. The streets of the City bear witness, at 9 a.m. and 5 p.m. to the coming and going of the vast black-coated army, hurried yet dignified, which brings life to the most powerful centre of business activity in Europe. The great regional capitals and many lesser towns, the great industrial zones based on coal, textiles and steel, all receive their daily quota of commuters from the sprawling English suburbs which, with their detached and semi-detached houses and gardens, are extending in ever-widening circles over the countryside.

In the *U.S.S.R.*, too, commuting exists and is spreading. About one-third of the active population of Moscow's suburbs works in the city centre; in 1955, 235,000 travelled daily from within the inner suburban zone (within the green belt) to the city centre, whilst 85,000 moved in the reverse direction. In the Donbas, more than 20 per cent of the miners live outside the mining area; at Kramatorsk, an iron and steel centre, 48 per cent of the working population come from outside the town, and at Voroshilovgrad, 23 per cent. These are but a few examples from many.

In *North America* also there are large commuting movements. In the U.S.A., in the thirty large towns which have over 400,000 inhabitants, there are 15,500,000 workers of whom 23·3 per cent commute from outside. Here again, the proportion is appreciably higher in some moderate-sized interior cities (34 per cent at Cincinnati, Minneapolis and Kansas City) than in the great metropolises (Philadelphia 22 per cent, Chicago 19). In New York the proportion is quite small (9 per cent) if one considers only those who come from outside the urban agglomeration (which extends from New Jersey to Connecticut); but the figures for entry into Manhattan Island are much more impressive—more than 1,125,000 people converge from all directions to join the 923,000 workers who already live there.

Means of transport. The transportation of such commuting crowds necessitates means which are numerous, strong and supple. There is sometimes collaboration between road and rail, and sometimes severe competition between them; the roads generally win, but the proportion of road and rail travellers varies with the degree of mechanisation reached in any area, varies also from time to time and in accordance with the distances involved.

To return to the United States for a first example, in the Boston region there are more than half a million commuters; in 1956, only 9 per cent of these used the railway, while 91 per cent used the roads (34 per cent in public or private buses and 57 per cent in private cars). In New York, the number of commuters by rail was 350,000 in the late 1920s, but only 208,000 thirty years later, whilst the road system was subject to an ever-increasing pressure.

In Paris, rather more than half the commuters use public transport; the *Métro* caters for almost 50 per cent of these, omnibuses for 25 per cent and trains 12 per cent, the remaining 13 per cent representing travellers who use more than one means of public transport during their daily journeys. In the United Kingdom, commuting in the Greater London region is often by multiple means—private car to the suburban station, where there are large car parks, then railway train to the terminus, followed perhaps by underground train or omnibus to the office.

In Amsterdam, a very detailed enquiry made it possible to outline a series of concentric zones, with radii of 12, 18, 24, and 30 km, corresponding to different modes of transport; within a radius of 12 km, one-half of the daily journeys were made by bicycle, with only 16·5 per cent of the commuters travelling by train and the rest almost equally divided between tramways, buses and private cars; from this inner zone came one-third of the daily commuters. Only 15 per cent of the commuters came from outside the 30-km circle; many of these did not travel every day, but those who did all used the railway. In the middle zone, between 12 and 24 km from the centre, tramways played the major role. Of all the Amsterdam commuters, only 7 per cent travelled by private car—and incidentally this is almost exactly the same figure as for the Paris region, a very different state of affairs from that which prevails in the United States.

Problems of the daily journey to work. Commuting is a system which clearly has its advantages; it enables great centres of economic activity to recruit a sufficiency of manpower which is able to live normally and often very pleasantly; but at the same time it places heavy burdens both on the individual and on the community.

There is no need to emphasise the enormous amount of time wasted on these daily journeys. It has been calculated that a Parisian wage-earner could work eight extra 40-hour weeks each year, without being absent from home one minute more or being deprived of a day's holiday; that represents the time he spends in getting to and from work! A somewhat similar statistic is that every Parisian spends annually the equivalent of thirteen days and nights in a public transport vehicle; when he reaches the age of retirement, he has spent a whole year of his life in a bus, on the *Métro* or in a suburban train!

To this loss of time must be added the fatigue and ill-health which result. On the 'pavé' roads of northern France which link the coalfield with the textile towns, vehicles bump their way for four or five hours a day, carrying the girls and young women who, in the interval between the outward and homeward journeys must remain standing for the greater part of the day at their work. This is a very tough endurance test for the female body; and it is recognised in many jobs which need considerable physical effort or great concentration, that accidents are most frequent amongst those who have the longest journeys to work.

Lastly, daily journeys represent a heavy economic charge, which falls on the individual purse. In France, though all wage-earners get a travel allowance, this still leaves them with a substantial proportion of their fares to pay themselves. Some firms spend considerable sums in this way—Philips of Eindhoven employ 110 motor-coaches to transport 8,500 workers daily over a distance which averages 43 km in all directions from the factory.

Added to this expenditure by the employee and employer is that which falls within the public sector. In Paris, the public transport networks sell weekly tickets at a much reduced rate; in 1951, with one of these tickets, a labourer's daily journey cost as much as he could earn in seven minutes, and by 1961 this had been reduced to six minutes. Between 1900 and 1960, the price of a ticket in relation to the wagebill of public transport has been reduced from 3·5 to 1. In 1975 the 'orange ticket' was introduced, a very cheap annual 'season ticket', valid on all omnibus and métro lines; its cost increases with the distance of the purchaser's residence from the city centre, and there are five concentric price-zones. This policy, adopted for obvious social and economic reasons, results in a crippling and ever-increasing deficit for the transport companies in the Paris region, a deficit which can only be countered by subventions from the public purse, regional or national.

On top of the expense is the inconvenience of the rush hour involving the provision of masses of vehicular equipment which is idle for twenty hours out of every twenty-four and which is yet inadequate at the morning and afternoon rush periods.

All these difficulties are much greater in western countries where there is free individual choice of transport media than in the U.S.S.R., for example, where public transport around cities consists largely of electrified railways and tramways.

In the United States, the craze for private cars is on the point of creating a catastrophe, and costs are becoming enormous: a train can carry 200 or 300 passengers at 90 km/p.h. using only 1,500 hp and a crew of three or four, whilst 200 people travelling by car consume ten times as much energy as the train, require at least 100 drivers, to say nothing of the police force required to control the traffic. It has been calculated that to replace a railway line at the peak hour would require 140 buses. In order to cope with the foreseen increase in peak-hour traffic around New York and Philadelphia, it will need seven times as much expenditure for Philadelphia and sixteen times as much for New York, to provide motorways than to increase the capacity of the railways. A paradoxical situation has thus developed: in 1957, the state of Connecticut devoted one-third of its governmental and local budget to its motorway network, a proportion higher than in any other state and representing more than was spent on education; the state of New Jersey has built a magnificent series of motorways for its commuter traffic, and 16·3 per cent of its budget goes in this direction, more than twice the expenditure on education. And at the same time it is necessary to subsidise the railways! The State of New York has considerably increased its subventions to urban transport since 1959, and New Jersey has signed contracts with the railway companies promising subventions if they maintain their services and their tariffs. Thus every effort is being made despite the defection of the commuters and the unbalanced budgets, to retain the railway network, for those responsible for planning in 'Megalopolis' are of the opinion that there is a danger of complete strangulation of the region if daily commuting by private car is allowed to go on unchecked.

This United States example of daily commuting which, like many other things in that country, has reached gigantic proportions, should indicate that even if such economic developments are inevitable, they must at least be carefully watched, and limited in every possible way to reasonable dimensions.

The movement of workers across political frontiers. We must place in a special category those whose daily journey to work takes them across a political frontier. This is not a common phenomenon outside Europe, where the density of population, the comparative smallness of the states, and political frontiers which have varied greatly in position during the centuries and which, as recently re-drawn, often cut across economic regions, help to explain its importance. It is only between the two parts of Europe separated by the 'iron curtain' that since the measures taken with regard to the Berliners, the frontier is completely uncrossable. Such movements take place between Eire and Northern Ireland, and in all the Rhineland countries of Europe, where they have been studied in detail. .

The motives for such movements are linked with the inequality of the economic situation on either side of the frontier—higher wages, better working conditions, more advanced social legislation, a more noticeable scarcity of manpower, these are the principal causes of the flow. Even though conditions may change in the course of time, the movements persist; thus Belgian Flemings were attracted to the French textile mills in Roubaix, Tourcoing and Armentières more than half a century ago, not only by the demand for mill-hands but also by the higher wages paid on the French side and the greater purchasing power of the French franc. These circumstances have changed since the war, however, with the textile crisis and the development of industry in Belgian Flanders, and trans-frontier movement has decreased greatly. On the contrary, the high level of wages in Germany now attracts migrants from Alsace and Lorraine, seeking remuneration better than they can get in France.

Transfrontier movements, like all the others, have been considerably helped by the growth and improvement of motorised transport. Postwar figures show very large increases over those of the 'twenties. But there has been a downturn in recent years in western Europe. Immediately after the second World War, about 150,000 people crossed the frontiers daily between Western Germany, the Benelux countries, France, Denmark, Switzerland and Italy. France and Switzerland were the main areas of attraction, and Germany and Belgium the countries of origin. But the hard times experienced by the textile industries in northern France have almost completely halted the flow of workers from Belgian Flanders since 1960, whilst the movement between Germany and France reversed after 1965. At the present time more than 10,000 French people work daily in the Saar and over 15,000 in the Rhineland. Several tens of thousands also move into Switzerland, where Basle and Geneva are the centres of attraction. In all, the number of 'frontiersmen' moving daily out of France approaches 80,000. Other daily trans-frontier movements take place between Belgium and the Netherlands.

These movements are thus of limited extent in comparison with the sum total of daily journeys to work; the major obstacles are not difficulties of transport but of currency conversion and social benefits, for the worker performs his task and receives his wages in one country, but lives, eats and falls ill on the other side of the frontier. Special agreements are generally made between governments to cater for such cases. Thus, in the case of those countries that have signed special agreements with France, French workers receive the same social security benefits and family allowances as are accorded within France itself.

In the particular case of the Common Market countries, the free circulation of people, envisaged by the Treaty of Rome, has had few important consequences so far: only the Italians and Irish seem to have profited by the arrangement. Out of about 10 million 'foreigners' within the nine member countries, about one-third come from countries within the group; this however, is not a matter of daily trans-frontier movement, but of permanent residence.

MIGRATIONS FOR LEISURE

Men do not work unceasingly. Their activity is broken by nocturnal repose, and this break is often accompanied, as we have seen, by a greater or less amount of daily travel; it is also interrupted at regular intervals for at least one day each week, and in many countries it is suspended for a holiday period of variable length.

These leisure periods may coincide with certain seasons: the agricultural rhythm gives the rural dweller a respite which in temperate latitude coincides with the winter, in tropical regions with the dry season; in school life, the fine weather and heat of summer mark the return of the holidays. They may also constitute an arbitrary break not necessarily coinciding with any natural phenomenon, nor accompanied by the interruption of industrial production. Though some factories may close so as to give all their personnel leave at once, many prefer to stagger their holidays.

Thus, freed from their occupations, individuals may take the opportunity of going away, and this produces the last of our classes of migratory movements—those which lead people on vacation towards a change of scenery and occupation, and then bring them back again after some days or weeks.

From the privileged to the masses

Such holiday journeys are on the increase—not indeed because the number of occupied people is diminishing or because work has become less absorbing, but simply by reason of economic and social progress. This form of escape which half a century or more ago was the privilege of the international idle rich, is now becoming the pre-rogative of the working classes in many countries, and is thus changing materially in character, with a whole series of different con-sequences.

For the sumptuous palaces which could only be found in excep-tional localities, holiday equipment of a more widespread and less luxurious character is being substituted. The few celebrated resorts of former times are giving way to a swarming crowd of smaller holiday establishments of all kinds; whole regions are being transformed by the penetration of the masses, in their search for nature, fresh air and sunshine, and these movements end by creating in the holiday resorts the very crowding from which the people sought to escape. Finally, as the clientele grows, tastes change and become diversified, and so the 'seasons' lengthen and perhaps merge.

An admirable example of all this is provided by the famous Côte d'Azur in southern France, with a yearly flow of over two million visitors, of whom 40 per cent are foreigners. At the beginning of this century, Nice was the winter resort of international millionaires; and there were no other places worth speaking of except a few towns such as Cannes. In 1920, there were six luxury hotels in Nice and eleven in Cannes, and between them they provided about 50 per cent of all hotel beds available in the two towns. In 1954, there were only two 'palaces' left at Nice and five at Cannes, representing only 29·4 per cent of the hotel capacity; but on the other hand, unpretentious 'pensions' and furnished apartments have multiplied enormously, whilst in every bay and on every cape of the whole Côte d'Azur hotels, villas and all kinds of holiday camps have grown like mush-rooms. The high season is now summer, and one-fifth of all the holi-day-makers stay there in August. The intense activity of all the means of transport is quite frightening, especially at the beginning and end of each month, when continuous streams of vehicles and trains creep like caterpillars in both directions, with frequent frustrating traffic jams, carrying pale creatures eager for the sun and those already tanned and satiated.

A similar to and fro movement takes place towards high mountain areas, both in summer, from June to August, and to an increasing extent also in winter, from December to April.

The intensity of these holiday migrations is closely related to the degree of socio-economic development found in any country. The first essential is the principle of annual leave of absence, and this is by no means always a feature of social legislation; in France, for example, holidays with pay for most industrial workers date only from 1936, and their duration was increased to five weeks annually in 1972. The second requirement is that wages shall be adequate to enable the workers to make financial provision for an annual holiday.

There is certainly a parallelism between average individual incomes and the number of people who take holidays away from home. Statistics and enquiries enable us to estimate that 64 per cent of Americans, 61 per cent of Swedes, 56 per cent of Canadians, 50 per cent of the French, 47 per cent of the English and of the Germans, take an annual holiday. But only 19 per cent of Soviet citizens. It is interesting to note that in those countries with a small proportion of holiday-makers, that is in which the custom is still confined to the privileged classes, the part played by foreign travel is much higher: thus 26 per cent of the Spaniards who have a holiday away from home go abroad to find their ideal spot, 20 per cent of the Italians, 14·3 per cent of the British and only 13 per cent of the French.

In any individual country, the higher the income and social class, the greater the number of holiday journeys; and to an increasing extent well-to-do families are taking several holidays during the year. It is not only the standard of living which matters, but also the way of life. In France, more than 25 millions take holidays; but whereas only 14.2 per cent of farm workers do so, and 29·3 per cent of those who have no occupation, 44·1 per cent of all artisans go on holiday, 54·9 per cent of the proprietors of small businesses and industries, 59·6 per cent of salaried staffs, 76 per cent of the middle class and 88·4 per cent of professional and upper-class people. Going on holiday is more characteristic of towns than of the rural areas: it is only quite recently that farm workers have begun to have vacations. And as the size of towns has increased, so has the percentage of holiday-makers among the population: in twenty years the proportion of French people enjoying this privilege rose from 38 to 50 per cent.

Thus one may say that in western Europe and North America—and the same thing goes for Australia and New Zealand—the majority of the people take part in these holiday migrations. In the communist countries of Europe, and in the U.S.S.R. too, holidays with pay are now the general rule. In other parts of the world, however, only a small minority of the population is able to take holidays—for example, the wealthier citizens of the great Brazilian cities Rio de Janeiro, São Paulo, Belo Horizonte, who are able to taste the refreshing coolness of the mountains or the delights of the beaches during their tropical summer.

Simple holiday journeys

In most cases, those who have the opportunity to take a holiday are content to seek relaxation in a single locality, more or less distant, where they remain for the whole period. The extreme examples of this are the week end and Sunday journeys which enable millions of town-dwellers to escape for a few hours from the crowded buildings and streets and seek the green, if not necessarily the calm, of the countryside. These day excursions are usually accompanied by shocking traffic jams on all the roads radiating from the great cities, which the townsman must endure twice over in order to visit his country cottage, or some other spot which attracts by the beauty of its site or the quality of its cuisine.

Other holiday migrations are of longer duration and wider amplitude, corresponding to the period of the annual vacation. They are of very varied character and one could define many different categories.

In all countries of the world, school children are allowed several intermissions during the course of a year's work, and in some of them they form in numbers the larger part of the holiday movement. As soon as the children are free, their parents send them away, to other families or relatives or to special camps, often far from home, and the same thing may happen several times a year. Sometimes the mother will accompany the children, and the father will join them at intervals in their temporary home, when he can get away from business. In this way journeys for business and pleasure get mixed up.

Many classes of workers now enjoy holidays with pay, and take advantage of the opportunity to shift their residence temporarily; this is general amongst salaried staffs and is becoming more and more common amongst wage-earners. In the United States even the farming population is beginning to share the same advantages; abandoning their snow-covered Middle West farms, they move to the mildness of Florida. The attraction of this State with its peculiarly privileged climate is such that many business men leave the fogs and the cold of the great north-eastern cities and set up subsidiary offices in Miami, from which they continue to direct their affairs by long-distance telephone.

These holiday migrations, then, may be of very variable duration, from a single day to several months. They may cross frontiers and even oceans; considerations of simple economics actually draw people from eastern United States to the winter sports centres of western Europe rather than to their own centres in the Rockies. The Côte d'Azur is one of the world's major tourist playgrounds, and 40 per cent of its visitors each year are foreigners, of whom about three-fifths come in almost equal numbers from the United Kingdom, the Benelux countries and Germany, another fifth from Italy and Switzerland and the remainder from Scandinavia, Latin America, the Iberian peninsula and North America.

Leisured nomadism, or migrations of the 'Cook's Tour' type

Many people prefer to have more than one holiday centre, or even to keep on the move the whole time. This is becoming more and more common with the improvement of transport and the development of a taste for travel, and we may call this leisured form of nomadism after the great English tourist agency established as long ago as 1844 by Thomas Cook, the 'Cook's Tour' type.

Organised holiday travel covering tours of a province, a country or even a whole continent, is expanding unceasingly. Often the tours are made by coach, sometimes by ship. In the case of overland tours, the journeying is done by day, and almost every night is passed in a different hotel; whilst on cruises the travel is effected by night and the days are spent at the ports visited.

In the United States, the use of electrically equipped caravans towed by automobiles and the existence of well-organised camps enables some lovers of constant change, particularly retired people and others who are not tied to one place by their means of livelihood, to live in Florida in the winter and in New England in the summer; and between these two terminals all kinds of holiday journeying is possible.

The development of individual tourism by automobile has been such, on both sides of the North Atlantic, as to give rise to what is almost a new form of civilisation, with motorways, scenic itineraries, *son et lumière* displays in old castles and chateaux, motels, service stations, and the proliferation of guide-books, maps, and souvenirs.

Consequences of holiday travel

In Western Europe alone, each year 150 million people make greater or less journeys for holiday purposes; statistics show a regular increase in the number of frontier crossings. In the U.S.A. the number of visitors quadrupled between 1951 and 1975 whilst the numbers leaving for foreign destinations rose from 5 million to 26 million. These movements have many consequences.

Changes of air and of occupation are good for human health, and the beneficent consequences of holidays are universally recognised. Thus all organisations concerned with social improvements, be they state or private, are concerned to ensure for the largest number of people a few days or weeks of holiday away from home; and children are especially privileged in this respect. It is not only the body which derives benefit from a temporary change of location. Remembrances accumulate, experience is enriched and new links are forged. The mingling of urban and rural, of dwellers in the hinterland and those on the coast, of citizens of many far-flung and varied countries, is of immense importance in the explanation of some aspects of definitive migration, for the accelerated evolution of areas which remain on the margin of modern progress (and so are particularly appreciated by tourists for the 'character' which they have preserved) and for the spread of uniformity in modern civilisation. Someone should study the influence of certain chains of international hotels, like the famous palaces of the Hilton group, or of the waves of English-speaking tourists, in particular the groups of American women who spend their savings on long international cruises, doing more to spread their own language than all the institutes put together. One sphere in which this interpenetration is most obvious to the much-travelled person is that of the kitchen. Year by year a world overrun by waves of tourists, ever more numerous and more inquisitive, is losing some of its mystery and also its diversity.

The tourist industry entails the growth of transport, commerce and buildings; it is a powerful stimulus of regional development and in some countries even plays an important part in the national economy.

Air and road travel now appear to be the transport media most willingly used by tourists. For transoceanic voyages, the aircraft has outmoded the ship which is often considered too slow: thus 71 per cent of transatlantic crossings are now made by air, 81 per cent of Iceland's visitors arrive by air, and even the United Kingdom, closer to the continent, receives 53 per cent by air. On the continents, the automobile, which is more supple than the train, has ousted the latter: 66 per cent of visitors to Spain arrive by road, and 70 per cent of those to Italy, compared respectively with 12 and 24 per cent cent by rail. The concentration of the majority of the travel upon short periods always creates difficulties; it involves the construction of ever wider and wider access roads and the multiplication of transport vehicles and personnel, and the congestion, which is inevitable provokes not only considerable inconvenience but also fatal accidents.

Arrived at his chosen locality, the tourist requires shopping facili-ties and usually a lodging or at least camping arrangements. In Switzerland, in 1970, no less than 30,684,000 nights were passed by visitors in hotel rooms or private houses, and more than 1 million under canvas. This necessitates planning and organisation on the part of the resorts. A tourist region is one which must develop or renew itself; in old Europe, the strings of villas and bathing-places that now hem almost all coasts represent new habits and new human settlements; on the contrary, the mountain villages, almost aban-doned by poverty-stricken peasants, begin a new life and modernise themselves when they are overtaken by summer or winter sports. The erection of hotels and shops is only the outward and visible sign of a fundamental change which brings a clean and adequate water supply, a new transport system, the local production or importation of con-siderable quantities of fresh food, the recruitment of labour for the hotel industry, for trade and other special services such as guides, ski-instructors, swimming pool attendants, etc. Thus not merely is the external appearance transformed, but also the fundamental economy of the region and its demographic rhythm.

However, such regional development is not without its difficulties; though most mountain resorts enjoy a fairly long double season, the same cannot often be said for the coastal resorts. Thus, in the northern French Alps and in the Swiss and Austrian Alps, the summer season lasts from June until the end of August, and the winter season from early December to the end of April in the snowiest parts. On the other hand, on the Channel and North Sea coasts, in Scotland and in Scandinavia, the coastal resort season is scarcely longer than six to eight weeks, and the hotel industry experiences great difficulties. All holiday regions are making great efforts to stagger the holidays so as to reduce the amount of high-season congestion.

The economic importance of tourism makes itself felt on a national scale. An examination of the balance between the receipts from the influx of tourists into any country and the amount paid by the inhabitants of that same country on foreign travel is interesting. Amongst the states of western Europe and North America, Spain has an easy lead; with 30 million visitors in 1975, it benefits from a large tourist income whilst its own nationals go abroad but little. The situation of Italy also appears to be very favourable, as is that of Switzerland; these two countries receive much more foreign currency from visitors than their own people spend abroad; the same thing is true of Austria and to a less extent of Greece and Portugal. On the contrary, Germany, the United States and Canada have a heavy deficit on their tourist balance-sheet and so do Japan and the Benelux countries. The United Kingdom and Norway have a roughly balanced tourism budget. As for France, its balance-sheet has changed over the years; it is now only seventh in Europe in numbers of holiday visitors, but it has many nationals who are eager to go abroad, and in some years the balance is negative. Thus, for some countries the income from tourism makes a large contribution towards balancing the national budget whilst in others the cash outflow is substantial, and this sometimes provokes governments into the imposition of restrictive measures, either on the movement of citizens or on the amounts of cash that they can take abroad.

PART V

OCCUPATIONS

Whether they are densely or sparsely distributed, gathered into towns or scattered over the countryside, whether they are prolific or sterile, tied to one spot or migratory, all human beings, in order to live, must either have some productive occupation themselves or receive their sustenance from someone else. To examine all the forms of human activity would be to write an economic geography of the world; we must here be content with something far less pretentious. Who works? What are the main forms of human activity and how are they changing? What is their framework, or background? In answering these questions we shall briefly review the whole field of human labour; and that is certainly something that no study of the geography of population can afford to neglect.

CHAPTER TWELVE

The Working Population

In any population, there are very few individuals to whom the universal need for work does not apply. The school-child labours at his studies, the housewife at her domestic chores; the efforts of the men bring life to the home and prosperity to the society of which they form a part. Statistics, however, take no account of the work of learning or of running a home, though they may throw into the same category producers, distributors and those whose labour is of the mind, and may include in the same column the agricultural peasant of an Asiatic delta and the rancher of the Great Plains of the United States. The figures, in short, select only those people whose labours contribute more or less directly to the national economy; and in this broad sense even the subsistence farmer who only produces enough for his own family's consumption, is included.

The 'active population', in the generally accepted, official sense of the term, comprises all those who are engaged in remunerative occupations and who seek a livelihood in such occupations. Thus the self-employed worker is included as well as all types of wage- and salary-earners and those who work without remuneration within a family.

Contrary to what one might at first expect, the 'active' proportion of the total population varies widely. According to official statistics, it ranges from 21·7 per cent in Algeria to 54·2 per cent in Romania. In the world as a whole, there are only six countries (amongst those with reliable statistics) having less than 25 per cent 'active' (three in Africa, one in Asia, and two island groups in Oceania). On the contrary, the highest percentages in the 'active' category are to be found in the socialist countries and in Japan—over 45 per cent. The European countries, except Spain, all have over 40 per cent, and it seems that this figure is general for countries with an advanced economy: thus in the U.S.A. it is 40·8, in Japan 48·9, in U.S.S.R. 48·4. How do these differences come about?

A comparison of male and female employment seems to provide the answer; for whilst the figures for male employment only range between 45 and 60 per cent over the whole world (with Europe and the U.S.A. round about 50), those for females may be anything between 1·8 (the world's low record, in Algeria) and 50 per cent or more.

Female labour

Since the enumeration of the active population disregards the many tasks of the housewife, the only females appearing in the statistics are those who work outside the home. But should the farmer's wife be included, who works in the fields alongside her husband? Many of the differences spring from the rules made by different countries to cover this point. Thus, in Salvador the records show 18 per cent of 'active' females, in Colombia 15·4 and in Mexico 10·2 per cent— though these three countries are not dissimilar in general character and civilisation and the pattern of female behaviour does not exhibit such differences. But whilst in Bolivia the official documentation shows female peasants to be one and a half times more numerous than male peasants—a superabundance of unpaid female family labour—on the contrary in most other Latin American countries there are only one or two females working in the fields to every ten men, and these are nearly all paid workers, the unpaid family helpers having disappeared from the statistics.

The question of the incorporation of female agricultural labour is therefore vital. Even in Europe, a country like France counts as 'active' the wives and daughters who lend a hand at harvest-time and are otherwise occupied with the treatment of produce at the farm. This kind of labour is characteristic especially of small family farms which are often scarcely profit-earning, and one is confronted thus with paradoxical situations. Thus, in northern France, the proportion of active females is particularly low in the coalfield (under 35 per cent) for the local industries of coal-mining and metallurgy do not lend themselves to female employment; it is moderate (40–45 per cent) in the fertile and prosperous countryside of Cambrésis where machines and paid agricultural labourers permit a high standard of living on fairly large estates where the wife is free to occupy herself solely with the home; it is highest (over 50 per cent) on the hills of Artois where on the small poor farms husband and wife can only keep body and soul together by working side by side for a meagre return.

Thus the French statistics showed, a few years ago, that 29 per cent of the female population was in active employment, but if we omit the agricultural sector the percentage falls to 21·7. Since 1954, however, the proportion of agricultural workers in the active population has fallen from 25 to 8 per cent; so that in 1975 the situation was somewhat different: the total active female population represented 30·2 per cent, and the omission of agriculture reduced this figure to 28. This corresponds to the position existing in the United Kingdom since about 1960 (27·4 and 26·2 per cent respectively), but on the British side of the Channel agriculture is a profession, and a very restricted one at that, and there is hardly anything corresponding to that maid-of-all-work, the peasant woman from the poorer regions of France, who herself, was until recently in some measure similar to her sisters from eastern Europe, from the Far East, from black Africa or Latin America.

We must therefore be on guard against these anomalies in the statistics. Amongst the countries with more than 35 per cent of 'active' females, most of those for which data are available are characterised by a high percentage of rural workers. There are several examples amongst the states of black Africa (Nigeria, Ghana, Upper Volta) and in the Andean states of Latin America (Bolivia), in which nearly four-fifths of the active females are in agricultural occupations; or again in the countries of south-east Asia (e.g. Thailand with 46 per cent). But much the same thing is true of certain developed countries, like the peoples' republics of eastern Europe, where the rural proportion of the total population remains high.

The first conclusion to be derived from these figures is that simple rural work, needing under primitive conditions a large but unskilled labour force, naturally recruits large numbers of women. This is generally noticeable in predominantly agricultural communities or in advanced communities which have preserved a substantial rural sector. The women give their free time to cultivation, throng at harvest time and stay at home during the slack season. In black Africa, it is often the women who wield the hoe and cultivate the fields, whilst the men devote themselves to the noble art of palaver or are employed in the mines or on public works. Even in Europe, it often happens that the husband and son will work in the factory whilst the daughters remain on the farm, and thus there are certain countries in the world—in Europe, as well as in other continents—in which the official statistics show women in agricultural employment to be almost as numerous, or even more so, than men. Such is the case, for example, in Bulgaria, where females represent 50 per cent of the agricultural work-force, in East Germany (46 per cent), U.S.S.R. (44 per cent), Japan (53 per cent) and Thailand (49·7 per cent).

Even if we try to escape from this preliminary difficulty of estimation caused by the uncertainties with regard to rural work, other variable factors appear. For example, is not female labour influenced by custom and civilisation? The Anglo-Saxon woman is freer and more inclined to work than her Latin counterpart, who is more closely enveloped in the shadow of her husband and home. In the United Kingdom and Spain, the proportion of active males is roughly the same (60·6 and 57·4 per cent) but for females outside the rural sector the figures are 32·9 and 13·4 per cent. The restraining influence of conservative catholicism, and the tradition of large families, seem to play a large part in this, and these factors remain more potent in Spain than elsewhere in the Mediterranean lands, so that Spain also has the smallest percentage of employed women, even outside the agricultural sector. The conservative Muslim societies also keep their women in subjection, and though the figures for such countries as Egypt (4 per cent) and Jordan (2·6 per cent) certainly take insufficient account of the labour of the fellahin, they are none the less indicative of the almost complete absence of female emancipation, particularly if they are compared with the figures for India and Pakistan, recently separated members of a former unity, the one Muslim and the other cast in a difference mould. We may assume that the methods of compilation and classification have remained similar, but the figures for India, where females streaming out of factories and offices or even working as navvies are common enough sights, show 11·9 per cent of the female population classed as active, compared with only 5·4 per cent of that of Pakistan.

The standard of living also plays a part, especially when it is associated with a different distribution of occupations. In generally favourable environments, female labour is less widespread, and is no longer an economic necessity, for the husbands' earnings suffice to keep the family.

Finally, the political regime may also exert an influence. The transformations in progress in the communist countries demand a large collective effort and enormous manpower; besides, those states strive to liberate the wives from domestic servitude by the creation of crèches, canteens and other social services which enable all those who wish to run a job and a family at the same time. Thus in the U.S.S.R. the very high figure for 'active' population is easily explained if one bears in mind that every other woman is employed—actually 45·3 per cent. Statistics of female employment in several other communist countries—Bulgaria, Czechoslovakia, East Germany, Poland, Romania and Yugoslavia—show rates higher than 40 per cent.

There are yet other factors which tend to magnify or decrease the amount of female labour, but they influence male employment at the same time and so will be dealt with under the heading of total employment.

The great variation in the published figures for female employment, and the unreliability of many of them, hinder the formulation of any further hypotheses or more precise classifications. We may note, however, that an active female percentage of 29 to 35 seems to be characteristic of the most advanced countries of the world (U.S.A. 29·9, U.K. 32·9, Sweden 29·9, Switzerland 32·4, France 30·2, Western Germany 30·2). On the other hand, in the same countries, where a whole range of varied occupations is available—in light industry and in offices—the development of female employment is in full swing; in the U.S.A. the percentage rose from 21·8 in 1950 to 29·9 in 1970.

It must, indeed, be stressed that figures for female employment are rising rapidly, for two main reasons. On the one hand, there is the availability, as with all other forms of demographic data, of better information, resulting from improvements in census data and statistical presentation. On the other hand, changes in economic and social conditions the world over have led to profound modifications. Thus in France, the female proportion of the active population rose from 34·8 per cent in 1954 to 38·4 per cent in 1974; in Poland where the lack of man-power is a special problem, the proportion rose from 32·8 in non-agricultural occupations in 1960 to 41 per cent in 1972. In all the communist countries of eastern Europe, with the exception of Albania, there are more women than men in the active population —though the actual proportions vary with the nature of the occupations. The Soviet Union provides a typical example (see below, p. 338). In the United States, females now represent 36·8 per cent of the total active population.

Finally we may note that in general, in comparison with men, women tend to be in the less favoured socio-professional classes. In

France as a whole, male earnings are half as much again as those of females. The following table speaks for itself:

Active Population in France, 1974[1]
(Socio-professional classes; per cent)

S-P Class	Men	Women	Total
Agricultural workers	8·2	8·6	8·4
(of which family helpers)	(1·2)	(7·3)	(3·6)
Agriculture, salaried	2·5	0·5	1·7
Small business and industrial proprietors	9·1	9·3	9·2
(of which family helpers)	(0·3)	(4·6)	(2·0)
Professional classes	1·0	0·2	0·7
Senior civil servants and executives	7·3	3·5	5·9
Medium-rank civil servants and executives	12·1	14·8	13·1
Office workers, etc.	9·3	27·4	16·2
Manual workers	45·5	22·9	36·9
Service personnel (hotels, etc.)	2·1	12·4	6·0
Other categories	2·9	0·4	1·9
Total numbers involved	13,027,083	8,096,183	21,123,206

[1] P. Laullie, *Enquête sur l'emploi 1974.* I.N.S.E.E.

It is clear that in the sphere of 'family help', whether in agriculture, small businesses or industries, female participation is important; whilst in some other categories, such as 'personal service' (e.g. hotels and catering) there is female dominance.

Age and employment

In countries with a high percentage of children or of old people, the proportion of adults—and so of the working population—is correspondingly less. This is even more noticeable in the more advanced countries, where there is universal education of long duration and where the existence of pensions and of public assistance allow old people to retire earlier and more completely from their labours. The age composition of the population, as well as the degree of social legislation, are therefore factors of importance, which should be considered together.

In primitive communities the proportion of active persons is undoubtedly high, but there are no statistics to prove this. Thus, in the early Industrial Revolution in Europe, children from the ages of five to eight upwards were employed in the fields, in mines and in textile mills; and so were women. It was the same thing in Egypt and in India until a few years ago; in the latter, the mining legislation, which is considered as progressive, has enacted that females may only be employed on the surface and between 10 a.m. and 5 p.m.; and that no miner may go underground under the age of eighteen. In poor rural districts, it is common for even very young children to help their parents, and as for the women, they work in the fields with their husbands or even, in some African communities, instead of their husbands. The cultivators never stop, and go on until they are ready to drop. A poor rural population thus has a large active proportion because it includes children, women and old people; but these labourers have a very low level of efficiency and the statistics can hardly take them into account.

Conversely, when schooling is compulsory up to a certain age, all the children under that age are withdrawn from the labour market. In advanced countries, the proportion is becoming ever larger; in France, almost one person in four is receiving some form of education, for the leaving age has been raised from twelve to fourteen years and even to sixteen. In such countries, also, when legislative measures are taken to improve the lot of old people, such folk cease work and disappear from the active list. In France, again, there is at present one retired person for every 3·1 active, and if present trends continue, by 1980 there will be one to 2·3. Discussions on the age of retirement take on a new significance when one realises that certain concerns such as the French National Railways are paying out three times as much in pensions as in wages.

There are thus complex and varied relations between the age composition of the population and the active proportion. France in 1977 has one of the highest percentages of old people in the world, a figure which it owed to the long period of low birth rate from the early nineteenth century to World War II; whilst the rise in the birth rate since 1945 also provided it with a large crop of children. The number of adults aged fifteen to sixty-four fell from 67·4 per cent in

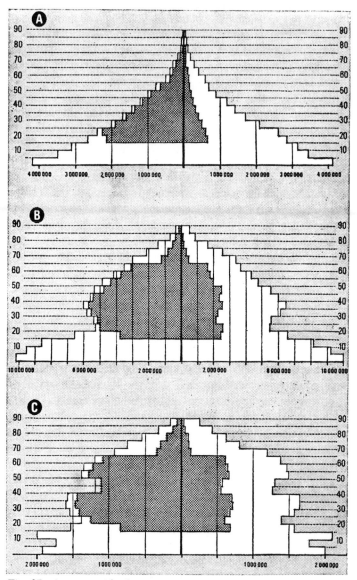

Fig. 37. *Age-pyramids showing proportion of 'active' persons in each age-group, in Brazil (A), the United States (B) and France (C).*

In each pyramid males shown left of the centre line, females to the right. Vertical scale of 5-year age-groups; horizontal scales of actual numbers of people. The stippled portions represent the active population, the blank areas the inactive.

1950 to only 62 per cent in 1960, and at the same time the working population dropped from 45·6 to 43·5 per cent. Conversely, the progressive and recently accelerated decline in the birth rate means that at the present time the adult population proportion has risen to 62·7 per cent, whilst the active sector, as a result of social and economic progress, has declined to a little over 41 per cent. In other words, many factors influence the proportion of the 'active', even within one country.

Within the different age groups there are variations in the proportions employed. Amongst the young ones, many are students, or if they are girls, are staying at home waiting to get married. Amongst the elderly, many are quietly enjoying their retirement. In the United States, less than one boy in two is at work between the ages of fourteen and nineteen, and under one girl in three; and as the decades have rolled on and social legislation has improved, it is noticeable that the number of boys with a job has decreased, whilst that of girls has a slight tendency to increase, a measure of the progress of female emancipation. As for those over sixty-five, one man in four is actually still employed (as against two in three at the beginning of the century and one in two in 1944); for females the figure is under 10 per cent. On the contrary, between thirty-five and forty-five, almost all the men are employed (98 per cent) and about half the women.

Here again, the nature of the employment and the standard of living have their significance. In Algeria, according to the census of 1954, the proportion of young Muslims aged fifteen to nineteen who were in employment was double that of the European boys; for the adults the proportions were almost equal, but in the case of the elderly the non-Europeans again formed a very much larger labour force, a fact which is easily understood when it is remembered that the non-Europeans were 82 per cent agricultural workers and the Europeans only 11 per cent in agriculture.

The proportion of workers in the various age groups depends on the youthfulness of the population: in France, there are proportionally more elderly workers than in the United States, but in the industrial regions with a very high birth rate, such as Pas-de-Calais, the youth of the labour force becomes very obvious.

Within the same population there is, however, a marked difference between the situation in the towns and in the countryside. In the advanced countries, the towns have a more precise framework of social legislation, schools of many grades, a regular pension for the elderly, and easier and more tempting occupations for females. The rural areas, heavily mechanised, need but little female labour. The behaviour of males and females in thus radically different; in the country a

Active population by age-groups

Age group	U.S.A. (1970)	France (1968)	Pas-de-Calais (1954)
Under 20	8·5	7·6	11·2
20–45	55·9	56·8	55·9
45–65	33·6	31·5	29·4
Over 65	3·9	4·0	3·5

man will work for almost his whole life, whilst in the town his period of activity will be much shorter; on the contrary, women are twice as active in towns as in the country.

Work and the family

The state of the family is another factor. It may be said that marriage urges a man to work since it gives him the responsibility of a home; amongst United States males aged twenty-five to fifty, almost all the married ones work (95 to 97 per cent), whereas the unmarried only show a proportion at work of 80 to 85 per cent, and the widowers and divorced even lower (75 to 80 per cent). Exactly the opposite is true for females: the married ones can leave to their husbands the task of earning a livelihood, whilst the others must fend for themselves. Referring again to the United States, 21 per cent of the married women aged thirty to thirty-four are in employment but 78 per cent of the spinsters and 60 per cent of the widowed and divorced.

The working life of the female is often complex. In the northern French coal-field, the young girls work in the textile mills until the time of their marriage, and then, after raising a family, sometimes seek employment once more. In the United States, women with children under six seldom work (only 15·9 per cent of them); when their children are older the percentage rises appreciably, especially in the towns.

There are thus a whole lot of circumstances, general or particular, that combine to control the expansion and contraction of the active population. The proportion may vary quite rapidly under the stimulus of urgent needs; thus during the war, many of the belligerent countries were led to the total employment of their manpower. In 1944, the proportion of the United States population classed as active rose to 63·1 per cent, a figure never equalled either before or since, and one due largely to the massive recruitment of female labour.

This shows, as does the example of the communist countries, that there exists a certain elasticity between the actual and potential labour force. All adults are potential workers, and a strong demand, and urgent necessity, or a policy of direction, can increase the proportion of workers in those categories that are not already fully employed, and especially the proportion of women.

Unemployment and underemployment

All the 'active' population is not in fact at work. Changes of residence, of employment, and adaptations to the economic rhythm represent an interruption of work for a certain relatively small number of individuals; this form of unemployment does not normally exceed 2 to 4 per cent. A country in which these changes are at a minimum may be said to experience 'full employment'. Such was the condition of France, in which the percentage of real unemployment fluctuated during the fifties between 0·1 and 0·3 per cent. This situation means in reality that there is a scarcity of labour; the number of unemployed being insufficient to permit a sufficiently wide range of employers' choice and the satisfaction of all existing needs.

A vigorous economic development allows jobs to be offered to an increasing proportion of the active population. The case of Western Germany since the last war is typical: as a result of the influx of refugees from beyond the Iron Curtain, one-fifth of the population in 1950 consisted of displaced persons, and in a disrupted economy in course of reconstruction the unemployment rate rose to more than 10 per cent. But as the 'West German miracle' developed, and graphs of production took an upward turn, the proportion of unemployed dropped progressively to 5·1 per cent in 1955, 2·4 in 1959 and less than 1 per cent since 1961, whilst at the same time the country has been drawing on foreign labour in increasing numbers from the Mediterranean region.

There is a delicate equilibrium, however, between labour requirements and availability. An economic accident, a halt in the pace of growth, a technical advance such as automation, a disharmony between productive capacity and the size of the market—any of these phenomena will result in an increase, perhaps serious, in the rate of unemployment. It was a concatenation of such features that caused the economic crisis of the early 1930s which was experienced by most of the advanced countries of the world. Some regions indeed suffered a veritable disaster: in South Wales one man in five was unemployed, and in the mines alone one in three. Even on the eve of the second World War, the United States still had 14 per cent unemployed, and the United Kingdom, Sweden and Switzerland over 10 per cent.

After a euphoric period of full employment that resulted, in some of the industrial countries of western Europe, in the attraction of large numbers of foreign workers, economic difficulties—linked in particular with the oil crisis and problems of international finance—have provoked a slackening of growth, or even a decline, with resultant unemployment. At the beginning of 1977 there were 7 million unemployed in the United States, 992,000 in Western Germany, more than a million in France. It must be pointed out that this unemployemnt is both an economic and a social phenomenon: in France, at the moment when 1,200,000 are unemployed, there are two and a half million foreign workers in the country. But the activities of the native and foreign workers are different, for nearly two-thirds of the foreigners are employed in industrial production, which only occupies 39 per cent of Frenchmen.

The curve of unemployment in the United States reflects in an

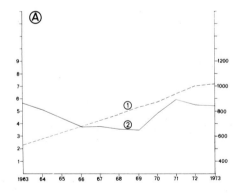

Fig. 38a. Unemployment and national income in the United States.
1. National income, scale of values on right. 2. Percentage of unemployed, scale on left.

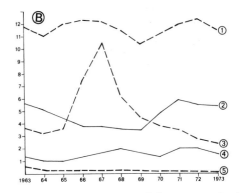

Fig. 38b. Trends in unemployment in different countries (per cent).
1. Puerto Rico; 2. United States; 3. Israel; 4. Sweden; 5. Switzerland.

interesting way the economic fluctuations of recent years. Greatly diminished during and immediately after the war, unemployment began to reappear towards 1949-50, when it reached 5 per cent of the active male population; the Korean war and subsequent rearmament programme caused the figure to diminish; the economic difficulties of 1954 and 1958 were each accompanied by a slight rise in unemployment, which again reached 6 per cent in 1961. The present situation is somewhat peculiar, for on the one hand technical progress, and especially automation, has permitted a considerable reduction in the labour force in certain industries—even the New York lift-boys lose their jobs by the installation of automatic elevators—and on the other hand, numerous industries can earn sufficient to pay their way by working at only 50 or 60 per cent of their capacity. In these circumstances unemployment must clearly rise again, but the fear of a deterioration in the social condition of the people has led to the passing of much legislation to counteract the danger—such as a large public works programme, special funds for the retraining of displaced workers, collective agreements and a reduction in the speed of progress of automation. The American economy was thus in a state of precarious 'underemployment equilibrium': the slightest economic crisis would be followed by a massive rise in unemployment. This indeed occurred during the recession that began at the end of 1973 and reached its nadir in 1975, at which time the unemployment rate was 9 per cent, a figure that is only slowly improving.

Who are the people most affected? First the juveniles aged fourteen to nineteen, usually seeking employment for the first time (16 per cent unemployment rate at the beginning of 1963); then, amongst the workers. the labouring classes are most affected (with 12·4 per cent), then skilled workers (7·5 per cent), qualified craftsmen (5·1 per cent) and lastly those who work in tertiary occupations (only 4 per cent). The Negroes make up half the unemployment roll; and indeed one might say that those most affected are those least equipped to earn a living. The length of the period of unemployment is increasing: in 1948, there were only 300,000 persons who had been out of work for more than fifteen weeks; in 1962 their numbers reached 1,100,000.

Being unemployed is hardly a profession; people are usually only temporarily out of work, and for the shortest possible time. And in addition to the variations in the rate which are linked with the general economic situation, there are other rapid and accidental fluctuations which accompany seasonal bad weather. All countries in the temperate zone have twice as much unemployment in winter as in summer, and in northern Europe three or four times as much; there are no such differences noticeable in the tropics, except where there is a well-marked dry season which stops all agricultural work.

We cannot, however, disguise the fact that data on unemployment are to be treated with great caution, and that it is often difficult to compare one country with another. In general, they only include the working classes and those with moderate wages who are subject to some form of unemployment registration; it is rare for the whole range of salaried staffs to be included. In certain countries—Canada, U.S.A., Japan, Italy, for example—sample surveys are undertaken which enable account to be taken of those who are not included in the unemployment insurance schemes, such as juveniles seeking their first jobs. Other countries make use of statistics furnished by the offices which ensure against unemployment, by the unemployment benefit organisation, by trade associations or employment bureaux. Thus there are important variations: in France, for example, the statistics of applications for jobs at the employment bureaux give numbers three or four times higher than figures of recipients of unemployment benefit. Also, the trade unions and the government are not in agreement on the numbers of persons involved. For other countries, e.g. the Irish Republic, the difference between statistics of unemployment insurance and those obtained from unemployment bureaux augments by two-fifths a figure which already fluctuates around 10 per cent.

The incidence of unemployment also cruelly affects the developing countries, in which the recent townward movement of impoverished peasants incapable of improving their lot in the countryside has engendered a state of chronic unemployment or under-employment. In Algeria, in 1966, there was officially 26·6 per cent unemployment in the towns, with 20 per cent in Abidjan and in Moroccan towns at the same date; and the rate was even higher, at 34·6 per cent, in Abeokuta in Nigeria. The cohorts of the unemployed are equally impressive in certain parts of Latin America: 36 per cent in Colombia in 1971, whilst in Peru, between 1965 and 1975, only one-fifth of the new entrants into the labour market found employment. The record must surely be held by India, however, where in recent years it is estimated that more than 220 millions are unemployed or under-employed, in fact 42 per cent of the entire population.

Unemployment, however, is the official state of being actually without work. It fails to take account of what is known as 'under-employment'. Many workers could be occupied for more days in the year, or for more hours in the week, or could work with greater efficiency if they had better materials to work with. These forms of underemployment are manifold; they have been well enough known in agriculture for a very long time, but they exist also in industry.

The spectacle of agricultural labourers waiting in the village square for a landowner to hire their services is a familiar one to all who have travelled through the Mediterranean lands; some of the men may wait all day for a call that never comes. In Italy, agricultural workers in regular employment work 280 days a year, but the day-labourers only 161 days. For 94 days out of the 270 to 280 workdays in the year, these 'disoccupati' have nothing to do, or in the best cases are unproductively employed. Several years ago a law was passed obliging landowners who bought machines to continue to employ the same number of workers. In India, it is estimated that the agricultural output could be maintained with only 65 to 75 per cent of the present rural labour force; agricultural workers do 289 days' labour in northern India but only 181 days in the south. This partial activity is only one aspect, however, of rural underemployment; when the size of the holding is minute, and the persons who work it could easily cope with a plot three or four times the size, one can equally say that there is underemployment. The Planning Commission in India estimated that 50 per cent of the holdings cultivated by peasant families were less than 0·5 ha (1¼ acres), a paltry size indeed.

As for underemployment in industry, it affects certain branches which are in a state of more or less concealed crisis and in which, in order to avoid dismissals, the hours of work are reduced. In the French textile industry the weekly hours are almost always fewer than in other industries; thus in 1955, they were only 41·7 as against 45 for all the other transformation industries. In the northern cotton mills the working week was actually reduced for a while to 30–35 hours. Here again one is justified in referring to under-employment.

It is naturally much more difficult to measure underemployment than unemployment, for it is an even more relative notion. There are in general only subjective and limited estimations or guesses, resulting from sample surveys.

The active section of the population is a fluctuating group on which the life and prosperity of the whole community depends; the fields of activity are as many and as diverse as the equipment, the organisation and the power of accomplishment. It would be fool-hardy to attempt to establish comparisons based merely on figures and generalisations; and in any case we must not disguise the fact that in this matter, as in so many others in the geography of population, it is easier to suggest than to draw firm conclusions.

CHAPTER THIRTEEN

The Main Occupational Types and their Evolution

Occupations are of almost infinite variety, and many classifications have been suggested, based on either the nature of the activities or on their social and professional characteristics. What is desirable is that as many countries as possible should adopt the same groupings, so as to facilitate international comparisons.

SOME COMMON CLASSIFICATIONS

From agriculture to miscellaneous services

The first scheme of classification, which is the simplest and is employed in the statistical documents of the I.L.O. (International Labour Office) distinguishes ten large groups including 'ill-defined activities'; these last are put into group 9, which is a 'rag-bag' into which all incomplete or ill-defined returns are consigned. Certain countries add an eleventh category—e.g. France, the unemployed; Italy and Thailand, those seeking their first job; Belgium, hotels and personal service and also the armed forces and unemployed as well as the usual groups.

The nine significant groups that one finds most frequently are as follows: agriculture, forestry, hunting and fishing (1); extractive industries (2); manufacturing industries (3); electricity, gas and water (4); construction (5); commerce, wholesale and retail, including hotels and restaurants (6); transport, warehousing and communications (7); banks, insurance, real estate and business services (8); community services, social and personal service (9).[1] The communist countries which publish statistics have various forms of presentation but they permit comparisons to be made.

This detailed classification is rendered additionally useful if it is possible, as in Belgium, to distinguish in the 'service' category between personal service and public service; but on the whole, as we shall see, it is very far from being sufficiently precise.

[1] These are the I.L.O. classes, re-defined in 1976.

Primary, secondary, tertiary
An alternative form of presentation puts the nine categories named above into three great groups, a primary group which includes agriculture, forestry, hunting and fishing, a secondary group comprising extractive and manufacturing industries together with building and constructional work, and a third or tertiary group which takes in all other branches of the economy.

This has the advantage of allowing a rapid comparison between the three major types of activity, for the first group includes all those branches which are concerned with the exploitation of natural resources, the second group those concerned with the transformation of those resources, and the third group all those which are not concerned with the actual production of material goods. The relative importance of these three groups categorises the stages in economic development throughout the world. However, it is unwise to generalise too soon; the subdivision of the tertiary group, in particular, can be very deceptive, for it includes such activities of advanced countries as banking, public and social services, as well as more elementary occupations like domestic service.

Besides, this classification, like the preceding one, takes no account of the social and professional hierarchy of labour but only of the general framework within which its more specialised forms are grouped. Thus it includes in the secondary group the office and research workers in this or that industry, though their activities are in fact typical of the tertiary group.

From employer to labourer
In order to analyse the economic structure of a country, or even of a branch of production, we can envisage a presentation which includes horizontal as well as vertical classification. This is a 'socio-professional' regrouping which takes account not only of the occupation (farmers, labourers, craftsmen, manual workers, traders) but also of the ranking within that occupation (employers, senior executives, officials and different classes of manual workers).

Such a grouping reveals interesting differences, not only between closely related types of occupation within a country, but also between the professional structure of one country and another. It is useful for giving a more complete picture than the general summary by groups. One can also get further precision by asking questions about the status of the individual within his occupational class, e.g. is he paid or does he work in the family? With this additional information the statistics cease to be mere abstract tabulations, and present a concrete and living image much closer to the geographer's needs.

Naturally, the more groups are subdivided and the more detailed the statistics, the fewer are the countries able to supply them; but we may hope that through the agency of international organisations we shall get more and more of what we really need.

The example of the United Kingdom. Most European countries, North America, Australia and New Zealand, and Japan, are already well supplied with occupational data. The communist countries of eastern Europe, and the U.S.S.R. also publish useful statistics though sometimes on a different basis. We may take the United Kingdom as an example.

Occupations in the U.K., 1976 (percentages)

Ordinary classification	Per cent	Major groups	Per cent
Agriculture, forestry & fishing	2·5	Primary	2·5
Extractive industry	1·6		
Manufacturing industry	32·6	Secondary[1]	42·3
Building	6·7		
Electricity, gas, water & sanitary services	1·4		
Commerce, banking, insurance, estate management	20·3	Tertiary	50·1
Transport and communications	6·3		
Services	22·8		
Miscellaneous	0·7		
Unemployed	5·1		

[1] Includes public works, not separately distinguished in the left-hand column.

As well as these two classifications, a third is available in the British statistics, dividing the active population into five social groups. These are (i) the administrative and professional classes, together with large employers and company directors (3·3 per cent); (ii) farmers, shopkeepers, small employers, officials (18·8 per cent); (iii) the general run of employees, including domestic servants, shop assistants, skilled workers and foremen (by far the largest group, 50·9 per cent); (iv) semi-skilled workers and agricultural workers (15·4 per cent); (v) labourers and other unskilled workers, military personnel (11·6 per cent). This classification has been based primarily on the earnings of the individual.

In parallel with this classification one could tabulate by age and education; from this it would be apparent that there is a certain normal progression up the social scale with age, whilst intellectual and professional qualifications are conducive to the rise of individuals into the first three classes.

We may perhaps sum this up in a more vivid manner by saying that of every 100 members of the active population, one is an important employer or director, two or three belong to a middle class of employers, two others are small employers like farmers and shopkeepers; a dozen make up the intellectual frame of the nation, including the higher professional classes as well as the minor officials; two or three are the agents of management (foremen and inspectors); five are self-employed, usually craftsmen but with very variable incomes; eight or nine are office workers or typists. All these make up about one-third of the active population; the other two-thirds are manual workers.

THE EVOLUTION OF OCCUPATIONAL GROUPINGS

None of the classifications given above is immutable. Even from one census to another, within a single country, variations appear, and over a long period quite revolutionary changes may be brought about. Thus in Canada, industrial occupations employed 28 per cent in 1921, 34·3 per cent in 1962 and 29·5 per cent in 1973; in Western Germany employment in the primary group represented 23·2 per cent in 1950, 13·8 per cent in 1960 and 8·2 per cent in 1972.

The examination of tendencies over long periods shows certain constant features, a general reduction in the primary group, growth and diversification in the secondary group, and an amplification and transformation of the tertiary group.

The 'primary' group

The primary group includes several occupations of which the most important is agriculture, and it is the evolution of this rural activity which will concern us most.

The world of agriculture is an extremely complex one, and we should be rash to include under the same heading the agriculture of North America or Australia, controlled by the profit motive, heavily mechanised, highly productive, and run by farmers who are substantial men of affairs; that of Western Europe, where the family tradition of generations of rural folk attached to the soil, has not yet completely disappeared, even though the techniques have been modernised (with notable exceptions like the United Kingdom which has the smallest proportion of agriculturists in the world); and that of the underdeveloped countries in which the cultivation of the soil is but the expression of the will to live on the part of men who scratch the soil with primitive tools in order to gain their daily nourishment.

One is tempted to add adjectives to the general term 'primary', to distinguish the elementary or primitive form from the transformed type characteristic of the countries of Western Europe and the European communist block, and this again from the transplanted type which has been developed in all the extra-European areas colonised by white folk of advanced civilisation. Even across the United States, however, one can still distinguish several sub-types, such as the small farming of New England which is closely related to its ancestral European form; that of the Old South which recalls the colonial period; and the exploitation of the Great Plains which is an expression of the conquest wrought by a powerful civilisation of advanced technique, a civilisation whose most recent upsurge is to be found in the development of the Pacific states, especially California.

Very diverse social structures are found to correspond to these differences in technical advancement and in the very concept of rural life. Some farmers own the land which they work; others exploit land which is not theirs; to aid them in their work, both types employ agricultural workers, either from within their own family or wage-earners from outside, who may be either temporary or permanent. The United Kingdom is probably the country which employs the highest proportion of agricultural workers in the world (59 per cent); it is followed by several Latin American countries of which the Argentine is the chief (59 per cent); on the contrary, in the whole of Europe there is generally less than 20 per cent of agricultural workers, except in Spain (29·6 per cent) and Italy (31 per cent); in the United States the figure is only 29·1 per cent.

In general, the countries that have a low percentage of agricultural wage-earners have a high proportion of family labour, as in most of the countries of black Africa. Amongst the more advanced countries, West Germany and Japan seem to hold the record with respectively 55 and 53 per cent of the agricultural workers being members of the farmers' families. In Europe, Greece with 39·2 per cent, France with 34, Italy and Spain all exceed 25 per cent, and Ireland almost reaches this figure. In the rest of the world the category is well represented in Asia (e.g. Pakistan 40·8 per cent), and in black Africa (e.g. Liberia 44 per cent). It is probable that the most interesting figures are not in fact available, since they would relate to countries that do not possess a reliable statistical service; we may note, however, that in these countries the proportion of farmers working on their own account is generally high. In Europe, the highest figures appear in Belgium (65.7 per cent), followed by countries such as France (45·3), Spain (41·8) and Italy. Outside Europe, the category is also well represented in the large developed countries such as the United States (53 per cent) and Canada (69 per cent), and in some Third World countries characterised by small peasant farmers (e.g. Ghana 67·8 per cent, Iran 58·5). The statistics of the communist countries are so presented that it is difficult to distinguish the three categories: thus in Poland, with 5,878,000 people employed in agriculture, 8·1 are alleged to be employees and 91·9 per cent individual proprietors.

The decline of the primary group. Since the primary group covers the most elementary activities, it is natural that with economic advancement it should decline, whilst other types of occupation delve deeply into its manpower in order to increase their own recruitment. There is thus in general a diminution in the part played by the primary group in the sum total of activity. But a relative decline does not necessarily mean an absolute regression and many countries have had, and still have, a diminishing proportion of agricultural population at the same time as an actual increase in the numbers engaged in agriculture. There are many different types of evolution for almost every country has its own peculiar circumstances which may notably alter the rhythm of its development within a few years. We may cite a few typical examples.

The United Kingdom is a somewhat exceptional case; the reduction in the rural population, which resulted from Free Trade and food imports from overseas, started very early, and still continues, though extremely slowly. Since 1881 the active agricultural population has diminished both in numbers (except in 1911) and in pro-

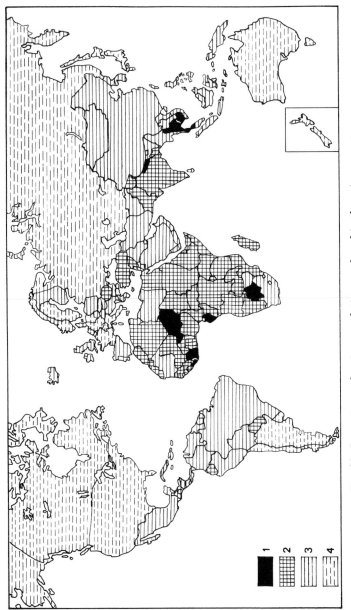

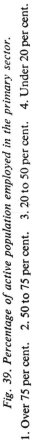

Fig. 39. Percentage of active population employed in the primary sector.

1. Over 75 per cent.   2. 50 to 75 per cent.   3. 20 to 50 per cent.   4. Under 20 per cent.

portion to the whole. Its proportion at present is really so small that the continued reduction is almost imperceptible (only 3·4 per cent lower in 1971 than in 1931).

In the majority of other economically advanced countries, the agricultural population went on increasing until about 1930 and then began to diminish, though its proportion of the whole active population began a slow decline about the end of last century or in the early 1900s, which has accelerated rapidly during the last two or three decades. Such is the case in the United States, which recorded a maximum agricultural labour force in 1910, in Canada (maximum 1931), and in Scandinavian countries, Germany and Italy. All these countries have not, however, reached the same stage; thus in Canada the agricultural population is only 6·2 per cent, and a little less in the United States (4 per cent), whilst it is still more than a sixth of the total active population in Italy (15·1) per cent. However, in Italy, after a moderate reduction of only 0·6 per cent per annum between 1936 and 1951, there has been a more rapid decline since 1952 with a reduction of over 2 per cent per annum; and Germany has had a similar experience, though with the proportion at a lower level (6·4 per cent in 1975).

Even in Europe, some countries have had uncommon experiences. Thus in France, where the general increase in population is but slight, the number of agricultural workers has diminished since 1921 but the proportion has remained quite high, for at that date two French workers in five were in agriculture, one in four in 1954 and only one in ten in 1975. At the present time, young rural workers are leaving the land at the rate of 180,000 a year, and even this seems insufficient to improve the profit-earning capacity of the farms. In the Netherlands, the rapid population growth and its high density, and the intensive use of the land, have resulted in a continued growth in agricultural occupations in parallel with the general growth in other sectors, but at a slower rate, so that there has been a slight reduction in the percentage, from 22·9 in 1920 to 19·6 in 1947; then a rapid decrease to 6·8 in 1975.

We may perhaps, though with a due sense of proportion, compare this Dutch example with that of Japan where the general conditions are very similar and the figures show but a slightly accelerated rhythm, albeit with much higher percentages (55 in 1920, 45 in 1954, 19·1 in 1970 and only 12·5 in 1975.)

In the communist countries the decline of the primary group is general and organised. It is made necessary by the transformation of the economic structure, the growth of manufacturing industries and of the tertiary group of occupations, and it has been reinforced by special measures—like agricultural mechanisation—designed to free as many as possible of the rural population. The governments in general hope to be able to accelerate the transformation of rural life so as to divert more people into other occupations. The fall has been sharp, as in Poland, where 42·5 per cent of the active population were engaged in agriculture in 1960, and only 35·5 per cent in 1970; but the levels are somewhat uneven, for the German Democratic Republic has only 11·7 per cent employed in agriculture, whilst the figure is still over 40 per cent in Bulgaria and Romania.

In the less well-developed countries, the evolution of the primary

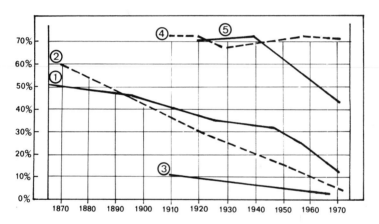

Fig. 40. Evolution of primary sector employment in different countries.
1. France. 2. United States. 3. United Kingdom. 4. India. 5. Brazil.

group is less closely bound up with the general economic development. Some of them have seen their economy turned upside down by the discovery of speculative riches such as the oil of Venezuela or Iraq. In Venezuela between 1941 and 1975 the percentage of the active population engaged in agriculture fell from 51 to 18·6 per cent, and the rate of rural exodus is here the highest in all Latin America and one of the highest in the whole world. Almost all investment is concentrated upon mining (petroleum, iron and manganese), whilst agriculture attracts but 4 per cent of it, and the standard of living in the countryside is very low. In the same class we can include Brazil;

here, the economic development increases daily, and there are regions and cities in the south which are abundantly prosperous, like São Paulo and Rio de Janeiro, attracting many migrants from the rural areas and providing them with jobs, whereas the great urban agglomerations in the north-east are quite incapable of absorbing and utilising the streams of migrants who converge on them. Between 1940 and 1970, however, the agricultural percentage dropped from 64 to 44, though the total numbers engaged in agriculture increased slightly.

A different case is that of India, which, despite five successive economic plans, has as yet hardly started the transformation of its economic structure. The number of agriculturalists continues to increase, as does the proportion which they represent. Between 1941 and 1951, of 20,200,000 new workers, 14,200,000, or 70·3 per cent, were absorbed by agriculture. The figures for 1971 show that agriculture still occupied 72 per cent of the active population, that is a figure slightly greater than at the beginning of the century.

The causes of the decline

The causes of the decline of the primary group of occupations are many, both psychological and economic. In all countries of the world the wages to be earned in agriculture are lower than those in industry and in certain sections of the tertiary group, but the number of jobs offered by these other groups is often insufficient to cater for the demands of the uprooted rural people. The hope of finding a better job thus plays a large part, even if there is little certainty of its fulfilment. In Denmark, in 1930, the daily earnings of an agricultural worker scarcely reached 50 per cent of those of a building labourer, but the countryside suffered little loss since there was an unemployment rate of 30 per cent. In 1950–54, progress in agriculture was such that the disparity in earnings was no more than 75 : 100, but as there was only 10 per cent unemployment and there were many jobs available, migrations from country to town were numerous. In the United Kingdom, it was the industrial growth in the nineteenth century that emptied the countryside, just as the great spurt in the Canadian economy since 1940 has drawn on the rural population for manpower. In the United States, between 1940 and 1950, the rate of rural exodus was only 28 per cent in the areas with average or high incomes, but rose to 36·9 per cent in the areas with the lowest incomes.

In the less developed countries there is no need to seek such precise economic correlations; it only requires the presence of large town to attract the crowds from the neighbouring villages in search of jobs, crowds who rather than expecting a clearly figured out rise in their standard of living are merely hoping against hope to escape from sheer misery. This is the case in the new African states, in many parts of Latin America and in Monsoon Asia. Naturally such movements are not irreversible; an economic accident or crisis soon causes the uprooted rural folk to hit the trail for their old localities. This is what happened in the United States during the depression of the 1930s, when the number of agricultural workers rose instead of continuing to decrease. In West Germany, after the second World War, it was into agriculture that a large numbers of the refugees and displaced persons drifted, before the younger and more energetic ones could find other employment; and the same thing happened in Japan with the repatriation of emigrants in 1945. The reason is that a family farm or work on the land offers, if not prosperity, at least an insurance against dying of hunger. The movement, however, is sometimes more systematic; in Africa, numerous workers get jobs in the mines under a contract lasting several years, and then return to their tribe and resume their agricultural way of life; many of the Algerians who lend their strength to support the French economy have no other ambition than to accumulate a small nest-egg which will enable them to retire to a piece of land in Algeria.

Who are those who leave the land with most willingness? All those who are least attached to it, either by reason of their age (because they have as yet no cultivable land at their disposal, or no family ties, or no accommodation, which might detain them), or because of their education, which they feel will fit them for other and better employment; and finally, the agricultural labourers and unpaid members of a farming family who are not themselves responsible for the farm.

In Canada between 1946 and 1955, the number of farmers decreased by 20 per cent, that of agricultural workers by 28 per cent and that of family helpers by 53 per cent. In Denmark, between 1938 and 1957, the number of farmers dropped by scarcely 8 per cent, but the number of agricultural workers and unpaid family helpers fell by more than 50 per cent. In southern Italy, and in north-eastern Brazil, it is usually the day-labourers who seek their fortunes elsewhere. Often the parents remain alone, living unpretentiously after their children have gone.

Agricultural workers do not necessarily have to change their abode to find alternative employment; in the United States between 1940 and 1950, 9·4 million agricultural workers changed their jobs, and of these 800,000 found other employment without moving from their houses. Around the large cities such a thing is very common—but it may occasionally happen in reverse. Thus in Saskatchewan, Canada, in 1956, no less than 16 per cent of the agricultural workers lived in towns and journeyed to their farms—an arrangement much more satisfactory from the point of view of children's schooling. Indeed, long journeys and poor scholastic facilities are serious difficulties to be overcome by forward-looking youth in the rural areas.

Adaptation of the primary group. In countries with a dynamic economy, most of the people who change their occupations do so by moving from the primary into the secondary group; this is what happens in the United Kingdom, Germany, France (since the last war), Canada, Australia and the United States. The tertiary group only attracts rural migrants in countries with a stagnant economy, like that of France between the wars, or in the underdeveloped countries; petty trading, domestic service and the police forces offer easy if not very productive occupations. A direct movement from the primary group into the more advanced sections of the tertiary group can only be made if the young country-dweller has sufficient intellectual ability or technical skill, and the same thing applies to recruitment into the specialised branches of industry. Thus a kind of pauperisation of the rural migrant develops, as when the sons of the sturdy Dutch farmers leave the family hearth and find themselves mere labourers in industry.

Another adaptation of the primary group is to be found in part-time work. In Canada, some 172,000 farm workers have another job as well, which in most cases is in forestry. In Germany, in 1956, no less than 4 million country folk were registered as having a second job, some 30 per cent more than in 1950, a growth which is due to the development of local industries and workshops set up to employ the excess rural population without uprooting it. In France, there are many cases of part-time workers who are called 'peasant-workers' or 'worker-peasants' according to the proportion of their time which they spend in field, factory or mine. In the United States, around the great cities, 'part-time farming' is a very practical way of solving the housing problem, which has been adopted by many families.

Even within the primary group important changes are occurring.

In most of the advanced countries of the world the number of agriculturists is not only becoming less and less but their technical equipment is increasing rapidly, so that it is difficult, for example, to compare a United States farmer of 1900 with one of 1975. The former produced sufficient food for eight people, but his successor of 75 years later produced sufficient for fifty, a spectacular rate of progress that can be attributed to the development of mechanisation—there were only 1,000 tractors in the U.S.A. in 1910, there are over 5 million now. During the last thirty years, agricultural production has more than doubled though the cultivated area has been reduced by 6 per cent and the working hours by one-fourth. In Northern France, including the Paris Basin, where the proportion of the population in agriculture is only half what it is in the rest of the country, land values and productivity are twice as high.

The reason for this is that the departure of part of the rural population from fertile and well-capitalised regions stimulates to greater activity those who remain. On the contrary, the depopulation of the less well-endowed areas may result in their ruination. Perhaps, however, this progressive abandonment of areas where the standard of living was too low is a necessary form of adaptation in the most advanced countries.

In the underdeveloped countries, the economic repercussions are much more delicate. If the rural population remains where it is, the very accumulation of numbers paralyses the prospects of improvement. If they leave the countryside, they only serve to swell the ranks of the hopeless unemployed in the cities; their influx floods the labour market and slows down or renders impossible the rise of wages and the progress of trade unionism and social organisation. In Japan, side by side with the permanent, organised and well-paid labour force, the factories recruit temporary workers who have no rights and are dismissed at the first sign of economic difficulty. And these labourers do not, by their townward migration, bring about an improvement in the conditions of life in the rural areas, for both capital and initiative are there lacking and demographic pressure remains very heavy. In such cases both the towns and the countryside are the losers.

The 'secondary' group

Under the title 'secondary' we include a whole series of diverse occupations whose only common denominator is the production of material goods. This group includes all kinds of extractive industries, the highly complex range of transformation industries and lastly building. Within the transformation industries, usually called 'manufacturing', some countries introduce a subsidiary classification, distinguishing the manufacture of durable goods, e.g. the framework of a steel bridge, and of non-durables such as tins of preserved food; or capital goods, such as machine tools, and consumer goods like motorcars or textiles.

It is perhaps awkward to have in the same statistical class the miner who hews his two or three tons of coal a day and the craftsman in the 'haute couture' establishment who embroiders silken gowns, but it is even more odd to have side by side the director of a great company and the labourer who unloads the raw materials from the lorry. The range of functions is even wider here than in agriculture: at the head is the managing director, supported by senior administrative and technical staffs (engineers or other specialists and personnel managers), who in turn are assisted by further ranks of minor officials, and then a whole series of manual workers, skilled and semi-skilled, down to the mere labourers, who, without any special skill, are absolutely anonymous and interchangeable, 'talliable and liable to forced labour at pleasure', and who earn the lowest wages of all (in France, this is the famous 'smig'—*salaire minimum interprofessionel garanti*—or basic wage from which the whole gamut of wage rates is calculated).

The secondary group of occupations is thus a world in itself. At one end it has very close relations with the primary group, for in the extractive industries man is scratching natural resources from the earth in a manner which is not fundamentally different from the woodman felling a tree. Indeed, to push the matter to its limit, one may well ask in which class to put the man who taps the rubber tree or the resin-bearing pine? Do they come into silviculture or are they extractors of vegetable produce? In Brazil, the statistics for extractive industries distinguish the workers who are concerned with minerals from those concerned with the vegetable world.

The interdigitation with the tertiary group is even more evident. Every factory has staff officers, both on the technical and the administrative side, whose functions are clearly more closely allied to the tertiary rather than the secondary group. In the United States, the percentage of non-manual workers is 10 per cent in the textile industry, 10·8 per cent in mining and 38 per cent in the chemical in-

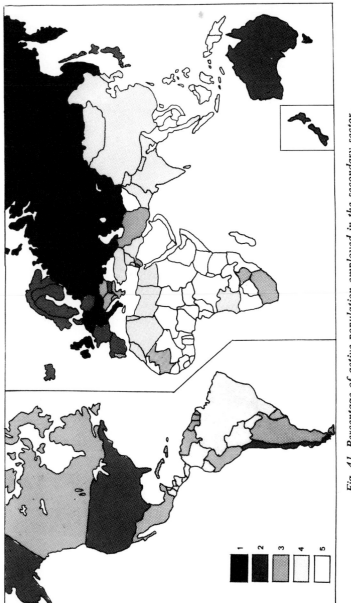

Fig. 41. Percentage of active population employed in the secondary sector.

1. Over 40 per cent.   2. 30 to 40 per cent.   3. 20 to 30 per cent.   4. 10 to 20 per cent.   5. Under 10 per cent.

dustry. In the last of these, the research teams and office staffs are becoming more and more important. The laboratories are often very large—the Dupont de Nemours Company devotes 3 per cent of its sales income to the financing of research; nylon was discovered in the laboratories of this firm after ten years of work by a large team of research chemists.

The label 'secondary', though convenient, thus conceals a great deal of ambiguity. For the detailed analysis of structures it would clearly be more realistic to study each type of industry separately and to make a horizontal subdivision into manual and non-manual workers or (using the American terms) into 'blue collar' and 'white collar' workers.

The cardinal importance of the secondary group

All the countries of the world are characterised by the increasing importance of the secondary group of occupations. This growth is the result of diverse influences, its rhythm is very variable and the stages reached differ profoundly. However, there is no doubt that the wave of industrialisation is an essential feature of the modern world.

This phenomenon began towards the end of the seventeenth century, in Europe; it developed throughout the nineteenth century, following on the industrial revolution which was based on coal and machinery. Its progress in Western Europe was spontaneous, helped by a whole series of discoveries and inventions, and it would be true to say that this region of the globe was the modern world's laboratory, where the techniques of manufacturing industries were worked out. From western Europe the movement spread to the United States, and to a few isolated pockets in the rest of Europe and in Russia. In these pioneer countries, the importance of the secondary group of occupations was thus already considerable by the beginning of the twentieth century, reaching 45 per cent in Switzerland and Belgium, 41 per cent in the United Kingdom, 40 per cent in Germany, 30 per cent in the United States, 29 per cent in France and in Canada, and 26 per cent in Australia.

This economic development of certain countries could hardly remain in isolation. The great transformatory industries needed raw materials, particularly mining products, and part of the preparation of these products had to be done in the producing countries themselves. On the other hand, the industrial countries, swollen with wealth, had capital to invest, and they created, as they do still, subsidiary companies in foreign lands; thus the great European motor-car firms have manufacturing and assembly plants in the Middle East and Latin America. Finally, the example of Europe could not remain unnoticed; gradually all countries of the world have come to realise that they must follow the path of industrialisation. So there have come into being industries which now rival those of Europe, industries whose beginning was often favoured by the periods of war which disorganised production and upset the rhythm of trade in Europe and the United States. Such was the origin of the great textile industries of Latin America. At the present time several of the developing countries are dependent, for the execution of their plans for industrialisation, on outside capital in the form of direct loans or international credit to be devoted to factory building and road-making.

In Australia, the proportion of the active population occupied in the secondary group rose from 26 per cent at the beginning of the century to 32 in 1933 and just over 40 at the present time. In Brazil, the secondary group increased by 23·5 per cent between 1950 and 1960. In Japan, the proportion rose from 22 per cent in 1950 to 37 in 1975. Even in those countries where development is less spectacular, the same trend is visible: in Colombia the percentage rose from 13 in 1938 to 19 in 1966, and in Pakistan from 7 in 1951 to 18 in 1972.

Finally, in the communist countries industrialisation is one of the fundamental dogmas of economic evolution. The governments of the various states have tried to accelerate the pace of industrial growth by all possible means, including massive investment, preferential labour recruitment, careful planning, propaganda, and rewards for inventions as well as for outstanding labour achievements. The transformation which is still in progress has been impressive and swift: in Hungary, the proportion in the secondary group rose from 27·7 per cent just before the war to 45·4 per cent in 1970, and in the U.S.S.R. from 24 to 45·1 per cent.

Industrialisation is indeed a veritable symbol of economic transformation. In making available to many people wages and salaries much higher than in primary occupations, it not only increases both individual and national incomes, but also increases·the capacity for production and consumption. An industrialising nation can gradually absolve itself from dependence on foreign countries by making use of its own resources. The real symbol of economic emancipation is the creation of heavy industry, which is the basis of all others. The construction of Volta Redonda iron and steel works in Brazil has been followed by others in Mexico, Chile and Peru. In all the communist countries, the plans have laid emphasis on heavy industries, and the greater part of the investments has been devoted to the production of capital goods. As for the welfare of the population and the raising of the standard of living, these both necessitate and encourage the production of a whole range of consumption goods.

Industry attracts industry; this is a well-known and frequently attested formula. To the extent that it necessitates the accumulation of investments and means of production, it allows a concentration of profits and so of re-investment. It attracts labour, moulds it to its needs and so hastens technical evolution; the promotion of workpeople within the factory is a frequent occurrence. In many countries the big firms have their own training centres and instruction courses for both technical and administrative staffs. But the workmen may also move from one factory to another. In France it is considered that the establishment of a motor factory is a good starting point for the absorption of unskilled labour, which after training can then move to the more complex techniques of the electrical and electronic industries. As an example of this capillarity of industrial labour we may quote the Peugeot company of Montbéliard, which recruits its workers in large measure from amongst the domestic clock-makers, only to lose them later to the electrical engineering works of Alsthom where wages are higher.

The progress of industrialisation, however, is not unlimited. It is estimated that for every 100 industrial workers, there must be 130 in ancillary occupations (commerce, service, and rural production for urban markets). Beyond a certain level, the secondary group of occupations becomes saturated. It is probable that the United Kingdom has already reached this ceiling, for 43 per cent of the active population were in this group as early as 1911 and there has been scarcely any increase since then; the figure reached 47 per cent in 1931, 46 in 1951 and 44·3 in 1970. The situation is stable, but that does not signify immobility.

The transformation of the secondary group. As the numbers employed in the secondary group of occupations grow, so the whole group changes its character. In the beginning, extractive industries are started, based on the exploitation of mineral resources. In Mexico, at the beginning of this century, they represented 9·8 per cent of the secondary group, a proportion which rose to 14·3 in 1940 and fell to 6 per cent at the present time. In Chile, they still make up 11·5 per cent of the group. In South Africa the proportion rises to 31 per cent, and Gabon must hold some sort of record with 47·8 per cent. A second category, that of the most simple food industries (milling and the slaughter of animals for meat), also has a tendency to develop rapidly, stimulated both by the productivity of the earth and the rising consumption; in the Argentine these trades occupy 10 per cent of the industrial workers. Textile manufactures, which can be based on local products and satisfy a large demand, and which often stem from old-established crafts, are also early developers; in Pakistan they employ 14·3 per cent of the industrial workers.

These early industries, however, are often but poorly equipped, unless they happen to have been set up by powerful foreign firms. Thus in India, 350,000 miners (20 per cent of them female) in the Damodar basin produce 38·2 million tons of coal; in the United States 250,000 miners produce 380 million tons, and in the United Kingdom 350,000 men raise 150 million tons.

If we follow the industrial development of a country like Australia or Brazil, we see in succession the growth of simple industries and then the appearance of new branches of manufacture, including heavy metallurgy. In Brazil, steel production was virtually non-existent on the eve of the second World War, but it has multiplied ninety times since then, and will soon satisfy the national demand; in Australia, iron ore production has multiplied forty times and steel production seven times, since 1938—and the same story holds good for Canada

Main branches of secondary industry (per cent)

Industries	Brazil	U.S.A. 1960	U.S.A. 1970
Extractive	3·8	4·8	2·5
Metallurgical	7·0	10·5	11·8
Textiles	24·1	6·5	3·8
Chemical	4·6	4·9	10·8
Food and Drink	14·0	7·3	6·2
Mechanical and transport engineering	3·0	13·8	23·4

and Argentina. Similarly, in the communist countries, even where heavy industry did not exist before the war, remarkable progress has been made.

A third stage now ensues, and the basic industries are followed by a proliferation of varied manufactures. The chemical industry, which needs large capital and a solid technical foundation, makes its appearance; and this third stage is also characterised by the development of automobile construction and consumer goods industries. In addition, the older branches of industry are transformed and become increasingly complex: in the food industries, for example, we find deep-freezing, dehydration, and the preparation of ready-made meals.

The result is a considerable diversification of the secondary group of occupations, with striking differences from one country to another. The examples provided by the United States and Brazil are instructive and characteristic.

In the United States, the diversification of industry has almost reached its peak. At the head of the list is the construction of vehicles, followed by general engineering, food industries and electrical industries. Important changes in ranking have occurred since the industrial census of 1947, for vehicle building has risen to the top (it was fourth in 1947) thanks to the spectacular growth of the automobile

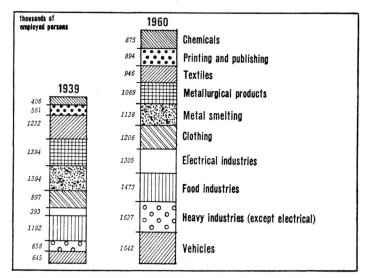

Fig. 42. Evolution of secondary sector employment in the United States between 1939-60.

and aircraft industries. Engineering, which occupied first place in 1947, has dropped to second place and the food industries have similarly fallen from second to third place. Electrical engineering, however, has risen from eighth place to fourth, and the number of persons employed therein has risen from 805,000 to 1,305,000. Primary metallurgy, conversely, has fallen from fifth to sixth place, and the most striking decline is that of textiles, from third place with 1,250,000 employees to eighth, with only 946,000. Wage rates to a large extent reflect these changes, for whilst vehicle building is among the best paid, with non-ferrous metals and coal-mining, textiles and clothing come at the bottom of the list with wage-levels only 56 per cent of those at the top of the scale. The chemical industry, too, has made great progress and has increased its employment roll by about 30 per cent. The changes are continuing, as the Table on p. 325 shows by comparing the relative importance of the various branches of secondary industry in 1960 and 1970.

Similar conclusions emerge from the examination of another highly-developed country, the United Kingdom. Here extractive industries are in decline, having lost 60 per cent of their manpower between 1921 and 1971, while the transformation industries have gained 42 per cent. Within the latter group one can distinguish the dynamic branches (mechanical and electrical engineering, rubber, chemicals, vehicle building) in which the employment increases vary from 63 to 105 per cent, and which represented 29 per cent of industrial employment in 1924 but 46 per cent at the present time, and the declining branches—textiles, clothing, leather, footwear—in which wages are low and the numbers employed are continually falling.

Even in Brazil, the same kind of modifications are in progress; all the industries concerned with metals and engineering are increasing rapidly (between 25 and 45 per cent employment increases between 1950 and 1960), whilst textiles remain stationary and the numbers employed in food industries are declining; the chemical industry (including pharmaceuticals) has grown more than 20 per cent, vehicle building has about quadrupled its manpower and electrical engineering has multiplied three times.

In addition to the simple rise and fall in importance of the various branches, there is the increasing complexity of the whole structure of the secondary group. In the United States, there is a continuous growth of industrial occupations which fall within the tertiary group: in 1970, as against 14·3 million people employed in industrial production, there were 5·1 million non-productive employees (buyers, salesmen, administrators, finance officers, accountants, legal advisers, production controllers, personnel managers, medical and welfare officers, and so on). Between 1919 and 1945, the proportion of non-productive personnel remained stable at around 20 per cent and even went down to 14 per cent under the stress of wartime circumstances, but since the end of the war it has risen sharply to more than 26 per cent since 1966. Between 1947 and 1956 the increase of non-productive employment was 50 per cent in the chemical industry, the oil ndustry and transport, that is in those branches in which investment and capital expenditure are highest; in part this is due to the considerable expansion of scientific research. On the contrary, the increase in the number of manual workers has been no more than 3 per cent, thanks to mechanisation which has reduced the demand for manpower by making each hour's work 4 per cent more productive than before. Between the early 1960s and the economic crisis of the mid-seventies, the numbers employed in the industrial sector increased by more than two-and-a-half millions, but 60·6 per cent of them were 'white collar' workers. In all, the total numbers employed in the secondary group of occupations are about 21 millions.

All these internal variations make for the existence of fundamental differences between one country and another in respect of the meaning to be attached to the same statistical categories. One needs only to see a public works contract in operation to realise that there is nothing in common between a 'building worker' in India and one in Europe or the United States. In the one case he is a man, or often a woman, carrying a small basket of earth on his head and working as close to his neighbour as any ant; in the other he is seated on a powerful machine that does the work of several dozen labourers.

With technical progress, the nature of the labour recruitment changes. At present in modern industry two groups of personnel are sought, in the first place a large body of unskilled workers who have simply to learn a single and preferably unchanging movement in the control of a machine that does the work for them, and secondly an *élite* of technicians who can repair the machines, devise better methods of operation and generally keep the productivity of the factory in motion. This development of the machine demands more and more capital investment and so larger and larger companies. In the United States in 1899, there were on an average 21·9 workers per establishment; at the present time there are 52. In the most modern petrochemical plants, enormous sums are invested for a very small number of employees.

Thus the secondary group of occupations, the basis of economic progress, is shown to be equally important for the breadth of its development in the modern world and for the internal evolution of its component parts.

The 'tertiary' group

More than either of the other two, the tertiary group is a composite one, so that the statistics relating to it need to be interpreted with great caution. It includes all those activities which are not productive of material goods, and so embraces transport and commerce, banking and insurance, public and private service.

It is obvious that banking and domestic service are poles apart; the one is the expression of vast financial and social organisation which can profoundly influence national affairs, the other is the most elementary occupation, found even in the least developed countries. Educational statistics are closely related to the structure of the tertiary group; thus in the United States we have the widest possible variation, between the liberal professions and higher technical occupations on the one hand, which demand sixteen years of study including one-third of this period at university level, and domestic service on the other, for which no more than the minimum imposed by the law, viz. seven years, is required. The difference is even more marked in the developing countries, like Brazil, where the doctor, the lawyer and the engineer have from fifteen to twenty years of study behind them whilst the domestic servant coming from the backwoods arrives completely illiterate.

Within the classes themselves, not all countries include the same occupations: for example, some countries include in transport the repair and maintenance of vehicles and rolling stock, whereas others put these into the secondary group.

Finally, as in both primary and secondary, the horizontal divisions are just as important as the vertical. Here again we can draw the distinction between manual workers and the 'white collar' staffs, and the percentages vary greatly from one branch to another. In the United States, within the category of 'communications and public works', there are 73·2 per cent of manual workers and 26·4 'white collar' employees, but in retail trade the proportions are exactly the reverse, viz. 72·9 per cent clerical, administrative and other staffs and 26·9 per cent manual workers.

Comparisons of crude figures are thus hazardous. We must distinguish at least two varieties of the tertiary group, which we may call the primitive and the developed.

The *primitive* form of the tertiary occupation group is characteristic of underdeveloped countries and those in the early stages of development. It includes a very high proportion of two classes which tend to disappear or at least to retract as the economic equilibrium improves. The first of these is domestic service: in Brazil, a working-class or middle-class urban family can easily have two servants, and in the country three or four; in the European cities in black Africa, the white families usually employ several coloured servants. In Brazil in 1950, the number of domestic servants represented one-fifth of all employment in the tertiary group, and in Mexico, in 1940, 16 per cent.

It is the same for certain types of commerce, for within this class are included not only the real distributive trades but also the petty shop-keepers who dole out a packet of cigarettes, or a pound of sugar, or home-made cakes. In Brazil, the statistics record no less than one quarter of the tertiary group as occupied in commerce.

In the *developed* form of the tertiary group the role of banking and finance increases rapidly, whilst many forms of service, especially the most elementary, diminish.

The major sectors of the tertiary group
(percentage of tertiary total)

Class	India 1971	France 1972	U.S.A. 1972
Banking, insurance, commerce	35·3	43·3	39·1
Transport	15·5	12·4	7·9
Services	49·2	44·3	48·5

Source: *I.L.O. annual statistics*, 1973.

In commerce there is a kind of internal mutation; the proliferation of petty traders who barely make both ends meet gives way to the development of the chain store with its numerous ancillary businesses such as warehousing and controlled storage; the total numbers employed may not greatly alter, but the character of the employment changes. In the United States, the sector including banking, insurance, and commerce has only 18·5 per cent of self-employed people, for the majority belong to salaried staffs, but in Brazil this figure rises to 45 per cent and in Mexico to 67 per cent.

It would need a great mass of detailed and comparable data to extend further the fascinating analysis of these developments in the tertiary group.

The development of the tertiary group. Like the secondary, the tertiary occupational group is one which is expanding as well as being in course of transformation in almost all countries of the world. Whilst the growth of the secondary group marks the consolidation of the economic potential of a country, that of the tertiary, bearing in mind the variety of its contents, indicates a real transformation of the internal economy. It is the expression of progress along three lines: (i) improvement of the basic services of transport, water supply and electricity, which permits the progress of industry and the development of new lands and resources; (ii) the progress of trade, commerce and finance which answers the development of production and consumption, of demand and supply in a more and more stimulated society with increasingly complex needs and a rising standard of living; (iii) the extension of public services, representing an increased effort by the State to organise the country and look after the welfare of its citizens. Far more than that of the secondary group, the growth of which accompanies the development of economic power, the growth of a well-balanced tertiary group reveals the full blossoming of national personality.

Looking in more detail into this general progress, one can put countries into different classes. The United States has by far the strongest tertiary group, which employed 37 per cent of the active population in 1910 and no less than 60·2 per cent in 1972. For the first time in the history of such economic statistics in any country, the number of non-productive workers represents more than 50 per cent of the active population; the tasks of administration, control and supervision are now greater than those of production. This is clear proof of the high degree of automation and the complexity of 'big business' in this great land of North America.

The proportions in other states, though moving in the same direction, are much lower. In the United Kingdom, which headed the lsit at the beginning of the century and had 43 per cent in the tertiary

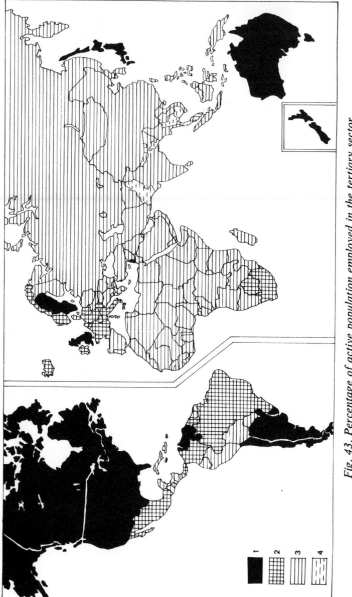

Fig. 43. Percentage of active population employed in the tertiary sector.
1. More than 45 per cent. 2. 30 to 45 per cent. 3. 15 to 30 per cent. 4. Under 15 per cent.

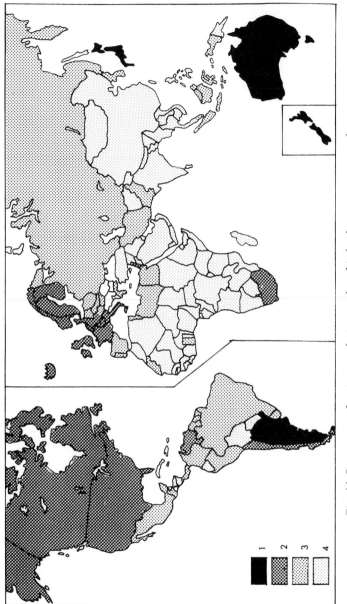

Fig. 44. Percentage of active population employed in banking, commerce and transport.
1. More than 30 per cent. 2. 20 to 30 per cent. 3. 10 to 20 per cent. 4. Under 10 per cent.

group in 1911, the figure had risen to 49·6 per cent in 1970; in France, the rise has been from 29 per cent in 1906 to 47 in 1972. Outside Europe there is the same trend: in Japan the figures are 25·6 in 1920 and 46 in 1970; in Mexico, 14 and 32, and in Colombia 14 and 30·3 (for these last two, the figures relate to the late 1930s and about 1964).

The simple percentages do not, however, always give a right impression of the increase in actual employment. Thus in Japan the numbers employed in the tertiary occupation group rose from 7 million in 1920 to 13 million in 1954, and 24 million in 1970, so that the proportion of the active population employed in the tertiary group is higher than in the secondary group. This is also the case in many other countries; first in those with a very advanced economy, like the United States, with the United Kingdom trending the same way, and secondly in those developing countries which have a 'primitive' type of tertiary group, such as Mexico and Brazil.

Within the tertiary group, the occasional availability of statistics allows us to analyse the movements of different classes of occupation.

In *transport*, the countries already well equipped have a stationary or falling manpower, as in the United Kingdom or the U.S.A. since 1920; but there are often internal compensations, the reduction in railway employment due to technical progress, and the virtual stability of waterways, being balanced by the great development of roads and airways. A general analysis of the situation should take account of these opposite movements. In countries where the transport network is still incomplete, important works are in progress that are accompanied by an appreciable increase in man-power. In Africa, employment increased by 104 per cent in Gabon between 1964 and 1970, by 30 per cent in Egypt and by 22 per cent in Uganda, during roughly the same period. There have been similar developments in Asia, for example, an increase of 187 per cent in North Korea. In countries undergoing vigorous economic expansion, there has likewise been an increase in employment, even though the transport system is already well developed: Japanese economic progress was accompanied, between 1954 and 1972, by an increase of 42·7 per cent in transport employment; and the communist countries of eastern Europe are in an analogous situation, with a 42 per cent increase in Bulgaria between 1963 and 1972 and similar expansion in Romania, Yugoslavia, Poland and Hungary, and even a 28 per cent increase in the Soviet Union. In North America also, during the same period, the employment roll has increased by one-fifth in both the United States and Canada. On the contrary, Switzerland, Netherlands, Western Germany and Austria have witnessed stability of employment, whilst a decline has occurred in Norway (−5 per cent) and the United Kingdom (−8 per cent).

In the *commercial* sector likewise there are great differences in rates of growth; the countries already fully developed show only a very slow progress or none at all; in the United Kingdom there has actually been a slight regression since 1931. In many countries a

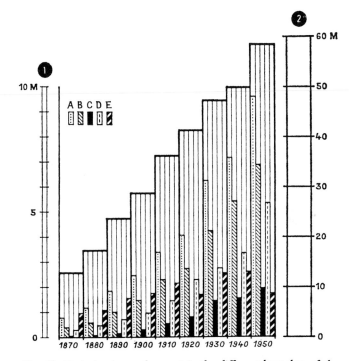

Fig. 45. Variation in employment in the different branches of the tertiary sector in the United States.

1 (*Left hand scale*): Millions of employees in the branches of the tertiary sector: A. Commerce; B. Professions, entertainment and personal service; C. Banking and estate management; D. Public services; E. Domestic service. 2 (*Right hand scale*): Total active population, in millions.

change in structure does not necessarily mean increased employment, but in the United States the number of employees in commerce rose by 44 per cent in the last forty years, and in the U.S.S.R., under rather special circumstances it is true, the figure has actually risen by 69 per cent since 1939.

Other classes also show outstanding increases, for they reflect the rising standard of life; such are *personal services* (laundries, hairdressers, etc.) which have risen by 24 per cent in the U.K. and by 41 per cent in the U.S.A. since 1930. Similarly the growth of the *liberal professions* and of the numbers of highly specialised technicians has been remarkable—a 30 per cent rise since 1950 in the U.S.A. for example; and in the U.S.S.R. the number of engineers has multiplied 3·4 times since 1939, and of doctors, 2·5 times.

All the branches of *public administration* are expanding—schools for more and more children, welfare and social security services which look after the health and well-being of the people in numerous countries, more efficient local and national administration—all of which need a large recruitment of personnel. In the United States, employment in public administration has gone up by 30 per cent since 1930, in Sweden it has doubled; in the United Kingdom, if we take account of modifications in classification in the sanitary services and in education, the increase has been not far short of 60 per cent; and in the U.S.S.R. between 1939 and 1959, the administrative staff of the communes increased by 10 per cent. Even in the less well developed countries the same trend is observable: in Mexico, though employment in public administration remained almost stationary from 1900 to 1921, it has since tripled, notably by the introduction of women, who represented only 1 per cent in 1921 and about 25 per cent now.

In the whole of the tertiary group there is one class of employment which is remarkable for its decline in all the well-developed countries, and that is *domestic service*. Between 1921 and 1951 the number of servants diminished by two-thirds in the United Kingdom, by more than one-half in Sweden and by 14 per cent in France. Domestic servants have indeed almost completely disappeared from American homes, and in western Europe their numbers are reduced year by year, and most of them are in any case foreign. In France, waves of young Spanish girls cross the frontier each year to serve in middle-class families; in the United Kingdom, private houses and hotels recruit their servants from Jamaica, Spain, Italy and elsewhere. In the underdeveloped countries, on the contrary, domestic service offers the daughters of rural migrants the means of helping their families to survive, and in Brazil between 1940 and 1950 the numbers of personal servants increased by 13 per cent.

A sketch of the 'quaternary' group

Confronted with the complexity of the tertiary group and the many variations within its manifestly heterogeneous sections, certain specialists have proposed the introduction of a fourth group. The proposal emanates from the United States, where systematic studies have been going on for more than thirty years, of the different occupational classes and their variation. The 'quaternary' group would include only the more intellectual occupations, the 'cream' of the nation's manpower, whose job it is above all to think, research and develop ideas. Naturally there are as yet no statistics relating to this fourth group and indeed it might be a delicate task to formulate its definition. It is, however, undeniable that certain categories of persons—scholars, authors, senior civil servants, leading bankers, etc.—play, both within and outside their own country, a very particular role which ought in some way to be distinguished in the statistics. Perhaps *Who's Who* would be a useful starting point (if only it did not contain so many who are no longer amongst the 'active' population)!

The volume of female employment

We have already outlined the part played by women in the active population; but their activity is far from being equally distributed amongst the different occupational groups and classes, and there are great variations from one type of country to another.

In the United States, since the beginning of the century, the proportion of females in the active population has risen from 18·3 per cent in 1900 to 36·8 per cent in 1970. At the present time, women are most numerous in domestic service, in which they represent almost the sum total (96 per cent), in office-work, in which they number almost two-thirds (63 per cent), in services other than domestic (45 per cent), and in the liberal professions and technical posts, commerce and industry. From a detailed list it is possible to see that they have almost a monopoly of professions which deal with child care, and of jobs as secretaries and domestic servants; that they play a large part in textile manufacture, the tobacco industry, dancing and music; whilst, in total, they make up 27·8 per cent of industrial employment, they represent only 23·5 per cent in transport, but 41·5 per cent in banking and commerce, and 57·6 per cent in community services, social and domestic service. They are, however, very poorly represented in such activities as mining (only 1·7 per cent), building (9 per cent) and agricultural labour (13 per cent). It is perhaps curious to note that they play but a very minor part in public administration, but that during the last few years their role as engineers, chemists, radio-operators and veterinarians has greatly increased.

A comparison with the statistics of female occupations for a communist country like the U.S.S.R. is very revealing. In the Soviet Union there has been a sharp rise of female employment from 28 per cent of the active population in 1929 to 51 per cent in 1970, but its role seems a little out of tune with the traditional conception of female frailty, for though there are only 9 per cent of women amongst the staffs of engine-sheds and tractor depots, there are 31 per cent in building, 48 per cent in manufacturing industry and, more normally, 83 per cent in catering, and 85 per cent in public health. The popular image of the Russian woman building a wall, sweeping a road, or driving a machine in a steelworks, has been fostered by the cinema and the press.

Female Share of employment in U.S.S.R.

Employment sector	per cent
Total active population	51
Industry	48
Agriculture	44
Transport	24
Posts and telecommunications	68
Social services	75
Health	85
Teaching	72
Arts	44
Sciences	47
Administration and management	61

In all the communist countries, the proportions are substantially the same, and we may note especially that in the field of teaching and health services, women represent three-quarters to four-fifths of the total numbers employed.

In the less well-developed countries, on the other hand, the part played by female labour, outside agriculture and petty commerce, is very restricted. Even in a country like Brazil, though there may be one female to nine males in the official statistics of agricultural employment (and there may be many more in domestic service in rural areas), there are only one in thirteen in industry and one in five in commerce. And the Latin American countries show a much higher proportion of female employment than those of Africa and the Far East.

Professional migration

It would be very interesting to follow the lives of individuals to try to discover the main trends of occupational change. The direction of such movements depends on the capacity of the individual, but also on the variety and strength of the demand from different sectors, and on what we might call the 'national mentality'.

When the primary group loses some of its labour, there is not always an exact adjustment between the numbers leaving and the jobs available in other occupations, and this may cause difficulties. Sometimes the rural exodus occurs too quickly, so that the labour market is satiated, as we have already noted. In other cases the migration rate is too slow and there is competition for labour between the various industries.

The best basis for the individual who wishes to change his job is education and technical skill. The greatest degree of social and professional capillarity is thus to be found in those countries where education is most widespread. The nation can thus draw on a large reservoir for the types of which it has most need, and the individuals themselves can change their jobs with relative ease. The huge numbers of engineers of all kinds produced by the Russians during recent years are often contrasted with the much more limited output of the Americans and with the poor development of this profession in France. One of the great difficulties of the underdeveloped countries is that they lack quality rather than quantity of manpower and personnel for the development of their potential wealth.

The amount of capital available for employment-creating investment is a second fundamental factor. Of what use are bodies and qualifications if there are no doors open to welcome them? The tragic case of the young Japanese students in the pre-war period, much more numerous than the jobs available, is an example of the under-employment of intellectuals, whilst the expatriation of rural Italians and Poles to the industrial areas of France and North America is another aspect of the difficulty and impossibility of change of occupation within the national framework. The creation of new employment indeed requires considerable preliminary expenditure—both on the preparation of sites and buildings and also on the organisation of the means of production. Communications, housing, urban services of one sort and another, have all to be provided. A family of workers leaving the French countryside or a small town for the Paris region, automatically costs the nation three times as much in public service expenditure. And when it is a question of starting a new factory building and all its equipment from scratch, the costs can be enormous: thus in Tunisia, in 1956, the establishment of a mere cellulose factory designed to employ 350 people was to cost 1,000 million francs. In Japan, the estimated cost of putting one new worker into the engineering industry is about £550, and for one new chemical worker, twenty times this amount, or just over £10,000, must be invested. It is easy then to understand the efforts made by governments to establish good statistical and economic forecasting services and to set in motion a system of planning which will help to equate supply and demand in the labour market, to avoid the disequilibrium which, both economically and socially, may have such distressing and even dangerous consequences and to develop production with as smooth a rhythm as possible. Such methods are made use of by all the countries that can.

As regards individual changes of occupation, however, the circumstances in all countries are not equally favourable to this supple and many-branched capillarity which enables the dynamic and well-equipped man to rise from one post to another. Though in most western democracies, social promotion is welcomed so that self-made men are rightfully proud of themselves, and though it is officially extolled and favoured in the communist countries, it is not the same everywhere. Sometimes there is a more or less official colour bar which places a barrier in the way of individual or collective progress; sometimes there is a social organisation like the caste system in India, which although legally abolished still retains an appreciable influence; sometimes it is just a tradition that is hard to disturb. In Japan, when

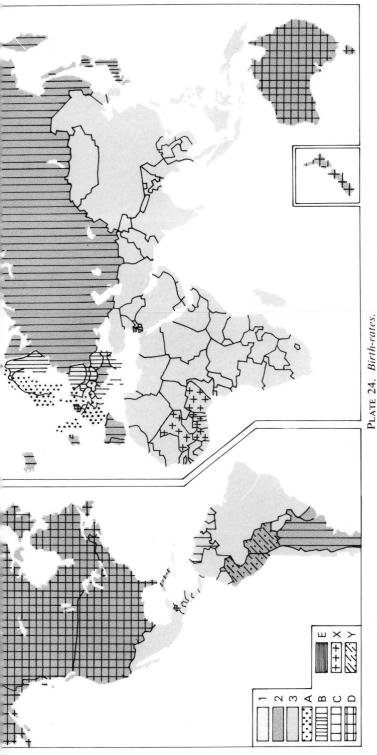

PLATE 24. *Birth-rates*:
1. Under 20 per thousand. 2. 20–30. 3. Over 30 per thousand. Types (explained in text, pp. 150–55) A and B, under 20 per thousand. C, D and E, 20 to 30 per thousand. X. Countries for which incomplete information indicates about 50 per thousand. Y. Information incomplete.

PLATE 25. *Belo Horizonte, Brazil: old Portuguese town and modern blocks*

PLATE 26. *Sydney suburbs laid out on geometrical plan*

PLATE 27. *London: part of the City, with old buildings and modern reconstruction after bomb damage during the Second World War*

PLATE 28. *The new town of Harlow, Essex*

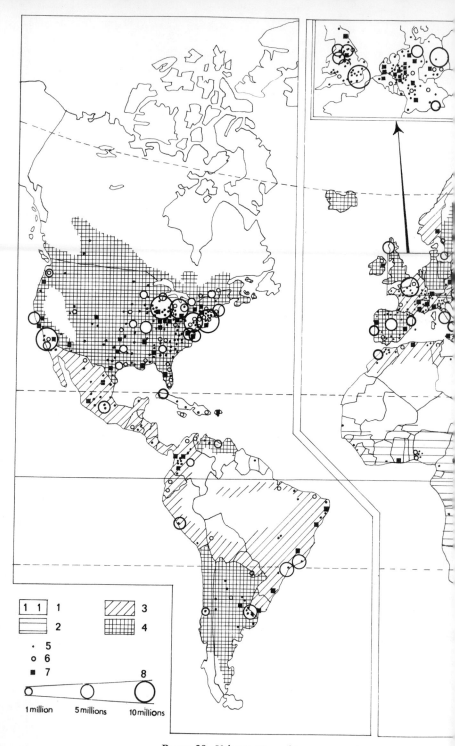

PLATE 29. *Urbanisation of towns*

URBAN POPULATION. 1. Proportion unknown. 2. Under 25 per cent. 3. 25 to 60 per cent. 4. Over 60 per cent urban.

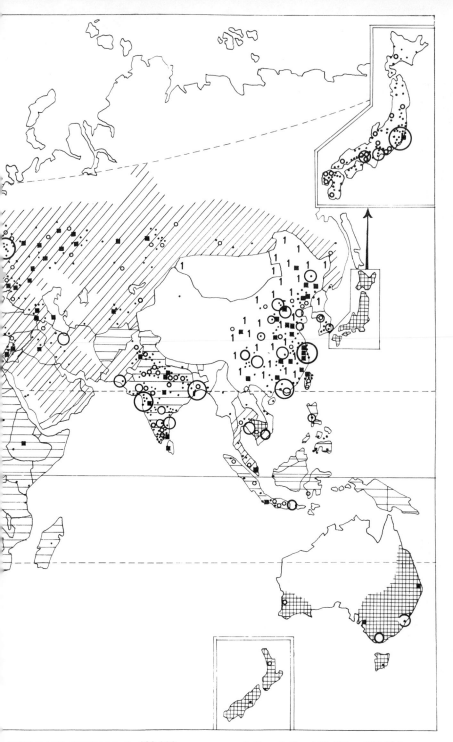

TOWNS AND CITIES OF OVER 100,000 POPULATION. 5. Population 100,000 to 300,000.
6. 300,000 to 500,000. 7. 500,000 to 1 million. 8. Over 1 million; circles proportional to population. Equatorial scale approximately 1:110 million.

PLATE 30. *A shanty-town* (favella) *in Brazil*

PLATE 31. *Preparation for a marriage at Ourgla, Algerian Sahara*

PLATE 32. *Temple of the Dawn at Bangkok*

PLATE 33. *Traditional Indian street architecture in Bombay*

PLATE 34. *A street in the new Siberian town of Angarsk*

PLATE 35. *Shopping centre of the new town of Vallingby, near Stockholm*

a worker is engaged by a firm, he is there for life; he thus obtains the promise of being retained whatever economic vicissitudes may ensue, but he may neither change his trade nor seek another firm which might pay higher wages. The workers are thus prisoners, and occupational changes are paralysed. This, however, is an exceptional case.

At the opposite extreme, some countries are experiencing a veritable flight of workers from certain particularly hard jobs, so that the gaps must be filled with foreigners from countries where the standard of life is much lower. The shortage of miners in France during the last sixty years, and indeed over the whole of north-west Europe at the present time, and their replacement by Italians, Poles and Africans is an example of a professional migration pushed to its conclusion. And much the same thing is true for labourers in agriculture and the building industry, for unskilled labourers generally, and for domestic servants.

In conclusion, the complexity of the occupational groups and of their evolution is a matter of considerable importance; we should now attempt a rough sketch of the distribution over the globe of the various types of active population.

CHAPTER FOURTEEN

Geographical Aspects of Human Activity

A simple journey suffices, without resort to statistics, to convey an impression of the diversity of human occupations. Everywhere there is the contrast between the open fields and the urban concentrations, but the latter may be few and far between, and almost exceptional, or widespread, expanding and dominating. Further, though the rural dweller generally lives by the land and belongs to the primary occupation group, city folk have varied occupations which put them into secondary or tertiary groups.

An obvious relationship exists between the intensity of urbanisation and the predominance of the last two groups: thus England and Wales, the most urbanised country in the world (80 per cent urban) is also the one with the lowest proportion in the primary group (only 3·1 per cent), and in the United States the population is 73·5 per cent urban and there are only 4 per cent in the primary group. In France, in the same year, the proportions were 70 per cent urban and 10 in the primary group, and in Brazil, 59 per cent urban and 44·4 per cent primary.

The great occupational groups, however, are not static but are constantly evolving, and there is thus a progression from one type of population structure to another, so that one can distinguish three fundamental stages—primitive, transitional and advanced.

PRIMITIVE SOCIETIES

In primitive social groups, two-handed man is the fundamental pivot of all activity; his conquest of nature is but feeble, his technical achievement almost nil; he is at some pains merely to survive and has but few possibilities of production in excess of his needs.

Predominance of the peasant world

Almost all human energy is devoted to the production of foodstuffs for local consumption, and agriculture occupies almost the entire active population; in black Africa the proportion is more than four-fifths, in south and south-east Asia often nearly three-quarters, and in Latin America, and the Middle East about two-thirds. Men and women work side by side. The hoe is still the fundamental implement, which scratches rather than turns the soil; there are no animals to assist, either because the natural conditions—for example, the presence of the tse-tse fly in Africa—may hinder their existence, or because land is so scarce and precious—as in the Far East—that not even the smallest area can be spared to feed cattle. The wooden plough is the first element of progress; it implies the presence of draught animals, however half-starved and ill-assorted these may be. The absence or scarcity of animals means that the use of manure is almost unknown. With such methods, in black Africa, yields are very small indeed; the soil is quickly exhausted and the cultivated patches must be moved after two or three years, allowing a fallow which may last ten or twelve years; in some cases the whole village community must change its location. Population densities are thus low, and the population is dispersed in small and widely separated hamlets, for only thus, in such precarious conditions, can the necessary amount of cultivable land be found within reasonable distance. The control of the landscape by man is almost imperceptible. All production is immediately consumed and there is always a hungry period between harvests, for means of conservation are primitive (large earthenware pots, or individual or collective store-houses raised above ground level); climatic and biological hazards are numerous, and the daily meal is a matter of uncertainty. More than 90 or 95 per cent of the inhabitants of the village are peasants pure and simple.

Such a state of extreme primitiveness only survives in isolated areas in black Africa and central South America, and even here it is tending to disappear as the tribesmen are subjected to taxation, which forces them to the use of money and so to the search for some saleable product in order to obtain it.

In other regions the role of water is fundamental; by permitting irrigation it promotes the development of a higher-yielding agriculture, more concentrated and permanently fixed in space. Even though the techniques may be primitive, the mastery of methods may be quite remarkable. The density of land occupation becomes very high, and man's presence makes itself very much felt in the landscape. Villages are larger, more closely-knit, and more permanent. In the dry lands of the Far East the geometrical subdivision is complete and not a square yard remains unoccupied. An excess of production over needs makes its appearance, and sometimes even rice is sold in exchange for poorer quality cereals so that a medium of trade develops. The structure of the village population becomes more complex and the proportion of peasants diminishes slightly.

It is in such primitive societies as these that one may still often find the dissociation of different activities within the primary group, and whole villages peopled by hunters and collectors (as among the pygmies of central Africa), or stock-raisers (on the margins of the humid areas and plains occupied by cultivators), or fishermen. Thus in north-eastern Brazil, on journeying from the coast towards the interior, one comes across first the coastal fishermen, living under the coconut palms whose nuts they gather, and launching their light *jangadas* on the rolling breakers of the Atlantic, then the cultivators, in the well-watered coastal belt where at many points colonisation of a more speculative nature is at present going on, and finally, when the rains get less and the land becomes more hilly, the first stock-raisers. In other parts of the world all the complexity of the primary group is found within the same village; for example in the reserves peopled by Canaques in eastern New Caledonia. Here nature provides everything for man except clothing, which indeed is hardly necessary in such a climate. Fishing, hunting, collecting and cultivation enable the inhabitants to satisfy almost all their needs, and this explains the labour difficulties that are encountered in the mines and in the towns. This is the paradise of the South Sea isles.

Poor development of trade and manufactures
The limited technical equipment and, more important still, the very low purchasing power militate against the development of other activities. At first, all efforts must be concentrated on the sole objective of producing in order to survive, and food production absorbs, in cultivation, in harvesting, in the preparation of eatables, an enormous amount of time and energy. Amongst the Turumdu of the Middle Congo, 4 per cent of human labour is devoted to forest clearance, 27 per cent to cultivation, and 56 per cent to the preparation of the produce (drying, threshing, retting, husking, milling, etc.), the remaining 13 per cent represents transport.

Thus few possibilities exist of producing surplus raw materials which might permit the development of transforming industries, and in any case the technical means are not available. At first, there is merely a rudimentary class of artisans devoted to the production of prime necessities; and the individuals concerned are as often as not agricultural workers at the same time, like the women who spin sheep's wool while guarding the flocks, and the men who get together to build a new hut. But other and more specialised artisans may also appear—shoemakers, blacksmiths, weavers and tailors; scattered about the countryside, they gather in the towns in specialised quarters, as can still be seen in the old centres of north Africa or of the East.

Finally the general standard of life is so low and the availability of money so restricted that the demand for clothing and other consumer goods is very small; and an almost non-existent market can hardly encourage production. In extreme cases, these primitive communities derive their whole livelihood from the local area and exist within a closed circle; in south-east Asia this has been called a 'vegetable civilisation', whilst in the northern polar regions, before contact was made with the civilised world, it was a life which revolved around the seal.

In such circumstances commercial exchanges are but embryonic. Many of the rural agglomerations lack a single trader, others have only a general shop—rather like the declining café-cum-grocery in small French villages—or the itinerant general salesmen or pedlars as in the remoter countryside of Latin America or black Africa; in Africa, these latter are often Syrians or Lebanese. Such shops or simple refreshment stalls still exist in these countries at cross-roads and traffic halts; it is only in the larger settlements that one will find more specialised traders, and even these may have only spasmodic dealings with a rural clientele. The occasion of a fair may bring many people into the town, and then a little money will be spent in the shops which appear like palaces of temptation. It is like a survival from the medieval period.

In such regions, which are without either administrative or social organisation, the rural areas are the domain of the peasantry, pure and simple. It is only in the towns that one finds anything different.

The anomalous role of the town

'Parasitic nucleus encysted in the countryside'—this is how the Middle East town has been described. Founded by conquerors or traders, perhaps both, a colony, a fortress or an administrative centre, it has but limited relationships with its surrounding region. The town makes little, and certainly nothing for the peasant; it is not a regional commercial centre because of the low purchasing power of the rural masses and their primitive subsistence economy. In the same way, in Africa, the town is often the result of modern colonisation; situated on the coast, or provided with greater opportunities for relations with the outside world than with the continental interior, it forms a separate economic and social unit. And the poverty of the rural hinterland and the lack of transport leave the mass of the people quite ignorant of the town. In north-eastern Brazil, many of the inhabitants living only twenty miles from a great regional capital of half a million population have never visited it.

Thus, in such primitive communities, the part played by the urban population is always very restricted. Moreover, the towns are ill-adjusted and there is a lack of medium-sized towns; there is nothing between the large village, which is in close relationship to the rural areas out of which it has generally grown, and the large artificial city, created from without in more or less recent times, and growing rapidly by the addition of the squalid shanty-towns built by uprooted rural dwellers or refugees. The population density around the towns may be quite low, and even the most elementary economic relations between the urban and rural people may be lacking.

Finally, the statistics of urban occupations can be very misleading. There is a high proportion in the tertiary group—commerce and the service industries. But let us not delude ourselves, for 'commerce' is often merely the sale of domestic objects on a very small scale, and domestic servants, especially female, are legion. Economic equilibrium is lacking, and there is an enormous concealed underemployment. Nevertheless, in overall statistics, these countries are better off in the tertiary sector than in the secondary sector; but it is necessary to emphasise the particular circumstances that such statistics cannot bring out.

The factors of transformation

In modern times, primitive communities are almost all penetrated by more or less active leavening agents which are modifying their fundamental characteristics. For the peasants, *the obligation to pay taxes* forces on them the cultivation of commercial crops, such as groundnuts in West Africa. Thus the idea of trade is introduced at the same time as the use of money. From this moment the die is cast: the attitude of the whole community changes and the appetite for gain may be so strong as to lead to the neglect of the traditional subsistence crops for more remunerative but inedible plants, a development which may in turn create grave food problems; thus the fellahin of the Nile delta have often sacrificed their cereals to the extension of the cotton crop when the price of the latter was high.

Technical progress, which enables the peasant to produce more than mere subsistence requires, may encourage him to sell the surplus and to buy things from the town or from other regions; in this way there is an imperceptible passage from pure subsistence agriculture to a mixed form of cropping, and the increased purchasing power of the countryside stimulates the whole economy. Urban expansion has similar results: by creating new resources and new needs, it involves in the early stages an increase in purchases from abroad to satisfy at least the requirements of the wealthier inhabitants, and then later the growth of local manufactures in accordance with available techniques and the demands of the masses.

The *injection of capital* is vital, whether it be derived from wealthy nationals who wish to increase their fortunes in their own country, or from foreign investments. In north-eastern Brazil, it is capital from big family businesses or important companies that has successfully established the sugar-cane plantations, and similarly with the development of vast irrigated basins like Kom-Ombo in Middle Egypt. In India, the great and powerful dynasty of Tata has established great national industries, christened new towns, built factories, and transformed a whole region. On the other hand it is United States capital that has developed the huge banana plantations of the United Fruit Company, scattered through Central America; it is North American or European investment that has opened up most of the exploited mineral deposits of Latin America and Africa. The creation of means of transport, banks and trading companies is part of the same process. All these factors, whether local or general, small or large, create employment, pay wages and extend the circulation of money whilst multiplying the list of necessities and increasing the possibility of complementary relations.

The importance of *mineral resources* in the financing of national development is well known; an obvious example is petroleum, which is almost all sold abroad by many of the producing countries. In the whole of the Middle East this 'black gold' plays a vital part, socially and politically, as well as financially. The great oil companies for long enjoyed monopolistic powers, and though their empire has been shaken they still exercise considerable influence; *Aramco* held Saudi

Arabia as firmly as any military garrison. On the technical side, the oil industry recruits workers, creates an urban and industrial proletariat, pays higher wages and engenders a dislike for the traditional occupations, whilst creating a pool of technicians and assisting the formation of a local élite. The petroleum installations are islands of modern life and progress planted in the midst of the almost medieval civilisation of the desert. The receipts from petroleum have always formed an essential component in the budgets of the Middle East producers, a privileged band that has recently been joined by Algeria, Nigeria and Libya; whilst the new oil politics of the OPEC countries and the rise in the price of this precious commodity have considerably augmented the revenues of the producing countries. A large part of these riches serves to finance development, and particularly industrialisation, creating a veritable revolution in the nature and rate of progress. A somewhat similar state of affairs exists in Venezuela, whose citizens, paying no taxes, have a per capita income which, according to the statistics, is one of the largest in Latin America (though it must be remembered that in fact much of the income is received by a small number of privileged persons). This influx of capital has enabled the construction of the best road system in South America, and of magnificent hospitals, and has even set the country on the road to an industrialisation based on native labour and technical skill.

These forms of economic colonisation by great commercial organisations, like the political colonisation of an earlier period, thus gradually exercise an undeniable power of transformation.

Finally, a last factor which may work in the same direction is the impulse given by a new political regime, which settles down to the task of thoroughly modifying the economic structure, using to this end its almost unlimited control over the life of the individual. The establishment of communism has thus permitted the transformation of hitherto mainly rural countries. The U.S.S.R. had 75 per cent of its population occupied in agriculture and forestry in 1913, and this proportion was reduced to only 38·8 per cent by 1960.

The remaining primitive societies

Under the influence of all the above factors, profound modifications are taking place all over the world and the ranks of the primitive communities are diminishing day by day; but the transformation is gradual and its incidence uneven, sometimes within a single country.

Thus the north of Brazil still remāins incontestably primitive whilst the south belongs to the second group, that of societies in transition.

As a working definition, we may suggest that countries with more than two-thirds of their population rural, and with an insignificant number in the 'secondary' occupation group, fall into the 'primitive' class. The list includes almost all the countries of Africa except the south and the northern fringe, several states or islands in Central America (Honduras, Haiti) and parts of the southern and eastern fringes of Asia (Bangladesh, India, Thailand). Statistics in those countries are naturally most inadequate, which prevents a precise delimitation.

SOCIETIES IN TRANSITION

Almost everywhere the strength of the factors of transformation has been sufficient to create a new world. This began in western Europe in the second half of the eighteenth century, in the United Kingdom; it spread gradually and continued to do so. From the moment when the threshold is crossed and industry is introduced into a country, there is no turning back; the movement progresses with greater or less impetus, eventually achieving an almost complete transformation of the environment.

The new possibilities

Man is no longer his own slave and limited to his own physical resources; he begins to have machines and money at his disposal, and the interdependence of individuals increases as life becomes more complex. The textile worker of Mulhouse operates an English or German loom, weaving cotton that has come from the United States or from black Africa and producing fabric that will clothe Frenchmen or distant foreigners; the farmer of Beauce turns his furrow with a machine made hundreds of miles away, and sells his wheat in Paris or in Europe, or if need be in China or India. This interdependence is felt everywhere; the African who grows groundnuts prepares oil which will feed the Europeans who have woven the cotton shirt that he wears; the rock-drills from the great industrial countries, controlled by large companies whose financial resources come from the same countries, bore for oil in the Middle East, in the Sahara, in Venezuela, and in the same way giant mechanical excavators dig the mineral deposits of Latin America.

Relations of all kinds intensify—exchanges of men and machines, of capital, of raw materials and finished products. In contrast with primitive societies which are inward-looking, the more advanced societies enter the field of world-wide economic relationships. This makes them at the same time richer but more susceptible. Their new equilibrium demands a spirit of collaboration and an atmosphere of peace and goodwill. A strike in a fundamental branch such as coal-mining, steel or transport not only fetters the whole national economy but may have repercussions from one end of the world to the other. Political difficulties between two states may be translated into a suspension of economic assistance, a withdrawal of technicians or of invested capital. Economic crises and wars, upsetting the system, may cause curious reversionary trends; some urban dwellers may return to the food-giving soil, as in the United States in the years following the 1929 crisis, or the peasants may reintroduce food crops when bread becomes scarce, as in France between 1940 and 1945, when wheat reappeared in mountain areas in which, owing to poor yields and low profitability, it had long since been abandoned.

On the other hand, the interdependence characteristic of advanced societies is more beneficial to mankind than the autonomy of primitive societies. When famine strikes in China or in India, no longer do millions suffer and starve to death, but shiploads of cereals converge on their ports from more favoured countries. The intensification of trade at all levels is the fundamental fact of this transformation—trade between individuals in the same country thanks to increasing specialisation in the different types of production, trade between different regions of the same country resulting from geographical differences, trade also between countries whose economies are complementary either because of their latitudinal situation or their unequal stages of development.

Transformation of the countryside

We have shown that it was the improvement of agricultural techniques that permitted demographic development and the expansion of industry and modern economy in Europe. This transformation has been universal and fundamental; it has resulted in the creation of new geographical landscapes.

The fields have intensified their production, but they have also rationalised it. Liberated from the fear of famine, and with a food supply assured by many and complex means of transport, farms tend increasingly to cultivate the crops for which their soil is most suitable, and thus a progressive specialisation develops. The rural folk thus have for disposal large harvests, and to cope with these it has been necessary to develop a transport network and a system of marketing to permit the outward flow of the food or industrial crops.

In the early stages of this spontaneous development it is to the regional markets and fairs that the rural surplus goes. The peasants themselves go to market and meet their customers; a complete hierarchy of rural market centres grows up, and on these focal points all commercial relations necessarily converge. The peasants who come in periodically spend on the spot much of the money which they have just acquired, and shops soon multiply, selling foreign produce as well as textiles and clothing, household equipment, and eventually a thousand and one less necessary articles. Thus the countryside itself becomes permeated by commerce, and at the same time the organisation of the environment progresses—administration, education, sanitary services, transport—and the 'tertiary' occupation group appears right in the heart of the primary.

Even in the remote interior of Africa, Asia or Latin America, it is possible to discern the beginnings of this transformation. The production of certain commercial crops creates currents of trade. The development of the castor-oil plant in the interior of north-eastern Brazil is accompanied by the movement of collectors employed by the big coast-centred companies, by the establishment of merchants who not only sell a variety of goods but also encourage and concentrate the local output and give credit, and by itinerant hawkers who sell things that the peasants have as yet no possibility of journeying far to purchase.

In the second stage, progress depends on the improvement of communications, on the extent to which education and the spirit of rationalisation influence the peasant mentality, and on the financial strength and speculative urge of the rural folk. The peasants are grouped in co-operatives and producers' associations, both for buying and for selling. Giant silos for the harvest, warehouses for the storage of seed and fertilisers, and agricultural stations to spread progress, all appear on the landscape whilst roads and railways multiply, and the number of vehicles rises rapidly; the mesh of rural centres becomes thinner, as the less important villages stagnate whilst better situated market towns add to their functions and become more urban.

The peasants themselves become less numerous and more efficient. Machines multiply and human labour decreases; the rural dwelling becomes transformed by the introduction of modern comforts. Though many quit their native village to seek other occupations in the towns, some remain in the family hearth, whilst some retired town-dwellers seek rural peace in their declining years. The village population becomes complex and farm-workers may not even be in the majority.

Transformation of the non-rural zones

Accompanying these developments, new human ant-hills come into being, which have nothing to do with agriculture, but towards which all the harvested products converge in order to supply essential food-stuffs. Sometimes these consist of vast zones where small towns jostle amidst a tangle of chimneys, murky canals and shining rails, dark conical heaps and geometrical-shaped factories that resound with the din of puffing and hammering engines. This was how it happened in the coal-fields, and such landscapes persist in the areas which were earliest industrialised; similar ones are still arising in new countries. In the U.S.S.R. since the Revolution, the area around Perm in the Urals has developed 'towns and workers' quarters on an area so restricted that they touch and often in fact merge one into another; in India, the town of Asansol in the Damodar basin was 'born and bred on coal; it is a shapeless invertebrate organism to which new cells are constantly being added'; it has no proper centre, and the town is part of a zone 'covered by a practically even stratum of human life'. A similar picture is presented by the coal-fields of western Europe with their clusters of small towns and workers' suburbs barely separated from each other.

Frequently there has been no industrial diversification in these coal-field areas, for the available manpower has been monopolised by the mines and the mining companies once viewed with a very jaundiced eye the competition of less arduous occupations. There is no female employment, and the mining towns are the most specialised in the world. The working population is almost entirely in mining and even the indispensable equipment of commerce and recreation is but feebly developed. A mining centre such as Pécquencourt in the northern French coal-field has 82 per cent of its employed population in the secondary group, and no less than 70 per cent in mining; but this is an extreme case.

These coalmining districts have drawn their manpower from the countryside, sometimes from far afield, and they now contain people from many different areas and perhaps countries. At first, the demands of increased industrial production attracted the masses in ever increasing densities, but later the growth of mechanisation and in some cases the exhaustion of the mineral deposits have brought about changes which are by no means simple. The heavy character of the work and the grim forbidding landscapes, despite recent town-planning and the construction of suburbs more stylish and comfortable than the miserable hovels of the earlier years, have tempted many people to go elsewhere and the coal-fields in countries of advanced economy act, as it were, as relay stations between immigration from rural areas or foreign countries and access to more attractive employment elsewhere.

Other industrial regions present characteristics analogous to those of the specialised coal-mining areas, namely the scattering of a large population in numerous closely-spaced and often highly specialised centres; such are the areas devoted to iron mining or to non-ferrous metals, or the traditional centres of the textile industries. The cotton region of Lancashire shows such a galaxy of towns of varying size, and at one time Burnley had 72·2 per cent of its active population in the cotton industry, and Blackburn 62·6 per cent. It was the mining and textile industries that grew first and it was usually these, in western Europe at any rate, that gave rise to the typical industrial conurbations.

In less advanced countries, mineral extraction is not always accompanied by industrialisation; only the miners are there, and the product of their labours is despatched, raw or semi-processed, to the industrial centres of the more advanced countries. The industrial overlay becomes more complex and more varied as the general state of development advances, so that not only does the labour force increase in mining areas but occupational variety is introduced.

To the mining and textile industries are soon added other more complex and more concentrated industries, seeking skilled labour, competent technicians and large consuming markets; the older towns thus become the seats of new industrial activities, whilst colonies of workers' houses spring up along the most suitable lines of communication or around the centres of activity which cluster in the neighbourhood. Industrialisation and urbanisation go hand in hand: in the U.S.S.R. during sixty years of communist rule, the urban population has increased by 290 per cent and industrial output has multiplied sixty times. In Japan, between 1955 and 1970, the urban population increased by 16 per cent, and the index of industrial production rose from 69 to 280. Individual regions show the same trends: in the Ukraine, overall industrial output has multiplied forty times since 1926 whilst the number of towns and other centres of essentially urban character has risen from 174 to 766. The successive creations of the capitalist period and of the new regime can be related to the growth of engineering, chemical and food industries. It is an urban blossoming, one might almost say an urban explosion, that accompanies industrial growth.

These towns cannot exist without the support of the tertiary group of occupations. The multiplication of industrial jobs means a continual rise in purchasing power, which in turn creates new and more exacting demands, so that the growth of the tertiary sector runs in parallel with that of the secondary sector. It is estimated that in a fully developed town, for every 100 new jobs in the secondary group, the addition of 130 in the service industries is necessary. In Japan between 1920 and 1970, the percentage of the working population employed in industry rose from 20·7 to 34 whilst for the tertiary group the percentages were respectively 25.5 and 46; even though there may be some parasitic augmentation of the tertiary group due to the peculiar population situation in Japan, the comparison of the two sets of figures is significant. In Western Germany between 1950 and 1960, the growth of employment in the secondary group was 39 per cent and in the tertiary group 45 per cent.

The blossoming of the towns
This congregation of human beings, this swelling of activities which have no relation to the land, may present a great variety of form and amplitude, and the number, character and importance of the towns which result from it are very diverse.

In the countries of early development, in which a firmly-established rural civilisation preceded the modern rash of urbanism, the urban 'systems'—the mesh and the hierarchy of towns and their industrial structure—are very complex. This is the case in the whole of Europe and in the U.S.S.R. as far east as the Urals, and also in the New England area of north-eastern U.S.A.; it is also true of Japan, and it is rapidly becoming true of certain parts of China.

The United Kingdom may serve as a model. Of the total population of towns with more than 50,000 inhabitants, one-third is originally or functionally connected with coal, and another one-third is in coastal towns, particularly on the great estuaries. Of the seven conurbations in Great Britain, five are situated, at least in part, on coal-fields, and the other two—London and Liverpool—on estuaries. The constitution of this urban mesh, which is the most important in the world in terms of the proportion of the population living in towns, has come about in four successive stages, each characterised by a different occupational structure. The first stage was one of slow urban growth in the midst of a rural environment of cultivators and domestic craftsmen, served by poor means of transport; it resulted in the birth of a series of agricultural market centres, distant from each other by no more than six miles or so. The birth of manufacturing industry, which in Britain preceded the transport revolution, ushered in the second stage, and gave rise to a large number of towns based on coal, or on textiles, or in the coastal zone, and a little later to the concentration of activity on certain nodal points in the new transport system. The multiplication of towns was accompanied by an increasing degree of differentiation in their evolution. The third stage was the outward spread of the towns; the congestion in the built-up areas became so great that people moved out to the comparative calm of the green fringes, leaving the town centres to the banks, the shops and offices and the factories; such developments were made possible by improvements in the transport facilities. Finally, we now seem to be entering a fourth cycle; all the earlier stages of growth had taken place in an atmosphere of 'laissez faire' and without conscious planning, and the results had sometimes been quite unbearable for the inhabitants. 'Town planning' now tries to become the rule.

This complex evolutionary process has given rise to many different sorts of town. The great metropolitan centres, surrounded by a whole galaxy of satellite towns, have very varied activities and strongly developed economic life in the midst of a vast urbanised area. Such town-clusters have been called 'conurbations'. Their growth has been progressive and has extended over centuries, and their functions are now extremely complex; they form a class on their own. A second variety comprises the ancient towns, which have not all developed in the same way; some historic centres have almost stood still, and indeed might even slowly decline if it were not for tourists and lovers of the past. There are numerous examples in Wales and Northern Ireland,

and Canterbury is a famous one. Thirdly, some ancient towns have been revived by the Industrial Revolution; on to their old historic quarters, more or less eviscerated and reshaped and with only a few scraps still piously preserved, have been grafted industrial quarters adjacent to modern means of transport, especially railways. Thus Cardiff, which had 2,000 inhabitants at the beginning of the nineteenth century, now has over 278,000, but its ancient castle remains at the heart, surrounded by a park created on the site of the old town, now demolished, and this in turn bordered by a swarm of factories, warehouses, railways, wharves, and working-class dwellings, all owing their origin to the coal traffic which the presence of the port engendered. The growth of industry did more than merely transform towns, however, it actually created them, as in the case of the innumerable mining towns of the coalfields, or of the railway-created towns like Crewe, Swindon and Middlesbrough. Industry even seeped into the old regional centres of eastern and southern England—like Norwich, for example—and also, to the disgust of many, into the ancient university town of Oxford, which is now divided into the collegiate quarter with its magnificent stone buildings, and the great automobile factories with their housing estates in grim geometrical pattern and monotonous colouring. The university has become, in the words of an Oxford don, 'the latin quarter of Cowley'. Finally, the fourth stage in urban evolution has given rise to the 'New Towns', planned from scratch to be ideal houses and work-places for populations of between 25,000 and 80,000. In these towns there are open spaces, sports grounds, and a rationally-planned location of work-places, dwellings and communal facilities, everything, in fact, to promote the good life both for individuals and the community.

In other countries, the richness of urban life is far less well developed. In countries settled by Europeans, like the two Americas and Australia, there are no ancient historic centres and even the country towns are very different. The urban 'system' is less coherent and the hierarchy less apparent. In countries colonised by the Anglo-Saxon race, the major rural centres have become progressively invaded by industry, such as food preparation and agricultural machinery, whilst the smaller towns are simply service centres, relatively far apart. The class of large and purely industrial cities is also much more widespread than in Europe, and most of the towns are scarcely more than one hundred years old. One looks in vain for historic relics, for there are none, but one is overwhelmed by the vigour and intensity of the urban life. The proportion of the population living in the large towns is high—in Australia more than 64 per cent of the population is in towns of over 100,000 inhabitants. Somewhat similar is the case of Asiatic Russia, where the towns are of even more recent growth, in the midst of a countryside which has lost its rural character.

In the territories colonised by the Latin races, on the other hand, the agricultural market towns depend much more closely upon the land; there are few specialised industrial towns, but a dominant influence is still exercised by the cities created in the early colonial period, and these, with their ancient churches, their narrow squares, their blocks of colonial houses, now fragmented by modern roads and other buildings, remain the great foci of urban life.

In Africa, where European colonisation is but a veneer of relatively recent origin, town development is much less vigorous and less diverse. However, there are some cities dating from earlier civilisations which have been given a new lease of life by modern administrative functions—like Fez, Marrakesh, Timbuctoo, and Antananarivo (Madagascar). But the major European-founded cities play the most important role, though this is often the result of a site which makes external relations easy rather than to any close association with the local area. There are some mining towns, but the few industrial cities are only found in the northern and southern extremities of the continent.

Lastly, in Asia (outside the Soviet territories), there is no lack of a historic past, but the urban population was but small in proportion to the total, and the recent economic evolution has not yet had much effect. There are some very large cities, and some examples of industrial agglomerations, but the vast majority of the towns are still rural markets, full of craftsmen and hardly touched by the great currents of trade. Less than 10 per cent of the population lives in towns of over 100,000 inhabitants, and there is neither the number of towns, nor the degree of specialisation, that characterises the more developed countries.

Stages in evolution

It is apparent that the societies in course of transformation have not all reached the same stage. There is an infinite gradation from the countries in the earliest stages of development, in which only the first stumbling attempts at industrialisation can be distinguished, to the developed European countries like France, Germany or Italy.

In a first class we find that the primary group of occupation represents one-half to two-thirds of the total employment; industry only occupies 10 to 15 per cent, whilst the tertiary group represents one-fifth. Countries like Egypt, most of the Latin American states (except the most advanced) and those of south and south-east Asia, fall into this class.

As the number of rural peasants declines, and the numbers employed in industry and the tertiary group rise slightly, a second class can be distinguished, into which fall Venezuela, Colombia, Paraguay, and Asiatic islands like Sri Lanka and Taiwan. The primary group now represents under one-half of the total, with the other half divided between secondary and tertiary occupations.

In a third stage, agriculture only occupies one-third of the active population, and we find a number of countries in which the three occupational groups are roughly equal. This was the case in France on the eve of the second World War, and it is still the case in Poland and Spain. Outside Europe, countries like South Africa and the U.S.S.R., which have respectively 28 and 24·7 per cent of the active population employed in the primary sector, belong more or less to this type. but they are changing rapidly, the U.S.S.R. especially so. Some Middle East countries such as Jordan, African territories such as Libya and Mauritania, and in Latin America the Dominican Republic, are still at this stage.

Finally, in a fourth stage, the secondary sector becomes important or even predominant. This is the case in the two Germanies and in Switzerland; and so it was until recently in numerous other European countries that have now taken a positive step in the direction of tertiary dominance. The United Kingdom, for example, had 46·6 per cent in the secondary sector and 49·6 in the tertiary, in 1966, but the most recent (1976) estimates show 42·3 and 50.1 per cent respectively. This evolution approximates to that of Belgium, France, Netherlands and Norway. In all these countries, the primary sector now generally employs under 10 per cent of the total labour force; and in most of them the next few years will witness an absolute preponderance of the tertiary sector.

FULLY-DEVELOPED SOCIETIES

As a result of their development, societies acquire a surplus of technical and financial power. The number of manual workers diminishes, and those engaged in actual production cease to form a majority in the active population.

Predominance of non-productive labour

In the countryside, machines replace men. In the United States, one agricultural worker who could produce enough to feed eight people in 1900, feeds fifty at the present time. The farmer becomes a technician and a business man. Systematic specialisation prevails; production is for sale, and the farmer himself becomes a customer of other farmers; thus the poultry-breeder of eastern U.S.A. buys cereals from the Corn Belt, and the dairy farmer seeks elsewhere a part of his fodder requirements. The countryside becomes the domain of the machine, and the soil a sort of raw material from which the maximum return is sought. As the ultimate development, contracts are signed with companies who finance the agricultural operations and pay the farmers for the crops harvested.

In such circumstances, is it any longer possible to speak of a rural way of life? The small townships which are sparsely scattered through the vast cultivated expanses are merely service stations to which the farmer drives by car, perhaps many miles, to buy a few necessities. The agriculturist has a comfortable house, with every modern convenience; his employees are largely mechanics; he takes long and distant holidays during the close season. This is the formula for rural life as one finds it developed on the vast plains in central U.S.A. and in certain parts of Canada and Australia.

In the field of industry, technical progress, and in particular the development of automation, is constantly reducing the amount of human labour. As in agriculture, output figures continue to rise whilst manpower falls. This trend, in which there is a tendency for the substitution of capital for labour, expresses itself in a considerable investment in sophisticated machines; true, it allows a reduction in human toil, but it also noticeably reduces the employment possibilities. A difficult equilibrium has thus to be sought between technological refinements and the use of human labour.

Parallel with the diminution in the number of manual workers, industry records a growing body of administrative personnel, of laboratory workers and other specialised technicians. Between 1950 and 1960, there was an increase of 43 per cent in specialist technical personnel in United States industry, and these now represent 10 per cent of the entire active population. The industries which are currently most vigorous in their development—chemical and electro-mechanical—are also those which have the highest proportion of non-manual workers in their total employment figures. There is thus, within the secondary occupational group, an expansion of non-productive labour.

The high standard of comfort and even of luxury attained by the mass of the population demands the multiplication of both public and private service occupations. Between 1950 and 1960, in the United States, the numbers employed in commerce and public services rose by 35 per cent, and this rapid increase in 'white collar workers' is the most notable feature of recent years. In the same period, the total number of manual workers—'blue collars'—rose by only 5 or 6 per cent.

All this results in a progressive diminution in the differences between rural and urban ways of life, which are brought nearer together by comforts, leisure, amusements and above all by incomes. Some farmers live in town and merely receive financial reports of the agricultural operations on their farms; many citizens prefer to remain in the country, commuting daily to their urban occupations. The spread of efficient transport media and the high purchasing power of the people make all sorts of town-country combinations possible. The urban transport pattern takes on the character of a gigantic spider's web, slowly invading the countryside; and infilling between the radial suburban tentacles produces a network or graticule that has been termed, borrowing an expression from the rural landscape, an 'urban bocage'.

This kind of spatial distribution of people has profound effects on the distribution of occupations: in some rural areas of the United States, agricultural workers are actually in a minority, and in order to record this outward spread from the towns the statistics distinguish between those rural dwellers who are farmers and those who are not.

In such circumstances economic exchanges proliferate; it is no longer merely a question of the simple movement of necessities, but of the thousand and one purchases of customers who are becoming more and more informed, discriminating and wealthy.

The expansion of developed societies

The numerical outstripping of the producers by the non-producers is taking place slowly but surely in all the most advanced countries. Both the fields and the factories need fewer and fewer men and women, and the productive capacity of the mechanised operative rises higher and higher, whilst the rising standard of life permits the multiplication and the unfettered development of all the desires and appetites of the people. The tertiary occupational group may become absolutely preponderant, exceeding 50 per cent of the total; such a situation has already been reached in Canada and the United States, and it would appear to be near to the possible limit. In some other countries like Australia and New Zealand the tertiary group is also dominant; and in Europe, Denmark, Norway, Belgium, the United Kingdom and Sweden each have more than half their employed population in the tertiary group. We may note also that in all these countries more than one-half of those occupied in the tertiary sector are in banking, commerce and transport. Outside these highly-developed countries, there are signs elsewhere in the world of a similar situation developing, as in Israel, Lebanon, Argentina and Kuwait. The last of these has a record 62·5 per cent in the tertiary sector, a situation explained by the virtual absence of the primary sector (1·7 per cent) and by the large numbers of foreigners—technicians, businessmen, teachers and instructors—attracted by the high salaries resulting from the success of oil exploitation. It is worth remarking that the net value of this state's output, per head of its population, is 11,652 dollars, or more than twice that of the countries that are reputed to be the richest in the world—Switzerland, Sweden, the U.S.A. and Canada.

We may well ask whether there is a limit to this evolutionary process. It has been noted that between 1946 and 1959 the numbers employed in banking in the United States increased by 65 per cent, whilst the numbers of non-agricultural workers went up by only 20 per cent. At this rate of progress, everybody would be employed in banking by A.D. 2100! This is hardly a conceivable prospect, however, and in the present state of our civilisation it would seem that 60 per cent of non-producers in the active population of a normal state is a figure difficult to exceed without a grave risk of economic disequilibrium.

CHAPTER FIFTEEN

Economic Aspects of Human Activity

Inequality is the fundamental basis of the relations between human societies. Unequal in health, unequal in fertility, unequally distributed over territories which are unequally rich, and unequally armed for the daily struggle for existence, the inhabitants of the present world suffer more severely than ever before from the unrelenting operation of the law of inequality. In times past, lack of technical and other means limited the possibility of any people achieving exceptional success, whether in the field of environmental control, of health or of production. Nowadays everything appears possible for some, whilst others are but little beyond the stone age. This poignant opposition is apparent not only between peoples widely separated on the earth's surface but also between individuals who rub shoulders within a single community. In this era of rapid and varied means of communication, of the almost instantaneous diffusion of news, and of permanent international contacts, the spectacle of such inequality can leave no one indifferent; solutions must be found, but the problem is by no means easy of solution.

THE FUNDAMENTAL INEQUALITIES

Food

The cry of alarm uttered by Josué de Castro in his book *The Geography of Hunger* was prompted by the tragic truth that almost half the world's population is under-nourished, quantitatively and certainly qualitatively. The entire population of Asia outside Japan, the Soviet lands and Turkey, a large part of Africa, the Latino-Indian states of north-western South America and part of Central America, have a daily calorie intake of less than 2,200 according to official estimates. More than one-half of the world's population (in southern Asia and the Far East) disposes of but one-quarter of its food resources (13 per cent of the world's animal foodstuffs and 44 per cent of vegetable foods), whilst the most favoured countries, which have but 29 per cent of the population (Europe, North America and Oceania) have 57 per cent of the food resources (69 per cent of the animal foodstuffs and 38 per cent of the vegetable).

Even this miserable ration is obtained with difficulty. Whilst in the United States the cost of food represents but 17 per cent of the family budget, and the figure is 33 per cent in Europe, in India it is 80 per cent. Out of the very meagre incomes the expense of feeding is thus a crushing burden. And what food it represents! The diet comprises little more than cereals: in India these make up 68·6 per cent of the total cost of food, whereas in Europe the comparable figure is only 15 per cent and in the United States less than 10 per cent. The consumption of richer foods is almost unknown; in India, where it is true the conditions are somewhat peculiar owing to religious proscriptions, only 3·3 per cent of the food budget is spent on meat and 5·2 per cent on sugar and non-alcoholic drinks, whereas in the United States the same commodities represent 30 per cent and 13 per cent respectively and in Europe, on an average, 20–30 per cent and 12 per cent.

The situation in India is particularly cruel, because it affects in a single country 15 per cent of the world's population and because it is intrinsically dramatic. And the signs of an improvement—contrary to what is happening in neighbouring China, which in the recent past was just as gravely afflicted—are difficult to discern, if indeed they are present at all, which is by no means certain. To understand the tragedy of undernourishment one must see these creatures of skin and bone performing heavy manual labour. Enfeebled by privations which start before birth, they have little resistance and are a prey to all kinds of diseases; their physical resources are cruelly limited. Death strikes most severely at young children, but it does not spare the adults. And there is the heavy toll of lost work-days due to the many maladies that assail these fragile bodies. In another continent the passiveness of the Andean Indians has been ascribed to many causes but it would seem that their spirit has been crushed by the endemic undernourishment, which has persisted for generations.

The uprooting of these miserable people and their transfer to the towns may relieve the actual hunger but often only serves to increase the incidence of deficiency diseases. Even the 'full stomach' policy practised by some organisations in colonial times, as in the mining regions of the Congo, is unsatisfactory, for it pays no regard to the requirements of a balanced diet. It is, moreover, difficult to repair

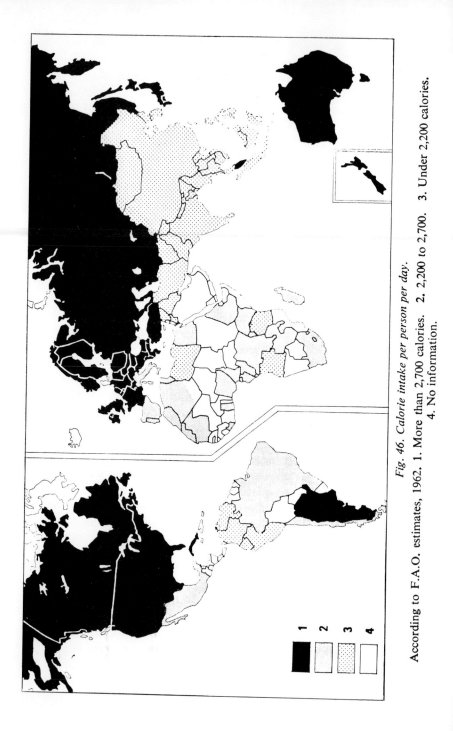

Fig. 46. Calorie intake per person per day.

According to F.A.O. estimates, 1962. 1. More than 2,700 calories. 2. 2,200 to 2,700. 3. Under 2,200 calories.
4. No information.

quickly the physiological damage, caused by serious deficiencies, which has been passed on from one generation to another. However, a better diet for the children leads to rapid progress and an obvious improvement in the general health of individuals.

Production

The weakest and poorest are also those least able to replace their failing strength by mechanical aids. The consumption of energy per inhabitant gives a good idea both of the technical power and the standard of life of a country. The United States is a long way in the lead with more than 11,600 kg of coal equivalent a year, and this is six times the average for the whole world (which is 1,984 kg) nearly twice the figure for the most favoured European country (Belgium with 6,500 kg), twenty-two times as great as in Brazil and fifty times as great as in India, which is a country by no means lacking in energy resources.

These figures imply a frightening inequality in the productive capacity of different countries, which can be illustrated by such pictures as these: Indian women breaking stones and carrying them one by one for the building of a dam, or processions of female navvies laden with baskets of earth from the foundations of a vast new building; the rice-planters of the Far East, blinded by the sun's reflection on the water in which they stand with bent backs; old-fashioned spinning mills in which the workers manipulate the cotton fibres in a hot and suffocating humidity or in an atmosphere filled with unbreathable dust; and at the other extreme, the splutter and roar of the machines that plough the fields, reap the harvests and carve out the roads, and the gigantic air-conditioned factories with their relentlessly moving production lines. On the one hand, human labour driven to inhuman limits, on the other, men aided but often enslaved rather than liberated by machines; and in any case, a considerable disproportion in the results.

If we seek once more the assistance of statistics, we can choose several significant datum-lines. The production of cereals per head rises to 1,082 kg in North America and 725 in the U.S.S.R., whilst, in view of the density of population, it is only 430 in Europe. In the other continents, however, it is much lower, and falls to a minimum of 172 kg in Africa; but if we consider only the rural population, which of course is much greater in the latter, the disproportion becomes much more striking. The yields of rice, the main Asiatic cereal, are typical: they scarcely reach 20 quintals per hectare in all the underdeveloped Far Eastern countries (excluding China for which there are no accurate figures), but rise to 36 qu./ha in the United States, more than 50 in Japan and in southern Europe. Deficient techniques and poor methods mean that the soil is not made to yield all that it could; certainly no one could accuse the Far Eastern peasant of not taking the utmost possible care—but he has no fertilisers, not even manure, and only the most primitive implements. The example of Japan, however, shows that remarkable progress can be achieved.

The 'green revolution' has encouraged great hopes, thanks to the early results obtained: between 1950 and 1970, the wheat yield in Mexico rose from 8 to 28 quintals per hectare; in the Philippines and Indonesia, output increased by an average of 20 per cent. This movement began in Latin America and spread to Asia, then much more slowly to Africa, where demographic pressures are less severe. As for the Chinese experiment, designed both to increase the area devoted to food crops and to increase yields, it would seem to have succeeded, if one discounts the climatic hazards and the internal political crises that reduced the harvest by 25 per cent between 1958 and 1960; between 1957 and 1970, the yield of rice increased from 26·9 to 31·5 qu./hect.

The situation is no better in respect of industrial production. Ninety-two per cent of the world's steel is made in countries which have less than one-third of its inhabitants; each United States citizen has annually at his disposal one-and-a-half times as much steel as the inhabitants of Western Europe or Soviet Russia, thirteen times as much as a Brazilian, forty times as much as an Indian and ninety times as much as a native of black Africa. Other fundamental and typical products tell a similar story: the fortunate inhabitants of the United States and Western Europe have roughly equal quantities of fertilisers at their disposal, but this represents three times as much as in the Soviet Union, ten times as much as in Brazil and forty times as much as in India. And so on, over and over again; the situation is the same in respect of chemicals such as fertilisers, sulphuric acid, of the major branches of metallurgy and of building construction. In the case of cement, so vital for modern constructional works, western Europe actually exceeds the United States, with 344 kg a head of population as against 309; but Brazil's consumption is only 64 kg a head, and that of India a mere 19 kg.

The dry bones of these statistics conceal a most unhappy situation, for they represent not something temporary but a 'slough of despond' from which it is very difficult to rise. There is certainly inequality of production, but also inequality in the possibilities of consumption, inequality in everyday life and well-being, and perhaps also a fundamental inequality in the very capacity for development.

In sum, these deficiencies are shown up in the disproportion between national revenues per head of population. The underdeveloped countries, with 46·6 per cent of the world's population, have only 11 per cent of its income, whilst North America, with less than 7 per cent of the world's inhabitants, has 35 per cent of the world's income. On an average, a citizen of the United States has nearly twice the income of a European who comes from the most favoured north-western section of the old continent, and more than four times that of the least favoured southern European (Portuguese); if one may believe the latest statistics for China, the disproportion between Chinese and American incomes is 1 : 25; and it is 1 : 37 for India.

The haves and have-nots

It is customary, when considering the profound disparities shown by such figures as these, to talk about underdevelopment. Certain human societies have developed the potential resources of their territories whilst others have hitherto shown themselves more or less incapable of so doing. A bright future, it would seem, is in store for these latter, if they wish to follow the modern evolutionary path. But this is only partly true, for whilst we may hope for the most rapid progress possible from the state of underdevelopment, we have to recognise the inequality of natural resources. Just as all men are born equal in the eyes of the law but are differently endowed with physical and intellectual aptitudes, so human societies have varied basic resources with which to attain, in the future, the ideal state of development.

We may pause for a moment to compare the situation of the United States with that of India. The former, with 6·9 per cent of the world's surface, has only 5·9 per cent of its inhabitants; its vast territory contains about one-third of the world's coal reserves, 15 per cent of the world's petroleum, half the natural gas, 7 per cent of the iron ore, and 20 per cent of the copper. Beneath the surface of the U.S.A. lies some

60 per cent of all the minerals consumed in its industry—the most powerful assemblage in the world; its citizens have vast plains at their disposal, and their sole agricultural problem is concerned with the absorption of the surplus production, with the disposal of stocks and with the reduction in the size of the harvest. India has 2·4 per cent of the world's surface, on which live 15 per cent of its population; in other words, with an area two-fifths of that of the United States (excluding Alaska) it has two-and-a-half times the population. The cultivable surface (that is the areas cultivated and those that could be) amounts to 2·38 hectares for every American and 0·5 hectares for every Indian. This is the fundamental inequality, but there are others; for the climate of India is such that irrigation and water-control are universally necessary, whereas the greater part of the agricultural land of the U.S.A. is free from this constraint. As for industry, it is

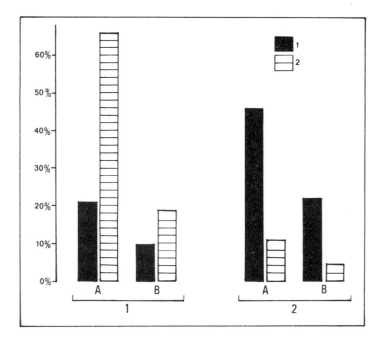

Fig. 47. Comparative graphs for 1970.
1. Population.   2. Gross National Product. Group 1: Developed Countries; Group 2: Under-developed countries.   A: Free market economy;   B. Planned economy. Scale: percentage of world total.

estimated that India could be completely self-sufficient in coal and iron ore, at least, but there are notable deficiencies, especially petroleum, which has so far been discovered only in very small quantities. And India is by no means the least well-endowed of the countries which are trying to improve the lot of their people.

A consideration of energy resources, the basis of all economic development, throws up other striking contrasts: the western world, with 17·9 per cent of the world's population, disposes of 57·5 per cent of the energy, and if we add the U.S.S.R. and eastern Europe (with 21·4 per cent of the population and 10·4 per cent of the energy) we see that less than two-fifths of the world's people consume more than two-thirds of the energy. The people of India, by comparison, representing 15 per cent of the world's population, consume only 1·4 per cent of the total energy.

Consumption, however, does not necessarily imply either production or reserves. Some countries, including the most powerful and well equipped, are not content with the resources developed within their now vast territories but draw also on the reserves of the poorer nations. The consumption of sources of energy provides two contrasting examples. In the case of coal, the United States consumes 14 per cent of the world total, but produces 19·5 per cent and holds 32·5 per cent of the world's reserves; in the U.S.S.R., comparable figures are 17·3 per cent consumption, 19 per cent production and 25·8 per cent reserves; but the underdeveloped countries consume 6 per cent, produce 3·5 per cent and have 6·9 per cent of the reserves. In this case the countries with the most important reserves do not push up their consumption to match output, but dispose of the surplus amongst the less well endowed countries. It is also true that if the consumption of the underdeveloped countries rises at a satisfactory rate the reserves will soon prove inadequate, even as present production is already insufficient to meet the meagre requirements. The case of oil is quite the reverse; here it is the underdeveloped countries that hold the major part—actually about 70 per cent—of the world's reserves, and the rate of production, together with the price level, is presently the subject of a fierce struggle between the producing countries, the foreign oil companies and the industrialised countries which are the main consumers and importers; the output is 52 per cent of the world's total, but the consumption of the poorer countries represents only 11·7 per cent.

Many more examples could be cited; they would all confirm the first impression, that there are some of the world's people that have prodigious riches at their disposal whilst others are most cruelly deprived. This fact has been the source of many conflicts in past times, from intertribal quarrels in primitive lands to murderous wars between highly civilised states in our own times. Australians are even now acutely conscious of occupying a large island continent so close to the teeming masses of Asia, even as the Russians in Soviet Asia are of their proximity to overpopulated China, and, more generally, fear must strike the heart of all the privileged nations as they contemplate a future in which the underprivileged ones, becoming fully aware of their state of utter destitution, may be driven to extreme measures. Already we have the organisation of a cartel of oil producers, and similarly for certain other minerals; and the rapid escalation in the price of raw materials is hitting the great industrial countries hard, for they can no longer exploit the sellers of raw materials and are obliged to bargain and to restrain consumption. Even the United States has become conscious of the limits of world resources and has launched a campaign against the wasteful consumption of energy. It is a course that will become obligatory for all in the coming decades.

ATTEMPTS AT IMPROVEMENT

The facts of unequal national endowments need not lead either to a negative attitude of blind acceptance or to revolution. One may attempt to transform the conditions of human activity in many countries and so remedy, at least in part, the intolerable inequalities in living standards which we find in the modern world. But the way is hard.

The poverty cycle—a vicious circle?

We have seen that many factors may contribute to the transformation of the economic structure of primitive societies. However, the results are often difficult to see and one may get the impression that certain structures are so steeped in conservatism that any progress is bound to be slow, if indeed it is possible at all under existing conditions.

Demographic growth is most rapid in the least favoured countries, so that each year there are more mouths to feed. Whilst, according to the statistics of the Food and Agricultural Organisation, the world's agricultural production index rose from 100 in 1950 to 184 in 1971, and production per head of population reached the not inconsiderable figure of 122, it still only needs the slightest climatic aberration or political upset to derange the whole machine. The index of agricultural output growth per inhabitant was actually negative in 1972, and the present progress margins are extremely slender and in fact point to a deterioration in the world situation. On the other hand, the available data show marked differences from one region to another. Calculations show that over the whole of the Far East and south-east Asia, agricultural production increased by 3 per cent during the last decade, whilst the population rose by 2 per cent; but this relative progress was insufficient to wipe out the consequences of the decade 1930–40, when population growth far outstripped the growth of food supplies. Thus in 1960 the standard of life was still 2 per cent worse than before the war, and it was only in 1961 (due, it is true, to an exceptionally good rice harvest) that the available food supply per head of population first regained its 1930 level. In 1962, with a poorer agricultural season, the food production per head dropped by 2 per cent. There is thus a very precarious balance between food and stomachs.

It is difficult to foresee any amelioration in the near future, for the rhythm of population growth is bound to accelerate by reason of the lowered death rate, and one cannot anticipate any correspondingly rapid fall in the birth rate. Even the Japanese experience shows that, if a remarkable reduction in the number of births were to take place in the very near future, it would be many years before this could ease the demographic pressure; even though, in Japan, the sharp fall in the birth rate began in 1950, the annual natural increase is still twelve per thousand and the expansion will not cease, other things being equal, until the end of the century. The limitation of population growth, though it appears indispensable for the future of mankind, is thus utterly ineffectual as a solution to the immediate difficulties. The major current problem is how to improve the economic condition of three-quarters of the world's people.

Social conditions present what is perhaps the most formidable obstacle. In primitive societies, the poverty and ignorance of the cultivators, and the fact that they are often descended from slaves, as in Africa, or from serfs known as 'peons' in Latin America, give them an attitude of resignation and passiveness that is inimical to progress. On the other hand, the property-owning classes do not want progress: the landed proprietor in Madras is opposed to the extension of irrigation works and the opening-up of new lands, giving as his reasons that 'if the cultivable area is increased the value of the land will decline, agricultural wages will rise because of the increased demand for labour, and the price of grain will fall because of the increased production'. The same attitude is found amongst the money lenders who almost always, in these poor lands, supply the peasants with their requirements in return for their crops, and when these are poor, for rights over the land; thus little by little are constituted the large estates on which the former peasant proprietors are in financial bondage, at the mercy of the money-lenders. The large commercial firms that trade in the areas are also hostile to the amelioration of the peasant's lot; and finally, the proprietors of the 'latifundia', so widespread in Latin America, are content with extensive exploitation, sterilising huge expanses for very meagre returns; in South America, only 2 per cent of the land is actually tilled!

Since, in these countries, it is the most powerful landowners who occupy all the key positions in politics, there can be no reform without a profound political transformation. Agrarian reform, which is absolutely vital in many Latin American states, is thus virtually impossible under present conditions. And a reform of this kind carried out without an overall policy may well be disastrous. Thus in Morocco, the breaking-up of certain large estates formerly worked by European colonists, and their distribution in small parcels to native Moroccans, resulted in the partial disappearance of vital export crops, in the chaotic proliferation of small individual crops of poor-yielding foodstuffs, and in the crowding, on a plot intended for a family of five or six persons, of sisters and cousins and aunts from near and far, thus re-constituting a poverty-stricken agricultural proletariat. Even in the communist countries, the redistribution of the land amongst those who formerly worked on it has not always given satisfactory results, for the necessity to group them together again into co-operatives and the creation of collective farms have in fact reconstituted the large estates. And difficulties in connection with the increase of disposable food surpluses are by no means confined to the underdeveloped countries.

Together with social conditions, technical conditions also present equally grave obstacles to progress. A physically weak population, undernourished and ignorant, is hardly conducive to improvement; the introduction of mechanical appliances is costly, and in any case these need a body of technicians to service them. And if the labour supply is abundant and cheap, is it not both inhuman and uneconomic to replace human labour by a machine? It has been pointed out that the manpower so liberated should devote itself to other occupations and so help to increase the overall production. But this is only possible in countries with a small labour force, as in Africa and certain Latin-American states. In areas where there is a superabundance of manpower and chronic underemployment, the Chinese solution of the human ant-hill type of labour is perhaps more sensible.

Technical improvements, meaning not merely the purchase of machines but also of fertilisers, better seed strains, selectively-bred animals, require large investments. Again, capital is required for building the transport media which are indispensable to the exploitation of resources and the feeding of the population, to the prospecting and development of minerals, and to the creation of the industrial nuclei which may eventually expand in proportion to the country's needs. The difficulties encountered by such large states as India and Pakistan in financing their development plans are well known. For those countries which happen to possess a commodity that is internationally in demand, there is a ray of hope, provided the financial returns do not all find their way into a few pockets. But for those which not only have to equip themselves technically, but also to feed a population much larger than the local agricultural output can support, the difficulties appear to be insurmountable, for they must import food products, capital goods and consumer goods all at the same time.

If we examine the indices of annual variation in the gross national product of the major countries of south-east Asia and the Far East between 1951 and 1961, we see that the only satisfactory increase is that recorded by Japan, which indeed, at 8·1 per cent per head of population, is quite remarkable. In all the others, except for Taiwan which is rather a special case, the growth has been less than 3 per cent, and even under 2 per cent in the case of Cambodia, Sri Lanka, India, Indonesia and Pakistan (there are no reliable figures for China). This can hardly be called progress.

Another disquieting feature of the situation is the inequality of development within the regions of a single country; the most favoured areas are incredibly prosperous, whereas the poorest seem to sink inevitably into even greater poverty. Thus in Brazil the average income per worker increased by one-quarter in the Federal District, between 1950 and 1960, and by one-third in the State of São Paulo, but it only rose by 4 per cent in the State of Paraiba (one of the poorest in the whole Federation), in which 80 per cent of the population work in the primary sector and only 6 per cent in the secondary sector.

Whilst preserving a due sense of proportion, can we not perhaps compare these extremes of development with the unequal fortunes during the past hundred years, of progressive northern Italy and the antiquated south, or of the Paris region and the rural west and south-west of France? Industry, it is said, attracts industry, and prosperity grows like a snowball: these commonplace expressions reflect a very real and deep-seated truth, that it is exceedingly difficult for the poor to rise from their state of misery. As the music-hall song of fifty years ago put it—'the rich get rich and the poor get poorer'.

The rhythm of development

It is possible to distinguish in the present world four different types of progress.

The *most advanced countries*, which are not subject to sharp changes, either demographic or political, give the impression of a flattening growth curve in recent years. The industrial boom during and after World War II was such that, despite the subsequent necessity for adaptation to peacetime conditions, so high a production level has been attained that it can scarcely be raised any further without encountering enormous difficulties in disposing of the output. The production curve in many branches has thus ceased to rise or has even begun to trend slightly downwards, and present efforts are concerned with getting higher and higher yields rather than with the total output. The United States is the best example of this type. Steel production and the output of automobiles and of certain important chemicals has fallen there since 1955, and recent years have been marked by a series of rapid booms and recessions. As to the causes of this instability, the saturation of the market has been suggested as a major one: 76 per cent of all American households have at least one motor car, 89 per cent have television, 92·5 per cent a washing machine and 95 per cent a refrigerator. Excess capacity is another, after the massive investment of the period 1955–57, for the production potential of the country is greater than its capacity for consumption, so that an equilibrium based on underemployment develops, and most of the large American industries are at present working beneath their capacity. As for agriculture, it made such progress with yields, that it had become necessary in some years to stop using part of the farmland, so as to avoid glutting the markets. In fact the recovery of agricultural production has been stimulated not by the home market but by the wish to export in order to satisfy the considerable needs of the international market. This might almost be called a state of 'overdevelopment'.

A second type comprises the countries with the *most vigorous recent development*. These are mostly states in which a change in political regime has brought about radical modifications in employment structure, as in the U.S.S.R. since the revolution, and in the peoples' republics under the tutelage of their powerful neighbour. Here the carefully planned changes are reflected in alterations in occupations, which increase in the secondary sector at the expense of the primary sector, and in a considerable growth of manufacturing industries. One example will suffice: Poland, since the end of the war, has increased elevenfold its output of steel, cement and electricity, and since 1970 the index of industrial production has risen by a further 71 per cent.

Also within this second group are countries which have been obliged, through an economy upset by the war, or through severe internal pressures due, for example, to rapid population growth, to undertake a policy of systematic redevelopment. These are countries whose resources and capacity for transformation have enabled them to forge rapidly ahead; some of them, like France since 1946, have had a succession of economic plans. In the list we find most of the states of Western Europe, together with Japan, Canada and Australia. Here too the changing occupational structure is accompanied by a powerful upsurge in the rhythm of industrial progress: in France and in Western Germany the industrial index has shown a rise of respectively 65 and 55 per cent since 1963, in Italy it has risen by 61 per cent and in Japan by 146 per cent.

In the third category we enter the ranks of the *countries in course of development*, but include only those which are making an effort and which have the means to ensure a measure of success. These are essentially the lands with considerable economic potential, which is being developed through various impulses, general economic development as in Brazil, political revolution as in mainland China, exploitation of a single highly valuable resource as in Venezuela. They all resemble each other in having a corpus of educated and experienced people who can make decisions and evolve an overall development plan; but they may differ in the means by which the plans are put into effect. In the Chinese Peoples' Republic it is by completely sacrificing the past and by a collective effort based on socialist principles; but in Brazil progress is under a capitalist regime which brings certain regions and social groups into full development whilst leaving others virtually abandoned. There is statistical evidence, though often of a very doubtful and disputable nature, of the extent of the progress made: in China the annual increase in gross national product per head of population for the decade 1950–60 was of the order of 10 per cent.

Finally, in the lowest class, are those parts of the globe which are advancing but slowly on the path of economic growth, some because they are weighed down by the millstone of overpopulation so that all their efforts are absorbed in coping with the annual increase in the numbers of mouths to feed, others because their uneducated population and the absence of an adequate resource basis paralyse them so that they cannot even start. The Indian example is typical: the index of gross national productivity showed a 3·6 per cent per annum rise between 1950 and 1960, but the rate per inhabitant was only 1·6 per cent, a trivial figure. The same thing is true of some of the Andean countries of South America and some in black Africa, which have scarcely as yet started on the cycle of development.

It is towards these last two groups that it is vital to direct help, to enable them to be released from their poverty and to commence a satisfactory rhythm of progressive development.

Relations between advanced and underdeveloped countries
The first care of the privileged countries should obviously be to see that their unhappy fellow-creatures do not simply die of starvation. It is indeed shocking to realise that whilst people were dying of hunger in Asia, the United States farmers were being paid to leave some of their land untilled in order to reduce the size of the harvest. But a world economy does not exist, and the surplus of one nation can only feed others through very complex mechanisms.

It has been estimated that in the underdeveloped countries foodstuffs make up about one-sixth of the total imports. These imports may thus be increased so as to raise the level of consumption without any corresponding increase in local output. On the other hand, the total quantity of exportable cereals might reach 100 million tons a year if all the developed countries made the necessary effort in production. There is thus ample scope for trade, even though the products available may not always meet the exact needs. Wheat, for example, is made abundantly available to the countries of the Far East—but they prefer rice; and the surpluses of alimentary fats, butter especially, find few takers.

In practice, different methods are applied within the framework of trade arrangements which are generally bilateral, for attempts to secure international agreement are fraught with difficulty. The United States, Canada, Australia, Argentina and France are the principal wheat exporters. Some 70 per cent of the U.S. exports are in the 'surplus' category. Shipments can be paid for in local currency, and the sums thus obtained are used on the spot by the vendor country for its own purposes (such as the maintenance of embassies, or common defence programmes), or granted as a loan to the local government to aid its expansion programme. These arrangements have their advantages, but also their disadvantages; they lower the price of cereals in the receiving countries and so reduce the income of the local farmers, and by allowing the rich countries to spend or lend local currency they deprive the poor countries of hard currency capital; and lastly, these special shipments may help to upset the international market equilibrium by causing a general fall of market prices and competing with the normal exporters. Another method consists in giving food supplies in exchange for work done by the available labour force; in this way public works may be engineered and lands improved or reclaimed. This arrangement, which helps to increase the labour force of the underdeveloped countries, both numerically and qualitatively, is an interesting one, but it must be noted that full payment of the workers in foodstuffs is impossible, so that some wages are also necessary, and these increase the budgetary expenditure of the already impecunious governments. Nevertheless this form of practical and direct assistance is praised by such agronomists as René Dumont, who regards it as a remarkably cheap and efficient way of ensuring rural improvements. Lastly, amongst other methods is the bartering of food products for strategic materials. This has been used occasionally by the United States, although money payments in local currency are usually preferred: some 60 per cent of their surplus wheat deals in recent years have been on this basis.

Assistance in the form of food is already being given on a vast scale, and it is usually given on such conditions that it provides both food and the incentive for further development. It has been estimated that if there were a world programme this form of aid ought to reach 20 to 30 per cent of the total capital assistance. But it is still insufficient to solve the problems of the underdeveloped countries, for by 1970, even though the countries with a surplus treble their exports, they will still furnish no more than 2 per cent of the agricultural products that the underdeveloped lands need.

Another form of aid which is therefore quite indispensable is technical assistance, which permits at the same time the transformation of the human environment and the formation of a corps of key workers for the establishment of all kinds of new enterprises. Teachers and doctors and their assistants help to raise the level of health and education, whilst engineers and technical advisers direct the teams of workers. A medium-sized country like France has 45,000 experts and teachers serving in the underdeveloped countries; one French teacher in every eight goes abroad. This sort of thing produces some very odd mixtures; in Upper Egypt, side by side with 2,000 Russian technicians working on the Aswan High Dam, was a huge chemical fertiliser plant being run by German engineers; and a small African state like Guinea has during the last few years received technical assistance from twenty-two different countries—with Chinese studying the possibility of constructing an airport and Czechs teaching French in the schools!

Lastly, all forms of aid are supported to a greater or less extent by investments. To render this aid more efficient, and to foster and coordinate it, sixteen industrialised countries, in 1961, formed the *Comité d'Aide au Développement* (Development Assistance Committee). This organisation supplied 8,115 million dollars in 1960 and 14,712 millions in 1970; just over half the latter total (7,948 millions) came from public sources and the remainder from private contributions. In addition, between 300 and 350 million dollars a year comes from the communist countries. This financial assistance is generally governed by strict rules. It is earmarked for carefully selected objectives which are parts of a more general plan of development. Preference is given to schemes which will quickly step up output and so act as catalysts in the general economic expansion.

Parts of this aid is again granted directly by one country to certain others; the developed countries present some 7,000 million dollars a year to the underdeveloped countries. France makes a particularly large contribution, and if all the rich countries gave in proportion, the total aid would reach 15,000 million dollars a year. In 1960, the United States and France between them provided 85 per cent of the bilateral aid from the industrial member-countries of O.E.C.D. The former's assistance goes mainly to Vietnam, Taiwan and South Korea, whilst 90 per cent of France's contributions go into the franc currency area. The methods of payment vary from country to country; in 1960 the United States citizen gave 14 dollars and lent 11, while the Frenchman gave 19 dollars and lent 11; France makes a free gift of 65 per cent of its total financial aid, England 27 per cent and Western Germany 20 per cent.

The disadvantages of these direct gifts from one country to another are that they often carry political implications, and they may in any case run the risk of wounding the susceptibilities of the recipients. International arrangements are perhaps preferable, as through the International Bank for Reconstruction and Development, or the grouping together of several countries in order to finance some particular enterprise or other in one of the underdeveloped states. Thus the 'Aid for India Club' which proposes to give financial assistance to the third five-year plan includes the International Bank, the United States, Canada, Western Germany, the United Kingdom, Japan and France. In such conditions the political neutrality of the assistance is much better assured. It must be admitted that the danger of political subjection is especially great for the smaller poor countries. But when the underdeveloped state is sufficiently large, powerful and well endowed, so that investments are obviously worth while, the competition is keen. Since Argentina offers favourable conditions for foreign capital, there is much rivalry between those willing to invest; thus the International Bank is financing the hydroelectric plan, French and German banks are furnishing credit for industrial and railway equipment, Swiss and German capital is going into chemical industries, British into atomic energy, and the Soviet bloc is also interested. In such conditions, a state of equilibrium is reached almost automatically, and this is equivalent to the system of international loans.

International obligations towards the underdeveloped countries thus have many aspects. The proffered help is not always completely disinterested, and whether it be incoherent or highly competitive, it is certainly insufficient. A better world organisation, accompanied by a lessening of tension between the great political blocs, would allow it to be more rational and clear-cut and so more efficient in reducing human suffering today and assuring a better and more worthy existence forthe people of tomorrow. But however massive the assistance, it should not relieve the beneficiaries of the need to help themselves, and it is this self-help above all that must be set in motion and sustained. Natural conditions as well as density of population are too diverse to permit the complete equality of human life all over the globe, but we must look forward at least to a reduction in the more shocking cases of disequilibrium. Can we continue to live with no twinge of remorse, knowing that our pigs are much better fed than many of the world's children, or that waste food in the garbage-cans of New York would suffice to feed the starving people of a city the size of Bombay?

Bibliography

It is impossible to give a full bibliography for this book, for three main reasons: first, it has been necessary to consult such a vast range of documents and publications from a wide range of disciplines, especially in order to make comparisons and syntheses, that it would be wearisome to list them all, particularly since often only a single chapter or even just a few lines or figures may have been selected from a large book. Secondly, many of the fundamental works deal with different aspects of our subject which are treated in different chapters of this book—for example, almost all the books dealing with the population of a country deal both with distribution and evolution—so that it would be necessary to repeat the list of such works in the bibliography for each chapter. Thirdly, there are several specialist journals in which all the articles are worth citing, sometimes several times; and similarly with the reports of demographic conferences.

A complete list of references would thus require a volume almost as long as the text itself, and it would be much more useful for the reader to have at his disposal the three excellent and quite recent bibliographies which are very well classified and from which it is readily possible to discover all the possible sources. Here we can do no more than list as precisely and completely as possible the basic documentation, and then give brief selections of the more important works. No papers from the specialist journals or conference proceedings are quoted. And in order to avoid repetition, the works have been listed not by chapters but regrouped in major topics.

List of Abbreviations used in Bibliography

A.A.A.G.   Annals of the Association of American Geographers
A.G.   Annales de Géographie
A.G.F.   Bulletin, Association de Géographes Francais
B.I.I.S.   Bulletin, Institut International de Statistiques
B.W.H.O.   Bulletin of the World Health Organization

C.O.M.	Cahiers d'Outre Mer
E.G.	Economic Geography
G.J.	Geographical Journal
G.R.	Geographical Review
I.E.D.E.S.	Institut d'Etudes pour the Développement Economique et Social
I.L.O.	International Labour Office (Bureau International du Travail)
I.N.E.D.	Institut National d'Etudes et d'Action Démographiques
J.G.	Journal of Geography
P.G.M.	Petermanns Geographische Mitteilungen
P.V.	Pacific Viewpoint
R.B.G.	Revista Brasileira de Geografia
R.G.I.	Revista Geografica Italiana
R.I.S.	Revista Internacional de Sociologia
S.A.	Scientific American
S.G.A.	Svensk Geografisk Arsbok
S.Q.	Sociological Quarterly
U.N.	United Nations

FUNDAMENTAL DOCUMENTS

(a) Statistical Summaries

United Nations, *Demographic Yearbook*.

United Nations, *Statistical Yearbook*.

International Labour Office, *Statistical Yearbook*, Geneva.

Congrès de population des Nations-Unies: Rome 1954, Belgrade 1965, Bucarest 1974;

Conférence mondiale de la population: Bucarest 1974;

Conférence mondiale de l'année de la femme: Mexico 1975.

(b) Journals and collections of papers

Population Bulletin of the United Nations. United Nations, Department of Social Affairs (annual, from 1951).

Population Index. Office of Population Research, Princeton University (from 1935).

Population. Revue de l'Institut National d'Etudes Démographiques, Paris (from 1946; summary tables for 15 years published in 1960).

Population Studies. A journal of demography. London School of Economics, London (from 1947).

Le Démographe. Bulletin of the International Union for the scientific study of population. Washington (from 1955).

Demography. Journal of the Population Association of America (annual, from 1964).

Milbank Memorial Fund. New York (from 1923).

Collected Papers, International Congress on World Population. Rome, 1954; Vienna, 1959; New York, 1961; Ottawa, 1963.

Actes de la 30e Session de l'Institut International de Statistique. Stockholm, 1958; also Bucarest, 1974.

Publications of the Population Council, New York (from 1952). Particularly:

 Studies in Family Planning;

 Bulletin of Demography and Family Planning;

 Country Profiles.

Problèmes économiques: recueil hebdomadaire d'extraits de publications internationales, published by Documentation Française, Paris.

Harward University, Center for Population studies: Research Papers.

Metropolitan Life Insurance Company, *Statistical Bulletin*.

(c) Bibliographical Works

ELDRIDGE, H. T. *The Materials of Demography*. New York, 1959. A selected and annotated bibliography (in English).

CHASTELAND, J. C. *Démographie*. Paris, 1961. Bibliography and analysis of books and articles, mainly 1945–58 (in French).

ZELINSKY, W. *A Bibliographic Guide to Population Geography*. Chicago, 1962. 2,588 items on population geography, with worldwide coverage, from the end of the nineteenth century to 1961.

(d) General Works

CARR-SAUNDERS, A. M. *World Population*. Oxford, 1936.

GEORGE P. *Introduction à l'étude géographique de la population*. I.N.E.D. handbook, No. 14, 1951.

THOMPSON, W. S. *Population Problems*. Chicago. 1953.

TREWARTHA, G. T. 'The case for population geography', *A.A.A.G.*, 1953, pp. 71–97.

BEAUJEU-GARNIER, J. *Géographie de la Population*. 2 vols. Paris, 1956, 1958.

WITTHAUER, K. 'Die Bevölkerung der Erde', P.G.M., No. 265, 1958.

GEORGE, P. *Questions de Géographie de la Population*. I.N.E.D. Handbook, No. 34, 1959.

VEYRET-VERNER, G. *Population*. Paris. 1959.

HAUSER, P. M. and DUNCAN, O. D. *The Study of Population*. Chicago. 1959.

PETERSEN, W. *Population*. New York. 1961.

TREWARTHA, G. T. *A Geography of Population: world patterns*, New York: London, 1969.

CLARKE, J. J. *Population Geography*, Pergamon, Oxford, 1965.

SPECIALISED WORKS

(a) On the evaluation and technical uses of demographic data

Demographic Yearbooks of U.N.O. Annual commentaries, each dealing with a different problem.

Other U.N. publications, including those on census data relating to fertility (Demographic Study, No. 6, New York, 1949); on urban and rural population (Demographic Study, No. 8, New York, 1950); and on active population (Demographic Study, No. 9, New York, 1954).

DEPOID, P. 'Rapport sur le degré de précision des statistiques démographiques', *B.I.I.S.* xxv. 119–230. Rio de Janeiro, 1957.

LANDRY, A. *Traité de Démographie*. Paris. 1945.

CHEVALIER, L. *Démographie générale*. Paris. 1951.

SPIEGELMAN, M. *Introduction to Demography*. Chicago. 1955.

BARCLAY, G. M. *Techniques of Population Analysis*. 1958.

LYNN SMITH, T. *Fundamentals of Population Study*. New York. 1960.

PRESSAT, R. *L'analyse démographique*. I.N.E.D. 1961.

(*b*) *On races and racial problems* (discussed in Chapter Three)

BIASUTTI, R. *et al. Le razze e i popoli della terra*. 4 vols. 3rd edn. 1959.

SCHWIDETZKY, I. *Das Menschenbild der Biologie*. Stuttgart. 1959.

SCHWIDETSKY I. *Die neue Rassenkunde*. Stuttgart. 1962.

LEROI-GOURHAN, A. *Ethnologie de l'Union Française*. 2 vols. 1952.

— *Handbook on Race Relations in South American Indians*.

AZEVEDO, A. *Geografia humania do Brasil*. 1951.

AZEVEDO, A. *Encyclopédie de l'Amerique Latine*. 1954.

JAMES, P. E. *Latin America*. 3rd edn. London. 1959.

— *Contribuçoes para o estudo de demografia do Brasil*. 1961 (esp. pp. 168–206).

— *Handbook on Race Relations in South Africa*. 1949.

BUCHANAN, K. and HURWITZ, N. 'The Asiatic immigrant community in the Union of South Africa', *G.R.* 1949, 440–9.

BUCHANAN, K. and HURWITZ, N. 'The 'coloured' community in the Union of South Africa', *G.R.* 1950, 397–414.

PATTERSON, S. *Colour and culture in South Africa*. London. 1953.

SAUVY, A. 'Le problème démographique et racial en Afrique du Sud', *Population*, 1953, 197.

(*c*) *On population distribution and its causes; and on the nature and results of demographic evolution*

Several general works, in addition to those already cited:

FROMONT, P. *Démographie économique*. Paris. 1947.

—*Findings of Studies on the Relationships between Population Trends and Economic and Social Factors*. U.N.O. 1951.

SAUVY, A. *Théorie générale de la population*. 2 vols. Paris. 1952, 1954.

REINHARD, M. R. *La population mondiale*. 2nd edn. Paris. 1962.

SORRE, M. *L'homme sur la terre*. Paris. 1961.

ZELINSKY, W., KOSINSKY, L. K. and PROTHERO, R. M. *Geography and a crowding world*, New York: London, 1970.

The following may serve as examples of detailed studies:

(*i*) *On distribution*

SANDER. E. 'Verbreitung des Menschen über die Erde', *Geogr. Rundschau* i, 1949, 330–4.

ZAVATTI, S. 'Il nuovo limite settentrionale dell' ecumene', *R.G.I.*, 1953, pp. 379–84.

ZAVATTI, S. 'Il nuovo limite australe dell' ecumene', *R.G.I.*, 1954, pp. 497–504.

(*ii*) *On density*

MOORE, W. E. *Economic Demography of Eastern and Southern Europe*. Geneva. 1954.

GEORGE, P. 'Sur un projet de calcul de la densité économique de population', *A.G.F.* 1953, pp. 142–5.

GOUROU, P. 'Le densité de la population au Ruanda Urundi', *Inst. Roy. Col. Belge Sc. Nat. et Medic.* vol. 21, part 6, 1953.

GOUROU, P. 'Le densité de la population rurale au Congo Belge', *Acad. Roy. des Sc. Coloniales*, i, 1955.

SESTINI, A. 'Densita tipiche di popolazione in Italia secondo le forme di utilizzazione del suolo', *R.G.I.*, 1959, pp. 231–41.

CLARK, C. 'Urban population densities', *B.I.I.S.*, 1958, pp. 60–68.

General descriptive works on distribution:

BURGDÖRFER, F. *Welt-Bevölkerungs-Atlas.* (publication sheet-by-sheet, since 1954).

— *Carte mondiale de la Population au 1/1,000,000e* (in course of publication).

TREWARTHA, G. T. 'New maps of China's population', *G.R.*, 1957, pp. 234–9.

General works on health:

MAY, J. M. *Ecology of Disease*. New York. 1958.

MAY, J. M. *Studies in Disease Ecology*. New York. 1961.

FOURNIER, E. *L'action médico-sociale dans les pays en voie de développement. I.E.D.E.S.*, 1961.

STAMP, L. D. *The geography of Life and Death*. London, 1964.

Amongst the innumerable publications dealing with different

parts of the world, the following are characteristic and of major importance:

AFRICA

KUCZYNSKI, R. R. *Demographic Survey of the British Colonial Empire.* 3 vols. London. 1948, 1949, 1953.

TREWARTHA, G. T. and ZELINSKY, W. 'The population geography of Belgian Africa', *A.A.A.G.*, 1954, pp. 163–93.

CHEVALIER, L. *Le problème démographique Nord-Africain.* I.N.E.D., Handbook No. 6, 1947.

CHEVALIER, L. *Madagascar, population et ressources.* I.N.E.D., Handbook, No. 15, 1952.

LORIMER, F. *Demographic Information on Tropical Africa.* Boston. 1961.

BARBOUR, K. M. and PROTHERO, R. M., eds. *Essays on African Population.* London. 1961.

United Nations, *Economic Commission for Africa* (1972).

CANTRELLE, P. *et al.* (Editors). *Population in African Development.* 2 vol; for the International Union for the Scientific Study of Population, 1974.

NORTH AMERICA

VEYRET, P. *La population du Canada.* Paris. 1953.

BOGUE, D. J. *The Population of the United States.* Glencoe, Illinois. 1959.

KLOVE, R. C. 'The growing population of the United States', *J.G.*, 1961, pp. 203–13.

CENTRAL AMERICA

GILBERTO, H. *La poblacion de Mexico: estado actual y tendencias, 1950–1980.* 1960.

ENJALBERT, H. 'La pression démographique au Mexique', *C.O.M.*, 1960, pp. 451–60.

— *Human resources of Central America, Panama and Mexico, 1950–1980. U.N.*, 1960.

SOUTH AMERICA

MORTARA, G., 'A populaçao do Brasil', *R.B.G.*, 1945, pp. 631–48.

— *Contribuçoes para o estudo da demografia do Brasil.* Bahia. 1961.

DE CARVALHO, A. V. *A populaçao brasileira.* 1960.

United Nations, *Economic Commission for Latin America* (1974).
ODELL, P. R. and PRESTON, D. A., *Economics and Societies in Latin America: A geographical interpretation*, London, 1973.

ASIA

Population Review: a Journal of Asian Demography. Indian Institute for Population Studies (from 1957).

CHEN, T. *Population in Modern China*. Tapei. 1946.

DRESCH, J. 'Population et ressources de la Chine nouvelle', *A.G.* 1955, pp. 161–201.

HO, P. T. *Studies of the Population of China, 1368–1953*. Cambridge 1959.

CHANDRASEKHAR, S. *China's Population: Census and Vital Statistics* Hong Kong. 1959.

TAEUBER, I. B. *The Population of Japan*. Princeton, N.J. 1958.

KISHIMOTO, M. 'Studies of population geography in Japan', *J. of Gakugli*, 1961, pp. 19–38.

DAVIS, K. *The Population of India and Pakistan*. Princeton, N.J. 1951.

NOUSS, I. *La population de la République Syrienne*. Paris. 1952.

EUROPE AND U.S.S.R.

SAUVY, A. *L'Europe et sa population*. 1953.

HUBER, M., BUNLE, H., and BOVERAT, F. *La population de la France*. 3rd edn. 1950.

DARIC, J. *Le fait démographique français et ses consequences*. Paris. 1956.

MYERS, P. F. and MAULDIN, W. P. *Population of the Federal Republic of Germany and West Berlin*. U.S. International Pop. Stat. Reports, Series 90, No. 1, 1952.

SIEGEL, J. S. *The population of Hungary*. U.S. International Pop. Stat. Reports, Series 90, No. 9, 1958.

In the same series as the above, No. 3 is devoted to Czechoslovakia and No. 4 to Poland.

KOSINSKI, L. *Procesy ludnosciowe na ziemiach odzyskanych w latach 1945–1960*. 1963 (summary in English). (Demographic changes in the 'recovered territories' of Poland between 1945 and 1960.)

CASA TORRES, J. M. 'Un plan para el estudio de la geografia de la poblacion española', *R.I.S.*, 1957, pp. 73–113.

— *Population trends in Eastern Europe, the U.S.S.R. and mainland, China*. Milbank Memorial Fund, 1960.

VINNIKOV, Y. R. and KOZLOV, V. I. 'Changes in the numerical strength and settlement of the peoples of the U.S.S.R.' *Soviet Geogr.* April 1962, p. 28.

HARRIS, CH. D. *Cities of the Soviet Union*, Chicago, 1970.

Population de la France. Special issue of *Population*, 1974.

BEAUJEU-GARNIER, J. *La population française*, Paris, 1976.

Substantial chapters on regional aspects of population will also be found in the major works devoted to different countries or different parts of the world; even a selection of these would take up too much space.

(d) On population mobility

A short bibliography on the classification of migrations is given in:

KANT, E. 'Migrationern as klassifikation och prolematik' (with summary in German), *S.G.A.* No. 317, 1953, pp. 180–209.

The most complete geographical work is:

SORRE, M. *Les migrations des peuples*. Paris. 1955.

Numerous aspects of the subject are dealt with in the following:

SCHWARZ, G. *Allgemeine Siedlungsgeographie*, 2nd edn. Berlin. 1961.

— *Les migrations internationales, 1945–1957*. I.L.O. Etudes et rapports, nouvelle série, No. 54. 1959.

SCHIEFER, J. *Marché du travail européen*. Paris. 1961.

LADAME, P. A. *Le rôle des migrations dans le monde*. 1958.

WARD, D. *Cities and immigrants*, New York: London. 1971.

GEORGE, P. *Les migrations internationales*. Paris, PUF. 1976.

On certain other themes, apart from the statistical, general and regional works already cited, the following will be found useful:

(a) On nomadism, African population movements, and some consequences of migration.

— *Nomades et nomadisme au Sahara*. UNESCO. 1963.

CLARKE, J. I. 'Studies of semi-nomadism in North Africa', *E.G.* 1959, pp. 95–108.

PROTHERO, R. M. 'Population movements and problems of malaria eradication in Africa', *B.W.H.O.* 24, 1961, pp. 405–25.

PROTHERO, R. M. 'Migrant labour in West Africa', *Journ. of Local Admin. Overseas*, 1962, pp. 149–55.

PROTHERO, R. M. 'A geographer with the World Health Organisation', *G.J.*, 1962, pp. 479–93.

PROTHERO, R. M. *Migrants and Malaria*, London. 1965.

TAPINOS, G. *L'économie des migrations internationales*, CNSP. 1974.

(*b*) *On urbanism, and migration to towns*

BEAUJEU-GARNIER, J. and CHABOT, G. *Traité de géographie urbaine.* Paris, 1964 (contains bibliography and extended treatment of these subjects).

Certain works cited in the above are quoted here, since they have been specially useful in the writing of the present volume:

LYNN SMITH, T. and MCMAHAN, C. A. *The Sociology of Urban Life.* New York, 1951.

LYNN SMITH, T. *The Sociology of Rural Life*, 3rd edn. New York, 1953.

— *Statistiques démographiques des grandes villes 1946–1951.* Inst. Internat. de Statistiques. The Hague, 1954.

BEAUJEU-GARNIER, J. 'Les migrations vers Salvador (Brésil)', *C.O.M.* 1962, 291–300.

HAUSER, P. M. *et al. L'urbanisation en Asie et en Extrême-Orient.* UNESCO. 1959

HAUSER, P. M. *L'urbanisation en Amérique Latine.* UNESCO. 1962.

DICKINSON, R. E. 'The geography of commuting: the Netherlands and Belgium', *G.R.*, 1957, pp. 521–38.

POKCHICHEVSKII, V. V. *Geografia migratsii nacelenia v Russii.* Moscow. 1949.

(Geography of population migration in Russia.)

POKCHICHEVSKII, V. V. 'Geografia nacelenia'. *Voproci Geografii*, 1962. (Population geography.)

POKCHICHEVSKII, V. V. *Goroda spoutniki.* Moscow. 1961. (Satellite towns.)

ROOF, M. K. and LEEDY, F. 'Population redistribution in the Soviet Union, 1939–1956', *G.R.*, 1959, p. 208.

ROSE, A. J. 'The geographical pattern of European immigration in Australia', *G.R.*, 1958, p. 512.

(*c*) *On tourism*

BURNET, L. *Tourisme et villégiature sur les côtes de France.* Paris. 1963.

— *Tourism in OECD member countries 1962.* Paris, 1962.

(*d*) *On the occupations of the people*

Statistical Yearbook published by the International Labour Office.

VIMONT, C. *La population active.* 1960.

FOURASTIE, J. *Migrations professionelles.* I.N.E.D. Handbook, No. 31, 1957.

— *Le vieillissement des populations et ses conséquences économiques et sociales.* U.N. 1956.

LONG, C. D. *The Labor Force under changing Income and Employment.* Nat. Bur. of Econ. Res. Princeton, 1958.

STIGLER, *Trusts in employment in the service industries.* Nat. Bur. of Econ. Res. Princeton, 1956.

— *Pourquoi les travailleurs abandonnent la terre?* I.L.O. 1960.

— *Labor mobility and population in agriculture.* Iowa, 1961.

SCHULTZ, T. W. *The Economic Organisation of Agriculture.* New York. 1953.

ZELINSKY, W. 'Rural population dynamics as an index to social and economic development', *S.Q.*, 1962, pp. 99–121.

ZELINSKY, W. 'Changes in the geographic patterns of rural population in the United States, 1790–1960', *G.R.*, 1962, pp. 492–524.

BEAVER, S. H. 'Technology and geography', *Advancement of Science*, 1961, pp. 315–27.

BRIGGS, A. 'Technology and economic development', *S.A.*, 1963, pp. 52–62.

DAVIS, K. 'Population', *S.A.*, 1963, pp. 63–72.

SCRIMSHAW, M. S. 'Food', *S.A.*, 1963, pp. 73–81.

THOMPSON, S. W. *Population and progress in the Far East.* Chicago. 1959.

WARD, M. W. 'Recent population growth and economic development in Asia', *P.V.*, 1960, p. 205.

RIALLIN, J. L. *Economie et population au Japon.* Paris, 1962.

DE CASTRO, J. *The Geography of Hunger.* London. 1952.

BUCHANAN, N. S. and ELLIS, H. S. *Approaches to Economic Development.* 1955.

BUQUET, L. *L'optimum de population.* Paris. 1956.

SAUVY, A. *De Malthus à Mao Tsé Toung.* Paris. 1958.

LEBRET, L. J. *Le drame du siècle.* 1960.

KOOL, R. *Tropical Agriculture and Economic Development.* Wageningen. 1960.

DUMONT, R. *Terres vivantes.* Paris. 1961.

PERROUX, F. *L'économie des jeunes nations.* Paris. 1962.

BOSERUP, E. *Woman's Role in Economic Development*, London. 1970.

ANGELOPOULOS, A. *Le Tiers Monde face aux pays riches*, Paris, PUF. 1972.

PITCHFORD, J. D. *The Economics of Population: an introduction*, Canberra. 1974.

Index

The more important references are in **bold** type